WENSLEYDALE REMEMBERED

THE SACRIFICE MADE BY THE FAMILIES OF A NORTHERN DALE
1914 – 1918 AND 1939 – 1945

Keith Taylor

COUNTRY BOOKS

Published by Country Books
Courtyard Cottage, Little Longstone, Bakewell, Derbyshire DE45 1NN

ISBN 1 898941 91 2

British Library Cataloguing in Publication Data.
A catalogue record for this book is available from the British Library.

By the same author:
DARLEY DALE REMEMBERED: THROUGH 50 YEARS OF WAR AND
PEACE

By the same author in conjunction with Trevor Brown:
A DERBYSHIRE PARISH AT WAR: SOUTH DARLEY AND THE GREAT
WAR
1914 – 1919

A DERBYSHIRE PARISH AT PEACE AND WAR
SOUTH DARLEY 1925 – 1955

Cover captions.
Front cover. Top left: *Leyburn market place 1914. Top right: Fred Shaw and family.
He was killed in 1917. Bottom: Haymaking in the Yorkshire Dales.*
Back cover. Top left: *Hawes market place 1904. Top right: Leyburn market place c1938.*
Bottom: *View of Wensleydale between Aysgarth and West Burton.*
(Photograph by John Morgan of Leyburn.)

Printed and bound by Antony Rowe Ltd.

DEDICATION

*This book is dedicated to the memory of my brother-in-law
Trevor Rhodes 1936-2001, a Yorkshireman who introduced me
to the splendours of 'God's Own Country' many years ago.*

Soldiers marching through Redmire in 1915.

Armoured vehicles on the village green at East Witton c1940.

CONTENTS

ACKNOWLEDGEMENTS AND THANKS

A special thanks to Dick Richardson at Country Books for all his help in getting the manuscript and photographs into book form.

Trevor Brown for proof reading and help on the background to the Great War.

Frank Dickens and Duncan Rhodes for help with computer work.

Curators of 25 Regimental Museums.

Staff of the Darlington Local Studies Library, Richmond Library, Skipton Local Studies Library and Matlock Local Studies Library.

The Dales Countryside Museum, Hawes, and Fiona Rosher and Debbie Allen in particular.

Ann Holubecki and Jose Hopper for their help, kindness and support, especially with regards to photography and providing photographs.

Editors of various church magazines and Wensleydale publications.

The Upper Wensleydale Family History Group.

John Morgan for permission to use his photograph of Wensleydale on the back cover of the book.

Special thanks for their time, information, memories and loan of photographs to the following people (I apologise if any person's name has been omitted from the list) :

M. Beswick, C. Flynne, O. Hutchinson, J. Cockett, D. Bowes. B. Stirling, M. Kilburn, K. Kilding, D. Goodall, J. T. Williams, M. Keeble, N. Croft, D. Atkinson, B. Chaytor, N. Pendlebury, B. Knowles, B. Scott, B. Alderson, G. Calvert, M. Harrison, M. Metcalfe, B. Allen, A. Kirkbride, Terry Kirkbride, T. Kirkbride, Mrs. T. Taylor, Mrs. Staveley, Colonel Le Mesurier, Mrs. Chapman, J. Iveson, N. Iveson, T. Gregg, A. Harrison, E. Cockbone, D. Weatherill, I. Weatherill, Mr. and Mrs. Chilton, E. Taylor, L. Houseman, A. Houseman, A. Roberts, D. Milner, P. Poulter, R. Handley, M. Edgley, J. Wells, D. Minnitt, R. Ward, U. Jackson, C. Wilkinson, Mrs. Wardman, Mrs. Mudd, M. Wilson, C. Dawson, A. Wilkinson, W. Thwaite, P. Leyland, E. Kirkbride, G. Marriott, J. Harrison, S. Bruce, M. Sanderson, W. Metcalfe, A. Peacock, G. Akrigg, J. Handley, H. Peacock, L. Kirby, K. Rider, C. Johnson, M. Kirby, W. & E. Banks, W. Metcalfe, A. Gitlin, S. Caygill, B. Iveson, D. Middleton, Mr. and Mrs. Hesp, K. Percival, G. Percival, M. Brown, Mr. J and Mrs. M. Sunter, Lord and Lady Bolton, P. Skidmore, B. Whitehead, A. Chapleo, P. Swainston, J. Taylor, A. Holstein, M. Howe, I. Spensley, S. Hemsley, B. Mawer, T. Dinsdale, C. Bustuard, M. Scarr, J. Cooper, R. Heseltine, Rita Richardson, R. Stephenson, M. Childs, G. Nicholson, P. Norrie, P. Pollit, M. Weatherald, E. Tull, Mr. James, D. Tinseley, R. Terry, Miss Craddock, P. Seckerson, N. McGregor, I. McGregor, C. Dodd, P. Hustwick, R. O'Connor, T. O'Connor, I. Jagger, M. Taylor, R. Greenhalgh, Mrs. Whitehead, W. Sharples, Mrs. Ewbank, Mr. and Mrs. James, R. Dinsdale, R. Kilding, R. Grufferty, Mrs. Hugill, Mrs. Turner, L. Hammerton, G. Guile, Mrs. Tuppling, F. Clarkson, J. Fawcett, F. Ligonnet, J. Burdon, M. Fairhurst, Mrs. Lofthouse, J. Robinson, M. Dinsdale, J. Whitton, L. and J. Peace, A. Naden, Mrs. Beaumont, Mrs. Heasman, D. Walker, R. Walker, A. Craske, Mrs. Moore, J. Sunter, J. Robinson, D. Shields, N. Harrison, A. Harrison, B. Whitehead, J. Roberts, A. Snaith, Mrs. Shields, R. Annison, M. Wilson, A. Silvester, D. Atkinson, C. Torrens, G. Walker, E. Myers, J. Moore, E. Young, Mrs. Bown, J.E.S. Hullah, M. Alderson, N.H. Morley, C.W. Nesbitt, R. Robson, P. Cooper (Green Howards).

BIBLIOGRAPHY AND SOURCES

Craven's part in the Great War Editor John T. Clayton

Squadron Histories by Peter Lewis, Putnam and Company

Fighter Squadrons of the R.A.F. by John Rawlins, Macdonald and Janes

Hitler's Naval War by Cajus Bekker, Purnell Book Services Ltd.

East Witton Parish Magazines Volume 1 (1910 – 1923) Volume 2 (1924 – 1950)

From the Dales to Jericho by A. E. Eaton, Recall Publications

Darlington and Stockton Times and *The Craven Herald* newspapers

Bomber Squadrons of the R.A.F. and their aircraft by Philip Mojes, Macdonald and Janes

History of the Green Howards 1914 – 1919

Wensleydale and Swaledale Almanac 1913

1890 Directory of North Yorkshire

1909 Directory of North Yorkshire

1901 census

6th Battalion Sherwood Foresters 1914 –1918 by W. D. Jamieson

World War II, Orbis Publications

Pen and Sword publications

The Story of the Durham Light Infantry, 1st Battalion 2nd World War

The Face of Battle by John Keegan, Jonathan Cape

History of the First World War by Liddell Hart

War Diaries from the following Regimental Museums: Green Howards, Northumberland Fusiliers, Durham Light Infantry, King's Own Yorkshire Light Infantry, Scots Guards, Coldstream Guards, Grenadier Guards, Royal Armoured Corps, Household Cavalry, Hussars, King's Royal Rifle Corps, Rifle Brigade, Cheshire Regiment, Royal Artillery, Lancashire Fusiliers, Royal Fusiliers, West Riding Regiment, York and Lancasters, East and West Yorkshire Regiments, Border Regiment, Manchester Regiment, Liverpool, Suffolk Regiment, Somerset Light Infantry, Hampshire Regiment,

A History of the 21st Battalion Manchester Regiment, Fleur de Lys Publishing

History of the First World War, Purnell

Up The Line To Death – The War Poets 1914 -1918, Methuen Paperbacks

Passchendaele In Perspective – The Third Battle of Ypres, Pen and Sword

Messines Ridge, Ypres by Peter Oldham, Pen and Sword

Chemical Soldiers by D. Richter, University of Kansas

The Story of the King's Regiment 1914 – 1948 by Burke-Gaffney, Sharpe and Kellet Ltd.

The Grenadier Guards in the Great War by Sir Frederick Ponsonby, Macmillan and Co.

Commonwealth War Graves Commission web site.

CD Rom of the soldiers who died in the Great War.

The most valuable sources of information and many accompanying photographs have been provided generously by people from the dale.

INTRODUCTION

The decisions reached by political leaders in London and the far flung capitals of Europe, resulting in the outbreak of world wide conflict in August 1914 and again in September 1939, appeared at first sight to have little impact on the beautiful, sleepy backwater of Wensleydale in North Yorkshire.

Yet inhabitants of the towns, villages, hamlets and farmsteads, looking out from their homes on the valley slopes towards the meanders of the River Ure, or, sheltering under the heights of Pen Hill, Addlebrough, Askrigg Common, Ellerkin and Widdale Fell, would find their ways of life disrupted and their families devastated by those same decisions, as the darkness engendered by the First and Second World Wars descended upon them to blight their existence.

The villages and hamlets of Thornton Steward, East Witton, Spennithorne, Harmby, Bellerby, Middleham, Coverham, Leyburn, Wensley, Preston under Scar, Carperby, Thoralby, Aysgarth, Walden, West Burton, Newbiggin, Castle Bolton, Redmire, West Witton, Worton, Cubeck, Thornton Rust, Nappa Scar, Newbiggin, Askrigg, Bainbridge, Countersett, Burtersett, Marsette, Stalling Busk, Sedbusk, Hawes, Gayle, Hardraw, Appersett, Cotterdale and The Moorcock bear testimony to the sacrifice made by the men of Wensleydale and their families.

War memorials are sited in virtually every parish, but who now remembers the "Pals" of 1914 – 1918? The First World War is passing from human memory into history, whilst many of those who survived the Second World War have passed away. 168 servicemen from this northern dale gave their lives for "King and Country" between 1914 and 1918, whilst the supreme sacrifice was again asked of 53 men during the years 1939 to 1945.

It is the aim of "Wensleydale Remembered — The Sacrifice Made By The Families Of A Northern Dale 1914 – 1918 and 1939 – 1945" to celebrate the lives of these lost generations, who did not live to see once again the view from Leyburn Shawl, the tumbling falls at Asgarth, the River Bain in full spate, Semer Water at sunset, the bustle of Tuesday market day at Hawes or hear the sound of lapwing and skylark as they wheeled high over the slopes of nearby hills and fells. Of greater importance, they did not live to return to their loved ones.

In the early years of this new millennium I believe we should still honour these men whose stories are part of a wider shared sense of history that has shaped our age. On the following pages I have attempted therefore to rekindle memories of these gallant Wensleydale parishioners by finding out, wherever possible, about their lives and deaths. In doing so I have felt privileged to be delving into their histories, and hope that it will help others to appreciate their supreme sacrifices.

Keith Taylor
2004

Voluntary Aid Detachment Nurses (VAD) on the steps of Bolton Hall, Wensley, 1914-1915. Lady Bolton stands at the front with the senior nurse, Helene Bowes stands second from the right on second step. Marguerite Campbell is first right on row behind and Maud Beswick is next to her, behind Lady Bolton (see page 42).

VAD nurses tending to convalescent soldiers, Bolton Hall. Marguerite Campbell is standing third from the left. (See page 42.)

Hawes Fair 1904.

DALES LIFE BEFORE THE GREAT WAR:
A PHOTOGRAPHIC RECORD

Hawes market place c1904. In the background are the Crown and Fountain Hotels. It received its Market Charter as recently as 1700, a recognition of the growth of trade in Hawes in the 16th century due mainly to packhorse traffic.

At Hawes Station c1914. Getting ready to re-stock the River Ure with fish on behalf of the Wensleydale and High Abbotside Fishing Association. (Founded in the 1840's.)

Town Foot, Hawes, c1908, showing the Queen's Hotel on the right.

Hawes Fair in 1904.

By permission of the Dales Countryside Museum.

Many of the Wensleydale farmers' horses were commandeered by the Army in 1914/1915.

By permission of the Dales Countryside Museum.

Hawes railway station c1905. (Nowadays housing the Dales Countryside Museum.) Hawes was the terminus of the Wensleydale line from Northallerton, built by the N.E.R. A branch line linked it with the Midland Company's Settle to Carlisle line at Hawes Junction (now Garsdale). The building was erected by the Midland Company in a style known as Derby Gothic but the station was manned by N.E.R. Staff. Milk floats and wagons can be seen on the right of the photograph.

By permission of the Dales Countryside Museum.

North Eastern Railway staff at Hawes Station c1908.

By permission of the Dales Countryside Museum.

The October 1905 Fair at Leyburn. Wilkinson's the saddlers can be seen in the background of Commercial Square.

Leyburn Fair (Grove Square) October 1906.

Leyburn Market Place 1915. It received its market charter only in 1684 when it was a village centred on Grove Square. The Regency style Market Hall was completed in 1856, the same year as the railway arrived from Northallerton. The bricks inside the building came from the Victorian brick works near Redmire Church.

Leyburn Sheep Fair c1910 in Grove Square.

Leyburn in 1914.

Farmers taking their churns of milk to Askrigg Station c1910.

Driving the cattle at Town Head, Askrigg, looking up Moor Road, c1910. Town Head Farm, home to the Kirkbride family, can just be seen on the left, in the middle distance. Much of the stock came from Swaledale.

The green at West Burton c1910. On March 10th and May 6th, during the late 1800's, fairs were held on the village green for horses, cattle and sheep.

Edwardian scene in Carperby c1907, showing the market cross.

Carperby village c1910, looking from the Askrigg side towards the high-stepped cross in the far distance, dated 1674. It tells of the time when Carperby had a market, granted in 1305.

The main street, Redmire, c1914. Amongst those talking are Jane Scott (Hawes), Janette Yates, Amy Hayton and Sarah Alice (Doddy) Scott. The stepped plinth of a vanished cross now supports a Victorian jubilee pillar of 1887. During the 18th and 19th centuries most villagers worked as lead miners and coal-miners in the mines and pits whose remains scar the moorland road towards Grinton and Reeth.

Redmire Railway Station 1908.
A few yards away was Redmire Dairy, where cheese was made

Photograph of part of Wensley village, taken from the church tower c1910. For a century after 1202, when it received its charter, Wensley had the only market in the dale, which continued until the 16th century.

Bainbridge c1910.

Fancy dress and sports in the year 1914 (Whitsuntide).
Outside the White Swan, Middleham.

The Main Street at West Witton, c1910. On the left hand side is Straffen's shop, followed by first Beacon Farm (now 'Whitecroft') and 'The Star' Public House.

By permission of Clive Torrens.

WEST WITTON

Moulds Gill Colliery, Tan Hill, Arkengarthdale, c1900. Before the Wensleydale railway was constructed, some coal found its way into Wensleydale to help fuel homes in the villages of the River Ure.

By permission of the Dales Countryside Museum.

Yore Mill carters c1890. (Aysgarth.) The carts are approaching the eastern end of the way through Freeholders Wood from Aysgarth Falls. The carts are returning to Yore Mill loaded with trestles, canvas and a set pot after a days celebration. Owen Dinsdale is holding the white horse's head. Robert Sarginson is driving the leading cart.

By permission of the Dales Countryside Museum.

CHAPTER ONE
1914 — INTO THE MAELSTROM

The men of Wensleydale would indeed serve their country. A few were regular servicemen, some volunteers whilst others were conscripts. 168 Wensleydale men would pay the supreme sacrifice and they are remembered on the war memorials that still stand in the parishes running between Thornton Steward in the east and Hardraw to the west.

My inspiration for writing the book came from a visit to the church at Stainforth, on the western fringes of the Dales. Not only was there a list of the fallen from the Great War inside the church, but also a brief history of each serviceman, together with a photograph wherever this was possible. I was determined to attempt something similar for the "lads" of Wensleydale.

Who were these men of the dale, born towards the end of the Victorian Age, with many destined to lie in "some corner of a foreign field that is forever England"? The vast majority worked locally, in the stone quarries above Burtersett, Preston under Scar, Leyburn and Harmby, or on the land, farming the fertile valley bottom of the River Ure or looking after the sheep higher up the dale.

Sheep, of course, were the life blood of the dale. The buildings, constructed in local slate and stone, were perfectly suited to the needs of a pastoral community, with their flagged ground floor rooms and the field barns, accommodating both young cattle and the hay needed for them to survive the severe winter months. A sturdy, independent type of person evolved in these dalehead farmsteads, which had been occupied for generations by the same farming families.

Their way of life was regulated by the natural rhythm of the seasons. Lambing took place in April, shearing at the beginning of July, hay cutting in late July, November witnessing tupping and always the twice daily routine of milking. The changelessness of the pastoral cycle in Wensleydale, set against a

Shearing sheep in the dales, c1900.
By permission of the Dales Countryside Museum.

Sheep shearing in the dales, c1900.
By permission of the Dales Countryside Museum.

Archduke Franz Ferdinand and his wife leave Sarajevo Town Hall on their last ride.
Sunday 28th June 1914.

background both green and generously wooded, was a satisfying anchorage for these people in a troubled world. These "troubles" intruded into their lives during the summer months of 1914.

Throughout the glorious sunny weekend of June 27th/28th 1914 many dales-folk were out in the fields and on the fell sides, gathering in the flocks and helping in the backbreaking task of clipping the sheep. However, these reassuring scenes of Edwardian working life, witnessed in the apparent idyllic settings around Hawes, Burtersett and Askrigg, were to be irretrievably affected by the consequences from two pistol shots ringing out on a street in the far away provincial Bosnian town of Sarajevo.

They came from the gun of a Bosnian/Serbian student nationalist, Gavrilo Princip. His assassination of the heir to the Austro – Hungarian Empire, Archduke Franz Ferdinand and his wife, the Duchess of Hohenberg, on the same gloriously sunny morning of Sunday 28th June would result in Wensleydale inhabitants finding their lives changed dramatically as Britain and the European powers became enmeshed on the road to violent conflict during the long hot days of July.

It was with the sound of those two gunshots ringing out in a mid-European town that the fates of 168 Wensleydale men were to be sealed and the lives of many others affected by hardship and sadness. The onset of the Great War on August 4th 1914 resulted in many men from the dale being despatched far afield to France, Belgium, Italy, Gallipoli, Egypt, Mesopotamia, the Pacific Ocean and the deep grey waters of the North Sea, off the coast of Denmark. Sadly, too many of the menfolk of Wensleydale would eventually be listed on their parish war memorials.

The bullets fired by Gavrilo Princip, from a distance of two feet, had found their targets. Blood was gushing from the Archduke's mouth over his green

Gavrilo Princip (centre) on his way to prison.

uniform. His wife was leaning on him, unconscious but with no visible wound. They were carried to a room in the nearby Government building in Sarajevo, next to the one in which the champagne was cooling for their lunch. A quarter of an hour later both were dead.

Their deaths triggered the march towards hostilities and it is true to say that enthusiasm for war was high amongst the populations of the belligerent nations. Throughout the European capitals, vast crowds swept onto the streets, each voicing support for their country's hostile stance. The belief in a successful, brief but bloody war was held by all armies.

The assassinations had resulted in Austria presenting Serbia with impossible conditions to avoid annexation; Russia immediately mobilised in support of her fellow Slavs, Germany responded at once and France followed suit.

On Tuesday, 4th August, 4300 trains, decorated with flowers and tricolour flags, overflowed with a noisy, enthusiastic mass of young men in old fashioned uniforms and resounded with an endless chanting of the "Marseillaise". The trains were carrying the French army towards the German army, which was moving to meet it in 11,000 trains.

Hopes that Great Britain could somehow stay out of the conflict were dashed when, following the long prepared Schlieffen Plan, German forces entered neutral Belgium, en route to Northern France.

The days before war was declared by Britain had been the Bank Holiday weekend and Monday 3rd August was the day for a trip out. The weather was beautiful, with brilliant blue skies and a warm temperature, ideal for a visit to the

Hay harvest in the dale. Similar methods were used in 1914.
By permission of the Dales Countryside Museum.

Collecting the hay harvest in the dale.
By permission of the Dales Countryside Museum.

Ready for harvesting the hay, c1908.
By permission of the Dales Countryside Museum.

Harvesting the hay in the dale.
By permission of the Dales Countryside Museum.

WENSLEYDALE REMEMBERED

The first cinema in Leyburn 1915.

The old Leyburn fire station and appliance on Shawl Terrace.

Wensley village war memorial. It is unusual in that it bears the names of both those who died in the Great War and those servicemen from the parish who survived. Instead, I have taken the names from the memorial inside Wensley Church.

To the memory of all the Wensleydale men
whose names are inscribed on the dale's war memorials.

THEY WERE NUMBERED AMONG THOSE WHO,
AT THE CALL OF KING AND COUNTRY, LEFT ALL
THAT WAS DEAR TO THEM, ENDURED HARDNESS,
FACED DANGER, AND FINALLY PASSED OUT OF
THE SIGHT OF MEN BY THE PATH OF DUTY
AND SELF-SACRIFICE, GIVING UP THEIR OWN
LIVES THAT OTHERS MIGHT LIVE IN FREEDOM.
LET THOSE WHO COME AFTER SEE TO IT
THAT THEIR NAMES BE NOT FORGOTTEN.

The Band of Hope at West Witton, taken in June 1914, just two months before the Great War broke out. Little did they realise how their lives would be affected.

seaside. Thousands flocked to the railway stations across Britain to catch special trains bound for the coast. However, the First Lord of the Admiralty, Winston Churchill, had mobilised the fleet and all excursion trains were taken over by naval reservists. London attractions, such as The Zoo, did a roaring trade, although far away in Wensleydale, where the weather was less favourable, many from the farming communities were still involved in gathering in the hay, after a period of inclement weather over the previous fortnight.

Numerous stooks of corn stood proudly in the hay meadows, the sheaves almost ready to be lifted by pitchfork onto the farm carts, ready for the lumbering ride back to the farmstead, or to be stored in the field barns that dotted the valley floor. But unbeknown to everyone, Armageddon was looming.

At 4p.m. the British Army was mobilised. Britain demanded that the German Army be withdrawn from Belgium by midnight 5th August or a state of war would exist between the British Empire and Germany. The ultimatum was ignored and war was declared at 11p.m. The Great War had begun.

In British cities everywhere, excitement reigned. On 5th August 1914 the pride of London's famous streets poured into the recruiting offices at Great Scotland Yard and elsewhere. They had come from watching Surrey play Notts at the Oval. They were sunburnt from a weekend at Brighton. They had been learning to dance the Tango. Some still carried memories of the scene outside Buckingham Palace the previous night when they had sung "God Save The King".

In the Wensleydale village of East Witton, the Church Choir and Sunday School outings for August 11th were both indefinitely postponed because of the outbreak of war and the requisitioning of the railways by the military. Instead of an outing to the seaside, the Sunday Sunday School treat was held in September in the form of a tea at the vicarage, provided by Canon George W. Garrod and his wife, with sports on the village green. It was a "throwback" to earlier treats, such as that of September 1910, when the day had begun with a cricket match, boys versus girls, with the boys batting left handed. Races of all kinds had been held and a tug of war, whilst at the close, schoolmaster William Greenhalgh had conducted the children in some excellent school songs. Meanwhile, on September 23rd 1914, the Church Choir finally made their trip to Scarborough, after the railways were back to dealing with their normal operations.

On Sunday evening, August 9th, the vicar, Canon Garrod, had preached on the subject of the war, taking for his text Saint Matthew Chapter 10, verse 34: "I came not to send Peace, but a Sword" and showing that terrible as war is, national dishonour and indifference to wrong doing was still more terrible, and that for England to have stood aloof at this present juncture would have been a national disgrace. Canon Garrod's son, Wilfred, had already joined the Yorkshire Regiment and, as a Captain attached to the King's Own Yorkshire Light Infantry, would be awarded the Military Cross in August 1918.

During this same period the town of Hawes decided to cancel their Agricultural Show. Lord Bolton, at Wensley, and other large landowners also abandoned their grouse shooting parties until further notice, although by 1915 they had once again started up. The owners of Simonstone Hall, near Hardraw, got into the spirit of things by offering many rooms as a convalescent home for wounded soldiers, but it was decided by the authorities that this plan would not be feasible.

In 1914 Britain was essentially a maritime power with only a small, if highly trained and professional army. Only 120,000 men would initially make up the British Expeditionary Force that embarked for France, compared with some four million Frenchmen and four and a half million Germans.

Lord Kitchener shocked a meeting of the War Council on August 6th by predicting a long war; countering the popular cry of, "It will be all over by Christmas." On August 7th Kitchener publicly called for 100,000 volunteers. By

September 12th an amazing total of 480,000 men had enlisted as volunteers.

The majority were from urban areas, where large numbers of work mates and neighbours joined together into the famous "Pals" Battalions such as the "Leeds Pals" and "Accrington Pals". In more scattered, isolated rural districts, such as Wensleydale, the rush to enlist was not quite so pronounced, but at various recruitment meetings the local dignitaries soon did their best to alter this situation.

Throughout the district during the first week of August it was noticeable that the price of provisions shot up because of panic buying, with the grocers' shops besieged by the local population. Meanwhile, the Reserves had been called out and the Territorial Battalions embodied and sent to the front. Horses were being bought up wholesale by the military authorities in this rural area.

Excitement was great in and around Richmond on Tuesday 4th August with officers and men arriving and departing by train. At 2-30p.m. a striking and enthusiastic demonstration took place in the market square when the respective regiments formed square and the proclamation was read by the mayor, Mr. William Walton. All the officers and men were armed and gave three ringing cheers for the King, with the large crowd joining in singing the National Anthem, played by the local Prize Silver Band. The bulk of the soldiers took part in a route march into the surrounding countryside, whilst local and district Territorials were dispatched to other quarters in the afternoon

The 3rd Yorkshire Special Reserve returned from camp at Barnard Castle on Wednesday 5th August and were billeted in the town. Cooking trenches were made opposite the Town Hall and market place and the cooks were busily employed all day.

On Thursday 6th August, following a long route march, the colours of the Battalion were deposited in the church during the evening. With fixed bayonets, the troops formed up in Frenchgate, opposite the entrance to the church.

The Darlington and Stockton Times newspaper recorded that in the first week of war Upper Wensleydale was stirred to its depths by the great conflict in operation. Dr. Pickles of Aysgarth travelled by the milk train on Sunday evening to join the Fleet as surgeon at Plymouth, whilst Reservist Robert Mudd had left Askrigg for York (we shall find later that Company Sergeant Major Mudd was killed on Friday 13th April 1917).

On Tuesday 22nd August a recruitment meeting was held at Hawes Market Hall. Mr. D'Arcy Wyvill, J.P., said that it was the young they saw going out with their guns, the young men they saw on the moors, that were wanted by their country. In the old days Wensleydale had a splendid corps of volunteers and the men he saw around him were quite as good as they were. They did not want their dalesmen to go out as conscipts (a voice shouted, "It will come to that!"), but as loyal volunteers (applause). Several volunteers were enrolled.

On the following day, Wednesday September 23rd , another well attended recruitment meeting was held at Bainbridge, Mr. J. C. Winn acting as Chairman. He reminded his audience of the days of the loyal dales "Volunteers" and made a strong personal appeal to the young men of the district.

In an able speach, Mr. D'Arcy Wyvill reviewed the situation and seconded Mr. Winn's appeal for recruits. He laid particular emphasis of the necessity of enlisting as many young men as possible who were accustomed to horses, as recruits of that class were not readily available in the large centres of population. Mr. W. Balderston also spoke.

It was hoped that this and other meetings in the district would be the means of securing a large increase in the number of recruits from a neighbourhood rich in fine, well set up young men familiar with horses and their management.

On that same sunny day, September 23rd, a fatigue party of the City of Leeds "Pals" Battalion, numbering over 100, arrived at Masham by train, to prepare the camp at Breary Banks, Colsterdale. The main body proceeded from Masham on the narrow gauge light railway with baggage, though some 30 soldiers went en route by foot. The march past was witnessed by large crowds in Masham. Cheers went up as the Company passed and the villages along the way were en fete for

Narrow gauge railway and engine between Masham and Colsterdale.
Used by the 'Leeds Pals' Battalion. 1914 – 1918.

Members of the 'Leeds Pals' in front of their wooden billet hut at Breary Banks, Colsterdale, 1915. Boar Lane is a well known street in Leeds. Most of these men would be killed within the first hour of the Battle of the Somme, 1st July 1916.

the occasion. Another 800 men would soon arrive. The little steam engine was powerful enough to pull three or four open wagons loaded with foodstuffs for the Battalion but the engine was very wide in proportion to the lines, making it top heavy and quite often it would run off the lines.

Tuesday 6th October witnessed a recruitment meeting held in Leyburn Town Hall where a large and enthusiastic audience came to hear a lecture on the war by Miss Gertrude Bell, the famous Middle East traveller and archaeologist (at Cairo she would later assist Lawrence of Arabia in his work to rouse the Arab tribes into rebellion against the Turks).

Mrs. Riddell sang "Land of Hope and Glory" and "The flag that shall never come down", the choruses being taken up by the audience. Then for an hour Gertrude Bell held the deep attention of the audience by tracing the events of the war and showing that it was utterly impossible for Britain, for the sake of our honour, truth and self-preservation, to have kept out of this dreadful conflict. She made a strong appeal to the men to come forward to defend their country, and to the women to use their best influence to get their men-folk to enlist.

Mr. D'Arcy Wyvill made a strong appeal for recruits, urging that the bad name the dale had got for not responding as it should to help the country in its time of need, ought to be removed. The dale used to muster a force of 700 strong, but now that was a thing of the past. Sir David Barclay, the local recruiting officer, also addressed the meeting, and the evening's events were wound up by Mrs. Riddell singing, "Your King and Country Need You", for which she was encored.

Exactly three weeks later, on Tuesday 27th October, Hawes Market Hall was filled to capacity at another recruitment meeting, but it was noted by the newspaper reporter that a large group of men preferred to stand outside the inner doors, rather than occupy seats within the Hall.

The speaker, Major Thompson, alluded to the unevenness of the recruiting within the county, stating that he had heard men say the Germans would not come to the moors. But that was where they made their mistake. The moors were the very places they would visit for purposes of observation and for supplies of sheep and cattle.

The Germans were not a gentle people, as the Belgian records could tell. He had been asked by Lord Kitchener to do what he could in Yorkshire, and he had accepted that duty. All employers should encourage their men to go and should keep their places open to them to return to. He hoped the cry of their country would ring through the dale, and when the dalesmen realised how great the country's necessity was, he believed they would not be long in coming forward to do their duty.

It was a glorious privilege, a great opportunity to take their part in defence of their home, country and all they held most dear (applause). Mr. Little, Mr. Penry Williams, M.P., and the Recruitment Officer, Sir David Barclay, also spoke, the latter soliciting the names of recruits, but none were forthcoming.

It may be the case that such meetings were received enthusiastically, but it becomes clear that certain individuals were not happy with the general response of the dale's menfolk to volunteer to fight the enemy. It is true that in rural areas there was not the rush to volunteer on the same scale as in an urban conurbation, but the men of Wensleydale did not deserve the vitriolic attack made upon them by an unnamed correspondent from Upper Wensleydale in the October 31st edition of the Darlington and Stockton Times. It is fortunate that he remained anonymous for otherwise he might have been forced physically to eat his words, which stated:

"Bitter disillusionment and an almost shattered faith in the loyalty of the dalesmen must have been the experience of such patriotic gentlemen as Alderman J.C. Winn, Sir David Barclay, Mr. D'Arcy Wyvill, and others, who, in their younger days responded without hesitation to the call of their country and who in the present crisis have so ably voiced through the dale the call of England for men. With a few gallant exceptions they have seen their call pass unheeded and even sneered at.

"Where is the patriotism of Wensleydale? Where its old time loyalty? Is it now comprehended only in the wearing and waving of toy flags and the unmusical bellowing of patriotic songs? Is all manly national feeling and heroic sentiment and enterprise gone? As Mr. D' Arcy Wyvill and others have so truly said, and as all who have even the most elementary knowledge of the causes which led England to take her stand on the side of France and Russia must know, this war is not of our seeking. We fight not for aggrandisement or for the sordid love for territorial acquisition, but for the independence of small states, for the maintenance of treaty obligations, for the suppression of a militarism that threatens our very existence as an Empire. We are fighting to keep our homes inviolate, to keep our beloved country free from the tread of a vindictive and cruel enemy, and to maintain our honour unblemished in the face of the whole civilised world. These are the great causes for which we are fighting, and can any Britisher be found who dares to say, "but that our cause is holy, righteous and pure"?

"In order to carry this fight to a successful issue our country asks for "Men" — brave, loyal, true men. What would we say of the man who stood with folded arms and turned an indifferent and unpitying eye on the torn and bleeding body of his mother as she wrestled against the ruffian's knife? And yet, is not this exactly the position of those who are able to fight and yet turn a deaf ear to the call of their Motherland? Surely, men of Wensleydale, it is in ignorance that you err; You surely cannot sin against the light.

"As a Wensleydale man myself, and proud of the fact, I say, "We dalesmen are not cowards, and if only the full meaning of all that defeat of the Allies portended was realised by them, the great majority would not be backward, nor could Lord Kitchener wish to own a finer, sturdier body of fighting men than could be recruited in Upper Wensleydale. Wake up, dalesmen! Cast your eyes for a moment across the seas. Look at India, at Canada, at Australia, New Zealand, aye, and at South Africa. Listen to the great, spontaneous outburst of love and loyalty that has rung across the seven seas and become the wonder and admiration of the world.

"Mother, we are coming!" Are you dalesmen content that future ages shall tell how that your brothers across the seas gave their lives, a sacrifice on the altar of Patriotism, while you stayed quietly at home?

"Then look to Belgium bleeding at every pore through the unspeakable atrocities of the German butchers; its cities desolate and its brave people home-less, penniless wanderers over the face of the earth. Can you look upon these sad and wretched ones and still remain inactive? Do their sufferings not cause you to tremble for the fate of your own homes and kindred should the enemy invade our shores?

"Then look once again right away yonder to the blood-stained land of France, where, with dauntless courage and magnificent heroism, thousands of our brave lads are fighting and yielding up their lives for our sakes. Are you not moved to the very depths of your being by the heroic deeds of our small but gallant force facing death with sublime fortitude and an unflinching courage, unyielding, though the odds be overwhelming, undismayed, though the carnage be fearful, and beating the enemy back step by step, winning glory and honour that shall never fade? The blood of thousands of brave and loyal Britishers drenches the soil of a foreign land, and though in that far-off country thousands have found their graves, yet those graves are graves of glory, and though dead yet they speak to us of duty nobly done, of a high and holy mission faithfully fulfilled.

"Men of Wensleydale, will you allow the cry of the living and the dead to pass unheeded? God forbid! Say, rather, we will go forth in our country's cause to act a man's part in our day and generation and make our dale not a shame but a glory, an object of commendation, and not of condemnation. Make up your minds ere it is too late, and see to it that the words of Harold Begbie's fine poem shall never apply to you ————-

"How will you fare, sonny, how will you fare,
In the far-off winter night,
When you sit by the fire, in an old man's chair,
And your neighbours talk of the fight?
Will you slide away as it were from a blow,
Your old head shamed and bent?
Or say — I was not with the first to go,
But I went, thank God, I went.

It is fair to say that the response from the countryside to Kitchener's call for volunteers was generally less enthusiastic than from the larger towns and cities throughout the whole of Britain. However, the writer of this particular article, possibly in his middle years of life and safe from any likelihood of fighting at the front himself, was being unfair to the men of Wensleydale. As we shall see, the call to arms was heeded by many men in Wensleydale and 168 of their names would be inscribed on the parish war memorials.

On Monday 16th November five recruits were given an enthusiastic send off from Hawes Station to Newcastle. At noon the Hawes Brass Band played patriotic selections in the market place and preceded the recruits to the station, where a large crowd had gathered. As the train steamed away, cheers were sent up, to which the lads responded by waving their handkerchiefs and caps. On the previous day John Kassell had left for Chatham to join the Royal Engineers and

The six Hawes recruits, 16th November 1914.
Back row: Lawrence Leach, Jack Moore, Albert Leach.
Front row: Charles Watson, John Kassel, Harold Heseltine.

the five others, all bound for the Royal Field Artillery, were Laurence Leach, Albert Leach, Harold Heseltine, Charlie Watson and John Moore (Albert Leach would be killed on the Somme in 1916).

Wensleydale should certainly feel no need for shame when we understand the sacrifice made by its many families. Indeed, it will be seen later that on the very day when the outspoken newspaper article was printed, news was being received of the first Wensleydale fatality.

On the Home Front, in October 1914, a number of ladies and gentlemen in Askrigg and Bainbridge formed themselves into a committee to provide a home for a family of Belgian refugees. Mr. H. Tunstill of Thornton Lodge had kindly placed a nine bedroomed house in Askrigg at the disposal of the Committee and furniture and the upkeep was to be

The five Field Artillery recruits,
November 1914.
Back row: Lawrence Leach, Albert Leach,
Jackie Moore.
Front row: Charles Watson, Harold
Heseltine.

provided by the people of the parish. Collections of money or kind were to be made each week by a brigade of boys appointed for the purpose. On Friday October 23rd, sixteen well dressed Belgian refugees arrived to find a hearty welcome. The Belgian flag fluttered proudly over the entrance. A large crowd, headed by the Relief Committee, wearing Belgian colours, awaited at Askrigg Station.

Meanwhile, two more Belgian refugee families, the Vander Bosch and the Marleins arrived at Hawes Station and settled in Gayle.

Charles Marlein from Ostende, was a sailor on the mail steam ships that crossed the Channel daily between Ostende and Dover. During his spare time he led an accordion band in Ostende and he would often entertain travellers on the cross Channel boats by playing for them.

As war broke out the shipping line gave their Belgian employees the chance to travel to the safety of England. Charles, together with his wife Natalie and children Emmerance, Margaret, Yvonne, Elvier, Madeleine, Theophiel (Phil) and Francis eventually arrived in Gayle, leaving their eldest son Auguste fighting in the Belgian army (he would later die for his country).

Billeted at Clints House, Gayle, they woke the next morning to find the local people on their doorstep with furniture, crockery and bedding, enough to equip the house. They never forgot the kindness shown to them. Two of their daughters earned their living by working for Mr. Martland, the Hawes tailor. Sadly, Francis, the youngest son, died from tuberculosis and was buried in

Belgian refugees. Maurice Vander Bosch, first on the left, came with his family to Gayle.

The Marlein children with their mother Natalie. Phil (Theophiel) Marlein stands second from the left. They came to Clints House, Gayle.

Hawes churchyard.

In early 1919 the Marlein family returned to Belgium but Phil could not settle and returned to the Dales to work for a local farmer at Swathgill Farm and then in Bishopdale, where he married a local girl. They settled in Gayle, with Phil working for Tom Allen, delivering animal meal to local farmers. Children Charles, Elvier and Madeleine were born at Gayle.

It is interesting to note that when Belgium was again occupied by the Germans in 1940, Phil's sister Madeleine, together with her family, once again arrived as a refugee in Gayle, whilst her husband joined the British Army. Phil was

'Jeanne', one of the Belgian refugees living at Burtersett and working in Hawes.

41

Adolf and Clemence Schaepherders and their family at Castle Bolton, in front of what became the village post office, next to the church. In Belgium Adolf was a tailor and the family arrived as refugees at Castle Bolton on 5th Decemeber 1914. A baby girl, Christiana, was born four days after their arrival, but died on 30th January 1915 and is buried in Redmire Churchyard.

already doing his duty by serving in the Hawes Home Guard as a sergeant.

October 30th saw a successful entertainment given at Stalling Busk school-room in connection with Raydaleside Band of Hope. There was a large attendance despite a stormy night. It opened with the Russian National Anthem, whilst songs were given by Mrs. T. Outhwaite and Miss Whitton, dialogue by Miss Fawcett, Miss Watson and younger members and recitations by Mr. Cloughton and Mr. M. Bell. A collection was taken for the Belgian Refugee Fund, whilst the Belgian and French National Anthems were played on the organ by Mrs. Hodgson.

By the end of the month the billiard room at Bolton Hall, Wensley, had been converted into a hospital ward, with thirteen beds installed. Wounded Belgian soldiers were being attended to by local Red Cross and Voluntary Aid Detachment (V.A.D.) nurses, who had been trained by local doctors over the previous year. (See photos on page 11.)

In an attempt to enable the local men-folk to be ready to help their country in its defence against the enemy, rifle clubs were set up in many villages through-out the dale. In October, at a meeting in Aysgarth Institute, it was decided to erect a rifle range in the Institute. The President, Alderman J.C.Winn, promised the use of one rifle and Mr. Brittain promised 1000 rounds of ammunition. By

The thirteen Belgian soldiers who arrived to convalesce from their wounds in late 1914
are shown relaxing in front of Bolton Hall.

Photograph by permission of Clive Torrens.

November 1914 the Institute had been taken over for the use of wounded soldiers and a range was set up instead in a garage at Palmer Flatts.

The Institute was to become a 12 bed convalescent hospital and Mr. George Dougal kindly lent White House, adjoining the Institute, as a nurses home. Aysgarth V.A.D. of the British Red Cross Society would undertake the nursing and ten soldiers were expected soon.

At the same time Mr. James Grime Lodge of Yore Bridge was elected President of the Askrigg Rifle Club, with Mr. James Preston acting as Secretary. An outdoor range had been erected in a field kindly lent by Mr. W. Balderston, J.P. The young people of Askrigg were showing a great deal of interest in the movement. Bainbridge set up a rifle range in the Temperance Hall, the Trustees having provided free use on two nights a week. They were also looking for an outdoor range and competitions were to be held. By February 1915, Aysgarth and Askrigg Rifle Clubs were holding regular competitions, with a team from Asgarth defeating the representatives of Askrigg Rifle Range by 23 points that same month.

Meanwhile, the professional and territorial units of the British Expeditionary Force had crossed the English Channel on declaration of war and moved into Belgium. Near Mons the British were struck by the full weight of the aggressive German First Army Group. Outnumbered, the British fought back stoutly, their rifle fire discipline taking heavy toll of the close German formations, but they were forced back onto a long retreat during August.

According to the historian of the "History of the First World War":

"During the thirteen days of the retreat, five of the seven German armies scythed down towards Paris, on a 75 mile front. For the troops on both sides they were days of endless marching under a scorching sun, marching until nearly every man seemed to have nails through the soles of his boots into his blistered feet, and the horses had worn their shoes wafer thin. Every movement was hampered by refugees. Order and counter order plagued both sides.

"In the days between Mons and the Battle of the Marne, the BEF, smallest of the Allied armies, played a vital role for it found itself at the outset right across the axis of advance of Kluck's army, the most powerful of all the German armies, with 320,000 men."

An important holding action took place at the Battle of Le Cateau, August 26th, when the BEF earned its place in history for the desperate and dogged resistance that took place when no one on either side could possibly have expected it. Again, the disciplined fire power of the professional British Army amazed the oncoming German soldiers as the British rifleman pumped out bullets at the rate of sixteen to the minute.

At the Battle of the Marne, September 5th to the 10th, the German advance was brought to a halt, and then turned back, with the BEF, severely mauled but showing great powers of recuperation, playing a vital role. Now came the "Race to the Sea", between September 15th and November 24th, as each side tried to outflank the other in a bid to take the Channel ports.

The final action of the "Race to the Sea" was the bloody First Battle of Ypres, October 30th to November 24th (there would be three further major battles here during the war), in which the BEF was nearly wiped out in a successful, gallant defence against a heavily reinforced German drive that was expected by them to capture the Channel ports.

It was during this crucial battle that Wensleydale received news of its first casualties, when two soldiers, one from Hawes and the other from Spennithorne, were killed during the desperate opening days of the conflict.

PRIVATE FREDERICK COCKETT
NO. 6006 1ST BATTALION SCOTS GUARDS
DIED THURSDAY 29TH OCTOBER 1914 AGE 28.

Frederick Cockett was born in Hawes in 1886 to 21 year old domestic servant and single parent Elizabeth Cockett, the sister of the local butcher Henry Cockett. A few years later she married the father of Fred, Joseph Moore, the

Hawes coal and coke merchant, and settled down to married life at the Holme, in Hawes, where five other children were born. Fred, however, retained the surname Cockett.

By 1901, fourteen year old Fred was to be found boarding with John Wear and his wife, the Hawes tailor and shopkeeper. Together with another boarder, 17 year old Robert Staveley, they worked as tailor's apprentices for Mr. Wear. Both lads would eventually go to fight for King and Country during the coming conflict, but only Robert would return safely to Hawes. It is also sad to relate that Fred Cockett's younger brother, John Moore, would also fall on the battlefield and his name too is commemorated in the church at Hawes. Elizabeth would therefore lose two sons during the five years of warfare.

Frederick Cockett (Hawes)

At some point well before the Great War began, Frederick had forsaken his career as a tailor by joining the regular British Army and serving in the Scots Guards. At the start of hostilities, in August 1914, Fred, who was married with a young child and living away from Wensleydale, had been on the Reserve List for one year. He was recalled to the Colours and joined his old Regiment, in the 1st Battalion. On the 14th August the BEF landed in France and Frederick found himself involved in the retreat from Mons, action at Le Cateau and in the Battle of the Marne.

CAPTAIN HUGH CLERVAUX CHAYTOR (26TH KING GEORGE'S OWN LIGHT CAVALRY) ATTACHED TO "B" SQUADRON 11TH HUSSARS (PRINCE ALBERT'S OWN) DIED SATURDAY 31ST OCTOBER 1914 AGE 30.

Hugh Clervaux Chaytor was born at Spennithorne Hall in 1883, the son of Clervaux Darley Chaytor and Frances Louisa Chaytor. An elder brother, Anthony Clervaux Chaytor and sisters Muriel and Violet, together with the youngest brother, Francis, completed the family (Violet married into the Orde-Powlett family of Thorney Hall, Spennithorne). The Chaytors, Orde-Powletts and Van Straubenzees were the three principal land owners in the parish of Spennithorne and Harmby.

Hugh followed a strong family tradition by joining the army in his early years and by 1914 had reached the rank of Captain in a Cavalry Regiment. Stationed in India, he enjoyed the military and social life of a young officer on the sub-continent, as a member of the 26th King George's Own Light Cavalry. By this time both his father and his mother were dead.

His brother Anthony had seen much foreign service, being gazetted from Public School to the King's Own Yorkshire Light Infantry during the Boer War 1901 and served with the Northern Nigerian Regiment 1904-1909 as a Captain. At the start of the Great War Anthony was attached to the Special Reserve of the K.O.Y.L.I. but by late August 1915 he had been promoted to temporary major with a battalion of the Lancashire Fusiliers in Kitchener's New Army. The youngest son, Francis, later became a Brigadier in The Royal Artillery during the Second World War.

By August 1914 Hugh Chaytor was no longer with the 26th Light Cavalry in India. The Regiment remained on the sub-continent until it arrived in France in mid-November but Hugh had been attached to 12th Reserve Cavalry Regiment. He left Aldershot on 14th September to be seconded to the 11th Hussars, who were already in France. During his short service of 46 days with the Regiment he made himself extremely popular with all ranks.

One of the most heroic actions fought by the BEF during the retreat from Mons to the Marne was that at Nery, a village near Compiegne, where, on September 1st, a single battery of Royal Horse Artillery, which, with the 1st Cavalry Brigade was covering the withdrawal of III Corps, held off for several hours the whole of the German 4th Cavalry Division. The 5th Dragoon Guards were stationed in the northern part of the village, with their horses in the open. The 11th Hussars covered the eastern side of the village with their horses under cover in houses, barns and sheds. On the western outskirts were the Queen's Bays. Three VC's were won by the artillery battery during the hours of battle and this combined action virtually destroyed the 4th German Cavalry Division as a fighting force.

Captain Chaytor was too late to take part in the Battle of the Marne in early September, which saw the German Army advance brought to a halt. However, by the 15th September he had arrived to join the 11th Hussars.

In the advance from Bethune to the Lys River the 11th Hussars distinguished themselves, playing their part in securing the Lys crossings. Its reconnaissance in flat, enclosed country dotted with houses and farms had meant casualties, all of which occurred mounted, at close range, but the necessary information had been secured. Sir John French wrote of this period 11th to 20th October, "Of all the splendid work performed by the cavalry, little can compare in results achieved with this advance." A large tract of country had been cleared of enemy, and the cavalry regiments had performed admiringly. But now the "Race to the Sea" was over, with neither side the winner, and over too, unfortunately, was mounted fighting cavalry work for the regiments of 1914.

On 14th October the first British troops, including Captain Hugh Chaytor, reached the ancient cloth centre of Ypres in Belgium. Here it was decided by the Allies to make a stand. Beyond was barely 20 miles of open country to the Channel ports. If the German Army broke through at Ypres, the war could be lost. By the 20th October Frederick Cockett had also arrived and prepared to take part in the action.

The First Battle of Ypres proved to be the graveyard of the old regular British Army. The Germans threw huge numbers of barely trained conscripts, many of them students, at the defending British and so terrible were the German casualties that the battle would be known to the Germans as the "Slaughter of the Innocents".

British casualties too, were enormous, and despite an heroic defence, the enemy advanced from three sides to within a few miles of Ypres.

The fighting for Messines Ridge, near Ypres, began in earnest on October 21st, with the Cavalry Corps to the east of Messines village. They were driven out of their rudimentary trenches and back towards Hollebeke. Orders came for Hugh and the rest of the British cavalrymen to abandon their horses and dig in and prepare defences for another German attempt to push them off the Ridge.

Tired but determined, the cavalrymen and infantry held the defences over the 22nd and 23rd October, with rifles and a limited number of machine-guns.

For a week the Germans attacked other parts of the line but then made a concerted effort to press the British again. A number of heavy guns had been placed and came into action again on the 29th/30th October, pounding the defences and hoping to annihilate the British cavalry and infantry who had dug in. It was on the day of 29th October that Private Frederick Cockett was killed whilst defending the line with the Scots Guards. His body was never recovered and he was later commemorated on Panel 11 of the Menin Gate at Ypres. Sadly for his family his death was not confirmed officially until December 1915, one year later.

On 26th October the Scots Guards had marched via Hooge to reinforce the line at Gheluvelt. An attack was made over very open ground but was held up by the enemy's artillery and machine-gun fire.

Whilst in the trenches at Gheluvelt over the next two days, they learned of an attack by the German 27th Reserve Regiment for 5.30a.m. on the 29th October. By 12 noon on that day the line held by the Gloucesters was broken and the

Coldstream Guards and Black Watch were forced to retire. Half of "B" Company and two sections of "C" Company Scots Guards, including Fred Cockett, were thus isolated and surrounded, and nothing more was ever heard of them.

Other sections of the Battalion held the enemy off all day and accounted for many Germans, until the 3rd Brigade was brought up in the evening and the line readjusted, but sadly, Fred Cockett was dead.

Meanwhile, on the morning of 30th October, heavy enemy artillery fire, some kilometres south of Gheluvelt, caused the Cavalry Brigade, with Hugh Chaytor, to vacate their position. The hamlet of Wambeke had already fallen to the attackers. Messines village, where the Queen's Bays, Dragoon Guards and 11th Hussars had made themselves ready with outer defences on the eastern side of the village, was attacked during the afternoon by Wurtembergers who were repulsed and unable to enter the village because of British rifle fire and the help of British 60 pounder artillery pieces.

German artillery shelled Messines church, as they believed the British were using the tower for artillery observation, and British troops entered the building to try and save some of the religious artefacts. German howitzers close to the edge of the village pounded the houses and defences throughout the night.

Just before dawn on 31st October, with the Kaiser himself present to direct operations, Germans of the 119 Grenadier and 125 Infantry Regiments, cheering and blowing horns, made a sudden attack and captured some of the British line, which was not a continuous trench but a series of short lengths. Further attacks were made but the Germans were forced back.

By now the front was along the main village street, and both the defenders and attackers were getting tired and desperate. British reinforcements worked their way up the western slope of the Ridge and into the village. Both sides fought hard, with the battle going on into the night, but the British were forced at last to withdraw from the village.

It was during the desperate actions taking place within the ruins of Messines village that Captain Hugh Clervaux Chaytor lost his life. As with Frederick Cockett, Hugh Chaytor's body could not be buried and instead his name was later commemorated on Panel 1 of the Menin Gate at Ypres.

The Commonwealth War Graves Commission give his date of death as the 31st October but in "The History of the 11th Hussars" it says that on the morning of the 30th October Captain Chaytor and Lieutenant Lawson-Smith and fourteen men were hopelessly buried and lost their lives when a number of shells burst at the end of their trench.

The Menin Gate, where the two names are inscribed, is on the site where thousands of Empire troops passed out of Ypres towards the Menin Road. It was

The Menin Gate at Ypres, showing the moat and Vauban's Ramparts.

unveiled and dedicated on 24th July 1927 by Field Marshall Plumer, in the presence of the King of the Belgians.

The Gate names those who fell between the 4th August 1914 and 15th August 1917, some 54,900, and who have no named grave. To let one's eye rove over the Panels of the dead is to appreciate to a tiny degree the price paid for Ypres' defence. Every night at 8p.m. precisely the traffic is halted through the Gate, and buglers from the local fire brigade play the Last Post. This ceremony has been carried out every night since 1929, except for the period of German occupation during World War II. Better still, to return late at night when the crowds have gone, the Gate floodlit, and one can wander alone onto Vauban's ramparts. Then it is not difficult to conjure up the ghosts of a lost generation that surround this now rebuilt, vibrant town.

On 31st October, the day that Hugh Chaytor died, the Grenadier Guards were "holding on by their eyelids" to the SE of Ypres. Casualties were high and the situation desperate. Regiments, battalions, all units became mingled and at one point in the afternoon, a message came from First Corps Commander, Sir Douglas Haig, that the Grenadiers were to hold their ground at all costs. Haig stated that he relied on the Grenadiers to save First Corps, and possibly the Army.

The Grenadiers held their ground and heroic actions elsewhere by the BEF blunted any further German advance. The Germans would continue to batter the thin line of defenders around Ypres, but the crisis had passed. The "immortal salient" had been created.

Back home in England, Wensleydale folk, especially the women, were already involved in making life a little more comfortable for the men who were fighting abroad or in training in England. In September 1914 at East Witton, a working party had been started by the vicar's wife, Mrs Garrod, to provide socks and shirts for soldiers at the Front or in hospital. 31 people joined the group. The ladies met on Saturdays at the school and already a fine pile of garments had been collected.

During the same month, a sum of £10 was forwarded from the funds of the late Hawes Troop of Boy Scouts to the "Good Luck" Fund of the "Carlyle Club", Piccadilly, to enable the Club to despatch 200 parcels of cigarettes and tobacco to the front. The King's Own Yorkshire Light Infantry had been chosen as the recipients. Hawes Cricket Club also sent £5-5-0d to the same fund in October for the benefit of the Yorkshire Regiment and each packet was to have "Hawes Cricket Club" printed on the side.

By December 1914, eight pairs of socks had been sent to the Belgian refugees being housed in Middleham. The 2nd Battalion Yorkshire Regiment (the Garrison Battalion at Richmond) had received 21 flannel shirts, with similar items distributed to the Lady Mayoress of Leeds for the Red Cross, and the 2nd Siege Battery of the Royal Field Artillery was the beneficiary of socks, mittens and mufflers. Miss Aydon, the church organist, had also organised a weekly collection amongst the Sunday School scholars on behalf of the Belgian Relief Fund. Throughout the dale, these tasks were being undertaken in each and every parish.

Whilst this work on the Home Front continued, further sad news reached Wensleydale, and the parish of Spennithorne and Harmby in particular, that another person associated with the parish had been killed, just one day after the death of Captain Hugh Chaytor. This tragic loss did not occur on the blood sodden battlefields of the Marne or Flanders' Fields, but far away on the vast open spaces of the Pacific Ocean.

LIEUTENANT COMMANDER
PERCIVAL VAN STRAUBENZEE, HMS "GOOD HOPE" R.N.
DIED SUNDAY 1ST NOVEMBER 1914 AGE 33.

Born in 1880, Percival was the son of Major General Turner van Straubenzee C.B. and Mrs. Florinda van Straubenzee of Spennithorne House.

The van Straubenzee family have their roots in Holland, but their arrival in England came about through their ancestor, Philip William Casimar van Straubenzee, born 1723 in Holland. He followed his father into the army but when the troops from the German state of Hesse came to England in 1745 under treaty obligations to defend Hanoverian King George II against the Jacobite rebellion, Philip got leave to join the Hessian force.

Whilst billeted in England he married Jane Turner, daughter of wealthy parents, against their wishes, and took her back to Holland. In 1748 he resigned his Dutch commission and returned to England with his wife. Naturalised by Act of Parliament, he settled down to country life, first at Kendal and then Kirkby Lonsdale. Three sons and a daughter were born and so was founded the English side of the van Straubenzee family. Eventually, the family home became Spennithorne House in the Wensleydale village of Spennithorne.

Their military tradition was to be perpetuated throughout the following generations. Phillip's great grandson, General Sir Charles Thomas van Straubenzee, served in the British Army in Coorg in 1834 and succeeded to the command of the 39th Regiment at the Battle of Maharajpore, India, in 1843. The General was in command of a Brigade in the Light Division in the Crimean Campaign 1854 – 1856 and, at the sacking of the Fortress of Sebastopol 1855, the Golden Cross from the Military Chapel in the White Barracks was brought home as a trophy to England by the General. It now stands on the family vault of the van Straubenzee's in Spennithorne chuchyard.

General Sir Charles went on to command the land forces at the capture of Canton, in China, and was Governor of Malta 1872 – 1878. Another member of the family, Major General Turner van Straubenzee, carried on the family tradition by commanding the Royal Artillery of the Indian Contingent in the Egyptian Campaign in 1882 and was General Officer Commanding the Madras District, India, 1891—1895. He and his wife Florinda had three sons and it was their second son, Percival, who was to die during the first year of the Great War.

Entering the Royal Navy as a Cadet, the young Percival van Straubenzee found himself engaged on matters of Empire and "Gunboat Diplomacy" in 1897, when, as a 16 year old, he was involved in the Benin Expedition in West Africa.

Benin City was the capital of one of the most highly organised states on the west coast of Africa between the 14th and 17th centuries, with political power residing with the Oba, or king. By 1702, however, a civil war had brought about severe depopulation and the fortunes of Benin fluctuated over the next two centuries, and after the abolition of the slave trade there appears to have been a general decline.

In 1885 the coastline was placed under British protection. Attempts were made to persuade the Oba (king) to end the custom of human sacrifices at state rituals and to enter into trading relations. In January 1897 an unarmed British mission set off for Benin despite a warning from the Oba that he was engaged in annual rites and would be unable to see its members. On the way, eight Europeans and many African carriers were massacred.

A punitive expedition, under Admiral Sir Harry Rawson, with young Percival van Straubenzee as one of the party, landed on the Benin River on February 12th, and after six days severe fighting the city was captured and partly burned; it was found to be reeking of human sacrifices. The Oba was deported to Calabar and seven chiefs held responsible for the massacre were executed. The government was entrusted to a council of chiefs under the guidance of British officials.

Seventeen years later, in early October 1914, Percival van Straubenzee, having risen to the rank of Lieutenant Commander in the Royal Navy, was to be found in the South Atlantic acting as the Gunnery Officer on board the heavy cruiser HMS "Good Hope", in the region of the Falkland Islands. The ship and its crew were soon to be lost at the Battle of Coronel, off the coast of Chile, on November 1st 1914.

This unlikely location for a sea battle between two European nations came about as a direct result of their Empire building rivalry. The Germans had built up a considerable number of possessions in the Pacific prior to 1914 and from

H.M.S. 'Good Hope', Flagship of Rear Admiral Sir Christopher Cradock. Its Gunnery Officer was Percival Van Straubenzee. The ship was sunk at the Battle of Coronel, 1st November 1914.

Rear Admiral Sir Christopher Cradock.

Robert C. Hutchinson (from Dent).

its Chinese base at Tsingtao, the East Asiatic Squadron, under the command of Admiral von Spee, patrolled the German Pacific "Empire".

With the outbreak of war this Squadron dispersed, with the light cruiser "Emden" causing chaos in the Bay of Bengal, while the other ships, "Scharnhorst", "Gneisenau", "Nurnberg", "Leipzig" and "Dresden" vanished into the Pacific. Eventually it became clear that the Squadron was heading for the Atlantic, via Cape Horn, and Britain feared that its supplies from Argentina could be cut off. The East Asiatic Squadron had to be stopped but the British ships available to do it were "not up to the job".

Some 2,200 fully trained long service German sailors, who were reckoned among the most efficient in the Imperial German Navy, were to fight a smaller number of Britons, the vast majority of whom had been happily pursuing civilian vocations less than six months before, and who now had little more than their pride and their courage to give them confidence.

The only British ships west of Cape Horn, South America, were the old armoured cruiser "Monmouth", the modern light cruiser "Glasgow" and the armed merchantman "Otranto", while just east of the Horn, at the British coaling base at Port Stanley on the Falkland Islands, the admiral commanding this collection of ships, Rear Admiral Sir Christopher Cradock, waited in the armoured cruiser "Good Hope", with Percival van Straubenzee as his Gunnery

Officer. These ships were too lightly gunned to take on the modern German Squadron, for they would soon be proved to be out-ranged and out-gunned.

However, by 4p.m. on Sunday November 1st 1914, Cradock's force arrived off the Chilean coast at Coronel, 250 miles to the south of Valparaiso. Everything favoured the German ships, but Rear Admiral Cradock felt he had no option and attacked at 6.18p.m., to the cheers of his 2000 men. Within the hour, the "Good Hope" and "Monmouth" were mangled wrecks of metal, burning from bow to stern, and out of action.

"Monmouth" especially received the full attention of the guns of "Gneisenau", which had won the Kaiser's Gold Cup for marksmanship only months before, and began to sag out of line. Flames belched from her quarter decks, water flooded through gaping holes in her bow, she listed badly to port and as darkness increased she disappeared to the south and her guns lapsed into silence.

Since action had commenced at 7.04p.m., Cradock's flagship "Good Hope" had received the individual attention of the gunners aboard "Scharnhorst", who had hit her with their third salvo, and who since then had been firing at her at a rate of four salvoes every minute.

At 7.40p.m. "Good Hope" was seen to slow and stagger under the rain of blows; her foredeck was ablaze, clouds of steam and smoke billowed around her, glowing sullenly. Blanketed under a dreadful fire from both the "Scharnhorst" and "Gneisenau", "Good Hope" was at last brought to a halt, with her upper deck a sea of flame, and she drifted down silently between the line of ships.

Then the fires reached a main magazine and at 7.53p.m., fifty minutes after the first salvo had been fired at her, "Good Hope" was shattered by a tremendous explosion. A broad column of flame rose upwards from beneath her main and after funnels until it towered 200 feet above her decks. Then the waves took the blazing hulk further off into the darkness, the flames dwindling as it drifted out of the battle.

At 8.35p.m. the "Nurnberg" found H.M.S. "Monmouth" painfully making her way towards the Chilean coast, and, as the British ship made no attempt to strike her colours, had little choice but to re-open the action and finally sink her. There were no survivors and none from the "Good Hope", which was never seen again after she drifted from the battle.

In two hours the Royal Navy had lost two ships and over 1000 men and boys, including Spennithorne's Lieutenant Commander Percival van Straubenzee and a young sailor from the village of Dent, in neighbouring Dentdale, Able Seaman Robert G. Hutchinson. The Germans had suffered just two wounded sailors. Both Percival and Robert's names are to be found on the Portsmouth Naval Memorial, on Southsea Common, commemorating Royal Navy personnel who have no known grave.

The German triumph was short lived. Admiral Von Spee's Squadron was to be destroyed a month later off the Falkland Islands by a powerful British force. Von Spee, planning to run into Port Stanley to raid the British wireless and coaling stations, discovered the British Squadron there, re-fuelling. The surprised Germans took to their heels, and the British, in hot pursuit, destroyed the German ships at long range. Of the five German ships, only the "Dresden" escaped. 2000 German sailors and their Admiral were lost. The "Good Hope" and Percival van Straubenzee were avenged.

Only two days after Percival's death, another Wensleydale sailor, from the neighbouring village of East Witton, went down with his craft, but on this occasion it was closer to home, in the murky grey waters of the North Sea.

LEADING STOKER JOHN ROBERT LEAKE
NO. 304084 H.M.S./D5
DIED TUESDAY 3RD NOVEMBER1914 AGE 30

John Robert Leake was the only son of the late John Leake and Jane Elizabeth Leake, a widow living with her daughter Hilda in the estate village of East Witton. Jane earned a living for her family as East Witton's post-mistress, the shop looking out across the large village green.

At the age of 18 years, Robert left the village in May 1903, to join the Royal Navy for a twelve year term of service. His Certificate of Service contained 12 annual reports, each being marked "Very good". He gained two Good Conduct Badges, one in 1906 and the other in 1911 and passed three examinations to qualify him for his special work. He had joined the Submarine Branch of the Royal Navy, in which section he progressed to become Leading Stoker.

By August 1914 the Royal Navy possessed 78 submarines in service, with 65 of these operating in home waters. One of these was "D" Class submarine No. 5, the vessel in which Robert Leake went off to war. Completed in 1912 at the Vickers Yard in Barrow-in-Furness, it had a complement of 25, including its Commanding Officer, Lieutenant Commander Godfrey Herbert.

On Tuesday 3rd November, German cruisers made a surprise raid on the British east coast off Gorleston, near Great Yarmouth, but were driven off. Submarine "D5", with Robert Leake on duty, was patrolling off Great Yarmouth at the time and struck a German mine, dropped by either a German submarine or one of the raiding enemy cruisers.

"D5" sank very quickly and only five crewmen on the bridge survived and were picked up by a local fishing drifter, "Faithful". Unfortunately, Robert was one of the 20 crewmen to lose their lives.

On Saturday November 14th at 2.30p.m. a memorial service was held at East Witton Church for John Robert Leake, taken by the vicar, Canon Garrod, There was a large congregation and a good attendance of the choir. The bell ringers gave a muffled peal, before and after the service.

The vicar expressed the deep sympathy which everyone in East Witton felt for Mrs. Leake and her daughter and friends in their terrible bereavement. Perhaps, by and by, when the first shock was over, mother and sister would be proud of the young hero who died fighting for his country, and would feel that his short life had not been spent in vain.

The preacher exhorted his congregation "to pray earnestly that the God of Battles would so direct the issue of the war that righteousness should prevail, and that the world should soon have the blessing of an honourable and lasting peace". It may be added that amongst the congregation were three wounded Belgian soldiers, who, with others, were being cared for through the kindness of Mr. and Mrs. Scrope of nearby Danby Hall, near Thornton Steward.

John Robert Leake's name is honoured on Panel 4 of the Portsmouth Naval Memorial.

We have seen that in the space of four terrible days Wensleydale had lost four fine men, but unfortunately this was to be just a portent of what was to come.

In France and Belgium throughout December 1914 an Allied offensive beat unsuccessfully for ten bloody days against the rapidly growing German system of field fortifications. The era of stabilised trench warfare from the North Sea to the Swiss border had begun; the spade, the machine-gun and barbed wire ringing down the curtain on manoeuvre.

As 1914 drew to a close and Wensleydale mourned the loss of Frederick Cockett, Hugh Clervaux Chaytor, Percival van Straubenzee and John Robert Leake, the enormity of the conflict became apparent to everyone as casualty lists were posted. By this time operations on the Western Front had already cost the Allies nearly one million casualties, with German losses almost as great. The Germans had not won a quick victory and now the Western Front would settle down to four years of bloody attrition. Wensleydale would not be spared its share of the country's heartache.

CHAPTER TWO
1915 — HOPES ARE DASHED

The realities of war in 1914 had dispelled all thoughts of an early end to the conflict. The eyes of the British public had been rudely opened by the widening of the conflict to new theatres of war and by the vast casualties resulting from the early campaigns. Nevertheless, the feeling persisted that once Kitchener's New Army of volunteers was ready in 1915, the combined efforts of the Allies would then soon defeat the enemy.

During the months of mid to late 1915, the war came physically into the realm of Wensleydale folk when huge tented army camps were pitched in the fields stretching between Leyburn and Wensley. Regiments, including battalions

Lines of the Durham Light Infantry, September 1915 in the fields at Westfield, between Wensley and Preston under Scar.

By permission of Clive Torrens.

Soldiers from the Wensley encampment marching along Redmire's village street 1915.
By permission of Clive Torrens.

Wensley camp near Leyburn, in June 1915. View taken from Leyburn Shawl and shows Penhill in the background.
By permission of Clive Torrens.

from several Scottish regiments and the Durham Light Infantry, came into the district to train, in readiness for service on battlefields overseas. Marching columns of soldiers, horse drawn army transport and soldiers taking part in military exercises became a common sight in Wensley, Redmire, East Witton and Middleham.

The soldiers in the camps had the Church Room and Town Hall at Leyburn put at their disposal. Newspapers, magazines and notepaper, as well as refreshments of tea, coffee and mineral water were provided by a Committee of ladies. Vocal and musical entertainment helped to pass the time when the soldiers were off duty.

At Middleham, a large marquee had been erected in the grounds around the Castle ruins and refreshments provided at a nominal fee. These arrangements had been carried out by the Local League of Honour. In Middleham Town Hall a reading and writing room was provided, whilst Middleham Weslyan Chapel had also provided a tea room. At Leyburn, a large hall had been erected in a field kindly lent by Lord Bolton, opposite the railway station, where cinema entertainment was organised for the benefit of the servicemen.

In August 1914 the men of Leeds had heeded the call by their Lord Mayor and rallied to the colours, many enlisting in the 15th Battalion, West Yorkshire Regiment ("The Leeds Pals"). Lord Swinton, with estates between East Witton

The photograph shows the first cinema in Leyburn, constructed in 1915 for the benefit of the soldiers encamped at Wensley Camp, at Westfield. The temporary wooden building, with canvas roof, was situated close to the present day Leyburn petrol filling station on Harmby Road, but by around 1917 it had been dismantled. After the war 'The Pavilion' cinema was built on this same site, which, together with the present-day 'Elite' cinema, provided Leyburn with two picture-houses.

By permission of Clive Torrens.

and Masham, in the Colsterdale area, gave permission for them to train at Breary Banks, near Colsterdale (part of the ecclesiastical district under the direction of Canon Garrod of East Witton Church).In September 1914, we have seen that an army camp for the "Leeds Pals" was set up in the hutted encampment previously occupied by the navvies who had worked to construct the nearby Leighton Reservoir.

On March 16th/17th 1915 the "Leeds Pals" were at East Witton when Field Operations between "C" and "D" Companies took place in the neighbourhood. "C" Company (Red Army) advanced from Coverdale on Bedale. "D" Company (Blue Army) were defending Bedale and early on 16th March took up a position west of Middleham, which the Red Army attacked later in the day and drove them back nearly to East Witton.

At night, outposts were posted by both sides, the Reds making Middleham their headquarters, whilst East Witton was occupied by the Blues. Early on the 17th March a spirited engagement between the outposts took place and eventually the Blue Company were compelled by superior numbers to evacuate East Witton and retire west. Here they took up a strong position, which they successfully held until the bugle sounded the "cease-fire".

After months of training in the area, the "Leeds Pals" embarked for Egypt in the latter part of 1915, their destination the new theatre of war at Gallipoli, where they would fight for real against the Turks. Some of the men who had fought in mock manoeuvres in Wensleydale would lose their lives on this battlefield, but it was to be on the first day of the Battle of the Somme, on July 1st 1916, that the vast majority of the Battalion would be decimated.

Just as with every other town and village throughout Wensleydale, East Witton continued to provide comforts for the Belgian refugees, for serving soldiers and wounded servicemen. On January 8th a concert was held in aid of the Belgian Relief Fund at the village schoolroom, whilst on February 12th the school children gave an entertainment to raise funds.

During April 1915, in East Witton, as

Memorial to the men of the 15th Battalion West Yorkshire Regiment ('The Leeds Pals') at Breary Banks, Colsterdale.

throughout the whole country, a movement began for a constant supply of fresh eggs for the wounded and sick soldiers in hospital. Something like 200,000 a week were required and each village school became the collection point.

A parcel of socks, mufflers and mittens was forwarded by Mrs. Garrod, through the War Office, to East Witton soldier Sergeant William Waite, and the following acknowledgement had been received:

"Madam, On behalf of Number 3 Section, 5th Division Ammunition Column, I wish to thank the ladies of the East Witton Working Party for the very useful articles they sent out for distribution by Sergeant Waite. They were very much appreciated by the men. Thanking the ladies for their kind gift."

On 19th September Sergeant William Waite, Royal Field Artillery, was writing from overseas to thank the children of East Witton:

"Dear children, One of the happiest surprises I have ever had occurred last week, when I received a parcel, and I am sure, if you only experience half the happiness that it has given to me, you will be happy indeed.

"Not only were the tobacco and cigarettes most welcome, but the fact that some of the dear little lasses and lads of England were thinking of me, afforded me the greatest delight and makes me more determined to go on doing my best to punish a wicked and cruel enemy."

During the early months of 1915 attempts were still being made to encourage the men of Wensleydale to join the Colours as William Waite had done. The first week in April witnessed a Recruitment March being made throughout the dale. The Darlington and Stockton Times announced on 10th April that "the sound of the bugle and the marching of men had been heard in Wensleydale that week and there had been stirring scenes of a military nature such as had seldom been witnessed in the North Yorkshire villages which dotted the valley of the Ure.

"The occasion had been a recruiting march of a contingent of the 4th Battalion Yorkshire Regiment and it was undertaken with the object of stirring up martial ardour with a view to securing at least some of the 500 men required to replace those falling out of the 4th Battalion, which was expected shortly to proceed to the Front. "D" Company was detailed for the purpose and the men, about 200 in number, were under the command of Major A.J. Fife.

"The men left Northallerton by special train on Tuesday morning, April 6th, to proceed to Hawes. News arrived at Hawes that the soldiers were arriving at 8a.m., instead of at noon, as previously arranged. A good number of towns people assembled at the station to witness and welcome them on arrival, but to their disappointment, only a few men — a fatigue party — arrived on the train. The rest of the party stopped at Askrigg at 8a.m. and after breakfasting and drilling there, set off accompanied by a bugle band, on their march to Hawes, where they arrived about noon.

"Rain fell heavily during the six mile march, making the conditions wretched indeed. When the sound of the bugle band accompanying the "Tommies" heralded their approach, large numbers of towns people lined the street "on the tip-toe of expectancy". At last the men were seen marching through the down-pour of rain with perfect precision. Their packs, which to the civilians seemed such a cumbersome load, were evidently no burden to them, and they marched at a remarkable pace. Their faces were ruddy with the glow of perfect health and they looked what they indeed were — a splendid body of highly trained and efficient men. Their mission was to obtain recruits, and how any young man eligible yet unwilling to follow their loyal example could look on them without a feeling of shame, passes understanding".

"Dinner was served for the hungry Territorials in the Market Hall (being provided by Mrs. T. Moore), and their healthy appetites testified to the splendid physical benefits resulting from a soldier's life. The continued rainfall prevented any drilling in the afternoon, but after they had partaken of tea the men were paraded in the market place and marched to the football field for drill. Hardly had they arrived, however, when down came the rain again, and they were marched back to the town, where the weather having cleared, they were put through military and physical drill by Captain F. Milbank. In this they showed themselves markedly efficient, demonstrating not only the thoroughness of their training, but also the enthusiasm of the men.

"During the spare hours of the day the sergeants and some of the privates

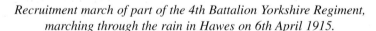

Recruitment march of part of the 4th Battalion Yorkshire Regiment,
marching through the rain in Hawes on 6th April 1915.

were busy among the many young men in the market place, trying to persuade them to join them, but with scanty success.

"In the evening the soldiers were entertained at a smoking concert in the Market Hall, which was crowded, the Reverend S.D. Crawford presiding. Songs and instrumental music were rendered by local artistes, and a most interesting singing competition was organised for the soldiers themselves, prizes being given for the best comic and best sentimental songs. Eight competed and some excellent singing was heard.

"The prizes, which consisted of pipes and tobacco, were distributed by Mrs. E.P. Gibson, who, in a brief address emphasised the need for recruits and urged all eligible young men to join at once. Sergeant Woodhead also spoke, calling upon the young men to come forward and do their duty to their King and Country. Six recruits were enrolled after the smoker.

"The soldiers were billeted for the night in the Market Hall and Council School, which provided ample accommodation. The men started for Aysgarth at 10a.m. on Wednesday 7th April, marching by way of Burtersett, Bainbridge and Worton. They departed in high spirits and all spoke highly of the way they had been entertained by the Hawes people. At Aysgarth the men were billeted at the Institute, in the school, by Mr. Dunbar and also by Mr. William Bell at the Flattlands. The soldiers received a hearty welcome and the same procedure was gone through as at Hawes. On Thursday, the route was via Carperby, Redmire and Preston to Leyburn and on Friday by Constable Burton to Bedale, whilst on Saturday 10th April the men returned to headquarters at Northallerton."

We find that at Bedale they had recruited seventeen men, who went up on stage to sign, which was in contrast to the nine men recruited throughout the rest of Wensleydale, between Hawes and Leyburn.

At the time that both Hawes and Middleham were deciding not to hold their Whitsuntide Sports for 1915, more attempts were being made to encourage the young men in the dale to join up voluntarily. At the Leyburn May Fair on Friday 14th May, the opportunity was taken to hold an open-air recruitment meeting, with addresses being delivered to the public from a motor car near the Town Hall.

One speaker stressed, "Some men up the dale have declared that they would go when they were fetched! That was not an English spirit." Another speaker said, "If my wife had come to Leyburn that day she would have been disgusted to see so many young men in the market who had not joined the army. If the men would not come forward freely, they would have to have some form of conscription." Six recruiting sergeants were busy in the town during that day and on the 17th May six recruits, John Moore, John Metcalfe, W. Johnson, John Fawcett, John Jackson and Simon Moore, all from the Hawes area, left that town for Richmond to join the Royal Field Artillery. It is sad to recount that we shall find five of these men would lose their lives before the war came to a close.

Most of the troops in training in the area were destined for service overseas and 1915 saw continued British involvement on the Western Front and in other theatres of war. Turkey's entrance into the war on Germany's side in October 1914 had changed the war's complexion. Russia, already shaken by the reverses of 1914, was now virtually cut-off from Franco-British war supplies. In an attempt to help Russia, a naval expedition was mounted to clear the Dardanelles for Russian ships in the Black Sea. When this venture stalled, an attack was planned on a little known peninsula called Gallipoli.

On the Western Front during 1915, the bulk of the BEF had remained in Flanders but as its size increased, it extended its front southwards, but only far enough to cross the wet levels of the River Lys into the dreary coal fields east of Lille, where, during 1915, it fought a series of minor, murderous trench to trench battles (Neuve Chapelle in March, Festubert May to June, and Givenchy) and also mounted one major, miscarried offensive at Loos in September to October. All were to be characterised by the extreme ferocity of the fighting and the miserable conditions which the terrain imposed.

Between Ypres and Armentieres, water was found everywhere close beneath the surface and much of the line had to be constructed of sandbag barricades instead of trenches. Almost everywhere, too, the Germans occupied what commanding heights there were. Near Ypres, the Passchendaele and Messines Ridges and in the coal fields, most of the slag heaps.

Compelled to struggle for possession of the higher, drier ground, the British had driven their lines in many places almost to within conversational distance of the Germans. British casualties mounted as these attacks were launched during 1915 and increased again when the Germans launched their own major assault at the Second Battle of Ypres (April to May), this latter assault seeing poison gas being used by the Germans for the first time in the west.

Increase of lethal fire-power had given the advantage to the defence, for a continuous battle line prevented classical offensive manoeuvres. The Germans, recognising the change long before the Allies, had adopted an elastic defence, in two or more lines, highly organised with entrenchments and barbed wire, heavy in machine-guns and supported by artillery. Assaulting troops broke through the first line only to be decimated by the fire from the succeeding lines.

As a consequence of these facts we find that the number of Wensleydale men who fell on the battlefield or died from wounds received throughout 1915, would gradually mount to a total of nine, with another "casualty" dying on home soil from natural causes, bringing the total for the year to ten.

RIFLEMAN CHARLES OSWALD SEWELL
NO. Z/74 3RD BATTALION RIFLE BRIGADE
DIED WEDNESDAY 17TH MARCH 1915.

Charles was born at Heckmondwike, near Dewsbury, Yorkshire, but in 1910 he arrived in Spennithorne and Harmby with his wife Annie and family to work as a quarryman at Harmby Quarry. Prior to that he had worked in the quarries at Horton-in-Ribblesdale, living at Foredale Cottage, Horton. In 1912 another child was born into the family. By the time that Charles went off to war, he and Annie had four children.

He enlisted at Leyburn in late August 1914 and by the early Spring of 1915 he was with his Regiment, 3rd Battalion Rifle Brigade, in the trenches in front of Armentieres. The Battalion spent five months from January 1915 in this sector of the front.

Charles Oswald Sewell (Harmby).

The War Diary states, "It was looked upon as a quiet bit of the line by other people, but we had our share of casualties, averaging four per day while in the trenches. Quite frequently we had a severe shelling from the Germans with 5·9 howitzers and it was seldom that our own shell allowance ran to more than 12 x 18 pounders a day in retaliation."

The Battalion Medical Officer, Lieutenant Somerville, would visit the trenches several times a day, coming up a communication trench with two feet of water in it.

So the Battalion, from January to May, carried out "routine trench warfare" and lost four men a day in a "quiet sector". It was on Wednesday 17th March that Charles Sewell helped to make up these statistics. A German shell landed in his trench and he was killed.

Charles is buried in grave VIII.A.20 in Ration Farm Military Cemetery, on the outskirts of Armentieres. He left a widow and four children, the eldest being six years old.

Just three weeks later another Wensleydale man died on home territory;

65

PRIVATE JOHN MILLS GOULD
NO. 17/1135 17TH (NORTH EASTERN RAILWAYS)
PIONEER BATTALION NORTHUMBERLAND FUSILIERS
DIED FRIDAY 9TH APRIL 1915 AGE 26.

John Gould was born in the town of Masham, North Yorkshire, in 1889, the son of George Gould, a draper, and Isabella Gould. Born at Exelby, near Bedale, George married Isabella, a County Durham girl, and set up business in Masham as a draper. Four children, Albert, May, John and George were all born at Masham, but by 1901 the family had travelled the short distance to live at Warnford House, Thoralby, with George still employed as a village draper. John Mills Gould was 12 years old and the second youngest in the family.

By 1914, the youngest child, George Sidney Gould, was living in Canada, having emigrated a few years earlier on one of the government schemes that took so many Wensleydale folk away to forge a new life in the Dominions. 26 year old John Gould was, however, working as a railway clerk at Ferrybridge when he enlisted in the army in January 1915, and prior to that job had worked on the clerical staff at Thirsk Station for six years.

John was in "E" Company 17th Northumberland Fusiliers and had been in training in the Hull area for just three months when the sad news of his death shocked his numerous friends in and around Thoralby and Aysgarth.

He was spending a few days leave with some friends at Ferrybridge and on Easter Sunday was taken ill, having contracted a chill. Pneumonia and pleurisy supervened and he passed away on the following Friday, 9th April.

His body was conveyed to Aysgarth Church on Monday and internment took place on Tuesday afternoon. Most of the Bishopdale homes were represented and 16 soldier comrades attended, with two buglers. His comrades fired three volleys over the grave and buglers sounded the Last Post. John Mills Gould is buried in the SW section of St. Andrew's Churchyard, Aysgarth.

John's younger brother, George Sidney Gould, volunteered to return to Britain with the Canadian Expeditionary Force and fight for Britain and the Dominions. He died, aged 26, on April 9th 1917 whilst attacking the Germans on Vimy Ridge. Within the space of a few years the Gould family had lost their two youngest children.

Across the Channel, however, the Allies were making preparations for another co-ordinated offensive in late April, early May, in the Ypres Salient, Belgium. These plans were spoiled by a surprise German attack on 22nd April, preceded by a cloud of chlorine gas emitted from some 5000 cylinders. This was the first use of poison gas in the West. The Second Battle of Ypres had begun.

Gas had an insidious effect, similar to pneumonia, with its victims slowly drowning as their lungs filled with fluid. Those who survived initial attacks could suffer from bronchial disease throughout their lives.

Two German Corps drove through two terrorised French Divisions and bit deeply into British lines, creating a wide gap. The Germans, however, had made no preparations to exploit such a breakthrough, and had few reserves available because of their build up of forces in the east, as they attempted to defeat the Russian armies.

Local counter-attacks by the British Second Army, including Canadian forces, finally stemmed the German advance by May 25th, after bitter fighting. German losses were some 35,000 men; the British lost 60,000 and the French about 10,000.

Two men associated with Wensleydale are included in these British losses:

SECOND LIEUTENANT GEORGE BARGH
KING'S REGIMENT (LIVERPOOL) ATTACHED TO THE
1ST BATTALION SUFFOLK REGIMENT
DIED MONDAY 10TH MAY 1915 AGE 25.

George was the son of Isaac (deceased) and Helen Bargh, of Proctor's Farm, Wray, near Lancaster. His people had farmed in Lunesdale for many years. He had received his early education at Halifax and subsequently obtained his B.Sc. at University College, Reading, where he was in the Officer Training Corps. In 1912 he became a very popular teacher at Hawes Council School, in Wensleydale, and was a keen player for the Hawes Football Club. He accepted his commission in the 4th Battalion King's Regiment (Liverpool) as a Reserve Army officer and at the summer vacation 1914 he left the area to join his Regiment.

During the fighting in the Second Battle of Ypres, George's Battalion was heavily involved. The sensible course for the defenders in the Ypres Salient would

George Bargh
(Hawes)

have been eventually to withdraw to the natural straight line of defence formed by the Ramparts of Ypres and the canal, but the political and sentimental objection to yielding ground, especially Belgian ground, led the British Commander, Sir John French, to order repeated counter-attacks and stay in the reduced Salient, "one huge artillery target", there to be pounded and gassed incessantly, with their scanty ammunition running low. This helps to explain the unusual position of the defenders losing almost twice as many men as the attackers during the Second Battle of Ypres.

Second Lieutenant George Bargh was killed in action on 10th May. His Battalion had lost 413 men in the fighting in front of St. Julien and he and the remnants had been attached to the 1st Battalion Suffolk Regiment to continue the fight. News of George's death reached his mother when she received a letter from Colonel Wallace, his Commanding Officer, who had been taken prisoner by the Germans during the bitter fighting. He reported that her son had been shot in the head just before the Germans took the trenches, as he was bandaging a wounded soldier, and was killed instantly.

In the confusion of battle, as attack was met by counter-attack, George's body was never recovered from the battlefield and his name is honoured on Panel 21 of the Menin Gate, Ypres.

Seven days later, Wensleydale lost a member of one of its most well known and respected families, the Orde-Powletts.

LIEUTENANT WILLIAM PERCY ORDE-POWLETT
4TH BATTALION YORKSHIRE REGIMENT
DIED 17TH MAY 1915 AGE 21.

Percy was the eldest child of the Honourable William G. Algar Orde-Powlett, M.P., and Mrs. Elizabeth Orde-Powlett (later the 5th Baron Bolton and Lady Bolton, of Bolton Hall, Wensley). Although born at Saltburn in 1894, by 1901 Percy was living at Wensley Hall with his parents, twin sister Elaine and younger brother Nigel.

He joined up on September 7th 1914 and was posted to the 4th Battalion Yorkshire Regiment, near Darlington, before leaving for Newcastle. The Battalion was stood to arms on November 3rd as firing had been heard off Lowestoft and Great Yarmouth, when German cruisers had fired at coastal targets. On December 16th they again stood by when Hartlepool, Scarborough and Whitby were bombarded by German heavy cruisers, with many civilians being killed and wounded in the raid.

On April 17th 1915 they left Newcastle for France and reached Boulogne at 2a.m. on the 18th. By train and route march they reached the Ypres Salient in Belgium.

At 1a.m. on 24th April, two days after the Germans had launched the offensive with a gas attack, the Battalion moved out to the Ypres Canal, where they experienced their first battlefield action. They lay under an intermittent shell fire, resulting in casualties, but at midday they were ordered to cross the Canal by a pontoon bridge.

As they dug a support line of trenches, a message arrived to say that the situation was critical, for the enemy had captured the village of St. Julien. The Battalion was to make good the village of Fortuin and push the enemy back into St. Julien and further.

They made their way through the wire for a mile under shell fire, crossing streams and meeting long range machine-gun fire from the left flank at Fortuin. St. Julien was strongly occupied by the enemy, who also held a muddy stream

Percy Orde-Powlett
(Wensley).

south of the village. Two companies advanced by rushes and the position was occupied, the enemy falling back in St. Julien. The Battalion had lost heavily whilst crossing the open level ground. At nightfall, orders came for them to fall back. This was the first action of the 4th Battalion in the Great War, a week after landing in France. The losses had been heavy, with 5 officers and 10 men killed, 1 officer and 59 men wounded and 17 missing.

Percy Orde-Powlett writes in a letter home , "This was the first time gas was used in the war, and our men had nothing but their handkerchiefs with which to keep it off, but people in London sat up all that night making respirators, which were despatched the next day."

Another extract from his diary relates to the first attack: "There was about 200 yards of open ground to cross. I confess that I did not expect that a single man would get over that open ground and reach the trenches. The fire was terrific; the ground was quite flat and was covered by German rifles and machine-guns; there seemed to be a shell bursting on every square yard of ground. However, it had to be done, and my platoon followed very well. We covered that ground pretty well. I went up to help the London Rifle Brigade. The company I got with had had all their officers wounded, but they were carrying on like heroes."

After a few days of so called "rest", with many casualties due to the shelling of their huts, they went back to the trenches for the next five days, shelled from the front and flank, gassed and attacked. They had their first touch of gas on May 1st and were also attacked on the 2nd, with casualties for this period being 34 killed and 80 wounded.

From the 9th to 12th May the Battalion was in reserve, spending the 14th in Ypres itself. Leaving the shattered town on the 15th May, the Battalion marched to the Railway Embankment. It was here, on May 17th, that Lieutenant Percy Orde-Powlett was killed. He had just left the cover of the first line of front trenches upon being relieved, when he was shot through the neck by a sniper, and died in a short time.

His Captain wrote, "It was a sad blow to us all to lose Percy, for we all loved him so. Gentle in nature, always cheerful and eager to work, brave and capable and confident —— the typical subaltern. Always thinking of the comfort of his men, he had turned to go along the trench with the intention of trying to drain it when he fell."

His Colonel wrote, "I had sent up Percy's name for mention in despatches, chiefly on account of the very gallant way he led his platoon in the first attack we made. He was always wonderful with his men and I think they adored him."

Percy Orde-Powlett's name is honoured on Panel 33 of the Menin Gate at Ypres.

The Darlington and Stockton Times of May 29th 1915 reported on the Memorial Service for the fallen officer at Wensley Church on Wednesday afternoon, 26th May. The paper reported that, "Wensleydale had lost in him one, who, if fate had permitted, would have been a public benefactor. He was a young man of high ideals, the future Lord Bolton, but his high sense of duty prompted him to run the imminent risk to his life by offering his services to his country in this terribly fatal war.

"After being at Eton College, where he was in the Officer Training Corps, he was an undergraduate at Cambridge University when the war broke out. He joined the 4th Battalion and on August 29th 1914 was gazetted 2nd Lieutenant, and on April 6th 1915 1st Lieutenant.

"Unselfishness was one of the outstanding features of his character, and he endeared himself to all those with whom he came in contact. In the 4th Yorkshires he was held in the highest regard and affection by both officers and men. By the men he was idolised and he would be particularly missed by the men of his own Platoon. The men knew to whom to apply to get a sympathetic hearing and a redress to grievances. He made it his particular care to look after the welfare of everyone of his men.

"Though, of course, a great deal away at school and college, the deceased loved his home at Wensley. He was extremely close to the schoolmaster, Mr. Briscoe, and a bond of sympathy and enjoyment of walks together was a common interest and a pleasure in nature study. The deceased made a special study of biology at Cambridge. He took an active interest in the Boy Scout Movement of Wensley and Leyburn, and acted as their scout leader at times. Had the nation been under its usual circumstances there would have been great rejoicings the previous month at Wensley for the celebration of his 21st birthday.

"At the Memorial Service in the old historic church of Wensley, the feeling with which the death was regarded and the sympathy for the deceased's parents was testified by the church being crowded. The service was conducted by the Reverend Ernest Orde-Powlett, Rector of Wensley, and half-cousin to the deceased. Percy's father was unable to attend on account of military duties."

21 months later, on 2nd February 1917, a beautiful stained glass window on the south side of Holy Trinity Church, Wensley, to the memory of Percy Orde-Powlett, was quietly dedicated by the Rector.

The Second Battle of Ypres came to a halt on May 25th after local counter-attacks by the British 2nd Army finally stemmed the German advance, after bitter fighting.

A week after the death of Percy Orde-Powlett, a soldier from Canada, but with strong connections in East Witton, was added to the list of the fallen from Wensleydale. He was killed some distance to the south, across the border in France, in the area known as the Artois.

CORPORAL BERTRAND (BERTIE) WILLIAM GREENHALGH NO. 13459 5TH BATTALION CANADIAN INFANTRY (SASKACHEWAN REGIMENT) DIED MONDAY MAY 24TH 1915 AGE 30.

Bertie Greenhalgh was born at Scarcliffe, near Bolsover in Derbyshire, in 1885, the son of William Greenhalgh, a Burnley man, and Nancy, a girl from Accrington. William was a schoolmaster who had married Nancy in 1870 and moved to the recently built Scarcliffe village school. By 1876 William was the headmaster. In 1871 a daughter Florence was born, in 1874 James Norman, in 1877 Edith and in 1885 Bertrand.

The family moved to Leeds some time after 1885 when William founded a private school "Springfield High School", with a colleague, Mr. Knightley. The school closed in 1889 and Bertie, a pupil at his father's school, went to Leeds Boys Modern School until the end of that year.

71

East Witton School and headmaster William Greenhalgh on extreme right, in 1910. William's son Bertie would be killed with the Canadian forces in 1915.

In late 1899 William took his family to East Witton, Wensleydale, to take up the post of village headmaster. Bertie and his brother James eventually joined the family at No. 14 East Witton and the two lads finished their education under the guidance of their father.

William Greenhalgh was the much loved and respected village headteacher for thirteen years until his retirement in 1913, aged 67. He became an indispensable member of village society, acting as organist and choirmaster at the church, parish clerk, Secretary of the Reading Room and of the Choral Society. In any social event, William was always heavily involved. He was also a highly accomplished artist and on his retirement from teaching would cycle over to Bedale Grammar School, where he gave lectures in Drawing.

William Greenhalgh, headmaster of East Witton School.

On the very day that war was declared by Britain, August 5th 1914, William was starting off from home on his bicycle when he collapsed and died. Practically the whole village population and estate workers on the Jervaulx Estate were in attendance at the funeral in East Witton Church on 8th August.

Bertie Greenhalgh was unable to attend his father's funeral. Since leaving school, the youngest son had spent some time employed in office work in Leeds, but before the war started Bertie had left England to make a new life for himself in Canada, encouraged by the government scheme to attract new settlers in the far-flung Dominion countries of the Empire.

He pursued a career in the Canadian Postal Services and became a mail clerk on the railway postal trains. Meeting his future wife Edith, from Keota, Iowa, USA, they settled down to married life in Wolseley, Saskatchewan, Canada, a town situated on the Canadian National Railway, 80 miles east of Regina, capital of the province.

When Britain declared war on Germany, the Dominions, including Canada, responded quickly and volunteers flocked to the Colours to go overseas and fight for the "Motherland". Bertie William Greenhalgh was amongst the first of his townsmen to enlist, being the only married man of the 42 volunteers from Wolseley.

Bertie enlisted on August 12th 1914 and by September 25th had been promoted to Corporal. With very little training behind them, the first Canadian contingent, 30,000 strong, reached Plymouth on October 14th 1914 and Bertie found himself on Salisbury Plain, involved in intensive training.

The Canadian First Division embarked for France on February 7th 1915 and after several route marches, arrived in billets at Hazebrouck on February 15th. Corporal Greenhalgh, 5th Battalion Canadian Infantry (Saskachewan Regiment) was one of two members of his Company chosen as grenade throwers. For whatever reason, on February 25th, just ten days after arriving in their billets, Bertie reverted back to the ranks.

By April 17th they had taken over a previously French held sector in the Ypres Salient and extremely heavy fighting developed in the St. Julien sector, held by the Canadians. By the time they were pulled out of the line and sent to rest near Bailleul on May 5th, Canadian casualties in the Second Battle of Ypres totalled 5,500.

Bertie had suffered slight wounds and was admitted to the 3rd Canadian Field Ambulance on May 6th but was discharged to duty on May 13th. There was to be very little respite for any of the Canadians for soon they were to be "sucked in" to the British attacks to the south, in the Battle of Festubert.

General Haig had been persuaded by Joffre, the French military leader, to commit British and Canadian forces to join in a French offensive aimed at capturing the heights of Vimy Ridge, with the objective of the British to capture Aubers Ridge and the village of Festubert.

The attack on Aubers Ridge on May 9th proved a costly failure but plans still went ahead to capture Festubert on the night of May 15th/16th, in support of the French offensive further south. It was the first major British night attack of the war, involving some 10,000 infantry, with the Canadian Division being held in reserve. The men wore white patches as distinguishing marks as they silently worked their way into no-man's land.

There was much confused fighting among the water-logged dykes. Once again, casualties were terrible and trivial progress was made. German opposition was hardening and on May 18th men were being killed by enfilading machine-gun fire almost before they had begun to move.

The collapse of the Battle of Festubert was now imminent. During the night of May 18th/19th Haig pulled out his men and replaced them with two British Divisions and the Canadian Division, in which Bertie Greenhalgh was a member. We have seen that the Canadians had suffered badly at 2nd Ypres and many of them were raw recruits.

Their short-scale ferocious attacks during the following eight days brought to a conclusion an action that had cost the lives of 710 officers and 15,938 men. Ammunition stocks were low and on May 26th the attack was called off. Two days earlier,one of the casualties had been Bertie Greenhalgh. In the vicious close encounter fighting that took place during those last few days of battle, Bertie had fallen on May 24th. He was one of 2,400 Canadian casualties.

It is believed that he was buried quickly in an unmarked grave but later his name was commemorated on the Vimy Memorial, on the highest point of Vimy Ridge, with these words in French and English around its base: "To the valour of their countrymen in the Great War and in memory of the 60,000 dead, this monument is raised by the people of Canada."

Bertie's name was also inscribed on the East Witton memorial in 1923 and, in

Vimy Memorial, France.

his home town of Wolseley, Canada, the flags were flown at half mast when the sad news of his death came to the town.

Further north, in the Ypres Salient, a serviceman with strong connections to Carperby was killed in early August, whilst serving in a working party behind the Front.

PRIVATE JOHN (JACK) GILBERT HARKER
NO. 8935 1ST/5TH BATTALION
SOUTH STAFFORDSHIRE REGIMENT
DIED 6TH AUGUST 1915 AGE 21.

Jack's grandfather, John Harker, was a lead miner from Gunnerside, Swaledale, who married his wife Nancy, a Morcambe girl. They were living at West Witton by 1861 and Carperby by 1871, as the lead mining industry declined. By 1881, however, Nancy was a widow farming 15 acres at Carperby cum Thoresby.

Four children resulted from the marriage, the second eldest being Edmund Harker. By 1891 Edmund, a railway clerk, was lodging with the Arnott family in Leeds, and married Minnie Arnott, one of the daughters. In 1894 a son, John (Jack) Gilbert Harker, was born at Bramley, but by the start of the Great War the family was living at Gravelly Hill, Birmingham, as Edmund's job on the railway meant that he moved around the country. However, most of Jack's uncles and aunts were still living in the Carperby area, either farming or working as postal assistants in the area, and Jack would visit on occasions.

Jack Harker volunteered to join the army in late 1914, enlisting at Handsworth, and by 1915 he was a private in the 1st/5th Battalion South Staffordshire Regiment. During July 1915 the Battalion was stationed in the Ypres Salient, SE of Ypres, defending the trenches in the Zillebeke, Armagh Wood and Hill 60 section of the line.

Although no major actions occurred, there was a constant trickle of casualties from shell fire, trench mortar, rifle grenade and sniper fire. Patrols and bombing parties were sent across no-man's land and the Royal Engineers reported that German sappers had been mining towards the South Staff's position on the SW slope of Hill 60. The engineers recovered 1,250 lbs. of German explosives from the mine gallery.

At 10.30p.m. on August 2nd the South Staffs were relieved in the line and went into Brigade Reserve at Railway Dugouts. For the next four days the time was passed in providing working parties for the Royal Engineers, repairing support trenches and communications systems. Although now behind the lines, danger was ever present from German artillery and on August 6th Jack Harker was killed by an exploding shell whilst helping the Royal Engineer's working party. Having been fortunate to escape death in the front line trenches, his luck ran out in a supposedly safer environment. His body was buried in grave 1.C.1 of the Railway Dugouts Burial Ground, close to where he was working.

It was to be many miles away from the Western Front, in the Turkish theatre of war, that the next casualty, a Middleham lad, was to fall in battle.

When Britain had gone to war with Germany, little or no thought had been given to the possibility of fighting Turkey. But Germany had built up a close relationship with Enver Pasha, the new Turkish leader, and encouraged a declaration of war by Turkey against Russia and Britain on October 29th 1914.

In January 1915, approval was given for a naval expedition to be mounted to clear the Dardanelles for Russian ships in the Black Sea. When this venture stalled, an amphibious operation led by General Ian Hamilton was planned on a little known peninsula called Gallipoli.

The plan provided for two daylight assaults on April 25th, one at Cape Helles on the tip of the Peninsula, the other by the Anzacs (Australian and New Zealand Army Corps) on the western side. At Cape Helles the British landed on five beaches in a welter of mismanagement, incurring murderous losses. The Anzacs were beaten back by a vicious Turkish counter-attack, with a loss of 5,000 men.

Both assaults had failed to capture the hill masses towering above the beaches and without these two critical heights the landings were doomed to failure. The Allied forces found themselves pinned down on their tiny beach heads, involved in the same kind of trench warfare experienced on the Western Front.

Between August 6th and 8th, following months of the bitterest fighting on the rocky slopes of the Peninsula, General Hamilton attempted a co-ordinated assault. The Anzacs were to make the main effort with a night attack. The newly arrived British Divisions, landing at Suvla Bay to the north, were to make a secondary attack, whilst from the Cape Helles position a holding attack was to pin down Turkish reserves.

The holding attack fulfilled its mission, but the Anzac attack bogged down in the darkness. Only the Suvla Bay landing, made without serious opposition, promised success. But the Corps Commander lacked vigour and drive. The advance lagged until Turkish reinforcements had time to come up, and again it was too late. The entire operation had failed.

It was to be in the fighting at Suvla Bay in August 1915 that a Middleham man was to lose his life.

CORPORAL CHARLES BALLAN MILLER
NO. 12374 6TH BATTALION YORKSHIRE REGIMENT
DIED SUNDAY 22ND AUGUST 1915 AGE 27.

Charles Ballan Miller was born in Middleham in 1888, the son of John Ernest Miller and Jane Miller, at Ivy Grove, the large house standing well back from the market place. John, a journalist and author, born in Chelsea, married Jane, a Middleham girl. Charles lived with his parents, elder sister Clara and younger siblings Florence and Hugh.

The family was well off, with John E. Miller making a living from newspaper writing about the horse racing scene, being well placed in living amongst the horse racing fraternity at Middleham.

As war was declared, the 26 year old Charles, married and with a young son, volunteered for service, enlisting at Middleham, and eventually joined the 6th Battalion Yorkshire Regiment.

In June 1915 the men were kitted out with Khaki uniforms and helmets and on July 3rd 1915 embarked on HMTS "Aquitania" in Liverpool docks. They passed Gibraltar, en route across the Mediterranean, their destination being the island of Lemnos, which they reached on Saturday July 10th. They disembarked the next day in the main harbour, Mudros Bay.

A fortnight was spent at Imbros, bivouacked on a sandy plain with no shelter at all. There they practiced night attacks, including night landings from small boats, as they prepared for the Suvla Bay attack.

At 10.30p.m. on August 6th the men were loaded into two lighters towed by destroyers, also packed with troops, and landed in pitch darkness on the beach, ready to attack the hilly area inland. Bursts of rifle fire greeted them as they charged up the slopes and took the hill. In the darkness confusion reigned, with battalions getting hopelessly mixed up.

The 6th Battalion had received heavy losses with 16 officers and 250 men killed and wounded. However, they remained in action over the next three days but by August 10th were pinned down in the trenches by heavy fire and withdrew on the night of August 11th/12th. No training was possible since, due to the shell fire, they were confined to a strip of beach twenty yards in width immediately below the cliffs.

On August 12th they moved forward to the fire trenches on Hill 50 whilst a fresh attack was being planned. They suffered dreadfully from the heat, want of water, the flies and dry rations. Turkish snipers trained their rifles on the few remaining wells.

Their objective was a nearby hill, 300 feet high. At 3p.m. the bombardment opened up, but the flat trajectory of the naval guns had done no damage to the

Turkish trenches which were deep and well concealed. At 3.30p.m. the attack began but there was a lack of direction, the shrapnel fire was heavy and Turkish machine-gunners were provided with a clear target. There could be no movement over the flat plain and the final attack was over by 4p.m.

The remnants of the Battalion stayed out until the next day but came back on the morning of the 22nd. When they reached the beach to go into reserve the decimated Battalion was only 285 strong, from a complement of 900, and was formed into a composite battalion. One of the many casualties was Charles Ballan Miller.

Charles's body was never recovered and he is commemorated on Panel 55 to 58 of the Helles Memorial, Turkey. The memorial is on the tip of the Gallipoli Peninsula. Its form is an obelisk 30 metres high, seen by ships passing through the Dardanelles. On the memorial are 21,000 names of the missing servicemen, who have no known graves.

It seems rather poignant to know that as Charles's life was ebbing away in far off Gallipoli, the people of Bainbridge and neighbouring parishes were making efforts in the August sunshine to help the cause of the wounded soldiers near the front line and in British hospitals. During the weeks of August large parties had

James Chapman in front of his shop in Bainbridge. The sphagmum moss bandages went on display here in 1915. He is holding the Bainbridge Horn. The custom of horn-blowing between 27th September and Shrovetide in early spring dates from the Middle Ages when Bainbridge was on the edge of a hunting forest of Wensleydale.

78

been organised to gather, dry and sort sphagmum moss in order to make special bandages for the wounded. It was collected from the Buttertubs Pass, Askrigg Moor, Wetherfell and Addlebrough. Soon, Bainbridge Green was dotted with considerable quantities, which had been laid in the sun to dry. The tedious task of picking out the grass was done in the Temperance Hall. Specimens were on view in Mr. James Chapman's Emporium.

Returning to events taking place on the Western Front, which was the main theatre of operations for the Allies, rumours abounded in September 1915 of a great Franco-British offensive which would shatter the German front. Kitchener's New Armies and Territorials were set to play a prominent role in the proceedings.

The British planned an assault on German positions near the village of Loos, in the bleak coal mining region between Bethune and Lens. The ground was unfavourable, being bare and open, swept by machine-gun and rifle fire from the German trenches and numerous fortified villages behind them. Many of those taking part on the British side were untried members of the New Army, with inadequate heavy artillery backing and shells. The omens were not good.

The Battle of Loos opened on September 25th 1915 with an artillery bombardment and the release of chlorine gas from over 5,000 cylinders. The gas carried fairly well over the German trenches on the right, but on the left was a failure, in some places drifting back and poisoning the British soldiers. Those who were able to advance were soon stopped and slaughtered by the un-gassed German machine-gunners.

When gaps did appear in the German defences, the British reserves were held too far back and could not exploit the opportunity. By September 26th these inexperienced reserves were marching across country in the dark and rain. Launched against a strong second line of defence on September 27th the attack broke down and survivors turned and flowed back.

On September 27th, during this day of ferocious fighting, a man with strong Spennithorne connections was killed in action. He had only been in France for sixteen days.

PRIVATE THOMAS WYNNE NO. 15518
14TH BATTALION DURHAM LIGHT INFANTRY
DIED MONDAY 27TH SEPTEMBER 1915 AGE 23.

Thomas Wynne was born at Burnley, in Lancashire, the son of Abraham Wynne, a joiner and carpenter. Abraham, a native of Liverpool, had married his wife Mary, who came from Leyburn, and settled in Burnley, where they raised their

The Old Horn Inn at Spennithorne c1911.
Abraham Wynne, father of Thomas, was landlord.

three sons, Thomas, William and Fred. However, by 1909, the family was living in Spennithorne, where Abraham was the landlord of the Old Horn Public House. By the outbreak of the Great War, Tom was living at Bedale and he enlisted as a volunteer in Kitchener's New Army at Sunderland, from where he was posted to the 14th Battalion Durham Light Infantry.

On the night of September 11th 1915 the Battalion crossed from Folkestone to Boulogne and entrained for the St. Omer district. Just one week later they marched off by night time route marches to take part in the tragic and dreadful fighting at the Battle of Loos.

At 7.15p.m. on September 25th they moved off in the rain in support of the 63rd Brigade. They were wet, tired and hungry, for all had been sacrificed to get the Division into the battle with the least possible delay. There was not even time to reconnoitre the ground.

Soon after 2a.m. on September 26th the old German front line was reached. When the mist lifted the German shell fire stopped all movement on the roads and casualties began to mount.

At 9.50a.m. a battalion was needed to reinforce the right flank in Chalk Pit Wood, on the slopes of Hill 70, a vital objective. The 14th Battalion was selected for the task and advanced steadily, nearing the western edge of the wood by 10.30a.m., under considerable shell and machine-gun fire. Retirement became necessary, however, but they rallied and advanced again.

The Durhams were pulled round towards Hill 70 and suffered heavily through machine-gun fire from Chalk Pit Wood and, followed by heavy shell fire, the troops came back over the Loos – La Bassee road.

At 2p.m. there came a spontaneous advance, in which the survivors of the Durham Battalion joined. Heavily punished in their flanks by shrapnel and machine-gun bullets, and unsupported by the British gunners, who had not been warned of the attempt, the infantry had no chance of success. The resulting retreat was shelled remorselessly and it continued until dusk.

Many of the severely wounded, including Tom Wynne, had to remain where they fell. The exhausted survivors, suffering tortures from thirst, remained in the old German trenches till they were relieved by the Guards Battalion in the early hours of September 27th. 16 officers and 277 men were killed or wounded. Private Thomas Wynne's name is commemorated on Panel 106 and 107 of the Loos Memorial, for his body was never recovered.

At the Battle of Loos the minor gains made were out of all proportion to the casualties suffered. British casualties were over 60,000 and one of the unfortunate souls was Thomas Wynne.

The main British operation of 1915 was of course the Battle of Loos, but the front line had to be defended day by day and these routine defensive duties consistently saw a loss of life and the constant haemorrhage of manpower in the New Army. One of these "statistics" was :

LANCE CORPORAL GEORGE MARTIN RAW
NO. 1154 1ST/5TH BATTALION WEST YORKSHIRE REGIMENT
DIED MONDAY 11TH OCTOBER 1915 AGE 27.

On October 11th Lance Corporal George Martin Raw died from wounds received when he was hit by shrapnel from a rifle grenade whilst on duty in the trenches on the Canal Bank, north of Ypres. There was no great battle unfolding at the time of his death; no blast from an officer's whistle to signal his men over the top with bayonets fixed, onward across the pock-marked landscape of no-man's land.

More soldiers died from shell fire, trench mortar, rifle grenade or bullet whilst waiting nervously in the trenches, than those who died during great offensives or retreats. George Raw may have survived if he had been standing a few more yards to left or right. Such was the uncertainty of life or death during wartime and his death was typical of how lives were lost during the great conflict.

George Martin Raw was born at Bellerby in 1888, the son of John and Margaret Raw. John, a Spennithorne man, had married Margaret, from Barnard

Moor Road, Bellerby, in 1905. The mill race that powered the corn mill is on the left and the chapel is shown on the right.

By permission of Clive Torrens.

Castle, and worked with his father George Raw as farmers and corn millers at the water powered Bellerby Mill, near Studda Farm. The picturesque beck that passes through the northern part of Bellerby was in actual fact the mill race for powering the Raw's corn mill. However, by 1901, John and Margaret were living with their family, John, George Martin, Fred and Edith, at Bewerley, just across the River Nidd from Pateley Bridge, where John was dealing in corn, flour, grain and hay.

By 1914, George Martin Raw had married Olivia, a Bradford girl. Early in the war he enlisted in the army at Pateley Bridge and joined the West Yorkshire Regiment. By mid 1915 he was with the 5th Battalion in the Ypres Salient.

Late September and early October were spent on the front line, both at the Canal Bank and at Glimpse Cottage Trenches, north of Ypres. On September 25th Allied guns bombarded the enemy trenches and the Battalion put up a successful smoke barrage. The enemy retaliated on the Canal Bank by sending "whizz bangs" and caused five casualties.

Whilst in Glimpse Cottage Trenches on September 27th, at 9.30a.m., there was a very heavy bombardment of the front line by trench mortars, howitzers and "whizz bangs". Dug-outs, trenches and parapets were flattened and as the bombardment ceased at 9.55a.m. a party, consisting of a German officer and ten soldiers rushed the Battalion trench. Two enemy got into a trench and knifed a bomber. Three enemy were hit on their return by Battalion rifle fire. 5th Battalion casualties were two killed and five wounded by the bombardment.

At 5a.m. on October 2nd the Battalion bombers threw 40 bombs into an enemy trench, with the enemy retaliating with rifle grenades. Whilst on the Canal Bank there was occasional shelling from howitzers, resulting in two men of a working party being wounded.

At 6.15p.m. on October 8th the Battalion relieved the 8th West Yorkshire Regiment in the trenches at Glimpse Cottage where all seemed very quiet. However, on October 9th, Lieutenant Brown and Lance Corporal George Martin Raw were wounded by rifle grenades. They were eventually taken to Essex Farm Cemetery, north of Ypres, which from April 1915 had been used as a dressing station and cemetery. Sadly, George succumbed to his wounds early on October 11th and was buried in the cemetery.

It had been in Essex Farm Cemetery in 1915 that Lieutenant Colonel John McCrae of the Canadian Army Medical Corps wrote the evocative war poem, "In Flanders' Fields"

In Flanders' fields the poppies blow
Between the crosses, row on row
That mark our place; and in the sky
The larks, still bravely singing, fly
Scarce heard amid the guns below.

We are the Dead. Short days ago
We lived, felt dawn, saw sunset glow,
Loved and were loved, and now we lie
In Flanders fields.

Take up our quarrel with the foe:
To you from failing hands, we throw
The torch; be yours to hold it high.
If ye break faith with us who die
We shall not sleep, though poppies grow
In Flanders fields.

John McCrae died from wounds in a Base Hospital in 1918.

George Martin Raw's name is to be found on both the Bellerby and Pateley Bridge War Memorials.

As the year 1915 came towards its close, the last Wensleydale casualty of the

year was not a serviceman, but a member of the Merchant Navy and his grave
was to be the watery depths of the North Sea.

JOSEPH ALDERSON, COXSWAIN, MERCANTILE MARINE, DIED TUESDAY 9TH NOVEMBER 1915 AGE 40.

Joseph's father, Edward Alderson, a Hawes man, had married Hannah, a
Swaledale girl from Muker, in the 1860's and throughout the following thirty
years Edward was a respected inn keeper and farmer in that dale, both at Thwaite
and Reeth.

Joseph, born in 1875 at Reeth, was second youngest in a family of nine
children. By 1901 his father Edward had travelled to Leyburn, where he was
landlord of the Bolton Arms Hotel and a farmer. However, by this time Joseph
had left the family home, for he had chosen a career in the Merchant Navy.

As war was declared in 1914, Joseph was living in London and had risen to
the rank of Coxswain in the Corporation of Trinity House, London, a maritime
society charged with the duty of erecting and maintaining lighthouses, light

Trinity House Yacht "Irene" in 1914.

The officers and men of the Trinity House Yachts "Irene" and "Stella", just before the Great War. The master of the "Irene", Captain Phillips, Coxswain Joseph Alderson and nineteen other crew members went down with the "Irene" when she hit a German mine on 9th November 1915.

ships and other sea marks around the coasts of England and Wales. It was also the principal pilotage authority in Britain.

On February 4th 1915 the Imperial German Navy initiated a submarine campaign, directed against merchantmen in waters surrounding the British Isles. By the year's end German U-boats, operating all over, had accounted for almost one million tons of Allied shipping.

On November 9th, 1915, Joseph Alderson was on board the Trinity House Yacht "Irene", in his capacity as Coxswain (or Helmsman and Senior Petty Officer). The 543 ton yacht, launched at Newcastle-on-Tyne in 1890, was loaded with ballast on its return journey from Harwich to London. Whilst in the mouth of the River Thames, one and a half miles ESE of the Tongue Light Ship, the "Irene" struck a mine laid by the little German U-boat UC1, a mine layer. The yacht sank quickly and 21 crew members, including its master, Captain Phillips, and Coxswain Joseph Alderson, were killed in the explosion or drowned in the surging waters.

Joseph Alderson is commemorated on Panel 9 in the Garden of

Remembrance at Tower Hill Memorial, London, on the south side of the garden of Trinity Square, close to the Tower of London. 3305 merchant ships were lost in the Great War, resulting in the deaths of 17,000 personnel. "Irene" was just one of many ships lost.

The Coxswain from Swaledale and Wensleydale is honoured on the war memorials for both Leyburn and Wensley.

The U-boat UC1 was the first of the little UC mine layers to be built, commissioned on May 7th 1915. Almost two years after the sinking of the "Irene", on July 14th 1917, the British acted to block the routes used by U-boats to and from the port of Zeebrugge by laying 150 mines in the shoals of Nieuport. Four days later, UC1, commanded by Oberleutnant zur See Mildenstein, left for a mine laying operation off Calais. She did not return and is presumed mined in one of these new fields. There were no survivors from the crew of 17.

Meanwhile, in the wider view of events on the world stage, Gallipoli was entering its final stages, with huge casualty lists posted but no success, whilst appalling losses had been suffered on the Western Front during 1915 on both sides. 612,000 Germans, 1,292,000 French and 279,000 British became casualties. The year ended with no appreciable shift in the hostile battle lines scarring the land from the North Sea to the Swiss Alps.

Both French and British had gained in experience, if not in wisdom, from the 1915 battles, but they had afforded the Germans still better experiences in the way to frustrate such attacks. In 1916 therefore, it was to be the Germans who profited heavily both by the offensive and the defensive lesson. Ten men from Wensleydale had lost their lives during 1915 but the sacrifice made by the dale in 1916 would prove even greater, with the loss of forty two dalesmen

CHAPTER THREE

1916... A SAD AWAKENING

Throughout 1916 the dales folk attempted to retain some form of normality in their lives. On Empire Day, May 24th, the public buildings in Upper Wensleydale were bedecked with flags, whilst pupils at Hawes Council School marched past and saluted the Union flag hoisted proudly for the occasion. Each child gave a contribution to the "Soldiers' and Sailors' Fund" and received in return an attractive souvenir of the day.

During January, Middleham Primitive Methodist Choir had contributed £8 12s 6d from their Christmas carol singing collection to bolster the "Methodist Fund" to provide a recreational hut for the Yorkshire Regiment's soldiers at Richmond Camp.

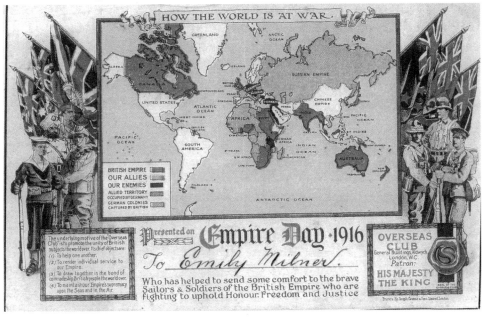

Schoolchildren's Empire Day Souvenir 1916. From Wensleydale.

Aysgarth Local Boys' Comforts Fund, October 1916.

INCOME.	£ s. d.	EXPENDITURE.	£ s. d.
Balance in hand	0 18 0	Parcels value 5/- to 32 men ...	8 0 0
Concert, Oct. 8th	9 15 6	Postage of Parcels	1 4 6
Subscription (Miss Bradley) ...	1 0 0	Use of Institute	1 10 0
		Curtains	0 5 0
		Bills—Posters	0 10 0
Total	£11 13 6	Total	£11 9 6

Balance in hand—4s.

BESSIE BRADLEY, Hon. Treasurer.

Aysgarth Local Boys' Comforts Fund, June 23rd, 1917.

INCOME.	£ s. d.	EXPENDITURE.	£ s. d.
Balance in hand	0 4 0	Parcels value 7/- to 44 men ...	15 8 0
Dramatic Performance June 23rd	17 0 0	Postage of Parcels	1 2 0
Total	£17 4 0	Total	£16 10 0

Balance in hand—14s.

BESSIE BRADLEY, Hon. Treasurer.

Plews & Sons, Leyburn.

A year later, at Christmas time 1916, East Witton parishioners raised money to send a New Year's gift to the East Witton lads at the front. 41 parcels, each to the value of 10 shillings, containing a tin of ham, tin of sausages, a cake, a camp pie, oxo cubes, coffee cubes, cocoa cubes, cigarettes, soap and one woollen garment, were sent off to the front.

On a Friday evening in early February a whist drive and dance was held in Redmire in aid of the Serbian Relief Fund. After the prizes had been distributed, dancing commenced about 11.30p.m. and went on until 4a.m. Music for the dancing was provided by Messres Metcalfe and Cockett from Hawes. A beautifully iced cake raised £7 in a competition and a Woodbine cigarette was sold for £7 0s 7d, helping to bring the total amount raised to £15.

From January 31st to May 11th the children of Raydaleside had sent 1198 eggs to the National Egg Collection, helping bring succour to the wounded soldiers convalescing in hospitals throughout Britain. Between March and May the children of Askrigg had contributed a total of 449 eggs.

In August, East Witton Church Choir decided that after two years of remaining at home, instead of going on an outing, they would travel to Ripon and Fountains Abbey. The war was lasting longer than expected and perhaps a day out would lighten their worries and concerns a little. Performing these mundane activities certainly helped to boost morale, for the people on the Home

Front could feel that they were doing something for their men folk away at the front. They definitely required something to take their minds off what was happening on the battlefields.

As if to show that civilians were not immune from the dangers of wartime, terrible news came to the hamlet of Gayle, concerning a horrific accident involving a local girl that had occurred in a munitions works on July 30th. Nancy Ann Raw, daughter of a Gayle farmer, who had volunteered for munitions work, met with an accident at Lancaster. She was without a cap owing to the heat and her hair was caught by an electric crane and she was scalped. Her condition was said to be extremely critical.

It was, however, a momentous event taking place in late May 1916 that held for a while the attention of the World's eyes, and cast the carnage taking place on the Western Front to the inside pages of the newspapers. For centuries, Britain's influence had rested with its control of the seas, as the supreme maritime power in the world. Just one week after the celebration of Empire Day within the dale, this supremacy was about to be challenged by the Kaiser's Imperial Navy in the waters of the North Sea. The Battle of Jutland was fought on May 31st and two sailors from Preston under Scar in Wensley parish would die in this clash of the Dreadnoughts, the only occasion during four years of war that the Grand Fleet of Britain and the High Seas Fleet of Germany met.

The two men from Preston under Scar were:

ENGINE ROOM ARTIFICER 3RD CLASS
ROBERT HENRY WILSON NO. M/129
H.M.S. "BLACK PRINCE"
DIED WEDNESDAY 31ST MAY 1916 AGE 19.

AND

ENGINE ROOM ARTIFICER 4TH CLASS
HAROLD WILLIAM SCRIVENER
NO. M/1502 H.M.S. "QUEEN MARY"
DIED WEDNESDAY 31ST MAY 1916 AGE 21.

Robert Wilson, born in 1896 at Preston under Scar, was the son of Arthur and Ada Wilson. Arthur had been born in Cleveland, Yorkshire, and in the late 1880's had come to Wensley to work for Lord and Lady Bolton at Bolton Hall, where he rose to the position of butler.

The family lived in a cottage, Hare Mire House, in the woods behind the Hall.

Robert Henry Wilson
(Wensley and Preston under Scar).

Harold William Scrivener
(Wensley and Preston under Scar).

The butler became a great friend of the younger members of the Orde-Powlett family and taught them about birds' eggs and fishing. Arthur had a bed made up in his pantry at the Hall and so could sleep there to be on hand for late night parties and special occasions.

Robert began his education at Wensley School, but removed to Basingstoke Council School the following year, 1902. Time was spent at Gosforth Council School before completing his education at Wensley, winning a scholarship for four years training as engine room artificer in 1911 and joining HMS Fisguard at Portsmouth.

At the end of his training he proceeded north to join HMS "Black Prince", a cruiser in Scapa Flow.

Harold William Scrivener was the youngest of two sons of Frederick and Clara Scrivener. Frederick from Suffolk and Clara from Somerset, had set up home at Bolton Hall, Wensley, where Frederick was the head gardener for Lord Bolton. The estate of 14,000 acres was almost self-contained with saw-mills, carpenters' shop, laundry and electricity generator.

The gardens were huge, employing many gardeners for their upkeep. They were mainly situated behind the Hall in the form of terraces leading upwards. Above them was the water garden and the enormous kitchen gardens containing glass houses.

Harold was educated at Wensley School, supplemented by private tuition. In 1909 he won the Naval Scholarship offered by the Education Committee of

Bolton Hall, Wensley, home to Lord and Lady Bolton. Note the splendid terraces and gardens in the background. Bolton Hall was built in 1678, with the village of Wensley at its gates. The present Bolton Hall is mainly an early 20th century construction built around the shell of the 17th century house, after a serious fire in 1902.

the North Riding County Council, which qualified him for admission to HMS Fisguard, the mechanical training ship at Portsmouth, which he joined as boy artificer in December 1909.

He had completed four years of training in the March before war was declared and was appointed to HMS "Queen Mary", a battle cruiser, as engine room artificer (His elder brother Charles Frederick Scrivener would enlist in March 1915, leaving his job as a mechanical engineer serving his apprenticeship with the Wolsley Works at Birmingham. He joined the R.A.S.C. as a driver and would survive the war).

On August 28th 1914 "Queen Mary" was in action against German naval vessels in the Battle of Heligoland Bight, when British cruisers raided into German waters, coaxing a fight.

In his diary Harold writes, "We are steaming for Heligoland and expect an engagement tomorrow." He records on the 28th, "We fired the first shots at

12.42 and finished about 13.15. I believe we sank two and the "Lion" one. One can't help but admire the Germans. The cruiser we sank went down with her flags flying, and was firing at us till she sank."

He later wrote about the action, "It was only a mild sort of scrap, but still it was a most interesting experience, especially for the men in the engine rooms, who had the added excitement of not knowing what was happening above. When we were allowed to come up on deck shortly after the action there was not the slightest sign of a German vessel to be seen. We were all disappointed, as we expected to see bits of wreckage and sinking German ships. I hope our next encounter will be a good dust up, and so settle things for a bit." Harold Scivener certainly had his wish fulfilled, for the "dust up" was to be the Battle of Jutland on Wednesday 31st May, 1916. Unfortunately, neither Harold nor Robert would escape with their lives.

In late May 1916 the German High Seas Fleet under Vice-Admiral Scheer put to sea, cruising north towards the Skagerrak, the expanse of often turbulent water which separates Denmark from Norway. Admiral Von Hipper's scouting fleet, forty fast vessels built around a nucleus of five battle cruisers, led the way. Well behind was the main fleet of 59 ships, 16 of them dreadnoughts and 6 older battleships.

Scheer's idea was to entice the British battle cruiser force of the British Grand Fleet, led by Vice-Admiral Sir David Beatty, into an engagement with his own battle cruisers led by Von Hipper. Scheer thus hoped to fall upon the British in overwhelming strength, Von Hipper being the bait he knew would attract Beatty.

However, British intelligence had acquired the German code and, warned of the sortie, the Grand Fleet, under Admiral Sir John Jellicoe, at once put to sea from Scapa Flow in the Orkney Islands on May 30th with his main force of 99 vessels, 24 of them dreadnoughts, with vessels such as the cruiser "Black Prince", with Robert Wilson on board, providing support and cover.

Vice-Admiral Beatty, on board his flagship HMS "Lion", also set sail from the Firth of Forth with his scouting force, the Battle Cruiser Fleet, including Harold Scrivener on board HMS "Queen Mary", the largest of Beatty's ships at 30,500 tons, and reputedly with the best gunners on board. This hard hitting, aggressive fighting force, known as the "Ocean Greyhounds", were allowed to take risks considered unacceptable to the main fleet. With their speed and fire-power they formed the spearhead of scouting and offensive operations.

The first contact between the opposing scouting cruisers was off the west coast of Denmark at 3.48p.m. The "Lion" leading, with "Princess Royal", "Queen Mary", "Tiger", "New Zealand" and "Indefatigable", in that order, opened fire. However, within forty minutes of the opening broadsides, Beatty had lost two of his great ships.

*Smoke billows from the 26,000 ton cruiser HMS Queen Mary,
as she sinks with her 1,200 strong crew, 31st May 1916.*

With a thunderous roar the "Indefatigable" went up in flames at 4.05p.m. and at 4.30p.m. "Queen Mary" succumbed. She had come under the concentrated fire power of "Der Fflinger" and "Seydlitz". With her propellers still turning she broke in two and disappeared in an enormous pall of smoke rising 800 feet high, taking down with her all but twenty of her company of 1266. Harold Scrivener did not survive. Vice-Admiral Beatty, viewing the disasters from his bridge, remarked, "There seems to be something wrong with our bloody ships today!" He then ordered his four surviving battle cruisers to alter course towards the enemy.

Good German gunnery played its part in the loss of the battle cruisers but something was indeed wrong with the ships. They had poor protection against flash from a gun turret penetrating to the magazine below if its doors were left open for speed and convenience in action. This ignoring of safety procedures in order to enable more shells to be fired off more quickly, plus the careless handling of their own cordite propellant explosive, led to a chain rection that resulted in the explosion of the ship's main magazine when these safety doors were left open.

The first capital ships from Jellicoe's fleet to engage the enemy were a group of three battle cruisers led by Rear-Admiral Hood, but at 6.30p.m. the same fate overtook his flagship HMS "Invincible" as that of "Queen Mary" and "Indefatigable".

When battle was fully joined, victory eluded Jellicoe. Twice, when the Germans appeared trapped, Admiral Scheer executed an extraordinary manoeuvre of "Battle turn about" and with the darkness to help them the Germans escaped back to their home ports.

But the battle was not yet quite over. After dark, Scheer boldly turned to the SE, deliberately crashing into the formation of light cruisers, including Robert Wilson's ship, "Black Prince", at the tail of Jellicoe's south bound fleet. He finally battered his way through in chaotic midnight battles of collisions, sinkings and gunfire. The "Black Prince", suddenly engulfed in the middle of the Germans, was sunk in four minutes, with the loss of Robert and his crew mates. The German battleship "Pommern" was cut in two, but by dawn Scheer was shepherding his cripples towards the Jade anchorage and Jellicoe realised that his quarry had escaped.

"Black Prince" had approached the centre of the German line in the confusion of battle. Too late she turned away, and in minutes was a blazing pyre. Without firing a single shot in the Battle, she disintegrated.

The British now turned back to their bases. They had lost three battle cruisers, three cruisers and eight destroyers, with a loss of 6784 men. The Germans lost one old battleship, one battle cruiser, four light cruisers and five destroyers, with 3039 casualties.

Jutland marked the end of an epoch in naval warfare. It was the last great fleet action in which the opponents slugged it out within sight of one another. A drawn battle tactically, it made no change to the strategic, other than to make the Germans realise that they had no chance of defeating the Grand Fleet.

However, between 4.30p.m. and midnight on May 31st 1916, Wensleydale had lost two fine young men.

But the lack of outright victory meant that Jutland could not for long take people's minds off the costly process of exhaustive slaughter on the land. For truly it has to be said, the year 1916 will always be remembered by the British and the French for its association with the names SOMME and VERDUN. The Battle of the Somme (July to November) and the Siege of Verdun (February to December) cost the British and French upwards of one million casualties and ground gained was minimal.

General Von Falkenhayn, German Chief of Staff, chose to attack Verdun in the certain knowledge that the French would defend the city to the last man, "to bleed France white". By June 1916 the French situation was desperate and General Petain begged his Commander-in-Chief, Joffre, to hasten a relieving action on the Somme.

General Haig would have much preferred to use his new armies in Flanders but political necessity demanded otherwise. The Somme area was chosen simply because here the British and French armies met and even though the allies knew the German defences were very strong the offensive was set for July 1st.

From that date no fresh German divisions would be sent to Verdun; the attack slowly stalled, then failed. The Somme battles saved Verdun but at a terrible cost to Britain's citizen army.

By the end of 1915 most people shared an optimistic view of how the war would progress, despite an increasing casualty list, but this view was shattered by the unfolding events of 1916. 42 Wensleydale men died in 1916 and 29 of these lost their lives during the Battle of the Somme. Twelve soldiers were lost in the first four weeks of battle, five of them on the very first day, July 1st. Another 17 men were killed during the later stages of the fighting. Sadly, Hawes with Gayle would pay homage to 11 of their men, Aysgarth parish to 5, Wensley with Leyburn, Askrigg, East Witton and Middleham 2 each, whilst Castle Bolton, West Witton, Bellerby and Carperby each lost one of their parishioners.

Voluntary enlistment was no longer an option for Britain and even before the Somme, casualties on the Western Front demanded replacements that could only be filled by conscription. In January 1916, by the Military Service Act, the voluntary system was abandoned and compulsory enlistment came into being.

As a result of these actions, all families were now deeply affected by the Great War. In addition, casualties were increasing from bombing raids from Zeppelins, food stuffs were not so readily available and a movement from the land and in service to munitions was mounting.

It is interesting to note that despite the York area being the nearest the Zeppelins got to Wensleydale, the authorities took the possibility of raids seriously. A system of observation posts was set up by the army. At Hawes, about six soldiers were billeted in the town to man a post close to the wall dividing Beulah Bank from the top graveyard. These soldiers appeared to be ones resting from the war or convalescing. Two soldiers would man the post, which was little more than a sentry box. This lasted for one winter, until the post was moved to a more comfortable hut with a telephone, close to Honeycott, Hawes.

The Battle of the Somme was launched on June 24th by a stupendous seven day artillery bombardment. On July 1st, 120,000 British and Empire infantry, following a rolling artillery barrage, dashed themselves against highly organised

German defensive positions on a 16 mile front. On that first day casualties were 50%, with 19,240 killed, 2,152 missing presumed killed, 35,493 wounded and 585 taken prisoner. These were the worst casualties in the history of the British Army. Losses on that one day easily exceeded the battle casualties sustained in the Crimean, Boer and Korean Wars, combined.

Despite the appalling losses of the first day, the British continued to forge ahead in a series of small, limited attacks, with the Allied offensive deteriorating into a succession of minor but costly small actions.

General Haig launched another major offensive in the Somme battle on September 15th , SW of Bapaume. Tanks had been secretly shipped to the front, and spearheaded the attack, but were too unreliable and few in numbers to gain a decisive victory. Gains were made but a breakthrough eluded them. Nevertheless, the British and French continued attacking, gaining small areas of ground through mid-November.

British losses in this campaign were 420,000; French 195,000, German casualties, including many pre-war officers and NCO's came to 650,000. The battles represented a watershed. The last traces of the "early carefree spirit" of the war had gone for good. From now on the men who moved into the trenches to replace the fallen would not see the war as a wonderful crusade, but as a bloody, deadly chore, to be slogged through, and if possible, survived.

Five Wensleydale men perished on the opening day of the battle. As historian Liddell Hart writes in his "History of the First World War": "July 1st dawned a swelteringly hot day. At 7.30a.m. the infantry advanced from their trenches, and thousands fell, littering no-man's land with their bodies, before the German front trench was even reached. While the shells flattened their trenches, the Germans sheltered in dug-outs or shell holes, and as the barrage lifted, dragged out their machine-guns, to pour a deadly hail of lead into the unduly dense wave of the attackers."

PRIVATE JAMES CHAPMAN
NO. 31388 21ST BATTALION MANCHESTER REGIMENT
DIED SATURDAY 1ST JULY 1916 AGE 22.

James Chapman was the son of Alexander Chapman, a Bainbridge farmer, and his wife Mary, a Lancashire girl. James was born in 1895 in a farmhouse at Borwins, a cluster of farmsteads near the River Ure, between Bainbridge and Hawes. By 1901, however, the family, including sisters Elizabeth and Violet, were living in Bainbridge, at Sunny Dene.

James left home to seek a career in Manchester and when war was declared in 1914 he was in the employ of Messrs Bagley and Chapman, wholesale meat stores, Manchester. In November 1915 he enlisted and was posted to the 21st Battalion Manchester Regiment. He proceeded to France in May 1916 as a new draft to the Battalion and immediately became involved in training for the coming battle.

The objective for the 21st Battalion was the capture of Mametz village. Instead of the signal for the attack being a blast from the officer's whistle, their signal, ten minutes ahead of zero hour, was to be the detonation of eight enormous mines which had been tunnelled under the German trenches and filled with dynamite.

At zero hour the barrage lifted and moved forward in progressive stages in front of the troops. On nearing "Cemetery Trench" they came under severe machine-gun fire from the outskirts of Mametz village. "A" Company split into groups, clearing and passing two enemy lines very quickly. A large number of prisoners were collected at Bulgar Point and sent back in batches.

"C" Company pushed over the parapet in waves of half companies, whilst "B" Company came up behind and they pushed through the village to reach a line of trenches, where they were subjected to heavy retaliatory bombardment and suffered many casualties. It was decided to hold the line with a few men whilst the rest retired to regroup and detail bombing parties to clear out the dug-outs in the village.

At 5.45p.m. the headquarters were moved into Mametz village and "D" Company moved up to the front line trench, but the position became untenable owing to heavy enemy artillery fire. As the Company advanced in waves to another position they came under heavy machine-gun fire, suffering severe casualties from German soldiers who had been by-passed and remained in the trenches. By 6.30p.m., however, the first objective, Mametz village had been secured.

Amongst the many casualties sustained by 21st Battalion was James Chapman. In the frightening hail of bullets and unceasing retaliatory shell fire, he was struck down and in the crater strewn landscape, his body was never recovered. He is commemorated on Piers and Face 13A and 14C of the Thiepval Memorial, on the Somme.

On a Sunday evening in late July a large congregation attended a memorial service held at Askrigg Church for the young soldier. After the second lesson, Reverend F.M. Squibb, accompanied by a chorister carrying a Union Jack draped in black, proceeded to the Chancel steps. The "Dead March" was played on the organ. The vicar said that the sorrow for the death of Private Chapman was not an unrelieved sorrow because there was sacrifice to it. He was the first young soldier in the parish to lay down his life for them. After the blessing the congregation sang the National Anthem.

SECOND LIEUTENANT FRANK DINSDALE
12TH BATTALION YORK AND LANCASTER REGIMENT
DIED SATURDAY 1ST JULY 1916 AGE 23.

In the year 1893 Frank Dinsdale was born at Litherskew, a small settlement of farmsteads close to Sedbusk, in High Abbotside. His father, James, a farmer, had married Sarah, a girl from Brough in Westmoreland. Robert, an elder brother of Frank's, helped his father on the farm and other brothers and sisters were George, Thomas, James, Esther and Ellen.

Frank Dinsdale was not destined for the farming life and after leaving Yorebridge Grammar School, between Askrigg and Bainbridge, he attended Garforth College and Leeds University. By this time the family were farming at Shawcote, on the way towards Askrigg.

When war broke out Frank was a member of the Leeds University Officer Training Corps, receiving his commission in September 1915 with the rank of 2nd Lieutenant in the 12th Battalion York and

Frank Dinsdale,
from Shawcote, Low Abbotside.

Lancaster Regiment. He went out to France in June 1916, only weeks away from his first and only experience of warfare.

The Battalion moved to Gezaincourt on June 5th, where they practised assembling in the trenches ready for the forthcoming engagement. At 9p.m., June 30th, they marched to assembly trenches near Courcelles, where tea was issued to the men. The Battalion was no sooner in position opposite the German positions of Serre, north of Beaumont Hamel, than the enemy bombardment opened with great violence and casualties mounted.

At 7.30a.m. the Companies moved forward and lay down about 100 yards in front of the trenches under cover of their own bombardment, but with enemy shell fire landing amongst them.

The first and second waves moved forward to the assault and were met at once with terribly severe shell, rifle and machine-gun fire; the left half of "C" Company being wiped out before reaching the enemy wire. The Battalion third and fourth waves suffered so heavily that by the time they had reached no-man's land they had lost half their numbers. The failure of the attack was wholly due to the wire being insufficiently cut.

One of those reported missing, believed wounded, was Frank Dinsdale, but it was not until much later that his parents received official notification that their son was presumed killed. The interval of time brought much suffering to his family and loved ones.

Some battalions' attacks failed because their supports could not or would not follow the trail they had blazed into the German positions, so leaving them cut off deep within the enemy lines. This seems to have been the fate of some of the 12th York and Lancasters, including Frank Dinsdale. Their graves were only found on November 13th, at the very end of the battle, when the village of Serre, one of the uncaptured first day objectives, at last fell into British hands. Frank's Company had reached the objective but had been cut off deep within the enemy lines at Serre.

He was a great favourite with both his brother officers and men of his Battalion and several of them had spoken in high terms of his splendid gallantry. The Vice Chairman of Leeds University had also testified to the high esteem in which he was held by his college chums. On leave he had expressed to his family the sentiment that if he was called to yield his life, they must not lament but rather feel proud that it was for his country and his King that he had died.

2nd Lieutenant Frank Dinsdale is buried in grave C.20. Queen's Cemetery, Pusieux, a village 15 kilometres north of Albert.

LANCE CORPORAL JOHN SHANNON
NO. 19978 10TH BATTALION WEST YORKSHIRE REGIMENT
DIED SATURDAY 1ST JULY 1916 AGE 38.

John Shannon's father, Thomas Shannon, was born in Scotland, but travelled throughout the north of England seeking employment as a gardener. His wife Emily was from York and their first child, John, was born at Long Bertham, Newcastle-on-Tyne, in 1878. By 1882 the family was living at Denton in Northumberland, where William, James, Emily and Laura were born, before relocating for a short stay in York in 1891, where another daughter, Hilda, was born.

However, by 1893, they were living near the Wheatsheaf Inn at Carperby, in Wensleydale, where children Thomas, Ellen and Lena became additions to the family. The eldest child, John, was no longer living with the family, for, aged 23 years, he had travelled into the Ripon area to seek employment. The family in Carperby later moved just outside the village, to the farming settlement at Bear Park, close to the banks of the River Ure.

With Kitchener's plea for volunteers in August 1914, it was not long before John Shannon enlisted at Ripon, before joining the 10th Battalion West Yorkshire Regiment, in which he rose to the rank of Lance Corporal. By this time both his parents had died.

The role of the 50th Infantry Brigade, of which the 10th Battalion was a part, was to attack Fricourt on July 1st, a ruined village in the little valley of the River Ancre, and then attack Fricourt Wood. Instructions were to advance against their objective, with the 7th Yorkshires and the 10th West Yorkshires ordered first to make a frontal attack on the village.

The two leading companies pressed on to their objective, the northern edge of Fricourt village, but the artillery fire which should have covered their right, keeping the enemy below ground until the assault of the 7th Yorkshire Regiment had taken place, was not sufficient protection and the enemy swarmed up from underground defences in large numbers.

The 3rd and 4th Companies had attempted to cross no-man's land in support but as they left the trenches, a murderous machine-gun and rifle fire swept along the leading ranks, practically annihilating the whole of the two companies.

Strenuous efforts were made by other battalions to reach the West Yorkshires, especially by the 7th East Yorkshire and 7th Yorkshire Regiments who again attacked at 7.30p.m., but the same murderous fire swept the attack away. In three minutes only, the 7th Yorkshire Regiment lost 13 officers and 300 men.

What little remained of the 10th Battalion West Yorkshire Regiment was withdrawn to Ville on the night of 1st/2nd July. Together with the 1st Battalion Newfoundland Regiment, the 10th Battalion lost the highest number of men of any battalion on that first day of battle — 700 men killed, wounded or missing, including all the officers. Despite the great gallantry shown throughout the day, it was sheer, bloody murder.

Lance Corporal John Shannon's body has no known grave but he is commemorated on Piers and Face 2A,2C and 2D of the Thiepval Memorial. His name is also honoured on the churchyard gatepost pillars at Aysgarth Church and on the small roadside memorial in the centre of Carperby.

SECOND LIEUTENANT JAMES WHALEY FRYER
22ND (TYNESIDE SCOTTISH) BATTALION
NORTHUMBERLAND FUSILIERS
DIED SATURDAY 1ST JULY 1916 AGE 24.

James Whaley Fryer was born in 1892 at Rookhurst, a large house in West End, Gayle, near Hawes (a hotel at the present time of writing). He was the only son of Major James Whaley Fryer and Edith Fryer. His father, James senior, had also served in the army and by 1901 he was aged 36 and living on his own means. A pillar of society, he was Chairman of Aysgarth Rural Council and a local Justice of the Peace. An only son, James junior had two younger sisters, Dorothy and Florence.

As an Old Bessonian from Yorebridge Grammar School, James left Hawes for employment as an articled clerk to Messrs. Dickinson, Millar and Turnbull, solicitors in Newcastle-on-Tyne, the city in which his mother Edith had been born. He had successfully passed his first examinations and was hoping to qualify his final when he joined the Colours in August 1914.

Second Lieutenant James Whaley Fryer embarked for France with his Battalion, 22nd Northumberland

James Whaley Fryer (Gayle).

Fusiliers, in January 1915 and remained there until his death on July 1st 1916. Around this period his father died and his mother Edith returned to Newcastle to be nearer her own people.

At 7.30a.m. on July 1st his Battalion moved forward to the attack on the enemy trenches south of La Boiselle, 2km. NE of Albert. Heavy enemy fire was experienced, with many casualties sustained, but the survivors reached the enemy second line of defence.

Between 8a.m. and 12.45p.m., six separate enemy counter-attacks were made to rush the Battalion flanks but they were repulsed. By this time the strength of the Battalion was only 7 officers and 200 men.

At 10.15p.m. a patrol got in touch with other troops sheltering in the New Crater, caused by an English mine that had been detonated that morning, ten minutes before the advance began..

Mrs. Edith Fryer received news of her son's death in a letter sent to her by the Captain of the Company James was in. The tragic news was that he had died just after he had climbed over the top of the trench parapet. Both his legs were taken off by the explosion of a shell. There is no known grave, and as with the many who fell during the conflict on the Somme during 1916 he is commemorated on the Thiepval Memorial, on Pier and Face 10B, 11B and 12B.

LANCE CORPORAL FRANK COLLINSON
NO. 22977 1ST BATTALION BORDER REGIMENT
DIED SATURDAY 1ST JULY 1916 AGE 19.

Albert Collinson, the father of Frank, had been born in the small East Riding village of Octon, seven miles to the north of Driffield. He became a rural post-man and by the early 1890's had married Martha, a girl from North Cowton, five miles east of Scotch Corner, on the present A1.

By 1895/96 Albert had become the rural postman at Middleham, in Wensleydale, and by 1901 the family, consisting of four year old Frank and his two year old sister Ethel, were living at Vale View, Middleham. An elder brother of Albert's, Dobson Collinson, was also living in Middleham and one of his sons, Harold, a cousin of Frank's, would also be killed before the war came to a close.

Volunteering in 1915, Frank enlisted at Middleham and eventually became a Lance Corporal in the 1st Battalion Border Regiment. At 7.30a.m. on July 1st 1916 he found himself just south of Beaumont Hamel, facing their objective for the day, Behucourt Redoubt.

They went over the top from their support line and over the first line by means of bridges. They met with heavy losses while crossing these bridges and passing through the lanes cut in the British wire. The men were magnificent, according to the war diaries, forming up as ordered outside their wire and advanced into no-man's land at a slow walk, also as ordered. The advance was continued until only little groups of six men were left here and there and these, finding that no reinforcements were in sight, took cover in shell holes or wherever they could. After just half an hour, the advance had been brought entirely to a standstill, with casualties totalling 625.

On July 2nd the remnants of the 1st Battalion were relieved. One of the men reported missing was Frank Collinson and it was not until March 1917 that his family received the news that he was

The Somme Memorial at Thiepval, unveiled by the then Prince of Wales in 1932.

102

confirmed as having been killed in action. Frank's name can be found on Pier and Face 6A and 7C of the Thiepval Memorial.

As the battle progressed throughout the month of July, eight more dalesmen would join the ranks of those who had fallen whilst serving their country :

SERGEANT JOHN SARGINSON
NO. 11505 11TH BATTALION WEST YORKSHIRE REGIMENT
DIED TUESDAY 4TH JULY 1916 AGE 27.

John's father, Thomas Sarginson, had been born at West Witton and later married Lilian, a girl from Sheffield. He was employed as a gardener and they lived at Castle View, Middleham, where they brought up a large family of five boys and three girls. Two of the brothers, John and Thomas, would die in the Great War.

By the outbreak of the war, their father Thomas had died and their mother, Lily, was living near to her married son Thomas, in Nelson, Lancashire. John Sarginson enlisted at York early in the war and rose to be Sergeant in the 11th Battalion, West Yorkshire Regiment.

On July 3rd 1916, the Battalion left its billets near Albert and moved forward to Becourt Wood. On the afternoon of July 4th they attacked the enemy lines in the direction of La Boisselle and gained their objective, an enemy trench, after incurring heavy losses. The inevitable German counter-attack forced the survivors to retire and fall back on their own lines.

Sergeant John Sarginson had been at the forefront of the advance but during the counter-attack by the German forces he was cut down by machine-gun and shell fire. He has no recorded grave and again, his name is to be found on the Thiepval Memorial, on Pier and Face 2A, 2C and 2D.

MAJOR JOHN CHAYTOR METCALFE
13TH BATTALION CHESHIRE REGIMENT
DIED FRIDAY 7TH JULY AGE 34.

John Chaytor Metcalfe came from a family with a strong military background. Born in 1882 at Ings House, Hawes, he was the only son of Major John Augustus Metcalfe. His grandfather had been chaplain to the Duke of Wellington's Regiment and his uncle, Dr. Parker, had for many years been the vicar at Hawes. John was educated at Marlborough College and later served in the 3rd Yorkshire Regiment at Malta during the Boer War, where he acted for some time as aide-de-camp to Lord Congleton, afterwards receiving a commission in the 13th Hussars.

In 1906 he left the army after inheriting extensive properties in the Hawes and Askrigg districts and took up horse racing, being successful as an amateur steeple chase rider and breeder of thoroughbred horses. At the outbreak of the war, he was residing at Ings House, Hawes, and at King Edward's Place, Wanborough, Wiltshire.

In August 1914 he enlisted in the Public School's Corps and a month later received a commission in the 13th Cheshire Regiment, raised at Port Sunlight as the result of an appeal by Lord Leverhulme to his employees. It left Aldershot for France on September 25th 1915, with John in charge of No. 1 Company.

John Chayter Metcalfe (Hawes).

The Battalion was deployed on July 7th 1916 against the village of Ovillers. The jumping-off point was from the newly won German trenches in La Boisselle. These trenches formed a salient in the German line, with the Germans still holding trenches flanking the line of advance from La Boisselle to Ovillers.

It had been arranged that the attack should be protected by smoke and by an intense barrage. But there was no smoke and the barrage was feeble. The advance, being thus unscreened, drew heavy artillery fire. This, together with machine-gun fire from front and flanks, stopped the attack about half way to Ovillers.

Casualties on this day were extremely heavy with 18 officers and 243 men being killed or wounded. John Chaytor Metcalfe's name is to be found on Special Memorial 24 in Ovillers Military Cemetery, 5 km. NE of Albert.

PRIVATE JOHN WILLIAM TEASDALE
NO. 3/9456 2ND BATTALION YORKSHIRE REGIMENT
DIED SATURDAY 8TH JULY 1916 AGE 38.

The Teasdale family had strong connections with Middleham, Leyburn and Wensley and John is commemorated in all three places. His father, also called John William, was born at Middleham and married a local girl, setting up their home close to the Rectory in the town. There, they raised three sons, John

William, Thomas and Alfred. John William senior worked in the local stone quarries at Leyburn and Harmby as a stone mason, but by 1891 he was already a widower.

The eldest son, John William, also became a stone mason and when war was declared, he was living at Wensley, aged 36. Enlisting at Richmond early in the war, John Teasdale joined the 2nd Battalion Yorkshire Regiment.

On July 1st 1916 the Battalion learnt that on July 8th they would make an attack upon Trones Wood, which was commanded by a large number of heavy German guns. At 7.15a.m. on July 8th ,"C" Company entered Bernafay Wood, followed by the Battalion bombing sections of the other companies. On "topping" some rising ground, heavy machine-gun and rifle fire poured into them, and the advancing front line was hit, almost to a man.

A few survivors got to a trench but German snipers located amongst the branches of trees stopped this attempt. A withdrawal to Bernafay Wood was ordered but there was no respite there, for the wood was bombarded heavily throughout the day. The cover was poor and the Battalion struggled to hold on.

It was with great relief that at 7p.m. orders were made for a withdrawal. Losses throughout the week had been terrible, a total of 433 casualties out of the 712 men who went into action.

John William Teasdale was killed whilst attacking Trones Wood. His body was recovered and he is buried in grave 5.C.20. in the London Cemetery and Extension at Longueval, 12 km. ENE of Albert.

GUNNER ALBERT LEACH
NO. 44227 88TH BATTERY
14TH BRIGADE ROYAL FIELD ARTILLERY
DIED WEDNESDAY 12TH JULY 1916 AGE 23.

Albert was the eldest child of Ambler and Joanna Leach. Ambler had been born in Bingley and became a journeyman tailor, employed by various tailors in the days when suits were made by hand. Whilst working in Wensleydale he met Joanna Kilburn from Bainbridge and they were married. Moving to the village of Cullingworth, between Keighley and Bradford in the early 1890's, their first child, Albert, was born in 1894, but a year later they were living in Askrigg, where their son Laurence was born. By 1896 they had finally settled down in Hawes, at Halfway House, on the Appersett side of the town, where Annie, Harold, Roland, Ethel, Mabel and Florence were born. Eventually, Ambler worked for the Hawes tailor, Mr. Mudd (the shop is now the outfitters "Whites of Wensleydale – Town and Country Wear").

Albert joined up in the Royal Field Artillery, with his brother Laurence and four other companions, and marched to the station on November 16th 1914, led by Hawes Brass Band. Posted to 88 Battery R.F.A., Albert was involved in the week long artillery bombardment of the German lines on the Somme battle front, from June 24th 1916, the greatest bombardment of the war up to that stage.

Albert Leach (Hawes).

However, retaliatory fire from enemy gun batteries could target the British gunners, and casualties were high. Amongst these casualties was Gunner Albert Leach, who was killed on July 12th. A letter was received by the family back in Rose Cottage, Hawes, from the officer commanding the Battery, stating :

"I hope you will find consolation in the fact that he died standing by his gun, and doing his duty as a true soldier should. Practically his last action was to load a shell and despatch it against the Germans. We were able to secure a clergyman of his own denomination to read the service and the grave is marked by a wooden cross with his name cut into it."

At the time of his death, his brother Laurence was also serving with the R.F.A. in France, whilst their younger brother Harold was serving as a Bombadier, in training at Newcastle.

The local paper reported that "Albert was a fine stalwart young fellow over six feet in height and a noted local athlete, a good sprinter and high jumper. He is the first of the Hawes recruits to make the supreme sacrifice."

The Leach brothers from Hawes. Left to right:
Gunner Albert Leach, Bombardier Harold Leach and Gunner Laurence Leach.

106

Albert Leach is buried in grave H.5. the Mesnil Ridge Cemetery, between Albert and Beaumont Hamel.

PRIVATE PERCY JEEVES
NO. 611 15TH BATTALION
ROYAL WARWICKSHIRE REGIMENT
DIED SATURDAY 22ND JULY 1916 AGE 28.

Although Percy Jeeves is not to be found on any memorial in Wensleydale, I have included him because he had close connections to Hawes. Born in Dewsbury, Yorkshire, it was in 1910, at the age of 22, that Percy Jeeves was engaged by Hawes Cricket Club as their professional player, this being his first entry into the professional ranks. In his first season he scored 206 runs in 15 innings and took 73 wickets at an average of 5.9 runs. Throughout 1911 he scored 536 runs and took 51 wickets at an average of 7. Percy scored centuries for Hawes against Constable Burton and the Yorkshire Clergy. Also, playing for Bedale, he scored 109 not out against York Trinity.

Percy Jeeves (Hawes).

It was through Mr. Crallon of the Stone House, near Sedbusk, Hawes, that Percy obtained a professional engagement with Warwickshire County Cricket Club and played for Warwickshire against the touring Australians. From that time his progress was rapid, and, according to the local paper, he joined the first flight of English fast bowlers. He played on four occasions against Yorkshire, his native county, with success. (amongst other ventures, Mr. Crallon owned "Gullivar", the Mineral Water Company making pop and ginger beer, by the side of Gayle Beck, in Hawes).

When war broke out Percy joined the 15th Battalion Warwickshire Regiment (the "Birmingham Pals"), which, in the summer of 1915, were in camp at Wensley. As with so many "Pals" Battalions it would be decimated during the fighting on the Somme.

In the third week of July a renewed assault was made along the whole of the narrow front from Guillemont to Bazentin-le-Petit. This failed completely and

107

during the first day of the renewed assault, Percy Jeeves was struck down. The sad news of the death was received by Mr. Crallon from Percy's parents in Dewsbury. He had been struck in the back by shrapnel from a shell on July 22nd and died shortly afterwards.

There is no marked grave for Percy and his name is honoured on Pier and Face 9A,9B and 10B of the Thiepval Memorial.

PRIVATE JAMES BANKS
NO. 5836 1ST/ 5TH BATTALION WEST RIDING REGIMENT
DIED WEDNESDAY 26TH JULY 1916 AGE 22.

Born at Hawes in 1894, James Banks was to be found with his family at Burtersett in 1901. His father William, from Aysgarth, married Ann, a Sedbergh girl and settled first at Garsdale, where their eldest son George was born. They then moved to Hawes, where James was born, before moving to Burtersett, where William was employed as an underground stonemason at one of the two Burtersett Quarries. Two daughters, Sarah and Agnes, were born to complete the family. Ann Banks ran a shop from one of her rooms to supplement the family income.

Burtersett underground quarry (an adit mine), on Quarry Hill, was worked from about 1860 and had seen a large expansion after the railway was opened

James Banks (Burtersett).

through Wensleydale in 1878. Production reached a peak in 1889/1890 and then gradually declined. It had a significant impact on the local economy, supporting as much as a quarter of the population of Hawes parish. A six day week was the norm, working for 18 shillings a week, from 7.30a.m. to 5p.m.. Burtersett stone was used for roofs, paving flags, stone setts (cobbles), drains and gullies, steps, railway platform edges, fireplaces and large stone tanks used on the farms. In 1890, 15,000 tons of stone flags went through Hawes Station each month. The best stone came from the drifts, pillars being left to support the roof. No explosives could be used and so the men used hard drills to work the stone. Underground illumination came from candle light, with a hundredweight of candles being bought at a time from "Candle Willie" Metcalfe of Hawes.

Miners at the Seavy Quarry, Burtersett, in 1895.

Miners standing at the entrance to Burtersett Quarry c 1895.

By permission of the Dales Countryside Museum.

Burtersett Quarry in 1895.

Before the war began, both of James's parents had died and he was living with his uncle, Mr. J. Dent and working for him at Halldale Farm, Fell End, Ravenstonedale. It was from there that James departed for Keighley, to enlist in the army and join the 1st/5th Battalion West Riding Regiment.

By July 3rd 1916 they were in Thiepval Wood, receiving severe casualties due to increased enemy shelling, but were relieved on July 6th and went into the assembly trenches.

The next few days passed relatively quietly in and around Thiepval Wood, with work on improving the trench system continuing. Between July 22nd and 25th the enemy artillery was active, with indiscriminate and prolonged shelling of the wood taking place during the night of 24th/25th. This was repeated with greater violence and heavier artillery from 11.30a.m. to 5.30p.m.on July 25th. Seventeen casualties were sustained, one of them being James Banks.

He was taken 8km behind the lines to the village of Warloy-Baillon, which had become a field ambulance station. There he died from his wounds on July

26th and was buried in Warloy-Baillon Communal Cemetery Extension in grave V. B. 7. The sad news of his death was received by his sister, Miss Sarah Banks, of Burtersett in late August.

PRIVATE HENRY ARMISTEAD STOREY
NO. 20524 9TH BATTALION YORKSHIRE REGIMENT
DIED WEDNESDAY 2ND AUGUST 1916.

Henry Storey was born into a farming family in the small village of Downholme, between Bellerby and Richmond, his parents being Fred and Maria Storey. Later in life they moved to Bardin Lane Farm, near Constable Burton.

Henry left home to work on a farm at Carperby and became engaged to a Carperby girl, Miss Wiseman, who later in life became the village shopkeeper. He enlisted and joined the 9th Battalion Yorkshire Regiment.

Three days into the Battle of the Somme, Henry's Battalion moved through Albert up the main Bapaume road. An attack was made on Horseshoe Trench on July 5th, the Battalion receiving heavy losses in capturing 146 German soldiers.

On July 10th an attack was launched against Contalmaison, a key village, with the Battalion crossing 1500 yards in the open. They burst through the wire and entered the village, taking 100 prisoners, but also receiving casualties. At 7.30p.m. a German counter-attack was repulsed, but the cost to the Battalion for the actions on July 5th and 10th had been a heavy one, with 438 men killed, wounded or missing. One of those wounded by shell fire was Henry Storey who died in a Field Ambulance Station on August 2nd and was buried in grave 1.M.52. in Albert Communal Cemetery Extension.

News of his death was received by his family and his fiance, Miss Wiseman. Devastated by his death, she remained a spinster and always dreaded Armistice Day coming round each year.

A month later, on September 3rd, another man from Carperby and one from West Burton, comrades in the same Battalion, died together as they attacked a strong-point at Thiepval.

PRIVATE WILLIAM HERBERT KILBURN
NO. 202833 1ST/4TH BATTALION WEST RIDING REGIMENT
DIED SUNDAY 3RD SEPTEMBER 1916 AGE 20.

Herbert Kilburn was born at Carperby in 1897, the second son of William and Mary Kilburn. William senior had been born in Bainbridge and married Mary, a West Burton girl, before arriving in Carperby as landlord of the Wheatsheaf Inn

111

*In the period before the Great War William Kilburn was landlord of the Wheatsheaf Inn,
Carperby and was the local butcher. He was father of Private William Herbert Kilburn.*

and also serving as the village butcher. An elder son Chapman, younger son Fred
and daughters Annie, Bessie, Jane and Blondie completed the family. By 1901
three of the daughters were employed as hotel waitresses at the Wheatsheaf. The
Kilburns were one of the families in Aysgarth parish to use their right to collect
firewood twice a year, between October and March, from Aysgarth Freeholder
Wood and to graze animals there. They kept goats and they used the milk at the
inn.

AND
PRIVATE GEORGE IVESON HAMMOND
NO. 202801 1ST/4TH WEST RIDING REGIMENT
DIED SUNDAY 3RD SEPTEMBER 1916 AGE 19.

George's father, Tunstall Hammond, a West Burton man, married Ann Iveson
from Gayle, setting up home in West Burton. Tunstall was a stonemason,
working in the quarries on the heights near Morpath Scar and in the quarries in
Bishopdale, near Aysgarth. George, born in 1896, had an elder sister and
brother, Esther and William and younger sister Annas. In 1915 he enlisted at
Barnoldswick and joined the same Battalion as Herbert Kilburn.

By August 31st 1916 Herbert and George were in the Forceville–Thiepval sector, with the Battalion preparing for an attack on a strong point in front of Thiepval village, part of a large attack to be made on both sides of the River Ancre. It was to prove a "Black Day" for the Battalion, with heavy losses sustained and no success to compensate for the casualties. At 5.10a.m. on September 3rd the companies swarmed over the parapet and a deadly cross-fire of machine-gun bullets opened from the direction of the enemy strong points, plus very heavy shelling embracing the whole of Thiepval Wood. At this early stage of the action most of the officers and NCO's were hit.

George Iveson Hammond (West Burton).

"B" Company charged and captured its first objective, but they were exposed in shell holes and they lost heavily from machine-gun fire. "A" Company passed through "B" Company but received heavy casualties, even being hit by their own shell fire. For some time the Company lay in the open, exchanging shots with the enemy. Casualties were piling up but the second objective was not yet taken. When they charged again, at 6a.m., only about 40 of the Battalion had reached the second objective and these were shelled heavily by howitzer and trench mortars.

No carrying parties had been able to get up to the captured position and they had to collect and use ammunition and bombs from the dead and wounded. The rest of the attack had failed and by 7a.m. the only British troops maintaining their position in the enemy defences were those of the Battalion

The Germans counter-attacked strongly and a slow withdrawal was ordered. Few, however, made it back across no-man's land to their own lines, with machine-gun fire taking its severe toll.

Only once, on October 11th 1918, has the Battalion had heavier casualties than on September 3rd. The total casualties for the day were 11 officers and 336 men killed or wounded, out of 18 officers and 629 men.

Two of the men killed by machine-gun fire during the ill-fated attack were Herbert Kilburn and George Hammond. Wensleydale men, they fought together, died together and are buried in the same cemetery on the Somme. Herbert is buried in grave X1X.A.7., and George in grave V11.D.9., both in Mill Road Cemetery, Thiepval.

On September 14th 1916, perhaps one of the most poignant incidents in our story of the Great War occurred when, on that same day, three Wensleydale men, comrades in the same Battalion, fell on the battlefield. Two of the men were cousins.

PRIVATE MATTHEW HESELTINE
NO. 20348 6TH BATTALION YORKSHIRE REGIMENT
DIED THURSDAY 14TH SEPTEMBER 1916 AGE 21.

Thomas Heseltine, the father of Matthew, was born into a Newbiggin farming family. He married Mary Jane Falshaw, a teacher from West Witton, and farmed at East Lane Farm, Bishopdale, near Street Head, where a son, John William, was born. By 1884 they had settled in the Toxteth area of Liverpool where Thomas ran a milk house, providing milk for the city. A daughter, Harriet, was born in Liverpool.

The heyday of the Liverpool milk house was just before the outbreak of the Great War. By this time 4,000 head of cattle were kept within Liverpool, with a milk house at the end of most streets. Fresh milk was therefore available at any time. The owners were often from the Yorkshire dales, hoping to earn enough money to obtain a farm of their own back home.

The milk house was purpose built, consisting of a large house with dairy, shippon, hay loft over the stable and muck midden, all enclosed within high walls and wooden gates. The dairy shop, usually managed by the female members of the family, was open from 8a.m. to 8p.m.

Cows were replenished when their yields dropped below three gallons a day. They were then sold for beef or sent back to the dales on the excellent railway network, to re-calve.

Cattle were fed on a mixture of brewery waste, molasses, Indian linseed and pea meal, mixed with water, with a later meal of hay. All the available grass cut from parks, cemeteries and verges was used during the summer months.

By 1887 the Heseltine family was back in Newbiggin, farming at East Barn Farm, with Thomas also working at the quarry as a stonemason. It was at Newbiggin that Thomas, Isabel, Robert, Margaret, Matthew and Mary were born. Thomas Heseltine senior and his eldest son, John William, were both Methodist lay preachers on the Bishopdale and Aysgarth circuit.

Before the Great War, their eldest son had become the egg, butter, poultry and rabbit dealer for the area, going to the local markets on his horse and trap. Farm hands on the local farms trapped and killed the rabbits, taking them to John to sell. He then despatched them by the night train to Castleford, Bradford and Middlesborough markets (his younger brother Robert was to continue this

The Heseltine family of Newbiggin, Aysgarth.
(Baby Matthew was later to be killed in the Great War.)
Back row: Thomas, Jane, Harriet.
Front row: Robert, Elizabeth, Thomas with baby Matthew, Maggie,
Mary Jane with May on knee, John Willian, Isabelle.

Robert Heseltine of Newbiggin.
Brother of Matthew.

business after the war). Poultry were kept and taken live in baskets to Thirsk and Northallerton markets, where members of the Jewish community from Leeds, would arrive to purchase them.

Brothers Thomas, Robert and Matthew eventually joined the army during the early stages of the war. It was Matthew who was to enlist at the same time as his elder cousin and namesake, Matthew Heseltine, from neighbouring Thoralby, and they joined the same Regiment.

PRIVATE MATTHEW HESELTINE
NO. 20349 6TH BATTALION YORKSHIRE REGIMENT
DIED 14TH SEPTEMBER 1916 AGE 22.

Matthew was born in 1893 at the family farm at Swinacote, by the gill flowing just outside Thoralby. His parents were Matthew and Margaret (nee Dinsdale from Reeth). Like his cousin, Matthew had three older brothers as well as having sisters, including Ann, Mary and Catherine, all three of whom emigrated to America before the Great War began.

Matthew Heseltine of Thoralby.

CORPORAL THOMAS WALTON
NO. 17799 6TH BATTALION YORKSHIRE REGIMENT
DIED THURSDAY 14TH SEPTEMBER 1916 .

Born in Appleby, Westmoreland, Thomas settled in Hawes before the Great War and married a local girl, daughter of James Fawcett. By 1916 they had a family of four young children. Thomas was a good footballer and rendered yeoman service as goalkeeper for Hawes Football Club for many years, playing in both the Westmoreland and Allertonshire Leagues. He was also a member of the Hawes Conservative Club billiards team that were so successful in the Orde-Powlett Cup competition, as well as member and once Secretary of the Hawes Brass Band. When he enlisted in December 1914 Tom was the first married man from Hawes to join the Colours.

All three men served with the 6th Battalion Yorkshire Regiment in the latter stages of the Dardanelles Campaign and in February 1916 found themselves in Egypt until the middle of May. The Battalion then embarked on board

"Arcadian" for Marseilles, reaching it on July 1st and then travelled by train across France to billets in Arras, taking over the trenches at Agny.

Playing no active part in the Battle of the Somme now in progress, they were eventually brought up to Senlis and on September 9th took over part of the front line trenches.

Opposite them the Allies still had to carry the enemy's original defences on the main ridge above Thiepval, and in the village itself, defences known as the "Wonderwork", that seemed almost impregnable.

On the night of September 14th the 6th Battalion was detailed to carry out the attack on the enemy position, his trenches being the primary objective and the "Wonderwork" the final target.

Tom Walton (Hawes).

At 6.30p.m. a very heavy artillery barrage was opened on the trench to be attacked and three minutes later "D" Company left its assembly trench and attacked the enemy trenches. These had somehow remained untouched by the bombardment and the attacking force was met by a heavy rifle and grenade fire, but nevertheless some still reached their objective and it was gained by a bombing attack about midnight.

The enemy counter-attacked violently, with bombs, at least three times during the night, but were repulsed. The losses in the Battalion, in this, its first fight on the Western Front, had been serious, with five officers and 130 men killed or wounded.

Tom Walton and the Heseltine cousins were amongst those killed. The officer in command of their Battalion, in a letter to Tom Walton's wife, stated that he was killed by a shell, death being instantaneous. Tom's death left a widow and four young children.

The heartache for both Heseltine families was immense. Both lads were the fourth sons in their families, both families also had four sons and six daughters. Both lads enlisted in February 1915, both their fathers were dead by this stage and both served in the same Battalion. Certainly Mary Jane Heseltine never got over the loss of her son Matthew and gradually deteriorated in health.

Tom Walton's body was recovered and he is buried in grave 111.M.1

Lonsdale Cemetery, just north of Albert. Neither of the cousin's bodies were recovered and their names are inscribed next to each other on Pier and Face 3A and 3D on the Thiepval Memorial. Even in death their names are closely linked.

The sacrifice and heartache for the families in Wensleydale was unrelenting. During the following three days, between September 15th and 17th , seven more men from the dale would forfeit their lives.

RIFLEMAN CHRISTOPHER GREGG
NO. G/12814 9TH BATTALION
KING'S ROYAL RIFLE CORPS
DIED FRIDAY 15TH SEPTEMBER 1916 AGE 23.

Christopher was the second son of Thomas Gregg, and the family of three sons and four daughters lived in Brown's Cottages at Bellerby. By 1901 Thomas was a widower and raised the family with the help of his elderly mother. He earned a living as a smallholder and by working as a quarryman at Bellerby and on the Hauxwell Estate.

Thomas was also a besom or broom maker. The heather (ling) for the besom heads came from the surrounding moorland and was held in a vice-like mechanism fixes to a bench. Ash saplings were used to bind the heather to the handle. These saplings were placed in the nearby beck to soften, and then smashed

Christopher Gregg (Bellerby).

to break them up into strips, to be used for the binding. The finished besoms were taken by horse and cart to be sold at Leyburn and Richmond markets.

Christopher's brother, Thomas, joined the Irish Fusiliers during the Great War and was twice wounded, in the shoulder and leg, and was eventually a POW for the last ten months of the conflict. Christopher, however, enlisted at Darlington and joined the 9th Battalion K.R.R C

Serious casualties occurred in the Battalion during ferocious fighting for Delville Wood on the Somme in late August 1916 but it was to be in the operation to capture the village of Guedecourt, near Flers, on September 15th that Christopher Gregg was to lose his life. It was here that tanks were used for the first time on the Western Front.

The Battalion's objective was to gain ground NE of Gird Support and then to dig in. A German machine-gun caused considerable casualties amongst the leading Companies "A" and "B", as well as at Battalion HQ in the rear, with the loss of many officers. Heavy shelling caught "D" Company at the rear of the operation.

A sergeant collected a small party of men and rushed two enemy field guns that were firing towards the village of Flers, killing most of the gunners and capturing the guns. The Battalion dug in whilst the Germans continued to mass troops ahead of them. Nothing happened all afternoon, but as dusk came on, the enemy attacked, but were thrown back and the night passed quietly.

However, Rifleman Christopher Gregg had been caught in the shell fire that had caught "D" Company and his body was not recovered. His name appears on Pier and Face 13A and 13B of the Thiepval Memorial.

Christopher Gregg.

PRIVATE LISTER STAVELEY NO. 29407
123RD COMPANY MACHINE GUN CORPS
DIED FRIDAY 15TH SEPTEMBER 1916 AGE 22.

Lister Staveley's mother, Mary Little, a Westmoreland girl from Norton, had married Edmund Staveley, a quarry worker from Hawes, who worked as a carter in the underground Burtersett quarry belonging to Tom Metcalfe. Two sons, Robert and Edmund were born and some years later a daughter Rachel and sons Lister and George were born at Burtersett. However, by 1901, Mary had been widowed and was eking out a living as a charwoman, with just Rachel, Lister and George at home. Robert was an apprentice tailor in Hawes and Edmund was working as an office boy for the local solicitor in Gayle.

Lister Staveley (Gayle and Hawes).

Robert Staveley, the half-brother of Lister. Out of the four Staveley brothers, Robert was the only one to survive the war.

Lister served as an apprentice to Mr. Tom Hiscock, the Hawes printer. His mother Mary, however, moved to number 3 Beech Street, Padiham, near Burnley, some years before the Great War, accompanied by Lister and George. At Padiham he acted as Secretary to the Horeb Congregational Secondary School and was employed as a letter press printer by Messrs. Spencer of Padiham.

Lister Staveley and his brother George enlisted in December 1915, with Lister joining the Lancashire Fusiliers but shortly afterwards both brothers transferred to the Machine Gun Corps. By mid-September 1916 Lister had been out in France for some five months. The Machine Gun Corps was founded in 1915 and originally sent its men out in companies which were attached at division level. It was a dangerous occupation, with the machine-gunners supporting any attack, by setting up their posts in shell holes in no-man's land and attempting to keep the heads of the enemy down whilst their comrades assaulted the enemy trenches. They became prime targets for enemy shelling and bombing attacks.

A letter from the chaplain to Mary Staveley reported, "I regret to inform you that your son died of gas poisoning on September 15th and was buried today. I saw your son before he died and he was quite patient and trusting in God. Everything possible was done for him, but the gas had got into his lungs. Your son has died for his country, and that sacrifice will not be in vain. It must one

120

day produce the fruit of liberty and righteousness."

Mary Staveley's sadness would increase as the war progressed, for in 1917 her son Edmund was killed and in 1918 her youngest son George fell in battle, resulting in the loss of three out of her four sons in this cruel war.

Lister Staveley is buried in grave 11.E.39. La Neuville British Cemetery, near Corbie, on the Somme.

Only one day later, another soldier from Hawes died from wounds and was buried in the same cemetery as Lister Staveley.

PRIVATE REGINALD WILLIAM MILBURN
NO. 24384 4TH BATTALION GRENADIER GUARDS
DIED SATURDAY 16TH SEPTEMBER 1916 AGE 27.

Reginald Milburn was born in 1889 at Hutton Rudby, near Stokesley, on the fringes of the North York Moors and south of Middlesborough. He was the second son of James Milburn, a draper and grocer, and wife Mary. Some time before the start of the Great War Reginald arrived in Hawes seeking employment. He enlisted at nearby Leyburn, and, being over six feet tall, he joined the 4th Battalion Grenadier Guards.

The Battalion was not involved in the Battle of the Somme until September 15th 1916, when tanks were brought into the action. The Grenadiers were to attack in the vicinity of Trones Wood, near Ginchy, passing through the rows of massed field guns taking part in the Allied bombardment. But when the guns began an intense fire, this became impossible and instead they moved by platoons along the old railway.

As they passed over what had been the first objective of the leading brigades, the heaps of dead Germans remained as evidence of the recent fighting. 500 yards north of Ginchy, they dug in, in a defensive position. A discarded British tank provided excellent cover for a dug-out, constructed underneath. At 5p.m. No's. 3 and 4 Companies were sent forward through the German barrage to protect the flanks, moving up to an empty trench. Thirty men were sent over the top to co-operate with the party working down the trench, and the Germans were soon driven back some distance.

During these actions, Reginald Milburn was wounded and taken to the Casualty Clearing Station but he died the following day, 16th September, and lies buried in grave 11.E.28 in La Neuville British Cemetery, Corbie, 15km. SW of Albert.

September 17th was another black day for Wensleydale, with confirmation that four men from the dale were killed on that day, with three of them belonging to the same Battalion, the 21st King's Royal Rifle Corps.

PRIVATE ROBERT STOCKDALE ATKINSON
NO. 6/2922 1ST BATTALION CANTERBURY REGIMENT
NEW ZEALAND EXPEDITIONARY FORCE
DIED SUNDAY 17TH SEPTEMBER 1916 AGE 21.

Robert was born in 1894. His father Nathan came from Brothay near Ambleside in the Lake District, marrying Mary Ann Tomlinson at New Hutton, near Sedbergh. Children Thomas, Richard, Nathan, Robert, Frank, Mary, Alice, Nellie and Phoebe were born and the family moved to Danzig Farm at Danby Hall, near Thornton Steward, in 1902. Nathan was working as a farm worker on the estate, eventually becoming a gamekeeper, and his sons too began work on the Danby Estate.

In 1912, however, sons Nathan and Richard (Dick) emigrated to New Zealand on a settlement scheme sponsored by the Scrope family of Danby Hall. As war was about to break out in

*Robert Stockdale Atkinson
(East Witton and Thornton Steward).*

1914, their brother Robert (Bob) went out to join them in New Zealand. It was not long, however, before all three brothers joined up and returned to Britain with the New Zealand Expeditionary Force. Meanwhile, back in England, their youngest brother Frank had joined the Hussars and Thomas joined the R.F.A. It was to be Robert and Frank who would fall on the battlefield and lie buried on the Western Front.

On July 23rd the Anzac Corps (Australia and New Zealand Forces) under General Birdwood was given the task of launching a renewed attack on a front opposite Pozieres, on the Somme. Nearly two months of bitter fighting followed, with very little progress made, but at great cost. The infantry on both sides became "compressed canon fodder for artillery consumption". The Anzac Corps was the main agent of this "nibbling" away at the enemy. It was like applying a battering ram ten or fifteen times against the same part of the enemy's battle-front, against one of the strongest points in the enemy's defence.

23,000 men were expended in these efforts for the ultimate gain, after six weeks, of a piece of ground just over a mile deep. One officer wrote, "We have just come out of a place so terrible that a raving lunatic could never imagine the horror of the last thirteen days."

Robert Atkinson survived the carnage of those last six weeks only to be killed in action on September 17th. His body was not recovered and his name is found on the Caterpillar (New Zealand) Memorial in Caterpillar Valley, 13km. east of Albert. Sadly, we shall see later that his brother Frank from East Witton was killed only a few kilometres away, near Pozieres, in March 1918.

A British poster of 1915 calling on the Empire for help.

RIFLEMAN JAMES HENRY MILNER
NO. C/13003 21ST BATTALION
KING'S ROYAL RIFLE CORPS
DIED SUNDAY 17TH SEPTEMBER 1916 AGE 19.

James was the youngest son of Thomas and Sarah Milner of Garsdale Head, near Hawes Junction. Thomas came from West Scale Park, near Kettlewell and was an engineer on the railway, servicing the locomotives at Hawes Junction. There, he met his future wife, Sarah, a Garsdale girl, and children Mary Ann, Mark, Emily, James, Margaret and Ethel Ann were born. In 1910, a sad loss occurred when Thomas was killed in an accident on the railway, leaving his widow to raise a large family.

James, who was living near Sedbergh when war began, enlisted with his older brother Mark at Leyburn in January 1916, both lads joining the 21st Battalion King's Royal Rifle Corps. By August 1916 they were on the Somme, ready to participate in the battle.

Brothers Mark Milner (standing) and James Henry Milner (Hawes).

AND
RIFLEMAN ROBERT HENRY LAMBERT
NO. C/12595 21ST BATTALION K.R.R.C.
DIED SUNDAY 17TH SEPTEMBER 1916 AGE 21.

One of three sons, Robert Lambert was born at Castle Bolton in 1895. His father Robert originated from Horsehouse in Coverdale and married Jane, from Redmire. They lived at the farm next to the Methodist Chapel at the top right hand side of the village green (the chapel is now a cottage), where children Christopher (Kit), Robert and William were born. As with James Milner, Robert enlisted at Leyburn and joined the same Battalion, the 21st.

Robert Henry Lambert of Castle Bolton.

AND

RIFLEMAN ALFRED CRADDOCK KILDING
NO. C/12880 21ST BATTALION K.R.R.C.
DIED SUNDAY 17TH SEPTEMBER 1916 AGE 24.

Alfred was born at Preston under Scar in 1892, the youngest son of James Kilding and wife Mary. James was a carter on a farm belonging to the Bolton Hall Estate. Other members of the family were Henry (Harry), George and Alice.

The war was to affect their lives dreadfully, for Alfred would die in 1916 and his older brother Henry a year later in 1917. Although living in Leyburn, Alfred enlisted at Middlesborough on December 16th 1915 and joined the 21st Battalion in France on May 4th 1916.

In the Autumn of 1915, in consequence of the number of men of the farmer and yeoman class who were believed to be holding back from enlisting, it was decided that a Battalion composed of such men should be raised in the hopes that they would welcome service with those of their own ideas and manner of life. This hope was amply justified in the 21st Battalion.

On May 4th 1916 it crossed to France and went into the line at Ploegsteert, in the Ypres Salient, until the middle of August, before it moved to the Somme.

On September 15th it took a notable part in an attack on the enemy's position to the east of Flers, where, over the next

Alfred Craddock Kilding.
(Wensley and Preston under Scar.)

two days, it carried three lines of trenches. Establishing itself, it held the captured ground until relieved by other troops. Tanks had been used in the attack for the first time. The Battalion lost heavily, including its Colonel, who fell at the head of the Riflemen he had led further into the enemy's lines than any troops penetrated over those days of battle. Sadly, three of the Riflemen who died in the attack were from Wensleydale.

James Milner's Commanding Officer wrote his widowed mother, Sarah, "It is my duty to inform you of news of your two brave sons. One of them, Mark, is wounded and is in hospital. The other, James, who was reported missing, is now officially reported killed. In giving you this news I can assure you that it is very painful to me, because not only were they both good soldiers, but really good lads. They were both very popular amongst the other lads in the Company and I can assure you they are both missed very much. From news we have received, it appears that James was killed instantaneously. My sympathies are with you."

They were going "over the top" behind some of the tanks when three men, James, Mark and George Walls from Hawes were hit by a shell, with James being killed. Mark suffered from his shrapnel wounds for the rest of his life.

James Milner is commemorated on Piers and Face 13A and 13B of the Thiepval Memorial, as is Robert Lambert. Alfred Kilding is buried in grave V.G.10. in the Guard's Cemetery, Lesboeufs.

The attack on Flers, between September 15th and 17th, was followed up on September 25th by another big attack, which, in conjunction with the French, compelled the Germans to evacuate Combles. Next day Thiepval at long last fell. The decisive break in the German front was caused by the appearance of three British tanks on the outskirts of Thiepval village. It was during the attack on Combles on the 25th and on Thiepval on the 26th and the follow up, that another two men, one from East Witton and the other from Hawes lost their lives.

PRIVATE EDWIN WRIGHT
NO. 34798 10TH BATTALION
KING'S OWN YORKSHIRE LIGHT INFANTRY
DIED MONDAY 25TH SEPTEMBER 1916.

Born at Masham, Edwin was working on the estates at Danby Hall, near Thornton Steward, when he enlisted in the army at Northallerton. His mother had come to Danby Hall as a cook for the Scrope family and she and Edwin lived at Eagle Lodge on the Danby estate. Killed in action whilst attacking Combles, near Thiepval, on September 25th, Edwin's name is commemorated on the Thiepval Memorial.

PRIVATE JOHN WILLIAM HORN
NO. 5176 4TH BATTALION YORKSHIRE REGIMENT
DIED WEDNESDAY 27TH SEPTEMBER 1916 AGE 20.

John Horn's father, Jeremiah, born at Leyburn, was married to Margaret, also from Leyburn, and in 1900 moved to Burtersett near Hawes, where Jeremiah worked as a stonemason and hewer of rock at Burtersett Quarry. Their three children, John, Anthony and George, had all been born in Leyburn.

John William Horn (Burtersett).

John, working at the quarry like his father, enlisted at Askrigg in October 1915, joining the 4th Battalion Yorkshire Regiment. He married a local girl, Jane Ann Dinsdale, in February 1916 and by the time of his death in September 1916, a child had been born.

Embarking for France in April 1916, the Battalion was not called upon to take part in the Battle of the Somme until September 15th, when the attack, supported by tanks, began. The Battalion held the line reached for the next two days, under heavy shell fire, which caused many casualties. Soaked through and exhausted, they were relieved on September 19th.

The plan for September 26th was to attack and capture the German trenches running from Flers. The Battalion attacked at 11p.m. in conjunction with the 5th Durham Light Infantry but by mistake the Durhams did not attack and the 4th Battalion found themselves in the German trenches with both flanks exposed and were driven out by strong counter-attacks on September 27th. The losses suffered were large and during the German counter-attack, John William Horn was killed.

He was posted as missing and it was not until early 1917 that Jane Horn was officially notified that her husband had been killed. His name is on Pier and Face 3A and 3D of the Thiepval Memorial.

PRIVATE JAMES PICKARD BELL
NO. 153353 79TH CAMERON HIGHLANDERS
(CANADIAN EXPEDITIONARY FORCE)
DIED WEDNESDAY 4TH OCTOBER 1916 AGE 28.

James Pickard Bell was born in Aysgarth in 1888, the son of the station master William Bell and his wife Barbara, who, in 1881 lived in the Station House, but later moved to the Flattlands. After attending Aysgarth Infant School, he completed his education at Leeds Boys Modern School before returning to live in Aysgarth. In 1910 he emigrated to Canada where he farmed on the prairies of Manitoba.

However, in 1915 he responded to the call for volunteers and enlisted in the 79th Battalion Cameron Highlanders, a Canadian Scottish Regiment. Training began in Canada and was completed in England, before they were sent to France in February 1916.

It was during the later stages of the Battle of the Somme, that on October 4th Private Bell was last seen leading a section of bombers towards the German lines facing Courcelette, a village halfway between Albert and Bapaume. He was never seen again and was reported "missing presumed dead". Official confirmation of his death did not arrive until July 1917. His body was never recovered and his name is commemorated on the Vimy Memorial.

These last days of September and early October had proved the continued strength of the German resistance and little hope was held out for a real break-through. The early onset of the autumn rains made this hope more slender daily.

The rains combined with the bombardments to make the ground a morass in which guns and transport were bogged, while even lightly equipped infantry could barely struggle forward.

It was during this period that a soldier with strong West Witton connections became the next fatality.

GUNNER JOHN A. HARLAND
NO. 96467 "D" BATTERY
92ND BRIGADE ROYAL FIELD ARTILLERY
DIED 23RD OCTOBER 1916 AGE 20.

John Harland's father, John Thomas Harland, was born at South Lodge, Bolton Hall Estate, on the main road between West Witton and Wensley. The Harlands worked on the estate, employed in the gardens and acting as gatekeepers. At the age of 4 John Thomas was living with his maternal grandparents at Castle Bolton. Later, he married Sarah, a Middleham girl, and they left to settle in the Newcastle area, where John A Harland was born.

Enlisting at Darlington, John Harland joined the Royal Field Artillery and in the rainy October days of 1916 was involved in supporting the fresh attacks through the mud towards Le Transloy, SE of Bapaume. The Battery struggled in the terrible conditions to push forward to new positions. As they lay down protective barrages for their own troops, retaliatory shelling by the Germans found its target and John A Harland was killed by shrapnel. He is buried in grave V.Q.4. at the Guard's Cemetery, Lesboeuf.

CORPORAL SIMON MOORE
NO. 20541 7TH BATTALION YORKSHIRE REGIMENT
DIED SUNDAY 5TH NOVEMBER 1916 AGE 20.

Simon was the youngest son of William Moore from Appersett. He was a native of Burtersett, but by 1901, aged 4 years, he was living with his brothers Edward, James and William and sister Ann in Appersett, at the home of his maternal grandparents, Francis and Ann Parker. It is possible that Simon's parents had gone to Liverpool to run a milk house in that city for we know that 18 months before the start of the war, Simon was in Liverpool employed in that occupation.

He came home to join his brother James Moore and some other companions, who all enlisted together at Leyburn in May 1915, before leaving for France on June 21st 1916. His two other brothers also went to the front as soldiers. Simon joined the 7th Battalion Yorkshire Regiment.

By October 29th 1916 they were preparing for an attack in terrible ground conditions. The filthy mire in the front line trenches was hip-deep and the fight against trench foot became most difficult.

A small attack was to take place at 11a.m. on November 5th against an enemy trench, using just 40 men of "A" Company, including Simon Moore, assisted by covering fire from "B" Company's Lewis guns and a Vickers Maxim. There was no telephone communication and because of the mud it took four hours for an orderly to reach the front line and return, even though the distance was only 500 yards. "A" Company had in fact failed in taking the objective and at 10p.m. a second attack was sent in with "D" Company but this too failed before the enemy's heavy machine-gun fire. 35 men were killed, 75 wounded and 10 were missing.

Simon Moore (Appersett).

Simon and James Moore, brothers, both in 19th Yorkshire Regimant.

Simon Moore is buried in grave 2.AA.13 at Sucrerie Military Cemetery, 16km. north of Albert.

A few days later the Battle of the Somme was brought to an end.

For ten other families in Wensleydale, bereavement came to them away from the blood soaked battleground of the Somme valley. Their grief, however, was just as strong.

PRIVATE MANSELL WAITE
NO. 9868 5TH BATTALION WILTSHIRE REGIMENT
DIED SUNDAY 16TH JANUARY 1916 AGE 19.

Mansell Waite was born in Malmesbury, Yorkshire, the son of William and Ada Waite. They came to Lime Tree House, at East Witton, where William worked on the Jervaulx Estate. Mansell had three other brothers, William, Edward and Samuel, but in 1909 Samuel emigrated to Australia as a foreman on the railway, whilst brother Edward emigrated in 1912. Mansell worked in the gardens on the nearby Jervaulx Estate.

He enlisted at Swindon in 1914 and went with the Wiltshire Regiment to Gallipoli to fight the Turks. His brother William became a Sergeant in the Artillery, whilst in Australia Edward joined the New South Wales Lancers and Samuel the 15th Queensland Mounted Infantry, eventually arriving to fight on the Western Front.

In September 1915 news came that Mansell had been wounded by a bullet in the left shoulder and forearm on August 9th, whilst further news reached his parents that he was again wounded, on December 8th 1915, this time near the shinbone. It did not appear too serious and he was transported by ship to a hospital on Malta, to receive surgical treatment.

Unfortunately, he developed typhoid fever after his arrival and died on January 16th 1916. It seems he contracted the fever before his arrival on Malta. It is not surprising since at both Cape Helles and Suvla Bay the heat had been terrific, water scarce and the sanitary conditions appalling. Helles was described as a midden and smelt like an opened cemetery.

By January 1916 the 9 month campaign had cost the Allies some 215,000 men, of whom 145,000 were due to sickness, 50,000 from dysentery.

Mansell Waite is buried in grave C.V1.6. in the Pita Military Cemetery on Malta.

TROOPER ARTHUR MAWER
NO. 3108 1ST LIFE GUARDS HOUSEHOLD CAVALRY
DIED FRIDAY 11TH FEBRUARY 1916 AGE 20.

Arthur Mawer in ceremonial uniform
(Aysgarth).

Arthur Mawer
in khaki.

By 1891 the Mawers had come from the Carlton area of Coverdale to farm at Barden Dykes, near Bellerby. By 1901, however, William and Jane Mawer had moved with their family to Hill Top Farm, Ellingstring, between East Witton and Masham, where they brought up their family of Elizabeth, John Thomas, Ellenor, Joseph, George, Esther, William, Florence and Arthur.

Arthur worked on his father's farm, whilst his oldest brother, John (Jack) farmed Lower Sowermire Farm, close to Leighton Reservoir, near Colsterdale. By 1914 Arthur was a farm worker at West Burton, in Aysgarth parish, and it was from there that he went to enlist at Richmond on August 28th 1914.

As a farmer's son, working with horses, it was only natural that he should join the 1st Lifeguards, Household Cavalry, and was sent out to the front on April 18th 1915. However, although the 1st Lifeguards retained their horses in horse lines just behind the front, they were used mainly as infantry in the trenches.

From April 1915 to January 1916 Arthur spent most of the time fighting in

132

the trenches in the Ypres Salient. On January 27th 1916 he was wounded in both legs and was taken to Calais Hospital, where he won everybody's esteem for his bright, cheery disposition. At one time recovery seemed possible, but he passed away on February 11th 1916.

At Ellingstring, groups of soldiers from the "Leeds Pals" camp at Breary Banks, Colsterdale, would come to Hill Top Farm on a Sunday and gather round the piano to sing songs. From Lower Sowermire Farm Jack Mawer delivered milk and eggs to the camp. He and the family were therefore upset when the "Leeds Pals" Battalion was decimated on July 1st 1916, especially as it was only four months since the death of Arthur.

Trooper Arthur Mawer is buried in grave 7.B.3. at Calais Southern Cemetery.

During February, two soldiers from the same Battalion, 4th Battalion Yorkshire Regiment, died whilst simply performing their defensive duties in the trenches.

PRIVATE DIGBY G BESWICK
NO. 3940 4TH BATTALION YORKSHIRE REGIMENT
DIED MONDAY 14TH FEBRUARY 1916.

Digby Beswick had connections with both Masham, from where he enlisted, and Middleham, where relations Samuel Malkin Beswick and his wife Jane kept the Commercial Hotel (nowadays Richard III Hotel).

The Commercial Hotel, Middleham (now The Richard III) in the late 1920's early 30's. It was run by Digby Beswick's relations before the Great War.

AND
CAPTAIN JOHN MAUGHAN
4TH BATTALION YORKSHIRE REGIMENT
DIED THURSDAY 17TH FEBRUARY 1916 AGE 26.

John Maughan was the eldest son of John and Annie Maughan, who lived at Abbey Hill, the large house overlooking Jervaulx Abbey. John senior was agent for the Jervaulx Estate. Their son was educated at Marlborough College and joined his Regiment in 1909, receiving his 2nd Star in 1911 and being gazetted Captain in November 1914. This was the same Regiment that Digby had joined. John went out to France in April 1915 and was in action at the 2nd Battle of Ypres a few days later. He took part in all subsequent engagements and was mentioned in Field Marshall Sir John French's despatches.

Captain John Maughan (East Witton).

On February 12th 1916 the Battalion occupied trenches round Hill 60. Work went on with repairing trenches. At 3p.m. on February 14th the Germans began to bombard them, whilst at 5p.m. the enemy exploded a mine under the bombing sap (trench), but did not attempt to

occupy the resulting crater. The bombardment continued until 8p.m. when it slackened slightly. Thirteen men had been killed and five men badly bruised by the explosion of the mine. Digby Beswick was one of those killed.

February 17th was a relatively quiet day, with good progress made in the work of repairing and renewing the trenches. However, there was some shelling and sadly Captain John Maughan was hit by shrapnel and was killed.

Digby Beswick was buried in grave 11.K.11. in Railway Dugouts Burial Ground, 2km. SE of Ypres. Captain John Maughan was buried in grave 1.G.25. in Poperinghe New Military Cemetery.

PRIVATE THOMAS JAMES ALLEN HODGSON NO. 27756 3RD BATTALION YORKSHIRE REGIMENT DIED SATURDAY 8TH APRIL 1916 AGE 24.

In 1901 nine year old Thomas was living with his grandfather William, a 69 year old widower and farmer at Stalling Busk. With them was Thomas's mother Eden Webster and his older brother William, a 19 year old shepherd on the family farm.

Thomas enlisted in late 1915 and was posted to the 3rd Battalion Yorkshire Regiment and proceeded to its war station at West Hartlepool to help in its duties of coastal defence. The Companies set about fortifying Hartlepool and district with trenches dug behind the sea beach. Maxim gun redoubts were constructed

3rd Battalion Yorkshire Regiment on inspection parade at West Hartlepool early 1916. Thomas James Allen Hodgson from Stalling Busk was a member.

and a huge furnace slag heap behind the town was put into a state of defence. Numerous guards had to be found daily to protect vital points in the harbour and exposed points along the coast.

Whilst helping in performing these duties Thomas Hodgson was taken ill and admitted to the VA Hospital at West Hartlepool. Sadly, he died on April 8th and was brought back to Wensleydale, where he was buried in the beautiful setting of the old Stalling Busk Church of St. Matthew, near to Semer Water (the church is in ruins today).

On April 22nd a Carperby man died from wounds, far from home in the heat and dust of Mesopotamia.

CAPTAIN ALBERT MORTON SENIOR
9TH PUNJABI (LIGHT INFANTRY) REGIMENT
DIED 22ND APRIL 1916 AGE 33.

Born 1883 in India and from a military background, Albert Senior was the youngest son of Colonel H.W.J. Senior, Indian Cavalry, and Mrs. Senior of Hall Garth, Carperby.

He followed in the family's military tradition by receiving his commission in January 1903 and was gazetted in the Indian Army a year later, being promoted to Captain in March 1912. In August 1914 Captain Senior married Winifred, second daughter of Sir V.H. Carewe of Calke Abbey in Derbyshire and they made their home in Earl's Court, London.

The oilfields near the Persian Gulf were of essential importance to Britain's oil supply and with war against nearby Turkey imminent, a small Indian force of one division was despatched to safeguard them.

Basra was captured in November 1914 but another Indian division was required to repulse the Turkish attacks of Spring 1915. General Townsend's Division was sent up the Tigris to take Amara and defeated the Turks at Kut in August 1915. The growing superiority in numbers of the Turkish forces compelled Townsend to retreat to Kut. Here, isolated and far from help his forces became besieged in December.

Two newly arrived Indian Divisions, with Captain Senior as one of the officers, battered futilely against the heavy Turkish defences surrounding Kut. Their attacks were repulsed throughout March and early April, with heavy losses sustained. One of the soldiers wounded was Captain Albert Senior.

With starvation near, Townsend capitulated, surrendering 2070 British and 6000 Indian troops on April 29th 1916.

The unsuccessful British relief force had suffered over 21,000 casualties.

Captain Senior died from his wounds on April 22nd but there is no known grave. Instead, his name is on Panel 49 and 66 of the Basra Memorial.

*** It is worth noting that in a 1916 Hawes parish magazine there is news of an urgent request from Northallerton for thousands of mittens etc. to be sent to Mesopotamia immediately.

SERGEANT JOHN EARNSHAW RIDER
NO. 11455 9TH BATTALION WEST RIDING REGIMENT
DIED WEDNESDAY 26TH APRIL 1916 AGE 23.

By 1901 Sergeant Rider's father, John Henry Rider from Redmire, together with his wife Margaret and sons John, Frederick and Frank, were living at Elm House Lodge, Redmire, in the grounds of Elm House, near Redmire Dairy and Railway Station. Their father worked as the gardener for retired solicitor Charles J Burrill at Elm House. Another son William and daughter Kate were born later.

Sergeant John Earnshaw Rider (Redmire).

Some years before the Great War, the family moved to Stanhope Terrace in Crook, County Durham, where John Henry went to work at Bankfoot Coke Ovens, attached to the Roddymoor Colliery. French ovens produced the coke. All the lads joined their father at the works.

Enlisting at Crook, brothers John, Fred and Frank all joined the army and sadly John and Frank would be killed in Belgium, whilst Fred would succumb to wounds some years after the war.

Between April 16th and 21st 1916 the Battalion spent their time in the town of Armentieres on the Franco-Belgian border. Innoculations against para typhoid commenced and bathing took place. Fatigue parties worked on cleaning the streets and the enemy dropped several shells into Place de la Republique, without any casualties occurring.

On April 22nd they relieved the 6th Dorset Regiment on the front line at Houplines, on the NE outskirts of Armentieres. Shelling was intense over the next few days.

From 6p.m. on April 26th very heavy trench mortars were fired into the trenches, which were absolutely wrecked. At 8p.m. the enemy attacked through dense smoke, with some of their soldiers reaching the trenches, but the West Riding Regiment held on and ejected them. A German officer was killed but the other soldiers got back, some badly wounded.

During the period of shelling by German trench mortars, Sergeant John Earnshaw Rider was killed. His body was never recovered and his name is commemorated on Panel 6 of the nearby Ploegsteert Memorial.

LANCE CORPORAL GEORGE WILLIAM STAYMAN
NO. 23217 4TH COMPANY
PRINCESS PATRICIA'S CANADIAN LIGHT INFANTRY
(EASTERN ONTARIO REGIMENT)
DIED FRIDAY 2ND JUNE 1916 AGE 31.

George was born in 1885, the son of James and Elizabeth Stayman. He was born in Sunderland and by 1916 his parents were living in Pelaw on Tyne, County Durham. His father James came from Appleby, but had left that town with his brother Thomas, James travelling to Southwick, County Durham, for work as a quarryman, and Thomas to Harmby in Wensleydale, where he married a local girl. Two older sisters plus George were born in County Durham, but for a period, the family moved to Harmby for James to work in the local quarry with his brother Thomas.

Some years before the war, George emigrated to Ontario in Canada, where he began work as a carpenter. In August 1914 he enlisted and sailed for England on October 3rd. In February 1915 he was transferred to Princess Patricia's Canadian Light Infantry and embarked for France.

Involved in actions against the enemy, George was wounded in the chest and back by gun shots and was admitted to Wimereux Hospital on May 10th 1915, Le Havre on the 12th and Base Hospital at Rouen on June 5th, before returning to his Battalion. On April 21st 1916 he was promoted to Lance Corporal.

By April 1916 the Canadians were in the Ypres Salient defending Sanctuary Wood and occupying Mt. Sorrell (Hill 59), the only high point on the ridge that was controlled by the Allies.

An attack was launched by the Germans just after 1p.m. on June 2nd 1916, announced by the firing of mines. They broke through from Mt. Sorrell to Tot Top and consolidated their line. During the vicious preliminary bombardment at 8.30a.m. they caught in the front line the Commander of the 3rd Division, Major General Mercer, who was killed, together with many soldiers.

The Colour of the Patricia's was buried under a direct hit but despite the ferocious shelling it was got to safety to the Ypres Ramparts.

The Germans were now attacking hard, overpowering eventually the companies holding the left hand part of the line, using flame throwers to eliminate their opponents. Despite this, the Battalion was to hold the line until June 4th, when they were relieved. The Canadians would retake the ridge in a counter-attack on June 13th.

It was in the bitter, desperate fighting on the first day of the attack that George Stayman was killed by shell fire. His name is one of thousands to be found on the Menin Gate, on Panel 10 - 26 - 28. How sad that another man who had gone to the New World to make a fresh start, should die defending his old country and leave grieving friends thousands of miles from his final resting place.

GUNNER THOMAS E. M. RUMFORD
NO. 87101 MEERUT DIVISION AMMUNITION COLUMN
ROYAL FIELD ARTILLERY
DIED SATURDAY 10TH JUNE 1916 AGE 37.

Thomas's father, James Rumford, married Frances, a girl from Grewelthorpe, and they lived at Castle Hill, Middleham, where James continued the family tradition by working as a tailor. The Rumfords were said to have been tailors to the powerful Neville family and were long standing keepers of the keys to Middleham Castle. James was certainly kept busy for he was also the Town Crier, parish clerk, sexton and keeper of the animal pound.

By 1901 Thomas had left home and it is my belief that he had joined the army. It is certainly the case that in 1916, long since married to Mary Margaret Pennington Rumford of East Witton Road, Middleham, he was to be found in Mesopotamia with the Meerut Division Ammunition Column, a British Artillery unit attached to the Indian Army.

The Indian Corps (2 Infantry Divisions, the Meerut and Lahore) had arrived in France in October 1914 and remained on the Western Front till the end of 1915 when it transferred to the Middle East. It was part of the relieving force sent out to break the siege of Kut, where Townsend's forces were pinned inside the town.

Unfortunately, Thomas was struck down with malaria and dysentery and died on June 10th at Amara, a hospital centre on the left bank of the River Tigris. He was buried in grave X1V.C.36 at Amara War Cemetery, Iraq.

PRIVATE JOHN FAWCETT TRENCH MORTAR BATTERY ROYAL FIELD ARTILLERY DIED 12TH DECEMBER 1916 AGE 35.

John was the second son of the late Henry Fawcett, for so many years the proprietor of the Fountain Hotel and Fawcett's grocery business in Hawes, and of Mrs. Thompson, Higher Broughton, Manchester. By 1901 Henry had died and James Burton was the proprietor. When his mother remarried, John went to live with her in Manchester and was employed by Messrs. Affleck and Brown, drapers, Manchester. He was 35 years of age, a large hearted, kindly man and was well liked by all who knew him at Hawes. Mrs Thompson's other two unmarried sons were with the Colours and her daughter had lost her husband in the war.

John Fawcett (Hawes).

A letter from the officer commanding the battery read, "I regret to state that your son was killed yesterday. He was hit by a shell splinter and died almost immediately. He fell on the Somme. Although he had only been with our Battery a short time, he was popular with men and officers, on account of his cheery spirit and readiness to work."

The final Wensleydale casualty for 1916 was a man who had been born in West Witton.

PRIVATE WILLIAM STANGER THOMPSON NO. 28/562 11TH BATTALION NORTHUMBERLAND FUSILIERS DIED 26TH DECEMBER 1916 AGE 35.

William was born in West Witton, his parents being Henry and Sarah Thompson. However, by 1891, Henry and Sarah were no longer living in the village and 9 year old William was boarding with 70 year old Hannah Smithson. He left West Witton to work as a dairyman in the Westgate area of Newcastle, but it was from

Darlington that he enlisted and joined the 11th Battalion Northumberland Fusiliers.

At the beginning of December 1916, the Battalion was in Toronto Camp in the Ypres Salient. On December 7th the soldiers' feet were treated, in preparation for them going into the front line trenches. Leaving the camp at 4p.m. they arrived at the "Hospice", Ypres, by 6.30p.m.

By night, working parties of over 200 men repaired the wire and trench system and a shell landed in the "Hospice" courtyard, wounding two men. On the 13th the line was trench mortared in the afternoon, killing one soldier and wounding three.

An intense bombardment began all along the Battalion's front line from 7a.m. to 10a.m. on December 15th and the trenches and wire badly knocked about, with one Company badly hit.

The heavy bombardment began again at 4.15p.m. An SOS was sent up at 4.18p.m. as a party of 40 Germans tried to raid the trench. They bombed one sap head, killing one man and wounding two, before retiring with the loss of three of their men. The intense bombardment continued until 5p.m., with the result that the trenches were practically obliterated. Large working parties were sent out at night and cut a way through. Two men were killed and seven wounded, one of the latter being William Thompson.

Sent first to a Casualty Clearing Station, he was soon transported by rail to Wimereux, on the Channel coast to the north of Boulogne. Here were a number of large hospital bases providing the best possible medical attention. However, on December 26th William Thompson died from his wounds and was buried in grave 11.B.14. in the Wimereux Communal Cemetery.

By the end of 1916, 42 men from Wensleydale had perished. The great increase in loss of life compared to the months of 1915 brought even greater sadness to the dale. The black months of the Somme Battle had alone accounted for 29 lives lost, and for so little gain.

The British armies could not stand up to machine-gun fire interlacing a defensive zone, stretching in depth for miles. In four and a half months of almost continuous attack, they were able to advance only a little more than eight miles.

The German defensive role was magnificent, but repeated German counter-attacks proved even more costly than Allied assaults. The German Army would never be the same again.

CHAPTER FOUR
1917 — ON FLANDERS FIELDS

1917 witnessed the gloomiest drama in British military history, the Third Battle of Ypres, more commonly spoken of by the title "Passchendaele" (July 31st to November 10th). It achieved little except loss and was so depressing in its direction that its name became associated with military failure. The seemingly inexhaustible powers of endurance and sacrifice shown by the soldiers was amazing and made even more poignant by the futility of the purpose and result.

48 men from Wensleydale died during 1917 and 17 of these met their deaths during a three month period, in the hellish quagmire that was Passchendaele. Another six died in the Battle for Messines Ridge, the preliminary preparation for the larger battle, or in its aftermath.

Earlier in the year the German General, Von Ludendorff, had prepared a much shorter, highly organised defensive zone — the Hindenburg Line, some 20 miles behind the over extended line from Arras to Soissons, to which they would withdraw.

Behind a lightly held outpost line, heavily sown with machine-guns, lay two successive defensive positions, highly fortified. Behind these again lay the German reserves, concentrated and prepared for counter-attack.

Between the original line and the new zone, the countryside had been devastated; towns and villages were razed, forests levelled, water sources contaminated and roads destroyed. The actual withdrawal, conducted in great secrecy, began on February 23rd and was completed by April 5th.

By the late Spring of 1917 the Allies were in disarray. The Hindenburg Line had proved too great a defensive line to break through and, more significantly, the French offensive directed by the hero of Verdun, Nivelle, had proved an expensive disaster. Elements of the French army mutinied and large numbers of soldiers stated that, although willing to defend their positions, they would refuse any order to attack. Great pressure was therefore placed upon the British to take up a greater proportion of the front and to take the fight to the enemy.

General Haig became encouraged to pursue his long-held aim — to break out of the Ypres Salient on to the Flanders Plain, and on to take the Channel ports used by the German U-boats. Sanctions for a limited offensive were given by the British Government.

The first part of the operation was a complete success. Nineteen huge mines were exploded under German positions in the southern end of the Salient and the British 2nd Army swept the enemy off the Messines — Wijtschate Ridge between 7th and 14th June.

Instead of an immediate follow up in the dry summer weather, six weeks passed before the main assault on the Gheluvelt — Passchendaele Ridge took place. This infamous battle began on July 31st and the rains began immediately. Empire troops were expected to advance through swamp-like terrain in full view of the defending Germans on the higher ground. Around 80,000 Empire troops were killed and twice that number wounded before Passchendaele was taken and the battle halted on November 10th 1917.

18 Wensleydale men would be among the fatalities, victims of one of the most awful battles in the annals of war. As General Kiggell, Haig's Chief-of-Staff, is purported to have stated after he visited the front, "Good God, did we really send men to fight in that?"

In the Battle for the Messines Ridge, the preparatory stage to the Battle of Passchendaele, a soldier from Thoralby was lost on the first day of the assault.

PRIVATE JAMES BELL FAWCETT
NO. 32973 8TH BATTALION YORKSHIRE REGIMENT
DIED THURSDAY 7TH JUNE 1917 AGE 38.

James Bell Fawcett was born at Thoralby in 1879, the eldest son and child of Robert and Ann Fawcett. The Fawcetts were farmers and by 1889 had moved to a farm at neighbouring Newbiggin, where Robert and Alice Ann were born. James worked on his father's farm, although by the time the war started, his father was dead and James was married to wife Elizabeth and they had one child.

He went to enlist at Leyburn and joined the 8th Battalion Yorkshire Regiment. At 3a.m. on June 7th 1917 they lay down in front of the assembly trench and ten minutes later 19 great mines exploded simultaneously beneath the enemy's defences, and supported by a barrage, the infantry went forward. The advance was difficult in intense darkness but they moved across the great craters with which the front was studded. The "Red Line" was captured with great dash while "C" Company advanced upon and captured the two mine craters.

"A" and "B" Companies had pushed on to the "Blue Line" as the enemy bolted from the shell holes they were occupying. At 3.40a.m. "D" Company passed through in artillery formation and occupied the "Black Line", meeting little opposition and receiving four casualties. The rest of the morning was then spent in reorganising, consolidating and putting in strong points in a state of defence.

Although the first day had been successful, one of the casualties was James Bell Fawcett. Killed by a shell burst, his body was never recovered and his name was inscribed on Panel 33 on the Menin Gate.

Sadly, five days after James's death, his mother Ann died and was buried in Aysgarth churchyard on June 15th..

Three men from Hawes in Wensleydale, who joined the same Regiment, had been hit on the first day of the assault, with one being killed and the other two dying some days later from wounds received.

PRIVATE FRED SHAW
NO. 28757 9TH BATTALION YORKSHIRE REGIMENT
DIED THURSDAY 7TH JUNE 1917 AGE 33.

Fred, the fourth child of Ned and Ann Shaw, was born at Slaithwaite, near Huddersfield. Elder siblings were Elizabeth, James and Frank, with younger brothers Charles and Arthur completing the family.

Ned was a signal man on the railway and also a part time photographer operating under the name "Shaw's Photographers". Two of Fred's brothers, Frank and Charles, who worked in the Huddersfield mills, emigrated to Canada before the Great War began.

Fred Shaw and wife Mary Elizabeth with children Ned (on left) and Jimmy c1916 (Hawes).

144

Fred, however, trained as a journeyman tailor, and travelled to seek employment. Whilst in the Hawes district he met and married a girl from Hawes, Mary Elizabeth Blades, in November 1909 and settled down on The Hill, Hawes, where two boys, Ned and Jimmy were born (sadly, Jimmy would die, aged 5 years, just four and a half months after his father was killed in action in Belgium, bringing even greater heartache for Mary).

Fred Shaw enlisted at Hawes in June 1916, joining the 9th Battalion Yorkshire Regiment, in which his two colleagues from Hawes, Edmund Staveley and Thomas Outhwaite, were already serving, and he went overseas in September 1916.

AND
PRIVATE EDMUND STAVELEY
NO. 28233 9TH BATTALION YORKSHIRE REGIMENT
DIED SATURDAY 9TH JUNE 1917 AGE 32.

Edmund's brother, Lister Staveley, had already been killed during the Battle of the Somme.

In 1901, sixteen year old Edmund was living at Park House, the Gayle home of Hawes solicitor Simon H. Willan, where he worked as an office boy. However, by the beginning of the war Edmund was married to Agnes Waggett, the daughter of a carter from Hardraw and they had a son William and a daughter Nora. Edmund was employed helping to run Strands Farm at Simonstone, near Hardraw. Enlisting at Leyburn he joined the 9th Battalion Yorkshire Regiment.

Edmund Staveley (Gayle and Hardraw).

AND
PRIVATE THOMAS PICKARD OUTHWAITE
NO. 28234 9TH BATTALION YORKSHIRE REGIMENT
DIED TUESDAY 19TH JUNE 1917 AGE 36.

Thomas Pickard Outhwaite
(Stalling Busk).

Thomas Pickard Outhwaite and Gertrude
Sherrington on their wedding day.

The Outhwaites originally came to Stalling Busk and the Raydaleside area in the 1730's to farm the land. Thomas's father, William Outhwaite, was born in Stalling Busk in 1845 and married Eleanor Pickard, a girl from neighbouring Newbiggin, near Aysgarth, and lived first in Raydaleside, where a daughter Agnes was born in 1871 and then near Ingleton, where William was born in 1875 and Thomas Pickard Outhwaite in 1880. William was farming 500 acres of land.

Shortly after 1880 they returned to Stalling Busk, where William senior farmed and eventually became the gamekeeper on the estate of Colonel Penry Williams, MP, of Raydale Grange. At Stalling Busk, daughters Maggie and Ann and son, John Matthew, were born.

Outside of the Outhwaite family home at Stalling Busk c1895.
Back row: Agnes, Eleanor (pregnant with John Matthew), William,
William (the ropemaker).
Front row: Maggie Ellen, Ann, Thomas Pickard.

It was in 1905 that Thomas's brother William took over the Ropeworks in Hawes from Johnny "Roper" Wharton, and which still operates under the Outhwaite name today. Thomas, who had worked away from home, had by now married Gertrude Sherrington, a girl from Tunsall, Catterick, and they settled down at Raydale Grange, where, for seven years he assisted his father as game-keeper on the Raydale Estate.

Thomas was a gifted elocutionist and assisted by his wife, was a popular figure at local entertainments. He enlisted in 1915, joining the 9th Battalion Yorkshire Regiment and became the first Raydaleside man to pay the supreme sacrifice.

The 9th Battalion took part on the first day of the Battle for Messines Ridge, their objective, the "Black Line". Beginning the assault at 6.50a.m. on June 7th, there was no great resistance for the first 200 yards, as they kept up close to their own barrage. However, in the thicker undergrowth, the snipers and machine-gun fire caused many casualties. They were forced to dig in on the southern part of Battle Wood because the machine-gun emplacements on rising ground in the

147

front and on the flanks had not been destroyed by the artillery. A great loss of life was experienced with 4 officers and 67 men killed, 7 officers and 178 men wounded and 9 missing.

Fred Shaw was killed in action and since his body was never recovered he is commemorated on Panel 33 of the Menin Gate. Both Edmund Staveley and Thomas Pickard Outhwaite were wounded in this day's action and died later. They were brought back for burial to Poperinge, Edmund in grave XV.1.6. and Thomas in XIV. E.12A.

A further two dalesmen died in the aftermath of the Battle for Messines Ridge.

GUNNER JAMES RAYMOND CLAPHAM
NO. 127074 294TH SIEGE BATTERY
ROYAL GARRISON ARTILLERY
DIED THURSDAY 21ST JUNE 1917 AGE 19.

The Clapham family had strong connections with the Leyburn and Middleham areas but Raymond Clapham had been born at Keighley in 1898, the son of Joseph and Ruth Clapham. Joseph was a blacksmith and wheelwright. It was in his home town of Keighley that Raymond enlisted and became a gunner in a Siege Battery.

AND
GUNNER WILLIAM HENRY TURNER
NO. 46137 40TH HOWITZER BATTERY
25TH BRIGADE ROYAL FIELD ARTILLERY
DIED TUESDAY 10TH JULY 1917 AGE 29.

William had been born in Middleham, the son of James and Christina Turner, who lived at Rosemount. James originated from Hunton and married a Scottish girl. He was a solicitor's law clerk, and the family was completed when a daughter, Olive, was born. William sought employment outside the dale and enlisted at South Shields, before being posted to the Royal Field Artillery as a Gunner.

The capture of Messines Ridge was almost the only true siege-warfare attack made throughout a siege war and secured the high ground that had given the enemy complete observation of the British trenches and forward gun battery positions.

The success of the battle was due to the effect of the mines and the artillery, which was so overwhelming. On a front of 9 miles, a total of 2338 guns, of which 828 were heavy, were concentrated. There were also 304 large trench mortars ie. one gun to every seven yards of front and five and a half tons of ammunition thrown onto each yard of front.

Both Raymond and William had been involved in the success of the Battle of Messines, in which the Ridge was taken at the cost of 25,000 German casualties and British casualties being 15,000. The artillery bombardment had lasted 17 days and both men survived the battle to fight another day.

Raymond Clapham was a gunner in the 294th Siege Battery, whilst William Turner was a gunner in the 40th Howitzer Battery. The Siege Battery consisted of six guns, each of 9.2 inch calibre, whilst the Howitzer Battery's six guns were of 6 inch calibre, both batteries being involved in bombardment and counter-bombardment roles.

However, during the six week interval between the conclusion of the Battle of Messines and the start of the Passchendaele offensive, these two gunners from the dale were killed as preparations were made for the imminent attack.

It was in the general day to day exchanges of artillery fire between the British and German batteries that both men were killed by enemy shell fire. Raymond Clapham lost his life on June 21st and was buried in grave 111.A. 3 at La Plus Douve Farm Cemetery, 10km. south of Ypres, whilst William Turner fell to a shell burst on July 10th. He lies buried in grave 11.D.4 at Ramscappelle Road Military Cemetery, Belgium.

Six weeks after the conclusion of the Battle of Messines the offensive to capture Passchendaele Ridge began. The bombardment proper opened on July 22nd and continued for ten days until at 3.30a.m. on July 31st the infantry of twelve divisions advanced on an eleven mile front, to the accompaniment of torrential rain. On that opening day of battle a Wensleydale fatality occurred, the first of 18 dalesmen to lose their lives during the horrendous fighting of the next three and a half months.

SECOND LIEUTENANT DOUGLAS BERNARD PRIESTLEY
2ND/5TH BATTALION LANCASHIRE FUSILIERS
DIED TUESDAY 31ST JULY 1917 AGE 20.

Douglas Priestley was the son of the Reverend Jonathan Priestley, who in 1903 arrived as the vicar of Thornton Steward Church. Jonathan had been born at Thornton, on the Yorkshire Wolds. His wife died shortly after Douglas's birth and the widower took up a new appointment as vicar of Bishop Monkton, near Ripon. In April 1916 Reverend Priestley died at Thornton Steward, shortly

The village pump at Thornton Steward, c1910. The Reverend Priestley, vicar, was to lose his son on the first day of the Battle of Passchendale, 1917.

Emily Batty (later Hamilton), winner of the first prize at Thornton Steward c1900. In the background is South View, on main street. She later became the village postmistress.

before he should have taken up an appointment at Farnley, Leeds.

Douglas had enlisted in the army and was promoted to Second Lieutenant in the Lancashire Fusiliers. On July 30th the Battalion moved into assembly trenches close to Wieltje and at 8a.m. on July 31st climbed out and formed up in artillery formation. When reaching the Hanebeek Stream they met with scattered rifle and machine-gun fire. 300 yards short of the "Black Line" the Battalion met with very heavy machine-gun fire and Companies at once "shook out" into extended order, but the severe casualties they incurred caused so much confusion that correct formations were never regained throughout the action.

Lieutenant-Colonel Best-Dunkley dashed forward, took command of the leading wave, and personally led them on through intense machine-gun fire until the "Black Line" was taken, and the attack proper could start in gaining the "Green Line", which fell around noon.

Within the hour the first German counter-attack was delivered and there was a grave risk of the survivors being cut off. A withdrawal was therefore ordered 700 yards to the rear.

German artillery fire became more intense and counter-attacks were delivered, preceded by four enemy aircraft which flew low and strafed the men with machine-gun fire. A further withdrawal took place to the "Black Line" after the loss of a further 80 men.

Lieutenant-Colonel Best-Dunkley collected all available men and personally led them to the attack, which succeeded in driving back the Germans. The artillery came to the rescue about 4.30p.m. with a heavy barrage which prevented the enemy from obtaining a footing in the "Black Line".

Of the 19 officers who went into action, 18 became casualties on the opening day, as did 473 other ranks out of a total of 593.

One of the officers killed was Douglas Priestley. His body was one of many that was not recovered and his name is honoured on Panel 33 of the Menin Gate.

PRIVATE BERTIE POTTER
NO. 205200 10TH BATTALION
ROYAL WEST KENT REGIMENT
DIED FRIDAY 10TH AUGUST 1917 AGE 19.

Bertie was next to youngest in a family of 9 children belonging to Fred and Annie Potter, who lived close to Clarendon House, Middleham. Fred Potter had been born at Boston Spa, between Wetherby and Tadcaster, Yorkshire, and had married Annie, a Middleham girl. He earned his living as the post-office assistant in Middleham, but Bertie, when he grew up, left the town to seek employment in the Newcastle area. He enlisted at Newcastle and was eventually posted to the 10th Battalion, Royal West Kent Regiment.

At 2a.m. on July 31st the Battalion reported in their position on the tapes, ready for attack in the vicinity of Zillebeke, just south of Ypres. The Battalion gained two objectives, consolidated and held their position. Throughout August 1st the enemy heavily shelled their position and snipers were active throughout the day and night. The weather was extremely bad. Men in some places were up to their waist in mud and water and communication was very difficult.

Similar conditions were experienced on August 2nd, but at 10p.m. on that evening the Battalion was relieved. Total casualties for the period up to August 3rd were 247 men killed, wounded or missing.

One of those wounded was Bertie, who was moved to the village of Godewaersvelde, just over the border in France. Three Casualty Clearing Stations had been set up in the village but the doctors and nursing staff were unable to save Bertie Potter, who died from his wounds on August 10th. He is buried in grave 1.C.57. at Godewaersvelde British Cemetery.

On the right of the attack, in the vital sector round the Menin Road, the advance was held up. And the rain continued day after day, hastening the conversion of the undrainable ground into a swamp in which first the tanks and before long even the infantry were bogged.

There was a short lull in proceedings until the second blow fell on August 16th, when a series of shallow advances towards the Ridge east of Ypres were made, although again little progress was made in the atrocious conditions. However, during this fresh attack and in its aftermath, four men from the dale would perish.

SECOND LIEUTENANT BERNARD GRIME LODGE
4TH BATTALION, BUT ATTACHED TO
10TH BATTALION DURHAM LIGHT INFANTRY
DIED FRIDAY 24TH AUGUST 1917 AGE 23.

Bernard's grandfather, Thomas Lodge, came from Oughtershaw and became the curate at Hawes Church. His father, John James Grime Lodge, a solicitor, married Sarah Preston, and whilst living at Dent, their son Bernard Grime Lodge was born in 1894. However, his mother Sarah died young and by 1901 Bernard and his father were boarding at Yorebridge Grammar School.

Bernard was educated at the Minster Yard School, York, Yorebridge Grammar School and Giggleswick School, where he was a member of the Officer Training Corps. After leaving Giggleswick School he entered Barclay's Bank at Northallerton, before transferring to the head office at Darlington.

In December 1914 he had joined the Royal Fusiliers but objected to trying for a commission until he had gained experience as a private. He went to France in November 1915, returning to England as a cadet in April 1916 and was gazetted on August 9th 1916 as a Second Lieutenant, Durham Light Infantry. In September 1916 he again went out to France, acting as the Company and then Battalion Bombing Officer and Intelligence Officer.

On August 22nd 1917 the 10th Battalion was brought up to the Menin Road, near Inverness Copse, and during that day and the 23rd were involved in heavy fighting, being severely shelled by the enemy.

It was on August 24th that Bernard Grime Lodge fell on the battlefield and later, Colonel

Bernard Grime Lodge (Askrigg).

Morrant wrote to his father to say,"A braver, cooler more reliable young officer could not be found. He had done wonderfully gallant work on patrol on numerous occasions. I know no officer in the Battalion I could have spared less than he. He was brave as a lion. We were counter-attacked on August 24th and I turned out all the men at Battalion HQ. He, without any orders, dashed off with the leading men right up to the point where danger threatened, at the corner of Inverness Copse. His body was found where the Adjutant of another battalion was also killed, evidently by a machine gun fired from our left flank. For the rest of the day this was a dangerous point and several others were killed there. I don't know how I shall replace him, as not only was he valuable as an officer, but I was very fond of him, as were all of us."

At a Memorial Service in St. Oswald's Church, Askrigg, a plain laurel wreath was attached to the seat where the deceased had worshipped in the church, bearing the words "From the garden of his home, Yorebridge House. In loving memory of my brave, noble boy, from his devoted Aunt Annie."

RIFLEMAN ROBERT PICKERING METCALFE
NO. R/24155 8TH BATTALION
KING'S ROYAL RIFLE CORPS
DIED FRIDAY 24TH AUGUST 1917 AGE 24.

Robert was born at Thornton Rust in 1894, the youngest son of George Metcalfe, a farmer, and his wife Grace, living at Ashfield House. Robert worked on the family farm, but during the war he enlisted at Leyburn and was posted to the 8th Battalion K.R.R.C.

On August 22nd 1917 they were in Sanctuary Wood, close by the position occupied by Bernard Grime Lodge, when they were heavily shelled and lost 50 men. As they were about to be relieved on August 24th, an SOS signal went up indicating a German counter-attack and "A" and "C" Companies defended part of Inverness Copse.

The counter-attack was a failure, except on the left, where a few patrols pushed through but did not get far. During the day 8th Battalion had to withdraw from Inverness Copse and suffered severely from shell fire, losing six officers killed, others wounded and 100 casualties in the other ranks. One of those killed was Robert Pickering Metcalfe, the first casualty from Thornton Rust. Rifleman Metcalfe, along with a party of ten others, were ordered to storm the front line of the enemy's trenches, when a shell burst amongst them, causing the death of all but two, who were slightly wounded.

His Captain wrote, in a letter to his mother Grace, "Your son has done extremely good work out here as a Lewis gunner, and his death is greatly deplored by all of us."

Both Bernard's and Robert's names are commemorated on the Tyne Cot Memorial, the former on Panels 128 to 131 and 162 and 162A, the latter on Panels 115 to 119 and 162A and 163A.

PRIVATE HENRY (HARRY) KILDING
NO. 36668 9TH BATTALION
WEST YORKSHIRE REGIMENT
DIED MONDAY 27TH AUGUST 1917 AGE 34.

Harry was born at Preston under Scar in 1883. We have already seen that his younger brother Alfred had been killed on the Somme in September 1916. Harry married Rose Peacock, a girl from Ripon, and they settled in that town, where Harry was employed at the Kearsley Varnish Works, on the Boroughbridge road. Sons Ernest and George were born and in 1916 a daughter, Renee.

Harry enlisted at Ripon in June 1916 and eventually sailed with his Battalion, the 9th West Yorkshires, on October 27th 1916. As with Bernard Lodge and Robert Metcalfe, Harry's Battalion was heavily involved in the fighting and on August 27th, during a period of intensive shelling by the Germans, he was killed. Harry Kilding is likewise honoured on the Tyne Cot Memorial, on Panels 42 to 47 and 162.

Henry (Harry) Kilding
(Preston under Scar and Ripon).

PRIVATE SYDNEY CHARLES ALLINSON NO. 25865 2ND BATTALION WEST YORKSHIRE REGIMENT DIED 8TH SEPTEMBER 1917 AGE 32.

Born in 1885 at the village of Ilton, west of Masham, Sydney's parents were George and Ada Allinson. In 1901, Sydney and his younger sisters Amelia and Amy were living in nearby Warthermaske, where their father George worked as an agricultural labourer. The family arrived in Harmby sometime before the Great War, attracted by work in the quarries.

It was at Ripon that Sydney enlisted, joining the 2nd Battalion West

Yorkshires and by June/July 1917 he was in the Ypres Salient. Involved in the second main blow against the enemy defences on August 16th , they attacked the heights of the Westhoek Ridge.

The 2nd Battalion advanced into Hannebeke Wood, where two machine-guns, still hot from firing, were found with German soldiers lying about killed or wounded by the barrage.

Heavy machine-gun fire came from the Battalion flank and a withdrawal was made to Hannebeke Wood, especially when large numbers of the enemy came over the Ridge at 9.30a.m.

At 3.30p.m. Very lights were sent up and a pigeon message despatched but the response from the British artillery was ragged. By 11p.m. they were ordered to withdraw to Railway Wood. Enemy aeroplanes had been active all day, flying very low and using their guns freely on the troops.

400 men had gone into the attack and of these 374 were casualties, either killed, wounded or missing. Sydney Allinson had been severely wounded and was eventually taken to the main hospital complex at Etaples, on the Channel coast, where he died from his wounds on 8th September. He was buried in grave XXV. P. 14A. in Etaples Military Cemetery, France.

Bad weather and the need for preparation delayed the resumption of the offensive until September 20th, when, that morning, the 2nd Army attack on a four mile front achieved some success on either side of the Menin Road. Of course, it had to come at a cost, including the lives of three men, from Bellerby, Leyburn and Hawes.

LANCE CORPORAL JAMES ROBINSON MAWER
NO. C/12811 21ST BATTALION
KING'S ROYAL RIFLE CORPS
DIED THURSDAY 20TH SEPTEMBER 1917 AGE 21

The Mawers came to Bellerby from Carlton in Coverdale, where James had been born, the son of Thomas and Jane Mawer. They were farmers and lived at Studda Farm, Bellerby. However, Jane died in 1903 and Thomas remarried, his second wife being the village post-mistress, Miss Thistlethwaite.

James worked on the family farm but in wartime he enlisted in Leyburn and joined the 21st Battalion K.R.R.C. On September 18th 1917 they moved into position for their attack on Shrewsbury Forest, their objectives being two enemy positions, the Red and Blue Lines.

They advanced at 5.40a.m. on September 20th with the enemy opening heavy machine-gun fire from dug-outs untouched by British artillery fire, causing many casualties. The Brigadier came up and personally rallied several parties of men until the Red Line was captured.

At 6p.m. the enemy put up a very heavy barrage and launched a counter-attack which was driven off. At 6.30p.m. an advance was made to the Blue Line, which was captured. A second counter-attack was driven off, although the enemy shelled the Battalion heavily during the night.

53 men were killed, 198 wounded and 44 were missing. Sadly, another man to be added to the Tyne Cot Memorial was James Mawer, whose body was not retrieved. His name is found on Panels 115 to 119 and 162A and 163A.

On the same day, September 20th, Harry Cockett, fighting with the South African Brigade, but a native of Hawes, also lost his life.

James Mawer (Bellerby).

PRIVATE HARRY COCKETT
SOUTH AFRICAN INFANTRY REGIMENT
DIED 20TH SEPTEMBER 1917 AGE 18.

Harry was the youngest son of Henry and Betsy Cockett of Johannesburg, South Africa, and formerly Hawes. Henry had been a butcher in Hawes but went out to seek a new life in South Africa. In 1910 Betsy Cockett left Hawes with her two sons and daughter to join her husband.

When war was declared, Henry joined the army in the Kalahari Horse Defence Force, helping to defeat the German forces in South West Africa, whilst his eldest son, Ronald, fought the Germans in East Africa.

Harry enlisted in February 1917 and came to Britain in June of that year. The South African Brigade, known as the "White Zulu", had a fine reputation as a fighting force.

On September 20th, the 4th Battalion advanced in dawn darkness over swampy ground and captured enemy outposts on the Zonnebeke Stream. The 3rd Battalion seized the fortified Vampir Farm and fanned out to overrun other

German positions in close quarter ferocious fighting.

The 3rd Transvaals were hit by machine-gun fire from Potsdam pill box strong point and began to falter. Under covering Lewis gun fire, troops vaulted through their own barrage, then waded across the Zonnebeke Stream and routed the German garrison.

The South Africans split into small parties to attack various points simultaneously. However, German rear-guard machine-gunners counter-attacked, accompanied by the incursion of German aircraft which mowed down exposed infantry, producing a large number of killed and wounded.

The second stage of the South African push saw men floundering through the sucking mud. They experienced a quagmire, sinking in chest high and losing equipment.

Harry Cockett
(Hawes and South Africa).

It was during this action that Harry Cockett lost his life. Having gone into battle 2576 strong the South African Brigade emerged with the horrendous casualty figures of 1255 killed, wounded or missing.

CORPORAL WILLIAM TRUEFITT DEIGHTON
NO. T2/14505 3RD COMPANY
23RD DIVISION TRAIN, ROYAL ARMY SERVICE CORPS
DIED FRIDAY 21ST SEPTEMBER 1917 AGE 30.

William's father, Thomas Deighton, was born at Kirby Sigston, near Northallerton, and joined the North Riding Police Force at North Ormesby, Middlesborough, in 1883. There he met his wife, Jane, a local girl, and they married. Their only son, William Truefitt, was born at Norh Ormesby, but they resided at Askrigg, West Burton, Middleham (1901), Northallerton, Bedale and finally Leyburn, where Thomas Deighton became Superintendent of Police. Three daughters completed the family. In July 1915 William's mother, Jane Deighton, passed away.

Whilst working in a draper's shop in Leyburn, William enlisted during the war, serving in France and Belgium in the Royal Army Service Corps. Part of his job was in getting men, munitions, artillery, fuel and food to the front line. The Corps even helped in operating the narrow and standard gauge railways up to the front line, and were often targetted by the enemy artillery.

In serving in this capacity, supplying munitions to the troops on the front line during the 20th September offensive, William was wounded and brought back behind the line. He succumbed to his wounds and was buried in grave 1V.E.21. of the Reninghelst New Military Cemetery, Poperinge, south of Ypres.

A fresh offensive began on September 26th, in which a Preston under Scar man was killed and two dalesmen serving together in the same battalion died during the following three days.

CORPORAL WILLIAM SMITH
NO. 45563 13TH SIEGE BATTERY
ROYAL GARRISON ARTILLERY
DIED WEDNESDAY 26TH SEPTEMBER 1917 AGE 29.

William Smith was born in 1887 in Leyburn to 19 year old Margaret Smith, a girl from Manchester. Born at Deansgate, Manchester, in 1868, she was the daughter of William Smith, a tobacconist. Her parents were both natives of Leyburn and in the early 1880's the family returned to that town, where William senior set up in business. By 1901, 14 year old William was living at Preston under Scar with his mother Margaret, now the wife of John Burnett, a general labourer working on the Bolton Estate, together with six half brothers and sisters. William was educated at Wensley School and sang in both the Wensley and Leyburn Church Choirs. By the start of the war he was travelling for a Leyburn firm.

He enlisted as a gunner in the Royal Garrison Artillery in 1914 and trained at Newhaven, Lydd and Portsmouth before

William Smith
(Wensley and Preston under Scar).

sailing for France on April 15th 1915. William saw action with the heavy 9.2 calibre howitzers in the battles at Givenchy, Loos, Aubers Ridge, Festubert and Ypres.

He went through many hardships and had many narrow escapes and finally in November 1916 he was awarded the Military Medal for bravery on the field; he was under very heavy shell fire, but held the position at great risk of losing his life.

In time, the Battery fought on the Ypres front, where, on September 26th he was killed in action in a trench at Inverness Copse. He is buried in Huts Military Cemetery NW of Dickebusch. Two thirds of the burials here were of gunners from nearby artillery positions.

PRIVATE JOHN WILLIAM DINSDALE
NO. 36063 8TH BATTALION YORKSHIRE REGIMENT
DIED FRIDAY 28TH SEPTEMBER 1917 AGE 24.

John's father, William Dinsdale, was in the building trade in Hawes with his brother Richard Blythe Dinsdale. His mother Ann kept a sweet shop in one of their rooms at the Garris, Gayle. When John left school he became a tailor by trade and enlisted in the town of Nelson, Lancashire, in March 1916. He sailed for France in July 1916 with the 8th Battalion Yorkshire Regiment, before being invalided home in December. He returned to the front in July 1917.

John Dinsdale
(Gayle and Hawes).

160

AND
PRIVATE FRED KILDING SHIELDS
NO. 26237 8TH BATTALION YORKSHIRE REGIMENT
DIED SATURDAY 29TH SEPTEMBER 1917 AGE 21.

Fred Shields of Castle Bolton in 'civvies' and in uniform.

Fred Shields was the youngest son and child of Joseph Shields, a Castle Bolton plumber and tinsmith, and wife Elizabeth Shields. They lived in a section of Bolton Castle, acting as caretakers, with Elizabeth providing refreshments for visitors. They also had a tinsmith's shop in a building across from the castle (nowadays a store room), where kettles, backpans etc. were made.

Fred enlisted at Northallerton and he too joined the 8th Battalion, becoming a colleague of his neighbour from Upper Wensleydale, John Dinsdale.

Early in July 1917 a large draft of 283 men, including John and Fred, arrived at Steenvoorde in the Salient to join the Battalion (50% of whom had seen no action).

On September 26th the 8th Battalion attacked Inverness Copse, whilst on the 27th they advanced into Sanctuary Wood, under atrocious ground conditions and hostile heavy fire from artillery and machine-guns. Prior to a German counter-attack, the enemy put down a very heavy barrage, causing a good many casualties. The battle continued over the next two days and saw the loss of John

Frank Shields, tinsmith at Redmire and a relation of Fred, making a back can for carrying milk. The family had been plumbers in the years before the Great War.

Dinsdale on the 28th and Fred Shields on September 29th.

John's Commanding Officer wrote to his parents, "He was killed at his post by a shell, which burst right in the trench and killed four of my brave platoon. I shall never forget your son's courage; he stood to his post, never flinching one inch as shells flew around us. All the platoon feel the loss very much, as he was always so bright and willing to volunteer for anything.

John's belongings, including his tin shaving mirror, a silver thimble from his tailoring days and a ring were sent back home by his platoon and the family still retain these items today.

Fred Shields is buried in grave XL1.C.14. of the Tyne Cot Cemetery, whilst John Dinsdale has no known grave and is honoured on Panels 52 to 54 and 162A of the Tyne Cot Memorial.

When another push was made on October 4th, on an eight mile front, it gave the British possession of the main Ridge east of Ypres, despite torrents of rain, which made the battlefield a worse morass than ever. On the opening day of the big push a further three dalesmen were killed, two of them serving in the same battalion.

PRIVATE NATHAN BURTON IVESON
NO. 39267 10TH BATTALION YORKSHIRE REGIMENT
DIED THURSDAY 4TH OCTOBER 1917 AGE 29.

John Iveson, father of Nathan, lived at the Gaits, Gayle, with his wife Mary and five children. He worked as a road length man for the Council, maintaining the surface of the local roads. Both John and Mary died relatively young before the Great War and the family was brought up by daughter Isabella. Nathan, or Nat as he was called, was employed by Aysgarth Rural District Council as a road man, following in his father's footsteps.

Enlisting at Leyburn in November 1916 he joined the 10th Battalion Yorkshire Regiment and went overseas in May 1917.

Nathan Burton Iveson (Gayle).

AND
CORPORAL WILLIAM HEMSLEY
NO. 10542 10TH BATTALION YORKSHIRE REGIMENT
DIED THURSDAY 4TH OCTOBER 1917 AGE 19.

William Hemsley was born in 1897 in the village of Thoralby, the youngest child of farmer John Hemsley and his wife Alice, living at Town Head Farm. William attended the local school and in his teens became an invaluable member of the Aysgarth Amateur Dramatic Society. At the outbreak of the war, aged 17, he enlisted in the 10th Battalion Yorkshire Regiment and went to France in October 1915.

At 9p.m. on October 3rd 1917 the Battalion formed up ready for the attack on Brooseinde, on the Ridge, the following day, but immediately came under intense shell fire and were told to find what shelter they could in shell holes.

At 5.15a.m. on October 4th they were in front of Polygon Wood, where the enemy, at zero hour, put down an intensive barrage. The Battalion was under heavy shell fire uninterruptedly from 9p.m. on October 3rd until 6p.m. on October 4th and had suffered serious losses. They simply held on under intense fire. The trench conditions were terrible with men standing in over a foot of slime.

Amongst the many who were lost during this day's actions were Nat and William. Both men from the same Yorkshire dale are commemorated on the same panels of the Tyne Cot Memorial, Panels 52 and 54 and 162A.

William Hemsley
(Thoralby – Aysgarth).

PRIVATE CHARLES SCOTT
NO. 42194 "D" COMPANY 9TH BATTALION
KING'S OWN YORKSHIRE LIGHT INFANTRY
DIED THURSDAY 4TH OCTOBER 1917 AGE 23.

Robert Scott, living at Post Office Yard, Preston under Scar, was a plate layer on the railway running through Wensleydale, and with his wife Mary, raised a family of seven. Charles was the second youngest of their children.

After leaving Wensley School he became a railway porter, but on June 4th 1916 he enlisted at Northallerton, joining the Northumberland Fusiliers. Later he transferred to the 9th Battalion K.O.Y.L.I., in "D" Company.

On October 4th 1917, in depressing rain, they fought their way onto the lower slopes of the Passchendaele Ridge, an advance of 700 yards that captured Poelcapelle and Polygon Wood.

The Germans had a grandstand view from the Passchendaele Ridge of the slow advance and rained shells down on the unfortunate troops. The massive use

The Tyne Cot Memorial, near Ypres. This is the largest British War Cemetery in the world with some 11,871 graves registered, but only 30% being named. This is evidence, if it was needed, of the vile swamp around Passchendale which swallowed up so many gallant men. To the rear of the cemetery is a wall on which are the names of almost 35,000 soldiers who have no known graves, and who died in the Salient from August 1917 to the end of the war. There is no air of triumph at Tyne Cot, more one of tragedy and mourning. Visitors come in large numbers but the cemetery keeps its atmosphere of quiet grieving. Wensleydale's gallant lads named at Tyne Cot are surely in immortal company.

of artillery had destroyed the ditches, drains and small streams which kept the water table below ground level. Combined with atrocious wet weather, this devastation left a landscape of nightmares. Shell craters now lay lip to lip, separated only by slimy mud. Guns, horses and men were drowned in hell.

"Joist Farm" was the first stumbling block but two sections of "D" Company mopped up this post and prisoners and four machine-guns were taken. There was a swamp to be crossed in the low ground, which proved to be a death trap; the men were up to their knees in slush and were swept by machine-gun fire.

On the right, the Germans attempted a counter-attack but "D" Company dealt with this. For an hour and forty minutes the men in the captured trench were subjected to a severe bombardment. About noon, the enemy advanced in force and massed near Polderhoek Chateau; an officer and party of men were sent out with two Lewis guns to get on their flank, but they disappeared and were never seen again.

Charles Scott of "D" Company was one of thousands whose body was never found and his name joins the multitude to be found on the Tyne Cot Memorial, on Panels 108 to 111.

PRIVATE HAROLD LINDLEY COLLINSON
NO. 202202 1ST/4TH BATTALION
NORTHUMBERLAND FUSILIERS
DIED FRIDAY 26TH OCTOBER 1917 AGE 30.

Harold was the son of Dobson Collinson and wife Mary Jane. Dobson, from the village of Scorton, had arrived at 4 North Road Middleham, where he earned his living as a house and carriage painter. By 1901 he was a widower.

Harold, at age 14, became a tailor's apprentice in Middleham but later left to seek employment in Darlington. It was there that he enlisted in the army, joining the Durham Light Infantry before transferring to the 4th Battalion Northumberland Fusiliers.

On October 26th at 5.40a.m. the attack began but the British barrage of shrapnel was useless against the line of concrete huts, which were the first objective. The rain fell heavily and the conditions of mud and water were appalling.

The attack was held up 80 yards west of the line of huts and machine-gun fire and sniping were so severe that any movement was quite impossible and casualties were very heavy. There was terrible difficulty in getting to the wounded as the slightest movement in the front line was checked by machine-guns and snipers.

The Battalion was relieved late on October 26th and proceeded by duckboard track across the swamp to Rose Cross Road Camp. Casualties were 10 officers and 256 men, including the death of Harold Collinson due to the explosion of a shell on his position. His name is to be found on Panels 19 to 23 and 162 on the Tyne Cot Memorial.

When, on November 4th, there was a sudden advance that gained the empty satisfaction of occupying the site of Passchendaele village, the official curtain was run down on the tragedy of "Third Ypres". It was the long-overdue close to a campaign which had brought the British armies to the verge of exhaustion.

However, two days before, on November 2nd, the final Wensleydale casualty at Passchendaele died from wounds received earlier in the action.

PRIVATE JAMES GRAHAM PRESTON
NO. 22738 18TH BATTALION LANCASHIRE FUSILIERS
DIED FRIDAY 2ND NOVEMBER 1917 AGE 20.

James was the son of Askrigg farmer James Preston and Margaret Ann Preston, who lived at West End House, Askrigg. The eldest son, Charles, went to Liverpool before the Great War to run one of the milk houses, but died as the war began. Another son, Jack, fought at Gallipoli and served in Egypt.

James Preston, or Jim as he was commonly known, was in training at Beckett's Park College, Leeds, training for the teaching profession, with his cousin Dick Chapman from Askrigg. He won two medals and a certificate for swimming and beat the 5 miles junior college record for running, doing the distance in 32 minutes 30 seconds. He was a member of Askrigg Church Choir and a Sunday School teacher for several

Private James Preston of Askrigg.

The Preston family of Askrigg (James had not yet been born).
James Preston (1859-1934), Charles Preston (1880-1914), Isobel Preston (1893-1974),
Margaret Preston (1860-1946), Frank Preston (– 194?).

West End, Askrigg 1930's. Chapman's shop and in the far distance,
the home of James Preston (with foliage growing up the front).

years. He was also a pupil teacher at Askrigg Day School.

Jim volunteered for the army whilst at Leeds, in 1915, and joined up in 1916, going to France in January 1917. He first joined the Royal Field Artillery but later transferred to the 18th Battalion Lancashire Fusiliers, where he became a bugler.

He twice refused a commission, preferring to serve as a private. On Jim Preston's 20th birthday, October 22nd 1917, the Battalion took part in the attack on Houthulst Forest in the Ypres Salient, pushing forward but receiving heavy casualties. Some concrete huts occupied by the Germans had not been dealt with and machine-gun fire from them caused numerous casualties all day.

The Battalion was in a very exhausted state, owing to the heavy and broken ground. Many of the men had lain all day in shell holes up to their waists in water. A number of wounded were brought in who had to be left out during daylight owing to the continual sniping of the Germans.

One of these wounded Fusiliers was Jim Preston, whose lung had been pierced by a bullet, and he was transferred to the vast hospital complex at Wimereux, on the coast north of Boulogne.

Sergeant Jack Preston, whose brother James was killed in action. Serving in 191 Depot Unit of Supply, Jack fought at Gallipoli, landing on 'A' Beach, Suvla Bay, on 7th August 1915. They unloaded hay, grain, food and medical comforts and organised their depot to supply the fighting divisions, often under severe shell fire. Jack left Suvla with his Depot Unit on 13th December 1915 and arrived at Alexandria, Egypt on 22nd December. He remained in Egypt until 1919. After the war he ran the farm at Askrigg.

Jim had returned to France six weeks before his death, after spending ten days leave at home. The matron wrote, "Your boy died at 11.30 this morning. All day yesterday he was becoming gradually worse and when I saw him this morning I felt he could not last long. He was perfectly conscious then, and when I asked

The Second Annual Re-union of the North East Gallipoli Association, held at the Imperial Hotel, Darlington, on 12th November 1938. Jack Preston, brother of James Preston was the organiser of the event and is sitting fourth from the left. The 1938 Munich Crisis had just passed, but nine months later, the Second World War began.

him how he felt he said, "I'm rather weak." I told him I would write to you today and he said, "Send my love and remember me to all my relatives." I am so very sorry, he was such a sweet boy."

Jim Preston had written home every day after he was wounded, right up to October 31st and he died on November 2nd. He is buried in grave V1.F.21. at Wimereux Communal Cemetery.

During 1916 Wensleydale folk had focused their attention on what was happening on the Somme. In 1917 the focus was once again on the main British offensive for that year, at Ypres.

However, action was taking place on other sections of the front line and death

occurred daily due to sniper fire or the deadly work of High Explosive shells. Life or death was a constant lottery, even on a "quiet day".

Throughout 1917, a further 24 Wensleydale men were killed or died, away from the actions in the Ypres Salient. The first of these was :

PRIVATE WILLIAM APPLETON
NO. 7227 1ST/9TH BATTALION
DURHAM LIGHT INFANTRY
DIED THURSDAY 25TH JANUARY 1917 AGE 21.

William was born at Dyke Heads, Gunnerside, in Swaledale in 1896, the son of George and Margaret Appleton. From a farming family, William was the second youngest of five sons and one daughter. By the start of the war he was working in the Askrigg district and enlisted in the army at Leyburn.

William joined the 9th Battalion Durham Light Infantry (Gateshead

Gurkhas). On November 5th 1916 the Battalion was on the Somme, near Warlencourt village, ready to attack the Butte de Warlencourt, a 40 foot high conical shaped hill and the quarry in front of it.

Initially they found success as they moved over and round the Butte and broke into the German lines beyond. The heavily reinforced enemy counter-attacked after 3p.m. and the Battalion was gradually forced back. Desperate hand to hand fighting took place during the afternoon, resulting in heavy losses on both sides.

After four hours of sustained bombardment a final counter-attack was launched against the Durhams at 11p.m. The men of the 9th Battalion were over-whelmed. Many died fighting. Others were compelled to surrender and only a handful of men found their way back.

42 men were killed, 230 wounded and 157 were missing.

One of the missing soldiers was William Appleton. He had been wounded in the fighting and was captured. Nursed by the Germans behind their lines he died from his wounds on January 25th 1917 and was buried by the Germans in grave 1V.C.9 in Valenciennes (St. Roch) Communal Cemetery, France. The cemetery was in German hands throughout the war, using it to bury their own dead, but William is one of 348 British soldiers buried there by the Germans.

PRIVATE CHARLES EDWARD BACON
NO. 1935 2ND/5TH BATTALION
WEST YORKSHIRE REGIMENT
DIED FRIDAY 26TH JANUARY 1917 AGE 38.

Born at Leyburn, Charles was the son of John and Emily Bacon. Born in Colchester, John had joined the army and risen to the rank of sergeant. When he married Emily, an Irish girl, in Southampton, she helped to buy him out of the army and he became a school teacher. He and Emily arrived in Leyburn, where John took up the position of headteacher at the Council School for the next 18 years, with Emily employed as the sewing mistress. He was also instrumental in establishing Leyburn Brass Band. Charles was the second youngest of their eight children.

Charles married a Middleham girl,

Charles Edward Bacon (Hawes).

Hilda Isabel Auton, of Clarendon House, whose father was a local printer.

Sadly Hilda Bacon received news at the family home, Lane House, Hawes, on January 28th 1917 that her husband had died of pneumonia in France, on January 26th. Charles had enlisted at Harrogate in December 1914, the third of the married men from Hawes to join up and was posted to the West Yorkshire Regiment.

Charles only went out to France in December 1916, but soon after disembarking he was taken ill and admitted to the Quai d'Escale Hospital at Le Havre (before embarking Charles was already ill and many said that he should never have been allowed to set off). His wife was summoned to visit him and went out to France

The family of Charles Edward Bacon, at Hawes, a few months after he died.
Richard Bacon, Jack Bacon, Hilda Bacon and Lucy, Victor Edward Bacon, Kathleen Bacon.

Hawes Brass Band 1912.
By permission of the Dales Countryside Museum.

immediately. After a few days she returned, leaving her husband apparently much better and hopeful of soon coming home.

Before joining the army, Charles was in business as a fish dealer in Hawes, having conducted a similar business at Ilkley, Newcastle and Middleham. He was a fine cricketer at that time and often rendered good service for the Middleham and Leyburn Cricket Clubs, being for some time groundsman for Leyburn,

He was a fine tenor singer and was a member of the Middleham Church Choir and the choir at Hawes. Charles was a valued member of Hawes Brass Band and a capital performer on the solo euphonium. In past years he had been a member of Leyburn Band which had been conducted by his father, John Bacon, and continued to play in Harrogate as a member of the Regimental Band during the war years.

Charles was buried in grave 3.E.13., Ste. Marie Cemetery, Le Havre. He left a widow and five young children, the eldest not yet 11 years old (Jack, Kathleen, Richard, Edward and Lucy).

PRIVATE JOSEPH AINDERBY ALLEN
NO. 28316 7TH BATTALION YORKSHIRE REGIMENT
DIED THURSDAY 8TH FEBRUARY 1917 AGE 33.

Joseph (Jos) Allen was born in Ainderby Steeple, near Northallerton, the eldest son of Thomas Allen. He came to live at Ulshaw Bridge and East Witton, working on the Jervaulx Estate. He married Agnes and they raised three children.

Joseph Allen was a fine athlete and this was witnessed on Coronation Day, June 22nd 1911, at East Witton. A new flag flew from the church tower and another on the green, whilst the houses were decorated. A large tent had been erected on the green with flags, foliage and flowers inside. Maypole dancing by 12 girls was enjoyed, with music provided on the school's harmonium by head-master Wiliam Greenhalgh. A presentation of Coronation mugs was made to the village children and then the sports commenced on the village green.

In the fell race to the top of Witton Fell and back, Joseph Allen came first. The parish magazine records, "From the top of the village, Jos Allen's lithe and active form could be followed as he climbed the steep and treacherous side of the Fell with surprising swiftness, and then he made a wonderful descent, which raised cheer after cheer from the spectators. It afforded a really graceful, gymnastic display. The time taken was 15 minutes, a wonderful performance."

Tea was taken inside the tent, a bonfire was lit on the Fell and in the evening dancing was enjoyed inside the same large tent. None could have realised what awful horrors lay in wait for certain families a few years hence, including that of Joseph Allen.

East Witton Pals, including Joseph Allen.
Left to right: Frank Shields, Joe ?, Joe (Jos) Allen, Jack Ryder.
Joe Allen would be killed in the Great War.

He enlisted at Middleham, joining the 7th Battalion Yorkshire Regiment. On the bitterly cold day of February 8th 1917 the Battalion was preparing for an attack across a frozen and snow covered no-man's land on the Somme, at Sailly-Saillisel, between Bapaume and Peronne.

The artillery barrage was ragged, with some shells landing on their own men. Pressing forward, "A" and "B" Companies lost many men, whilst "C" Company suffered even more from their own artillery. German counter-attacks were destroyed by Lewis gun fire but bombing attacks appeared threatening. By 3.15p.m. the enemy had made five attacks which were beaten off.

Casualties were heavy and wiring parties sent out at 6.30p.m. to help consolidate, were issued with white coats to be less conspicuous against the snow.

A number of the stretcher cases had been placed in a cellar at Headquarters to await removal, but a shell blew the place in, killing most of the men. 60% of the Battalion were casualties during the day and one who was reported missing was Joseph Allen.

A Memorial Service was held at East Witton Church on March 3rd. Tragically, a month after the service, on March 28th, his widow Agnes Allen died, aged 33, leaving three young orphans.

Joseph Allen's name is commemorated on Pier and Face 3A of the Thiepval Memorial.

GUNNER ALEXANDER KIRKBRIDE
NO. 129805 "Y" 56TH HEAVY TRENCH
MORTAR BATTERY ROYAL FIELD ARTILLERY
DIED SATURDAY 17TH FEBRUARY 1917 AGE 22.

Alexander Kirkbride had been born at Beckstones, Gayle, the youngest son of an agricultural labourer, Alexander Kirkbride and his wife Mary Elizabeth (nee Allen). By 1914 they were farming at Faws Head Farm, Gayle, near Gayle Beck.

Alexander enlisted at Leyburn in March 1916 and went to France in June of that year, having become a gunner in a heavy trench mortar battery.

These batteries, using Stokes Mortars with a calibre between 2 inches and 9.4 inches, were not officially connected to the Royal Artillery. They were ad hoc units made up from 90% ordinary infantry, who were simply trained in the use of the weapons.It was a dangerous occupation since they were serving in the front line and were targetted by enemy mortar and howitzer batteries.

Alexander Kirkbride (Gayle).

On a Tuesday morning in early March his parents received a wire that their son had been dangerously wounded. This was followed on the Thursday by another conveying the sad news that he had died from wounds on February 17th. Their elder son Tom, also serving in the army, was home on leave when the news arrived. Alexander Kirkbride (whose cousin, Herbert Allen from Gayle, would die in 1918 whilst serving in the RAF) was buried in grave 1.B.14. Merville Communal Cemetery Extension, 15km. north oh Bethune, France.

PRIVATE ROBERT WALTON
NO. 34584 1ST GARRISON BATTALION
SOMERSET LIGHT INFANTRY
DIED TUESDAY 6TH MARCH 1917 AGE 43.

Born at West Witton, Robert Walton was the fourth son of Mr. and Mrs. J. Walton of Hawes and the husband of Mary Jane Walton of Ardwick, Burnley. Robert had been in the regular army in the late 1890's when he took part in the Chitral Campaign in India., with the East Lancashire Regiment.

To control the North West Frontier, British forces in 1895 advanced through the Malakand Pass to occupy the magnificent and fertile valleys of Chitral, whose horsemen were famous for their skill at polo. Cut off by a rising of the tribesmen, the British had to be relieved in 1897 by the Malakand Field Force, one of whose officers was the young Winston Churchill.

With the Lancashire Fusiliers, Robert went through the Boer War without injury. Although he had finished his term of

Robert Walton (Hawes).

service with the army in 1914 and was living in Burnley with his wife, he was one of the first to respond to the call for men and enlisted at Blackburn.

He was sent to France early in the war and was wounded in the head at the latter part of 1915. Sent into hospital in England he eventually recovered and was posted to the 1st Garrison Battalion Somerset Light Infantry, a Battalion made up of older soldiers at Plymouth in January 1917 and deployed to India in February to act as garrison troops.

Robert Walton succumbed to pneumonia on March 6th, whilst on board his troopship and was buried at sea. His name is commemorated on Panel 12 of the Basra Memorial in Iraq (Mesopotamia).

We have seen that in early Spring the Germans had withdrawn to new defensive positions on and behind the Hindenburg Line. John Iveson, a soldier from Gayle, lost his life as the British Army pursued the retreating German forces.

PRIVATE JOHN (JACK) IVESON
NO. 18622 2ND BATTALION COLDSTREAM GUARDS
DIED WEDNESDAY 14TH MARCH 1917 AGE 31.

Jack's father Edward and mother Mary lived at Bridge End, Gayle, where Edward farmed and did odd jobs to earn extra money. Jack was the third son, with brothers William, Arthur and James and sisters Isabelle and Mary completing the family.

Jack was an excellent footballer with the Hawes team, as were all the brothers. As a centre forward he was known throughout the Richmondshire and Westmoreland areas. Standing well over 6 feet tall, large, athletic, nimble and fast, he scored more goals than any other player. Jack had trials with Burnley and played in some team games.

Owing to the large number of Iveson

John (Jack) Iveson (Gayle).

The Hawes Football Team early 1900's.
John (Jack) Iveson is the team captain, sitting immediately behind the cup.

Corporal Earnshaw XI, Coldstream Guards, (played 6, won 6) September 1916, just six months before Jack Iveson was killed. Jack stands second from the left on the back row.

families in the dale, Jack's family members all had the name "Molly" affixed to their name (coming from their mother's Christian name Mary) e.g. Molly Jack, Molly Bill etc.

Jack worked on the farm but before the Great War he travelled to Vancouver, Canada, together with his friend Jack Dougill, and worked as a lumberjack. When he returned he married Margaret Kirkbride and resumed work on his father's farm.

In July 1916 he enlisted at Richmond and, partly due to his size and strength, was posted to the 2nd Battalion Coldstream Guards. All four brothers were eventually to join the Colours.

A daughter, Mary, was born in January 1915, whilst a second daughter, Isabella Dinsdale Iveson was born in January 1917 (she was seven weeks old when Jack died, never having seen his second daughter).

On February 23rd 1917 the German forces began their methodical retirement to the Hindenburg Line, a 70 mile long stronghold of bunkers, three lines of wire and fortified gun emplacements between Arras and St. Quentin. The Allies cautiously pursued the retiring Germans over the "scorched earth" they had left behind, and during the many actions fought in this fighting retreat, Jack Iveson was wounded.

On Wednesday March 14th 1917 Margaret Iveson received a telegram stating that her husband had been dangerously wounded and on Monday March 19th another telegram arrived conveying the sad news that he had died on the 14th.

Jack Iveson is buried in grave 1V.C.13. in Grove Town Cemetery, Meaulte, just south of Albert, France.

On April 9th 1917 the British Army attacked the Hindenburg Line in the Battle of Arras (April 9th to April 15th), as a preliminary to the main French offensive launched by General Nivelle a few days later, further south. As part of the Arras Offensive, a Canadian Corps attempted to capture the heights of Vimy Ridge, a long term thorn in the side of the Allies. Fighting in the Canadian forces was a former resident of the Wensleydale village of Thoralby.

PRIVATE GEORGE SIDNEY GOULD
NO. 423027 29TH BATTALION CANADIAN INFANTRY
DIED MONDAY 9TH APRIL 1917 AGE 27.

In Chapter Two we saw that George's brother, John Mills Gould, died in England whilst serving in the army and was buried in Aysgarth Churchyard.

Years before the war began George Gould emigrated to Canada from Thoralby and settled as a farmer at Eriksdale, inland from the eastern shore of Lake Manitoba. He enlisted there on April 30th 1915 and eventually sailed for England on the S.S. "Missanabic", arriving on September 13th 1915.

As a member of the 29th Battalion Canadian Infantry he arrived in France on May 8th 1916. On May 9th 1917, one year later, they gathered themselves to attack Vimy Ridge, to cover the flank of the British 3rd Army as it attacked out of the subterranean tunnels and caves of Arras,

An advertisement of 1913 by Tom Hiscock, the Hawes printer.

towards Cambrai.

The Canadian Infantry surged across the wreckage of the German first line before the few survivors could get out of their dug-outs and by 6.05a.m. were in possession of the trench system. The second line was reached, but machine-gunners caused mounting casualties as the Canadians fought for the ruins of a large cellar containing two German Battalion Headquarters.

Machine-guns on Hill 145 took a further toll on the advance up the slope of the Ridge and the Canadian 4th Division ground to a halt. Resistance southwards was lighter and by 1p.m. three woods fell into Canadian hands.

The northern part of the Ridge line was only gained after the tenacious German machine-gunners on Hill 145 had been dealt with. Scattered groups of Germans withdrew hastily from the far foot of the Ridge. The forward slopes were stormed before nightfall and the crest fell in the early hours of April 10th.

By April 12th the Canadians were in full control of Vimy Ridge, standing 200 feet above the Douai Plain below, overlooking the coal mines and slag heaps of the Lens district. Its capture was a remarkable feat of arms and gave signal proof of the Canadians' courage, skill and ability.

George Sidney Gould did not survive the first day's battle for Vimy Ridge. His name is commemorated on the imposing Vimy Memorial.

On that same opening day of the Arras Offensive, 9th April, a man from Hawes also died and another from Askrigg was killed as the battle reached its final stages.

The environs of Arras were honeycombed with tunnels and caves, combined with an underworld of sewers. In these caves was accommodation for an army of 30,000, the springboard for the attack.

PRIVATE JOHN MITTON
NO. 30383 2ND BATTALION YORKSHIRE REGIMENT
DIED MONDAY 9TH APRIL 1917 AGE 40.

John Mitton was the eldest son of Warrin and Ellen Mitton of the "Cattle Market", Hawes. Warrin was both a joiner and a farmer. John was married to a girl from the Leyburn/Finghall area, Mary Teresa Mitton, and they had two young daughters.

Before joining the army he was for four years postman on the Raydaleside Road and lived at Askrigg. Previous to that he was for about 14 years rural post-man at Finghall and was married whilst there. He was presented on leaving Finghall by the people on his round with a marble clock, pipe and pouch and a purse containing money.

For many years a player member of Hawes Football Team, he was for two years its secretary. He was also a fine billiards player and while at Finghall played many times for Leyburn Conservative Club in the Orde-Powlett cup matches. As a youth he was a member of Hawes Church Choir and latterly a member of the choir at Askrigg. A fine, cheery fellow, he possessed a host of friends.

John Mitton (Hawes).

John Mitton enlisted at Leyburn and joined the 2nd Battalion Yorkshire Regiment, embarking for France at the end of July 1916.

On April 7th 1917 the Battalion moved from Bellacourt to Blairville, south of Arras, ready for the start of the Arras Offensive on the 9th. They followed the first wave as "moppers up" over open ground until held up by the German wire. One party established itself in shell holes, joining them up by digging trenches during the day and here they remained under shell and rifle fire until relieved at 1a.m. on April 10th.

By the end of the day 24 men were killed, 89 wounded and two were missing. One of those killed was John Mitton and he lies buried in grave D15 of the Neuville-Vitasse Road Cemetery, 6miles SE of Arras.

COMPANY SERGEANT MAJOR ROBERT MUDD
NO. 35532 10TH BATTALION
WEST YORKSHIRE REGIMENT
DIED FRIDAY 13TH APRIL 1917 AGE 37.

Born in Ripon, Robert was the son of Edward and Margaret Mudd of Masham and husband of Mary Jane (nee Heslop). He joined the army in 1899 and went through the Boer War, in which he was wounded. He held the South African Medal 1901–1902 with five bars viz. Laings Neck, Transvaal, Relief of Ladysmith, Orange Free State and Tugella Heights.

When war was declared he was in the 2nd Reserve, and his time would have expired in November 1914. He was one of the first to be called to the Colours and left his wife and three children in Askrigg to enlist at York, where he joined the 10th Battalion West Yorkshire Regiment.

He acted for some months as drill instructor but was sent to France on July 12th 1915 and remained until December of that year, when he claimed and obtained his discharge. He resumed civilian life, being employed by G. Dougill and sons, Contractors, Aysgarth.

Robert was again called up on June 28th 1916 and sent to France on July 11th that same year, where he was joined in the Battalion by his two brothers. On April 13th 1917, during the Battle of Arras, the Battalion was in the vicinity of Monchy-le-Preux, just to the east of Arras. All day long the enemy, assisted by his aeroplanes, heavily shelled the front line trenches and casualties were severe.

Robert Mudd (Askrigg).

Company Sergeant Major Robert Mudd and two officers in close proximity were all killed when a shell dropped into their position. There is no known grave and Robert's name is found on Bay 4 of the Arras Memorial.

Although the Battle of Arras officially ended on April 15th with no breakthrough gained, the British continued with operations of a smaller scale on April 23rd, in order to again support Nivelle's French Offensive. Three more men sacrificed their lives on the opening day of the battle.

PRIVATE WILLIAM MOORE
NO. 28278 "B" COMPANY 7TH BATTALION
EAST YORKSHIRE REGIMENT
DIED MONDAY 23RD APRIL 1917 AGE 24.

William was born at Sedbusk, High Abbotside, in 1889, the son of farmer, stonemason and builder Simon Moore and his wife Ann (nee Tennant from Askrigg). The Moores were strong chapel folk and had been instrumental in the building of Sedbusk Chapel.

13 children were born and it is sad to relate that all seven lads died or were killed when only young men, two of them as a result of the Great War.

By 1914 the family was living at Litherskew Farm, where William and his father were joint tenants. When William Moore enlisted at Richmond he joined the 7th Battalion East Yorkshire Regiment.

On April 22nd 1917 the Battalion moved into the trenches near Arras in preparation for the attack at 6p.m. on St. George's Day, April 23rd.

At 5.45p.m. they moved up to the original front line in the Sunken Road, passing through a heavy barrage on the way. Several casualties were suffered and while the Battalion occupied the Sunken Road it was heavily shelled the whole time.

During this prolonged shelling, William Moore was hit by the blast from a shell and his body was never recovered. His name is to be found on Bays 4 and 5

William Moore (Litherskew, Hawes).

of the Arras Memorial. Several times William and his brother James had come home on leave and with everyone tearful as they departed once again, both lads had been very fearful that they would not survive.

James was to die in 1919 as a result of wounds received on the battlefield.

PRIVATE ROBERT SHARPLES
NO. 235110 4TH BATTALION YORKSHIRE REGIMENT
DIED MONDAY 23RD APRIL 1917.

Robert was the eldest son of Mr. and Mrs. Sharples of Scar End, near Hardraw Falls. He was a well-known local athlete and was on many occasions a successful competitor at local sports. His father worked in the quarry on Stag Fell, as did Robert and his brother John. However, by 1916 their father had died.

Robert enlisted at Hawes in March 1916 and left for France in December of the same year, having joined the 4th Battalion Yorkshire Regiment.

On April 12th 1917 they reached Arras after a long march in Arctic conditions, to be accommodated in the caves. They were to take part in the offensive close to the village of Wancourt, SE of Arras.

On April 23rd they met with considerable opposition from machine-gun and rifle fire and had to take up positions in shell holes 50 yards from the enemy line.

They rushed the trench and took many prisoners, finding the trench full of German dead and wounded.

Moving on to the support trenches they captured a howitzer battery of three guns and started to dig in. Machine-gun fire was severe from the left flank and by now only 150 men remained. Retirement began back to the British lines, the whole time being subjected to heavy machine-gun fire. 360 men had been killed, wounded or were missing and one of those whose body was never found was Robert Sharples. Bay 5 of the Arras Memorial proudly bears his name.

PRIVATE JOHN WILLIAM WEATHERILL
NO. 19025 13TH BATTALION ROYAL FUSILIERS
DIED MONDAY 23RD APRIL 1917.

John William, or William as he was known, was the son of John and Jane Weatherill of Castle Hill, Middleham. William had been born at Maunby, between Thirsk and Leeming Bar and the family arrived in Middleham when

their parents took over a small pub. Brothers George and Harry and sisters Mary and Eliza completed the family group. Their father eventually became a farm man at West Park, Middleham.

William enlisted at Leyburn and joined the 13th Battalion Royal Fusiliers. Brother Harry also joined the army and was wounded by shrapnel, which affected him for many years afterwards.

On April 22nd 1917 the Battalion proceeded to assembly positions for an attack towards Greenland Hill, near Gavrelle, NE of Arras, set for 4.45a.m. the following day. By midnight they were in position, with the loss of six casualties.

As with so many men in the Battalion, the following day saw John William Weatherill killed by shell fire as his Company advanced

Harry Weatherill (Middleham).

185

under a rolling barrage and his name is commemorated on Bay 3 of the Arras Memorial.

PRIVATE HENRY PEACOCK
NO. 241634 5TH BATTALION YORKSHIRE REGIMENT
DIED SATURDAY 28TH APRIL 1917.

Henry Peacock was living in Middleham when he enlisted in that town during the Great War. However, I have been unable to find out anything about his background. Although there was a son of Matthew Dobson Peacock (the race horse trainer at Manor House) called Henry, it was not he who was killed during the war.

Henry joined the 5th Battalion Yorkshire Regiment and during February and March 1917 they were in training in France. When the Arras Offensive began on April 9th they were kept in Corps Reserve in the Arras area until April 11th.

During this period Henry and his colleagues were just behind the lines constructing roads and repairing them to enable munitions and other supplies and men to be "fed into" the unfolding battle. It was not without considerable danger, since daily shelling was an occupational hazard and it resulted in over 60 casualties durind this short period.

One of these men was Henry Peacock. He was moved south to the town of Rouen on the River Seine, where there had been set up numerous hospitals to deal with the large influx of wounded men. It was here that 17 days later Henry Peacock died from his wounds.

He lies buried in grave P.1.E.9B. in St. Sever Cemetery Extension, Rouen.

Following the Nivelle Offensive of April 16th to 20th, to the south of Arras, there was widespread mutiny in the French Army between April 29th and May 20th. Renewed British attacks attempted to draw German reserves to the northern front and so distract the German attention from finding out about the mutiny. In this they succeeded, but at the cost of many lives, including a dale's headmaster's son and a Bellerby man.

CORPORAL FRANK LESLIE LOFTUS
NO. 17596 11TH BATTALION
EAST YORKSHIRE REGIMENT
DIED THURSDAY 3RD MAY 1917 AGE 21.

In November 1916, Mr. Briscoe, headmaster of Wensley School for the previous five years, left to take up a post as headmaster at Bedale Council School. Mr.

Francis Loftus of Birmingham arrived in Wensley with his wife Sarah, to become the new headteacher. It was the head-teacher's son, Leslie, who would go missing, presumed killed, on May 3rd 1917, six months after the headteacher arrived in the dale.

Leslie Loftus was born in Great Yarmouth, Norfolk, in 1895. Educated at Great Yarmouth Grammar School, he began training to be a teacher at Sheffield Training College.

He joined up in March 1915 when 95% of the College students volunteered to join the armed services. Leslie assisted in the training of recruits and also took drafts of men across the Channel.

Finally, in December 1916, he embarked for France with the 11th

Frank Leslie Loftus (Wensley).

Battalion East Yorkshire Regiment. All through the winter he and his friend

Wensley School and teachers c1907. A number of the lads served in the Great War and some did not return. Mr. Loftus took over as headmaster from Mr. Briscoe in 1916 and the following year his son Leslie Loftus was killed in action.

Corporal Sutton took part in trench warfare, and during the intervals of rest, these two made a point of visiting the country churches and sent an account home.

At 9p.m. on May 2nd 1917 the Battalion assembled ready for an attack early next morning against Oppy Wood, NE of Arras. To get to the assembly positions the Companies had to go over the top of a rise within 1000 yards of the enemy, with a moon low in the sky behind them, whilst the Germans sent Very lights flaring into the night sky.

It was no surprise that at 1.40a.m. on May 3rd, the Germans started an intensive barrage on the Battalion, which never really stopped all day.

The main objective was to be Oppy Support Trench. At zero hour, 3.45a.m., the Battalion, which had been lying out in the open under a hostile enemy barrage for two hours, began the attack in the dark, advancing towards a dark wood.

Enemy machine-guns were firing from within the wood from trees, as well as from the front trenches. Nevertheless, the men went forward, attacked, and were repulsed. Reforming in no-man's land under hostile fire, they attacked again, and again were repulsed. Some even attacked a third time, isolated parties getting through the wood to Oppy village and were reported there by 6a.m. These men were cut off and surrounded later.

The Battalion received 270 casualties. Leslie Loftus was killed by machine-gun fire but his body was found and buried by his friend, Corporal Sutton, a few hours later. Just before nightfall Sutton was captured and for two years was detained in Germany. No authentic information respecting Leslie reached his parents. He had been posted missing, but till Corporal Sutton returned, his actual fate had been unknown.

Frank Leslie Loftus has his name inscribed on Bay 4 and 5 of the Arras Memorial.

PRIVATE ANTHONY WARD
NO. 34714 "C" COMPANY 10TH BATTALION
KING'S OWN YORKSHIRE LIGHT INFANTRY
DIED THURSDAY 3RD MAY 1917 AGE 23.

Anthony Ward was born into a large family in Bellerby, living in a small cottage on Moor Lane. His father, Thomas, was lame and for many years worked on the gate at Leyburn Auction Mart.

All four sons joined the Colours, with Anthony enlisting at Leyburn and joining the Yorkshire Regiment before being transferred to the 10th Battalion K.O.Y.L.I.

On the same day that Leslie Loftus was killed, May 3rd, Anthony Ward also fell and his body was buried in grave 1.B.6. in Henin Communal Cemetery Extension, 8km. SE of Arras.

Before dawn on May 3rd, during a general attack on the Hindenburg Line, the 10th Battalion K.O.Y.L.I. moved up to the front line west of Wancourt, in the second line of their Brigade. Even so, they were involved in the fighting and came under shell fire, resulting in casualties, one of which was Anthony Ward.

Sadly, Anthony's mother, who worked as the caretaker at Bellerby Church, never recovered from the news of her son's death. It affected her mind over the following years and she could often be heard talking to her son.

Anthony Ward (Bellerby).

Just 18 days later another Bellerby man, who had won the Military Medal, died some distance to the north, in the Ypres Salient, whilst serving in the front line trenches.

RIFLEMAN (SIGNALLER) GEORGE C. BECK (M.M.)
NO. 12812 18TH BATTALION
KING'S ROYAL RIFLE CORPS
DIED MONDAY 21ST MAY 1917 AGE 24.

John Beck, the father of George, had been born in Lofthouse, Nidderdale. He was a shepherd, and whilst employed in Coverdale, he married Mary Jane, who came from Horsehouse. By 1881 they were living at The Lilacs in Bellerby and raising a family that eventually consisted of three boys and two girls. George was the youngest son.

Some time after 1901 John and Mary ran the Cross Keys Pub in Bellerby, until Mary died in 1912 and John one year later. Their eldest daughter, Jennie, continued as landlady until she married.

George Beck enlisted at nearby Leyburn and joined the 18th Battalion

189

K.R.R.C. In March 1917 Signaller George Beck was awarded the Military Medal for bravery on the field of action. The Colonel sent for him and personally congratulated him. The events that led up to the honour conferred were as follows :

He, along with other men, were out doing certain work, when, after completion, and upon arriving back at headquarters, they found one of their number missing. The officer in charge and George at once set out in search of the missing man. When they found him he was badly wounded and George gallantly volunteered to remain behind with his wounded comrade until help came and the man was conveyed safely back. Signaller Beck was himself wounded and brought

George Beck (Bellerby).

to England in September 1916 and upon recovering returned to his military duties in France two days before Christmas Day 1916.

January to April 1917 was spent between duty in the trenches in the Ypres Salient and at rest camp or training. By May 19th they were at St. Eloi, SE of Ypres. The artillery on both sides was very active (** part of the artillery bombardment by the British in preparation for the Battle of Messines in June). The enemy began to pay a good deal of attention to the Battalion's back areas, causing great annoyance to working parties and transport.

At 9.30p.m. May 21st the enemy heavily shelled the Battalion front, especially on the left. Here was a detached post, partly in no-man's land, garrisoned by 15 men, including George Beck. Of these, he and eight others were killed outright and three wounded, but the other three stuck to their post gallantly, mounting and firing their one remaining Lewis gun.

There was, of course, no grave for George Beck, His name is inscribed on Panels 51 and 53 of the Menin Gate.

In Bellerby, George had been courting Miss Copley, the maid at the vicarage. At George's Memorial Service it was his elder brother, William, who comforted Miss Copley during the proceedings. Later, she and William were married and settled in Leeds, where they ran a grocery business and market stall.

Meanwhile, news arrived in Hawes about the death of a local hotel keeper's son, on the Arras front.

CORPORAL CHARLES HESELTINE JONES
NO. 42986 9TH BATTALION
KING'S OWN YORKSHIRE LIGHT INFANTRY
DIED FRIDAY 1ST JUNE 1917 AGE 19.

Charles Heseltine Jones (Hawes).

Charlie, as he was known, was the eldest son and child of Christopher Jones, landlord of the Crown Hotel in Hawes, and his wife Ann (nee Heseltine). Children Mabel, Jack, Richard (later to be killed during the Second World War) and Jennie completed the family.

Christopher Jones, always known as Kit, was born on a farm in Redmire and lived a very varied life. As a young lad he worked in service to a wealthy family in Sheffield and then travelled to America and Canada. After marriage to Ann Heseltine, he settled in Lancahire, where Charlie was born, and sometime after 1901 he came to Hawes to take over the running of the Crown Hotel from the previous landlord, James Burton.

Kit was quite a character who liked a drink and a gamble and had a passion for following the horse racing. He was friendly with Matthew Dobson Peacock, the "Uncrowned King of Middleham" and attended most of the important race meetings. He was also an accomplished ventriloquist and accordion (concertina) player, entertaining at village halls and pubs across a wide area, including Sedbergh.

(***On May 4th 1940, during the Second World War, the BBC van from Manchester came to the King's Arms at Redmire to make a broadcast of local talent for a Forces programme. Singers who performed included landlord Joe Alderson, Ernest Heseltine, Jim Lambert, Dick and Bill Balderstone and Bob Bushby. Kit sang to the accompaniment of his concertina.).

The following is an extract from the Craven Herald newspaper in early June 1917 about the death of Charles Jones on the Western Front :

"The sad news was conveyed in the following letter received on Tuesday from the Chaplain; "It is with the very greatest regret that I write to inform you of the death in action of your boy, Corporal Charles Jones. I understand that his

The Jones family of the Crown Hotel, Hawes, during the Great War.
Mabel Jones, Charles Heseltine Jones
Jack Jones, Christopher (Kit) Jones, Jennie Jones, Ann Jones, Richard Heseltine Jones.

death was practically instantaneous as a shell fell amongst the troops, and I am sure he did not suffer. I said the Burial Service over him the day after he was killed. Please accept my deep sympathy in your great bereavement. May God help you to bear it bravely."

"Charlie Jones was a lad whose cheery spirit made him a great favourite with all who knew him, yet this was allied with a studious nature, always thoughtful and considerate. His short career as a pupil teacher at Hawes Council School was marked with nothing but success. Just after he joined the Colours he received his certificate as a Certificated teacher and was to have entered the Leeds Training College.

"He had a high sense of duty and the call of his country found with him a ready response. He volunteered his services in November 1914, but owing to a recent attack of rheumatic fever he was rejected. Recovering his health he again volunteered early in 1916 and was accepted into the Royal Field Artillery. He was shortly afterwards transferred into the Northumberland Fusiliers and later

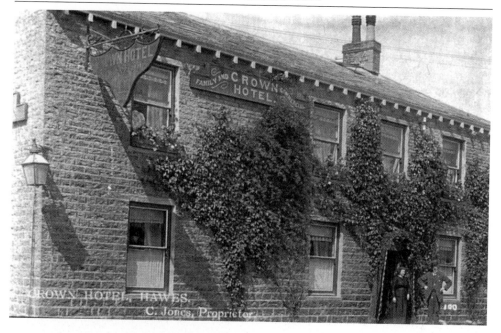

Christopher (Kit) Jones and wife Ann
outside their inn 'The Crown Hotel', Hawes, pre-Great War.

again into the K.O.Y.L.I.

"He went into France in December 1916 and has been in action practically ever since. The following extract, taken from one of his letters, proves his noble sense of duty: "As I look round I ponder to myself which of us is destined to make the big sacrifice. If it be my fate to make the supreme sacrifice I know it won't have been in vain, as our cause is the cause of righteousness."

"He was a valued member of Hawes Church Choir from his early boyhood up to the time of his joining the army, and when on leave he always occupied his place in the choir."

Charles Heseltine Jones was killed in action just to the SE of Arras on June 1st 1917 and was buried in the cemetery nearby. His resting place is grave 11.A.16. in Henin Communal Cemetery Extension.

PRIVATE JAMES CHILTON
NO. 28145 16TH BATTALION
WEST YORKSHIRE REGIMENT
DIED THURSDAY 14TH JUNE 1917 AGE 20.

James was born at Low Street, Kirby Fleetham, Yorkshire, the son of James and Mary Chilton. James senior had married Mary Pearson from Bellerby and by

1901 he had brought his family of seven children to live at Railway Street, Leyburn. He worked as the horseman for Edward Alderson, landlord of the Bolton Arms, Leyburn, who also had a farm on which James worked. One son, Frederick, was employed by Reeds Store, Leyburn, providing agricultural feedstuff to the farmers, while daughters Alice and Lizzie were seamstresses.

James Chilton junior enlisted at York in late 1916 and by April 1917 was serving with the 16th Battalion West Yorkshire Regiment in training at Earsdon Camp, near Whitley Bay, Northumberland. Writing to his sister Lizzie he mentioned how the food was good at first but was now very poor, with rice served instead of potatoes and less of everything (** this was due to the German U-boat campaign of 1917 that resulted in the loss of many ships transporting food, and an increase in the

James Chilton (Leyburn).

rationing of food). He wrote, "Just fancy, they are calling men up to 50 years of age to join the army. That shows we are getting short of men, but we are doing very well now. I am sure it won't last long now as America has started war on Germany."

James's older brother Amos was already in the army, serving in the Royal Army Service Corps in France. A short time after writing the letter to his sister, James was also out in France, but within six weeks of arriving he would be dead.

By June 6th the Arras Offensive was over and the West Yorkshires went into the front line just north of Arras, to man the trenches. Fatigue parties began work on the Bailleul Road.

On June 9th they took over the line in the Gavrelle sector, nearby. The 11th June saw terrible storms which flooded the trenches in places The artillery was more active during the night and on the 12th three casualties were reported, all wounded.

June 13th saw considerable improvement made to the trenches, with new fire-bays constructed, trenches deepened, new sump holes made and floorboards laid. However, during these routine trench duties, on a "quiet day", Captain

Amos Chilton, extreme right on front row. Somewhere in France.

Croxford and six men were wounded by shell fire and shrapnel.

One of those wounded was James Chilton who was transferred to the western fringes of Arras for treatment, but succumbed to his wounds the following day, June 14th. James is buried in grave 1V. J.28.in Duisans British Cemetery, Etrun, on the outskirts of Arras.

PRIVATE JOHN FAWCETT
NO. 40330 18TH BATTALION
WEST YORKSHIRE REGIMENT
DIED SATURDAY 16TH JUNE 1917 AGE 37.

John was born at Castle Bolton in 1880, into a farming family keeping dairy cattle. By 1901 he was living with his mother Ann, a single woman of 58 years, and working on the family farm. However, by 1914, his mother had died and he was living with his cousin, Annie Wade, at Japonica House, Halton East, between Embsay and Bolton Abbey, near Skipton.

Enlisting at Halifax, he joined the 18th Battalion West Yorkshire Regiment and by June 10th 1917 they were providing working parties on the front line near Arras. 100 men, under the supervision of the Royal Engineers, carried trench boards to the support line and helped widen the trenches.

Orders arrived on June 14th to say they were to relieve the 15th and 16th Battalions West Yorkshires in the front line south of the Arras-Gavrelle road.

At 10p.m. on June 15th the Battalion left the trenches, following these orders. At 9p.m., however, a High Velocity shell had exploded, causing 13 casualties, one of them being John Fawcett.

He was taken to the Casualty Clearing Station but died the next day, June 16th, and was buried in grave 111.H.36. in Aubigny Communal Cemetery Extension, 15km. NW of Arras, on the road to St. Pol.

LANCE CORPORAL CHARLES ROBERT NICHOLSON "W" COMPANY 19TH BATTALION NORTHUMBERLAND FUSILIERS DIED SATURDAY 14TH JULY 1917 AGE 38.

Born in Middleham in 1880, Charles is next to be found in Newcastle-on-Tyne in 1901, where he was employed as a factory checker. He entered service in the army in 1912 and by 1917 he was serving as a Lance Corporal in France on the Epehy Sector, between Bapaume and St. Quentin.

As with John Fawcett, Charles was involved with improving the trench system in his sector. Excavation work was carried out and duck boarding laid down on July 12th.

On the night of July 12th/13th the enemy opened up a concentrated bombardment. No. 2 Platoon of "W" Company, including Charles Nicholson, moved up to reinforce the garrison of the post in Bird Cage Trench. The enemy attempted a determined raid, but withdrew under the fire of the Fusiliers.

The bombardment was then resumed as intensely until 1.15a.m. of the 13th. No. 2 Platoon remained with the garrison until it was reorganised. 6 men were killed and 23 wounded during the action, one of these being Charles Nicholson.

He was brought back to the village of Tincourt, 7km. east of Peronne, where there was a Casualty Clearing Station, and he died the next day, July 14th. Charles is buried in grave 1.B.1. in Tincourt New British Cemetery.

GUNNER WILLIAM HUNTER TOMLINSON WEBSTER NO. 696260 "Z" 57TH TRENCH MORTAR BATTERY R.F.A. DIED SUNDAY 5TH AUGUST 1917 AGE 22.

William's father, John Anthony Webster, had been born in the village of Barningham, south of Barnard Castle, and married his wife Jane, a Grassington girl, before arriving to farm at Nappa Scar, near Askrigg. They raised a family of four daughters and three sons, the youngest child being William. In his years

William Webster (Nappa Scar, Askrigg).

at Nappa Scar, William was a member of Askrigg Church Choir.

He was working in a milk house at Garston in Liverpool when he enlisted in the army in May 1915, eventually becoming a gunner in a trench mortar battery. His two brothers, Thomas and Samuel, also joined the Colours during the war.

In August 1917 sad news was received by William's parents at Nappa Scar that he had died in hospital in France. He had been overseas since late December 1916 and was slightly wounded on July 7th 1917. However, on the night of July 29th his billet was heavily shelled with gas shells. He nobly assisted his comrades who suffered more than himself and he was afterwards removed to one of the numerous hospitals at the large military base of Etaples, 27km. south of Boulogne.

Pneumonia supervened and he died suddenly on August 5th. William Webster is buried in grave XX11.O.21A. in Etaples Military Cemetery.

COLONEL JOHN WILLIAM LODGE
COLONEL OF 3RD BATTALION YORKSHIRE REGIMENT.
COMMANDING 2ND (HOME SERVICE)
GARRISON BATTALION
DIED THURSDAY 23RD AUGUST 1917 AGE 60.

John William Lodge was born in 1856, the only son of Robert and Mary Lodge of "The Rookery", Bishopdale, and was educated at St. Peter's School, York. Thence he went to Caius College, Cambridge, where he took his Degree of MA and in 1883 he was called to the Bar at the Inner Temple. At the age of 18 he had joined the 5th West York Militia, which became the 3rd Battalion Yorkshire Regiment in 1881. With this Battalion he served in the Boer War, and, for 6 years (1906-1912) he commanded the Battalion.

On the outbreak of the Great War, Colonel Lodge at once offered his services and returned to his old Battalion as a Major, remaining with it until May 5th 1916, when he was appointed to the command of a Garrison Battalion, which he held at the time of his death.

As Squire of Bishopdale, Colonel Lodge interested himself in local and County affairs. He was JP for the North Riding and was on the Yorkshire Fisheries Board. A skilled angler and excellent shot, he was for many years an enthusiastic follower of Otter hounds. He passed away, after a very brief illness, on August 23rd at "The Rookery".

He was laid to rest in the SW part of the churchyard of St. Andrew at Aysgarth on the afternoon of Monday August 27th, with military honours. The band of the Regiment met the funeral procession outside the village and, in addition to the firing party, detachments from two battalions were present. Volleys were fired over the grave and buglers sounded the "Last Post".

John William Lodge (Bishopdale and Aysgarth).

The Rookery (long since demolished), Bishopdale, c1900, home of Colonel Lodge.

Richmond 1893 3rd Battalion Yorkshire Regiment.
Major Lodge second from the left on the second row.

PRIVATE SAMUEL KIRK LAMBERT
NO. 30337 6TH BATTALION YORKSHIRE REGIMENT
DIED MONDAY 12TH NOVEMBER 1917 AGE 23.

Frances Lambert, the mother of Samuel, was born at Askrigg in 1874 and, as a 20 year old single woman, gave birth to Samuel Lambert in 1894. Five years later, in 1899, she married Wilfred Kirk, a man 18 years older than her, and the likely father of her child. He was a farmer living at Middle Farm in the beautiful but isolated hamlet of Cotterdale, west of Hawes. Children Margaret, Sarah, Frances and Lena were born to complete the family. Samuel Kirk Lambert attended Hardraw School and worked on the family farm.

Samuel enlisted at Leyburn in June 1916, joining the 6th Battalion Yorkshire Regiment and went overseas later that year.

On November 1st 1917 the Battalion was in the support line SE of Loos, in the desolate coal mining region of Northern France, where a little shelling of the trenches took place. Between November 4th and 6th work was spent on improving their own trenches, whilst the nights were spent on the reserve line.

On November 9th preparations were made for a raid by the 9th West Yorkshires. Samuel and his colleagues helped by cutting gaps in the wire and placing ladders in position in the trenches.

On the evening of the 9th, however, retaliatory shelling by the enemy on the trenches was heavy and during this period one man died of wounds and six others were wounded.

Samuel was brought to Chocques, 4km. NW of Bethune, to the site of No. 1 Casualty Clearing Station, but on November 12th he died from his wounds and was buried in grave 1.M.30. in Chocques Military Cemetery.

Samuel Kirk Lambert
(Cotterdale and Hardraw).

The Chaplain sent his parents the following letter: "News will have already reached you that your son died of wounds yesterday, — news the meaning of which to you I can only guess. But in spite of the sorrow it must bring, is there not also in it a note of triumph for those of us who believe in the love of God? I was with your boy before he passed away, and he sent you the message of his love. He was a splendid boy, and you may well be proud of such a son. It was my privilege to lay him to rest today, in a little cemetery behind the lines. Your son gave his life for his country and for the love of you. I pray that God will give you his comfort and the peace that passeth understanding."

PRIVATE HERBERT LAWSON METCALFE
NO. 16077 2ND BATTALION ROYAL IRISH REGIMENT
DIED TUESDAY 20TH NOVEMBER 1917 AGE 19.

Herbert (Bert) Metcalfe was born at Countersett, between Bainbridge and Semer Water, the son of a farmer, William Metcalfe and his wife Emma Jane. In early married life, they suffered sadness when in 1901 their son John William died, aged 18 months, followed in 1903 by Richard, aged 15 months and in 1910 their daughter Alice died, aged 6 years. Bert, their eldest son, Robert, Margaret and

Cissie were the remaining surviving children.

At the time Bert Metcalfe enlisted on January 30th 1917, he was assisting Mr. T. Paley in a milk house in Liverpool. Not of robust health, he went into hospital in England for some time, but went out to France and Flanders on June 19th 1917, with the 2nd Battalion Royal Irish Regiment.

Herbert Lawson Metcalfe
(Countersett and Stalling Busk).

It played a prominent role in the Battle of Cambrai, 20th November to December 3rd 1917, with Bert losing his life on the opening day of the attack. At dawn on November 20th some 200 tanks followed a sudden burst of artillery fire into the German wire. Behind them moved wave after wave of infantry. Success came initially but the British leading tanks became casualties, mainly from mechanical breakdown, and the advance slowed down. German counter-attacks fell on the salient on November 30th and a partial withdrawal was made on December 3rd. Casualties on both sides were equal; about 45,000, but Cambrai marked a turning point in Western Front tactics on two counts: successful assault without long preliminary bombardment and the first mass use of tanks.

The 2nd Battalion was involved in an attack on a front of 2000 yards in front of Fontaine-les-Croisilles, the main objective for the Battalion being Tunnel Trench and The Tunnel.

Tunnel Trench was taken with slight opposition after six minutes, and four minutes later Tunnel Support was captured. The Tunnel itself, running 40 feet below the parapet of Tunnel Trench, with upward shafts every 20 yards, was being cleared by bombing parties. The enemy below ground showed some resistance at first, firing up some shafts with machine-guns, but soon gave up.

The Royal Irish killed 50 Germans and took 210 prisoners, capturing machine-guns and mortars. Mines within the Tunnel were disconnected and so unarmed. The enemy made some slight local efforts at counter-attacks, which were easily dealt with, although their shelling was at times severe. Casualties during the attack were 9 killed and 51 wounded, and one of those killed in the shell fire was Herbert Lawson Metcalfe. His body was never retrieved and his name is found on Bay 5 of the Arras Memorial, not the Cambrai Memorial.

The final casualty from Wensleydale for the year 1917 was:

PRIVATE RALPH TIPLADY METCALFE
NO. 45122 12TH BATTALION DURHAM LIGHT INFANTRY
DIED WEDNESDAY 21ST NOVEMBER 1917 AGE 33.

Ralph was born in 1884 at Bainbridge Ings (nowadays the site of a caravan park) on the outskirts of Hawes, the only son of John and Jane Metcalfe. By 1901, Jane had died and Ralph was working on his father's farm.

By 1914 he was in partnership with his father but in the Spring of 1917 he sold the whole of his stock and enlisted at Richmond, joining the East Yorkshire Regiment, before being transferred to the 12th Durham Light Infantry and going overseas at the beginning of November 1917.

The new draft of men was absorbed into the Battalion, which was to leave France by rail to join the fighting on the Italian Front, where the defeat of the Italian forces by the Austrians at the Battle of Caporetto in the autumn, threatened the complete overthrow of the Italian Armies.

The 12th Battalion, including Ralph Metcalfe, entrained at Arques on November 8th on two trains, journeying via Abbeville and Amiens to Paris and thence south by Dijon and Arles to Marseilles.

They travelled along the French and Italian Rivieras in the golden sunshine of Sunday November 11th, where a short halt was made at Nice, Monaco, Monte Carlo, Mentone and San Remo. At each place the station platforms were crowded with people who had turned out to see the British troops pass through.

Cigarettes, apples, grapes, flowers and chocolate were showered on the men, whilst all along the line the people cheered, waved flags and threw bunches of flowers.

However, all was not well with Ralph Metcalfe. A letter from the Chaplain was received by his father saying that he had caught a chill and had been taken off the train at San Remo. It was reported that he was going on well and would soon be fit and well again. Three days later another letter was received with news that he was suffering from pneumonia. On November 21st 1917 Ralph Tiplady Metcalfe died and was buried in grave 111.B.2. in Bordighera British Cemetery, between Bordighera and San Remo on the Italian Riviera coastline.

As the last Wensleydale man to die in 1917, Ralph Metcalfe's death brought the total of local servicemen who had been killed in action or died during the year to 48. The pain and heartache for their loved ones must have been virtually unbearable, but there was to be no "let up" in 1918.

Even more dalesmen would become eligible for service overseas in 1918 as conscription now included married men with children, exemptions became rarer than ever and still no prospect of victory was in sight.

For the Wensleydale soldiers home on leave there was no greater contrast than between the beauty of their dale and the desolation of the morass that was Passchendaele.

The dale between Aysgarth and West Burton.
By permission of John Morgan.

The quagmire landscape of Passchendaele, Belgium.

CHAPTER FIVE

1918 — TOWARDS VICTORY BUT AT A PRICE

The first news of the death of another dalesman came in March 1918 when a man from the Upper Dale died from his wounds, received during a small scale enemy raid. He would be the first of 51 men to die during the last year of war.

PRIVATE MICHAEL AKRIGG NO. 268427
1ST/7TH BATTALION WEST YORKSHIRE REGIMENT
DIED WEDNESDAY 13TH MARCH 1918 AGE 23.

Michael's father, Michael Akrigg senior, was one of a family of eleven, born on the family farm at Hartley, near Kirkby Stephen. From the mid-17th century the Akrigg's had lived and farmed in Grisedale.

Michael's mother was Margaret Kirk from Cotterdale. This little dale was once populated by just three families, the Halls, the Kirks and the Kings, hence an old couplet:

> "Three halls, two kirks and a king
> The same road out as goes in."

Eventually, by 1901, the Akriggs were farming at White Birk Farm, South Lunds, not far from the Moorcock Inn. Michael, who worked on the family farm, was an only son, with sisters Margaret, Mary Jane, Lydia, Sarah and Agnes for company.

Michael Akrigg enlisted at Sedbergh and joined the 1st/7th West Yorkshire Regiment. By February 22nd 1918 the Battalion was in the Ypres Salient, working on the Corps line in the vicinity of Zonnebeke, but on the 23rd they moved into the lines on the Broodseinde Ridge.

On the night of February 23rd/24th there was an attempted enemy raid on their trenches. At 11.20p.m. the enemy opened a heavy barrage along the

Battalion front. At the same time a strong enemy party of 100 men approached the advanced post, manned by Corporal Moss ("D" Company) and 8 other ranks.

The post immediately opened fire with Lewis gun and rifles and the enemy attempted to surround them and threw stick bombs. After putting up as strong a resistance as possible, Corporal Moss withdrew his party to the front line posts. This he succeeded in doing, but by this time he had had two men killed and two wounded, one of the wounded being Michael Akrigg.

During the remainder of the action, 15 German prisoners were taken, but on the 24th February, Michael Akrigg was transferred to a Casualty Clearing Station to be treated for his wounds. He died on March 13th and was buried in grave 111.F.14. in Menin Road South Military Cemetery, 2km. east of Ypres.

Meanwhile on April 6th 1917 America had declared war against Germany, but with her small army of 210,000 men, it would take some while before her manpower resources could become a decisive factor.

During the winter of 1917/18 General Ludendorff realised that Germany's only hope of winning the war lay in a decisive victory in the West in 1918 before the weight of American man power began to tell. The Bolshevik Revolution of 1917 in Russia had resulted in that country being knocked out of the war.

Ludendorff shifted most German forces from the East and prepared for an all out offensive to be launched as early as possible in the spring, using "shock troops" as spearheads for the assault. He planned to smash the Allied armies in a series of hammer blows, driving a wedge between the British and French forces, and then destroy the British in subsequent assaults. Preparations were made for this massive attack in the Somme area to begin on March 21st between St. Quentin and Arras, towards the goal of capturing Amiens.

Three more Wensleydale men would lose their lives on the very first day of the "Kaiser's Battle", when overwhelming German forces would roll forward and swallow them up.

The British were well aware of German intentions and made preparations for the inevitable attack. One of the most ironic re-deployments was to abandon the Passchendaele Ridge and form a tight defensive line around Ypres. All the sacrifices of the previous Autumn seemed as nought.

Liddell Hart, the military historian, wrote: "At 4.30a.m. on March 21st the sudden crash of some 6000 German guns heralded the breaking of a storm which, in grandeur of scale, of awe and of destruction, surpassed any other in the World War. By nightfall a German flood had inundated 40 miles of the British front; a week later it had reached a depth of nearly 40 miles and was almost lapping the outskirts of Amiens, and in the ensuing weeks the Allied cause itself was almost submerged. Germany came desperately near to regaining that lost chance of victory which she had forfeited in early September 1914."

During the first week of battle eight men from the dale were killed.

On the first day of battle, March 21st, the Germans were favoured by a thick fog that cloaked the infiltrating soldiers as much as it masked the defending machine-guns. The specially trained German "shock troops" rolled through the fog, behind a rolling barrage, and passed around the British strong points, which would be later "mopped up" by reserves.

Wensleydale's first three casualties on this opening day of battle were Thomas Storey, Henry Beswick and Gunner J. Horn.

RIFLEMAN THOMAS STOREY
NO. C/12597 7TH BATTALION
KING'S ROYAL RIFLE CORPS
DIED THURSDAY 21ST MARCH 1918 AGE 24.

The Storey family was of long standing in Castle Bolton, living at the "Nookin", and employed as stonemasons and builders. Past members of the family were involved in the building of Leyburn Town Hall in 1856.

At the "Nookin", parents Henry and Elizabeth lived with their children John, Dorothy, James, Thomas, Henry and Hannah. Thomas Storey was serving his apprenticeship with shoe maker Thomas Haw of Aysgarth and engaged to a Stockton girl when he enlisted at Leyburn on November 17th 1915 and joined the 7th Battalion K.R.R.C. He departed for France on May 1st 1916.

On March 21st 1918 the Battalion was in the south of the Somme area, where the defences were the weakest, and the German 18th Army advanced without serious check from its opponents. Following a surprise 5 hour bombardment by more than 6000 guns the specially trained German shock troops infiltrated behind the rolling barrage.

Private Thomas Storey of Castle Bolton.

The British 5th Army, spread thin on a 42 mile front lately taken over from the French, collapsed and withdrew. Thomas was caught up by the full force of the German attack on the first day of battle, and fell on the battlefild, his body never being recovered. His name is inscribed on Panel 61 to 64 of the Pozieres Memorial, 6km. NE of Albert.

Further sadness struck the Storey family when Thomas's brother, James, was wounded by a bullet entering one side of his jaw and passing out of the other side. He was then taken prisoner by the Germans for the duration of the war. Earlier, in 1917, their eldest son, John, had died of tuberculosis, aged 31. We have seen that such sadness weighed heavily on many families, and 1918 would see more such gloom descend upon the dale.

Rifleman Jim Storey, brother of Thomas Storey, Castle Bolton, at Aldershot February 1916. Jim eventually became a Prisoner of War in Germany.

Jim Storey and fellow Prisoners of War in their camp in Berlin 1918. Jim is standing fourth from the left on the back row.

PIONEER HENRY BESWICK
NO. 224934 "G" SPECIAL COMPANY ROYAL ENGINEERS
DIED THURSDAY 21ST MARCH 1918 AGE 21.

Henry Beswick (Leyburn).

Henry was born at Leyburn in 1897, the son of Thomas Beswick and his wife Elizabeth (nee Imeson). Children Thomas, Maude, John, Henry, Horace and Walter were born.

Thomas Beswick had worked as a coachman at Agglethorpe Hall, near Melmerby, before he arrived in Leyburn as landlord, first at the King's Head and then the Black Swan. He also ran a farm at Craken House, off the Harmby Road. When Henry Beswick left school he went as an apprentice chemist in the employment of H.C. Brierly, with premises at Leyburn and Middleham.

Henry enlisted at Leyburn on June 6th 1916 and mobilised on March 6th 1917, being posted to the Royal Engineers. He joined his unit, "G" Special Company and embarked for France on May 12th 1917.

Mr. Brierly, his employer, had been influential in his selection for the Special Gas Unit when he wrote to the army explaining that Henry had been one of his best pupils, having been a student at the Westminster College of Chemistry for two years. Many of the men recruited into these Special Companies were chemists. Except for the gas shells fired by the artillery, it was this small Brigade that operated the release of gas on the Western Front.

By 1916 the main way of releasing the gas was from cylinders, brought up into the front line trenches and the valves on the nozzles opened. Cylindrical tube projectors, dug into the ground, and firing drums of gas , were also used. By early 1917 there were 21 Special Companies, each given a letter, instead of a number, Henry Beswick being in "G" Company. From April 1917 to the close of the year, the Brigade employed 12,000 cylinders, fired off 100,000 projectors, together with 120,000 Stokes mortar gas bombs and released a total of 2050 tons of gas.

As the Germans launched their offensive on March 21st 1918, the "gas men"

Loading British gas cylinder projectors.

A German machine gun crew protected from a gas attack.

fought side by side with the infantry in the desperate fighting of rearguard defensive operations.

Henry Beswick had been home on leave in late February and returned to France on March 14th. Seven days later he would be dead. On March 21st "G" Special Company was helping to defend the village of Vaux-Vracourt, just north of the main road from Bapaume to Cambrai. A large number of the enemy approached over the ridge at 11.30a.m.and were engaged by low flying British planes.

At noon the Germans advanced in mass up the valley and formed up in Vracourt Copse, where they were shelled. Enemy machine-gunners swept the ground, whilst one advanced post was shelled by "whizz-bangs". The garrison stubbornly held on.

Captain Laycock and twelve men went forward to the line through heavy machine-gun fire, with the Captain and two men wounded by 3p.m. An enemy aircraft fired on the party from 150 feet and as the men opened fire on it, it crashed in flames. A small party of Germans came forward, one man carrying a white flag, but when one soldier stood up to beckon them forward, he was shot at. Firing was ordered and the man with the white flag was seen to fall.

Attempts by the Germans to get through the wire were repulsed, with shell fire coming in strongly, and machine-gun fire continued intermittently throughout the night. The casualties on March 21st were 1 officer wounded, 5 men killed and 11 wounded. One of those killed was Henry Beswick. His Company was unable to recover his body and he is commemorated on Bay 1 of the Arras Memorial.

GUNNER J. HORN NO. 123539
126TH SIEGE BATTERY ROYAL GARRISON ARTILLERY
DIED THURSDAY 21ST MARCH AGE 22.

In 1914 Gunner J. Horn was living with his father, Joseph, a farm worker, and mother Christiana at Thornton Steward. After enlistment he joined the Royal Garrison Artillery, where he was part of a gunnery team in the 126th Siege Battery.

The 9.2 inch howitzers of his Battery attempted to stem the flow of the German advance by counter-bombarding the attacking forces, especially the opposing artillery batteries that rained down a devastating number of shells from 6000 guns.

However, the shock troop tactics of the Germans by-passed Allied strong points on the first day of the battle and the Battery felt the full weight of the enemy bombardment. Gunner Horn was caught by the blast of a shell whilst tending his gun and was mortally wounded on March 21st. He lies buried in grave 1V.B.24. in the Lebucquiere Communal Cemetery Extension, 8km. east of Bapaume.

PRIVATE HAROLD BINKS
NO. 235223 13TH BATTALION YORKSHIRE REGIMENT
DIED 22ND MARCH 1918 AGE 23.

Harold was born in 1894 in the hamlet of Well, to the east of Masham, the eldest child of Thomas and Elizabeth Binks. Thomas, also born at Well, had married Elizabeth from Thornton Watlass, near Bedale, and was employed as a gamekeeper on the nearby estate of Snape Park. Two daughters and another son, besides Harold, completed the family. By 1914, however, Harold Binks was living at West Burton.

He enlisted at Leyburn in 1915 and joined the 13th Battalion Yorkshire

Regiment. At 1.15p.m. on March 21st 1918 the Battalion marched on Hamelincourt, between Arras and Bapaume, to occupy the front trenches to the east of St. Leger. There was tremendous confusion as the Germans had broken through the British lines.

At midnight on March 21st "A" Company occupied the front line trench and, with a Lewis gun team and bombing party, succeeded in killing or dispersing the enemy. At 7a.m. on the 22nd, Captain Simpkin, with two platoons of "D" Company, made a bombing attack on the German opposition trench, clearing it, killing 20 defenders and capturing 7 machine-guns. Within a few minutes some 300 Germans counter-attacked and drove out "D" Company, the Captain being killed.

*Harold Binks
(West Burton and Aysgarth).*

A frontal attack on the trench with "B" Company was made after a barrage, and the enemy bolted, after sustaining heavy casualties. At 6.45p.m. the order was received for a gradual withdrawal, with "B" Company covering the retirement. By this time the Company was almost completely surrounded, with some being captured.

Harold Binks was killed during this action, and, with his body never being recovered, he is honoured on Bay 5 of the Arras Memorial.

PRIVATE FRANK ATKINSON
NO. 12694 10TH HUSSARS
DIED SATURDAY 23RD MARCH 1918 AGE 21.

We have already seen how Frank's brother, Robert Atkinson, had been killed fighting with the New Zealand forces on the Somme in 1916. Frank, a great favourite in East Witton, remained in the village, being engaged in work on the Jervaulx Estate.

He enlisted in October 1914 and joined the 18th Hussars, a cavalry regiment, but when they served in France, they mainly acted as infantry men in the trenches, whilst keeping their horses safely back behind the front line. Here they could be kept ready for any operation requiring rapid movement. Unfortunately they remained dismounted for the greater part of the war.

By 1918 Frank had been transferred to the 10th Hussars and on March 21st, marched to Beaumont, near Ham, and bivouacked in the open. Early on the 22nd, a dismounted Brigade was formed from cavalry units, with Frank and colleagues from the 10th Hussars being part of it. Their horses were moved to Ollencourt, where the Brigade rejoined them on March 26th. However, Frank would not be with them, for he died in action on March 23rd.

By midday on March 22nd the Germans were up against the Crozat Canal and the dismounted cavalry units were brought in as reinfocements, and found themselves heavily engaged the following day.

Frank Atkinson (East Witton) and sister.

East Witton 1917.
Mary Atkinson, Nellie Atkinson, Alice Atkinson, Frank Atkinson.

They arrived at Noureuil, south of St. Quentin, at 5a.m. on March 22nd and that night dug a line of defence in the village. At 11.30a.m. on the 23rd the Germans broke through the French defences at nearby Tergnier and orders came through at 1.30p.m. to retire west of Noureuil. The new line was held until 4.30p.m. when the left was driven in by overwhelming force and the enemy occupied the village.

During this fierce engagement, Frank Atkinson was killed. He has no known grave and his name is on Panel 4 of the Pozieres Memorial 6km. NE of Albert.

PRIVATE THOMAS LAWSON WARDMAN
NO. 300157 1ST/7TH BATTALION
LANCASHIRE FUSILIERS
DIED MONDAY 25TH MARCH 1918 AGE 20.

Thomas's father, Taylor Wardman, was born at Middlemoor, Nidderdale, near Pateley Bridge and married Eliza, a local Nidderdale girl. Their family consisted of Alice, Thomas, Ellen, Jenny, Annie, James, William, Martha, Mary and Marjorie. Some time was spent in Leeds, where Thomas was born, but well before the Great War, they came to live at Riseber Lane, Leyburn.

Taylor Wardman worked for the firm of Reeds, of Railway Street, Leyburn, delivering groceries throughout the district on a horse and cart. Deliveries were made as far as Reeth and he would stay overnight on such occasions. He also helped to transport lead from the Keld Head Lead Mine, above Preston under Scar, to Leyburn Station on his horse and cart (when later, the quarrying came to Preston, an aerial rope way helped to bring the stone down to Wensley Station in large buckets. The weight of the loaded descending buckets helped to power the returning empty containers upwards. A similar rope way was used in the Redmire Quarry).

When Thomas Wardman enlisted at Leyburn he joined the 1st/7th Battalion Lancashire Fusiliers and on March 24th 1918 the Battalion had been brought into the line to try and stem the German advance.

They were diverted to the village of Sapignies, just north of Bapaume, and from early morning on March 25th had a very gruelling time, fighting many "ding-dong" battles on the ridge which runs south from Sapignies.

A Lieutenant collected scattered troops, organised them and led them through a heavy barrage to reinforce a hard-pressed sector of the line. Another Lieutenant organised and gallantly led a counter-attack which drove the enemy out of a part of his line.

Another officer ran through heavy machine-gun fire to rally his troops and inflicted heavy losses on the enemy by firing the Lewis gun. They held on for

Taylor Wardman, father of Thomas Lawson Wardman, on the road between Wensley and West Witton, on Alma Corner, delivering groceries for 'Reeds' of Railway Street, Leyburn.

three hours although practically surrounded and under heavy fire. Eleven NCO's and men of the Battalion won the Military Medal for their share in this magnificent defence.

However, during this defence of the line, Thomas Lawson Wardman was killed, and as with so many others, his name is to be found on the Arras Memorial, on Bay 5.

PRIVATE RALPH ALDERSON
NO. 24371 NO. 1 COMPANY
3RD BATTALION GRENADIER GUARDS
DIED WEDNESDAY 28TH MARCH 1918 AGE 38.

Ralph's grandfather, Ralph Alderson senior, was a joiner from Keld, in Swaledale, who settled in Hawes. He continued his joinery business and took over Gayle Mill, a former water-powered corn mill, and ran it as a sawmill.

In 1865 he also took over the tenancy of Foss (Force) Head Farm at Gayle, which was run by his son Thomas. Land was farmed on the fells above, on nearby fields and in fields between Hawes Station and the River Ure. Thomas had married a Gayle girl, Jane Kirkbride, and their surviving children were Thomas, Ralph, Fred, Jim, George, William, Hannah, May, Polly and Jinny.

Ralph Alderson, junior, a single man living at the family farm, worked at the water-driven corn mill in Hawes (today the Conservative Club) and also at the Cheese Factory. An extremely powerful man, he took part in local trials of strength and proved himself to be the strongest man in the area when, in the Station yard at Hawes, he succeeded in lifting a number of railway track, where others failed.

Ralph Alderson (Gayle).

Force Head Farm, Gayle. The home of Ralph Alderson.

The corn mill at Hawes, beside Duerly Beck, in which Ralph Alderson worked.
By permission of the Dales Countryside Museum.

216

The Wensleydale Dairy was established by the beck in Hawes in 1898. The old mill building was used at the start of the Wensleydale cheese industry in Hawes. Edward Chapman, a Hawes corn merchant, was the biggest local buyer of farmhouse cheeses, and in 1897 he decided to buy milk in bulk from the farms and manufacture the cheese for himself, in a cheese factory by Gayle Beck, based on a daily intake of 200 gallons of milk. When threatened with closure in 1935, the late Kit Calvert put up some capital and persuaded local farmers to support him in buying the factory.
Wensleydale Cheese had first been made by the tenants of Cistercian monks from Jervaulx Abbey, using the milk of ewes grazing on the land between Askrigg and the hills beyond Hawes, still known as Low and High Abbotside (only later was cow's milk used). A process known as 'pickling' was used, involving running the cheese into tins coated with brine.

Annual fairs were held at Hawes and the "Rope King" would attend, challenging local people to tie him up to prevent him escaping. Ralph was the only person successful in stopping him.

Whenever his mother required extra flour for baking, Ralph would carry a 16 stone bag across his shoulders from his place of work, across Bealah Bank, to the farm at Gayle.

Three brothers, Fred, Jim and Ralph would eventually join the Colours. On November 3rd 1915, at the age of nearly 36, Ralph enlisted at Leyburn, and with his height and strength, it was not surprising that he joined the Grenadier Guards, in the 3rd Battalion. On January 19th 1917 he crossed the Channel to join his Battalion in France.

Ralph had been selected as a stretcher bearer for the Battalion, partly due to his great strength and physique. The evacuation of the wounded in a battalion fell on 32 stretcher bearers, capable of carrying 16 wounded between them, and needing an hour or more for each journey. It was an extremely hazardous occupation, as, unarmed, they crossed no-man's land to collect the wounded.

Whilst in France and Belgium, Ralph kept a diary, a copy of which is still in the possession of his relatives in Gayle:

Ypres. 23rd/24th July 1917 — Stretcher bearing, with Brewer, Munn, Wing and Haylewood all killed.
31st July 1917 (Battle of Passchendaele) Went over the top 4a.m. Started dressing the wounded up to the Black Line.
1st August 1917. Dressing wounds and bringing in the wounded. Raining, knee deep in mud.
9th October 1917 "Went over the top" (The crossing of the Broembeek stream by the Guards Division)

By mid-November 1917 the 3rd Battalion had moved south into France, and on November 27th participated in fierce fighting during the latter stages of the Battle of Cambrai and Gouzeaucourt. During this Autumn period Ralph gained the Military Medal for conspicuous bravery on the field of battle. It tells something of his character that he never mentioned this when later he was home on leave in his native Gayle.

On December 25th 1917 Ralph was on leave for the last time. Early on January 7th 1918 he walked with his brother Thomas to Hawes Station and as he took his leave, said to his brother, "I won't be coming back, Tommy!" The next day he was back in France.

As the train left Hawes Station, taking him on his final journey down the dale, he would travel through fields belonging to the Aldersons, fields in which he had spent many happy hours of his youth during haymaking time. The contrast of the beautiful dale of his birth with the desolate battlefields of France, could not have been more stark.

The 3rd Battalion was not involved in the opening day of the Ludendorff Offensive. By the 23rd, however, they were in position, south of Arras, at Boyelles, in support but under heavy shelling.

On the 24th the Germans advanced by two's and three's but were scattered by rifle fire. At 10p.m. on March 25th orders were received to retire to a new line

Arras Memorial, France.

and fresh trenches were quickly dug by the men, under the falling of enemy shells.

The Battalion was just west of Boyelles on March 28th when the German artillery shelled the back area and particularly the valley in which the 3rd Battalion headquarters was situated. The Germans advanced towards No.2 Company, but were met with accurate fire from Lewis and machine-guns, which decimated their ranks. They were unable to make an impression on the Battalion's frontage, although the 3rd Battalion's 131 casualties were heavy and one of these was Ralph Alderson.

Although buried hurriedly on the battlefield, today his name is to be found on Bay 1 of the Arras Memorial.

Two poignant letters were received by his family. The first came from a close colleague, the Chaplain, Captain the Reverend Phillimore, MC:

"He was a splendid fellow and we were very fond of him. He had been so long with us, done such magnificent work, that we all recognised him as a prince amongst Stretcher Bearers, because he was always dependable and so good. He never shirked his duty, but was always first to be on the spot, helping people forward.

He was killed carrying out his duty, of helping the wounded under heavy shell fire.

He was buried by me on the field of battle with the service of the church. I want you to feel in his death, not the great sort of loss, but a sort of gain. He was so splendid, that one feels sure that his sacrifice must have won for himself an Eternal Reward or Renown.

He surely passes into the presence of his Master to receive the reward of those who have washed themselves in the Blood of the Lamb.

God help you in your sorrow, and give you strength to bear up and face the trouble which is his reward and your sorrow."

The second letter came from his Platoon Officer, 2nd Lieutenant Ellison:

"I am writing to you because I was the Platoon Officer of Private R. Alderson on the day he was killed. I myself was wounded twice that same day.

The Battalion marched out from Arras and by the morning of the 28th we were at Boyelles. My Platoon was in an advanced post, the Germans attacking at 6.15a.m. Private Alderson was hit in the head and died instantaneously.

He had been perfectly splendid as he always was. He really was a good man and I can't tell you how sorry I am to lose him. He always did his very best at everything, and he was always cheerful and very willing, you ought indeed to be proud of him. It was a splendid death (we were all with our backs to the wall) and in such cases the lot of a stretcher bearer is not a cheerful one.

If there is anything I can do for you please let me know. I can only give you my deepest sympathy and tell you again that he was one of the very best. He was buried the same evening."

Sometime after his death the family received a mounted silver chalice, inscribed with the words: "Private R. Alderson MM. From the admirers of a hero."

At the Arras Memorial, France.
Photograph of Ralph Alderson
and the memorial chalice
presented by his colleagues after his death.

It almost certainly came from the Chaplain and his comrades and today is still in the possession of relatives in Gayle.

PRIVATE GEORGE BECKWITH
NO. 22371 2ND/4TH BATTALION
WEST RIDING REGIMENT
DIED SATURDAY 30TH MARCH 1918 AGE 19.

William Beckwith, the father of George, was a shepherd from Arkleside in Arkengarthdale, north of Reeth, who married Mary, a native of Bellerby. In 1901 they were living with their youngest son George at The Swan, Redmire.

George had been born at Castle Bolton and the family returned there to live, but by 1914 his mother, Mary Beckwith, had died. He enlisted at Keighley and joined the 2nd/4th Battalion West Riding Regiment. He was joined by a neighbour from nearby Stalling Busk, James Bell, who would die 12 days after George.

On March 25th 1918 the Battalion marched to Bucquoy and collected extra ammunition and bombs before marching off to take up a position near Achiet-Le-Petit, just NW of Bapaume, to perform a defensive buffer.

At 2.30a.m. on the 26th orders came to withdraw, as a large number of the enemy were reported to be working round their right flank. On the 27th the Battalion was defending SE of Bucquoy and at 10a.m. the whole line was heavily shelled and the enemy developed an attack on their front, which was beaten back by Lewis gun and rifle fire.

The following day, March 28th, the enemy shelled the position continually all day, but no attacks developed. However, during the shelling George Beckwith had been severely wounded. He was removed to behind the lines and was transferred to the main hospital and Casualty Clearing Station Base for that area, at nearby Doullens. His comrade from Stalling Busk, James Bell, was also wounded in the same action but survived long enough to be transferred to Etaples Hospital on the French coast.

It was at Doullens that two days after arriving, George Beckwith died, on March 30th. He was buried in grave V1.G.40. in Doullens Communal Cemetery Extension.

PRIVATE JAMES PRATT
NO. 49716 8TH BATTALION LINCOLNSHIRE REGIMENT
DIED FRIDAY 5TH APRIL 1918 AGE 19.

James Pratt was born at the Gaits, in Gayle, the second youngest child of John and Agnes Pratt. John Pratt worked on the railway as a plate layer and kept a smallholding at Bands, near Gayle.

Dick was the eldest son, followed by William (who milked the cows in the early morning and then did a full days work at Burtersett Quarry), Mary, Elizabeth, James and Jack.

Enlisting at Richmond, James Pratt eventually joined the 8th Battalion Lincolnshire Regiment and was involved in the latter stages of the first phase of Ludendorff's Offensive.

By March 30th 1918 the German surge towards Amiens was almost stagnant. Roads were blocked, transport "scuppered", reserves harassed by the British air attacks, troops were exhausted, and in some cases they were becoming involved in looting the abundant supplies of food, drink and materials that German soldiers had been denied over the past two years.

John Pratt, father of James Pratt at the farmhouse at Bands, Gayle.

Nearly a week passed before, on April 4th , a further German effort was made by 15 divisions. Meeting a reinforced defence, this had still less success and Ludendorff suspended the attack towards Amiens on April 5th. However, on that very day, James Pratt was killed in action helping to stem the German advance. He was buried in grave 111.G.8. in Gommecourt British Cemetery, 19km. SW of Arras.

Within the space of twelve days in early April, thirteen more dalesmen's lives were lost, two of them serving in the same battalion. The Germans, finding that their advance was being brought to a standstill in the direction of Amiens, turned their attention further north and determined to threaten the Channel ports. On April 9th they began a concentrated attack along the River Lys, on the British and Portuguese front between Armentieres and La Bassee, and the fighting spread to Messines in Belgium.

PRIVATE FRED LEALMAN
NO. 241657 5TH BATTALION YORKSHIRE REGIMENT
DIED WEDNESDAY 10TH APRIL 1918 AGE 29.

Fred Lealman was born at Coxwold, east of Thirsk, in 1889. His father, Henry, had been born in nearby Kilburn and married Mary, a girl from Hornby, a village between Northallerton and Darlington. Daughter Jane was born at Crayke and sons Robert and Fred at nearby Coxwold, where their father was a gamekeeper. By 1901 Henry had taken his family to live at Downholme, a village between Bellerby and Richmond, where he was again in employment as a gamekeeper.

On enlisting at Leyburn, Fred joined the 5th Battalion Yorkshire Regiment and was joined by another dalesman, Thomas Thwaite from Hawes.

During the Ludendorff Offensive, the Battalion moved to Hancourt, east of Peronne, on March 22nd,1918 but was forced to retire when engaged by the enemy, and fought a rearguard action as they crossed the River Somme at Brie.

Two Companies maintained their ground on the 25th, with "B" Company holding on until the end. At 8a.m. on the 26th the enemy again attacked and there was a general retirement to the Rosieres line, but the rearguard platoon were either killed or captured.

On March 27th, at 7p.m., the enemy launched a further attack but were driven back with heavy casualties. However, by now the Battalion's losses were so great that it became a composite battalion and by March 30th was involved in desperate fighting in the valley of the River Luce, as attack and counter-attack took their toll. A casualty during this period of fighting was Fred Lealman who was wounded and taken to the billeting and Casualty Clearing Station centre of Merville, 15km. north of Bethune, where he died on April 10th. He is buried in grave 1.D.68. of Merville Communal Cemetery Extension.

PRIVATE FREDERICK CLARKSON
NO. 241764 8TH BATTALION BORDER REGIMENT
DIED WEDNESDAY 10TH APRIL 1918 AGE 29.

The Clarkson family was long established in Middleham and lived on North Road. James Clarkson was a stonemason's labourer, and, with his wife Elizabeth, raised a large family. Frederick was the eldest, with siblings Cissie, Bertha, John, Harry, Violet, Elizabeth, Ida, Charlie, Johnson and Jack. Most of the lads were farm labourers or worked in the nearby quarries.

Frederick enlisted at Leyburn and at first was posted to the Yorkshire Regiment, but by March 1918 he was serving with the 8th Battalion Border Regiment in France.

During the first phase of Ludendorff's Offensive the Battalion was heavily involved, suffering severe casualties on March 22nd at Vaulx Wood.

By the 28th they had been pulled out of the line and on March 31st entrained to Belgium for duty in the Le Touquet sector of the front line, on the River Lys, just north of Armentieres. Sadly, they were to have little respite, for this area of the front was involved when Ludendorff launched the second stage of his offensive between Armentieres and La Bassee.

On April 9th the Le Touquet sector was heavily shelled in the afternoon with gas, high explosive and shrapnel. At 5.30a.m. on April 10th the Germans attacked after a

Mrs. Elizabeth Clarkson holding her son, Johnson, together with daughter Elizabeth and a friend, Nellie Brooks, in North Road, Middleham, before the Great War. Lower down North Road was the Gas Yard, run by the Handley family.

heavy bombardment. "A" Company was practically cut off and other Companies retired to the Reserve Line, which was soon enveloped.

At some stage in the day's actions Fred Clarkson was killed and his body was never recovered. His name is honoured on Panel 6 of the Ploegsteert Memorial, Belgium, south of Ypres. His mother, a very hard working woman, who took in people's washing to make ends meet, received Fred's pension but refused to spend it for she always called it "blood money".

PRIVATE HAROLD BELL
NO. 80885 8TH BATTALION DURHAM LIGHT INFANTRY
DIED WEDNESDAY 10TH APRIL 1918.

Harold Bell was born at Burnby, near Pocklington, on the Yorkshire Wolds, but by 1914 he was living in Wensleydale, between Hawes and Hardraw. Enlisting at Richmond, he eventually joined the 8th Battalion Durham Light Infantry.

By April 8th 1918 the Battalion was to be found near Estaires, on the River Lys. The fighting of the 9th to 12th April was very stubborn, the Germans only succeeding in advancing about five miles in these four days, despite the men of the Battalion being so worn out by the March retreat that throughout these days

The Ploegsteert Memorial in Belgium. The entrance, flanked by lions, leads to the circular memorial, on which the panels of the interior and exterior walls contain the names of Harold Bell and three other Wensleydale men, all killed in the Spring of 1918: Fred Clarkson, John Thomas Moore and Francis Henry Rider.

of fighting some fell asleep even in the act of firing.

On hearing the bombardment, the Battalion hurriedly stood to arms on April 9th and occupied positions in the neighbourhood of Lestrem, on the eastern bank of the canalised River Lawe. At 1.30a.m. on April 10th the Germans attacked the bridge head there and the shelling was intense, the German artillery firing over open sights. Most of the bridge head garrison were killed or wounded and casualties elsewhere were severe. As it was impossible to counter-attack with the few men available it was decided to withdraw to the west bank and destroy the bridge.

At 6p.m. considerable numbers of the enemy advanced and a heavy bombardment fell on the remains of the Battalion near Lestrem Post, with shells bursting on the Company Headquarters.

During the early morning bombardment of the bridge head garrison, Harold Bell had been killed by shell fire. His name is commemorated on Panels 8 and 9 of the nearby Ploegsteert Memorial.

PRIVATE THOMAS THWAITE
NO. 242720 5TH BATTALION YORKSHIRE REGIMENT
DIED THURSDAY 11TH APRIL 1918 AGE 37.

Thomas was the second youngest of nine children in the family of Simon and Mary Ann Thwaite (nee Metcalfe), a farming family from Hawes. The children were Alexander, Agnes, Ninion, Simon, James, Ninion, Simon, Thomas and Christopher (Agnes, Simon and Ninion died early in childhood, from Scarlet Fever).

By 1901, Mary Ann Thwaite was a widow, living with her son James and his family at Mid Mossdale Farm, near the Moorcock Inn.

Thomas Thwaite enlisted at Leyburn and joined the same Battalion as Fred Lealman, the 5th Yorkshire Regiment. After desperate action between March 21st and March 30th, in which Fred became one of 388 casualties, the Battalion was withdrawn and by April 9th had travelled north with orders to dig in at Laventie, south of the River Lys and SW of Armentieres. The following day they were to feel the full weight of the second German thrust between Armentieres and La Bassee.

At 11a.m. news came that the enemy was over the River Lys and occupying La Boudrelle. Three Companies moved up to form a defensive flank astride the road but came under direct and heavy fire from machine-guns and light field artillery and suffered some loss. Parts of the line were driven in by the weight of the enemy attack, but it held out through the night.

In the early hours of April 11th the Germans attacked the left flank heavily and Companies of the Battalion, holding a salient in the line, maintained their ground till practically surrounded and many were captured, while the wounded had to be left behind. Many casualties were caused by the fire from an enemy field gun and at 8.30p.m. the remains of the Battalion withdrew.

One of the casualties left behind was Thomas Thwaite, whose body was never recovered, and is honoured on the Special Memorial E.8. at the Croix-du-Bac British Cemetery.

PRIVATE JAMES BELL
NO. 204943 2ND/4TH BATTALION
WEST RIDING REGIMENT
DIED THURSDAY 11TH APRIL 1918 AGE 30.

James's father, John Bell, came from Simonstone to work as a woodman on a Stalling Busk farm. His wife, Isabella Iveson, came from nearby Carr End and together they raised their children James, Arthur and Matthew.

Before enlisting, James was in the employ of Mr. Penry Williams, M.P. on his Raydale Estate, and married a Stalling Busk girl, Ann Outhwaite. We have already seen that Ann's brother, Thomas Pickard Outhwaite, had been killed whilst fighting for his country in 1917.

James Bell joined the 2nd/4th Battalion West Riding Regiment in July 1917 and went to France in December of that year where he joined a fellow dalesman,

George Beckwith, from Castle Bolton. Sadly, we saw that both men were wounded during the fighting on March 28th, with George dying on the 30th. James was taken to No. 4 General Hospital at Etaples, on the French coast, but on April 11th he succumbed to his wounds and was buried in grave XXX111.G.12. Etaples Military Cemetery.

A Memorial Service was held at Stalling Busk Church (the old church) on Thursday May 1st when Reverend Squibb paid a tribute to the deceased. The church was crowded and great sympathy was shown to the widow and relatives.

PRIVATE ROBERT THOMAS DAVISON
NO. 365812 1ST BATTALION
NORTHUMBERLAND FUSILIERS
DIED THURSDAY 11TH APRIL 1918 AGE 39.

Robert's father, also named Robert, was a farmer at The Lilacs, Bellerby, close to South View Farm. He married Lucy, a Bellerby girl, and Robert was the second eldest child. Their eldest son, Christopher, sadly died in 1904, aged 25, a year after the death of their father.

Robert married Mabel Lonsdale and they lived at Prospect Cottage, Bellerby, with Robert employed locally as a draper's assistant. However, he was called up to the Colours, enlisting at Sunderland, and joined first of all the Durham Light Infantry and was then transferred to the 1st Battalion Northumberland Fusiliers.

On April 9th the Battalion was in the Lys area between La Bassee and

Robert Davison (Bellerby).

Armentieres, recovering from the strains of the battle it had taken part in two weeks earlier, further south. Suddenly, they were engulfed in the fresh German attack, as an intense bombardment began along the front, the flanks being deluged with mustard gas, as 9 German divisions launched themselves against 3 Allied divisions.

The Battalion was engaged in fierce fighting throughout the next three days in a fighting retreat and holding operation, but on April 11th Robert Davison was killed in action. With no known grave to his name, he is commemorated on Panels 20 to 22 on the Loos Memorial, France.

GUNNER EDWARD SPENCE
NO. 65594 20TH SIEGE BATTERY
ROYAL GARRISON ARTILLERY
DIED FRIDAY 12TH APRIL 1918 AGE 22.

Edward was the fourth son of Wensley farmer Simon Spence and wife Hannah. Born at Wensley, where he went to school under Mr. Myers, Edward was a member of Wensley Church Choir, the Sunday School and was also a bell ringer. He was employed as an apprentice joiner by Mr. John Chapleo of Middleham, but he joined up on November 8th 1915, enlisting at Leyburn, and became a gunner in a siege battery.

During the German advance on the Lys front in 1918 he was killed by a shell landing near his gun whilst his Battery was counter-bombarding the enemy forces on April 12th.

The family received a letter from Major Bell: "Gunner Spence had always done exceptionally good work, especially in the heavy fighting last Autumn during the Battle of Passchendaele and he was a splendid example of coolness under fire."

Edward Spence was buried in grave 1V.B.10. in Noeux-Les-Mines Communal Cemetery Extension, 6km. south of Bethune.

PRIVATE FRANCIS HENRY RIDER
NO. G/67587 "Z" COMPANY 2ND BATTALION
ROYAL FUSILIERS
DIED SATURDAY 13TH APRIL 1918 AGE 20.

We have already seen in Chapter Three how Frank's brother, John Rider, had been killed on April 26th 1916. Born at Redmire but living and working at Crook, Co. Durham, he enlisted from there and joined the 2nd Battalion Royal Fusiliers.

On April 12th 1918 the Battalion was in the village of Vieux Berquin to the north of the River Lys, between Armentieres and Hazebruck, waiting for the approach of the German forces.

Early in the morning of April 13th a heavy attack was launched by the enemy on the left, which was finally held up. The ammunition dump caught fire, causing considerable confusion to the enemy who were forming up close by. A large number of Germans were killed with machine-gun fire from the Battalion's left post.

The enemy attacked again but was held up 800 yards from the line by machine-gun fire and so began to dig himself in. By nightfall, however, a withdrawal of the Battalion was ordered since its flanks were "in the air".

During this day's actions Frank Rider had been killed and his name is inscribed on Panel 3 of the Ploegsteert Memorial, across the border in Belgium.

PRIVATE JOHN JOSEPH CARRUTHERS
NO. 94581 1ST/6TH BATTALION SHERWOOD FORESTERS
DIED MONDAY 15TH APRIL 1918 AGE 19.

John Joseph Carruthers was the eldest child of Joseph and Ellen Carruthers. Joseph, a Cumberland man, had joined the police force and whilst serving near Easingwold, had married Ellen, a girl from the village of Terrington, in the Howardian Hills. In 1899 John Joseph was born at Hutton-le-Hole, on the North York Moors, where Joseph was serving as the village police constable. By April 1901, however, John Joseph and his two month old sister Mary, were living with their parents in Leyburn, where Joseph was working as the police constable in the town. In 1917 John Joseph Carruthers enlisted at Beverley and was eventually transferred to the 6th Battalion Sherwood Foresters.

The Germans attacked the Portuguese with mustard gas April 9th, causing them to give way and so created a sharp salient 15 miles deep. The Sherwood Foresters became involved in establishing and holding the southern flank of this salient which was a series of shell holes hastily surrounded with a few strands of barbed wire.

The action took place in unspoilt agricultural country, low lying, and the fields interconnected by deep and wide drainage ditches, which connected with the La Bassee Canal, two miles to the rear. The whole area was continuously bombed by gas shells and gas casualties were frequent, the men sometimes having to sleep in their gas masks.

The town of Bethune was burning and destroyed and for the first time since 1915 pitiful groups of refugee peasants were to be seen on every road.

During the period of shelling John Carruthers was wounded and taken to the Casualty Clearing Station where, on April 15th, he died from his wounds and was buried.

PRIVATE THOMAS MILLER
NO. 30292 10TH BATTALION
EAST YORKSHIRE REGIMENT
DIED WEDNESDAY 17TH APRIL 1918 AGE 19.

George Coates Miller was the father of Thomas. He was a farmer at West End Farm, Woodhall, near Askrigg, who had married Margaret Holmes from Carlton

Thomas Miller convalescing in hospital, extreme right in photograph.
He came from Woodhall, near Askrigg.

in Coverdale. Three sons, Jack, Thomas and James and three daughters, Margaret, Alice and Mary were born at Woodhall.

Thomas worked on his father's farm, but in February 1917 he enlisted at Richmond and joined a West Yorkshire battalion. With them he embarked for France in October 1917 and fought at the Battle of Cambrai. He wrote to his sister that they "went over the lid" on November 20th 1917.

On Christmas Day 1917, however, he entered the 1st General Canadian Hospital in France, suffering from boils, and was eventually transferred to a Carlisle hospital on January 12th 1918, before spending leave with his family at Woodhall.

When he returned to France he was drafted into the 10th Battalion East Yorkshire Regiment and between March 26th and March 31st was heavily engaged in stemming the Ludendorff Offensive in an area to the NW of Bapaume. Total casualties were 4 officers and 207 men.

When the second thrust of the Offensive began on April 9th the Battalion was in the vicinity of Armentieres, on the northern side of the River Lys and was again heavily engaged by the enemy.

On April 13th Tommy Miller was badly wounded in the spine, causing paralysis, and was sent to a hospital at Etaples. He died from his wounds on April 17th and was buried in grave XX1X. E.9. in Etaples Military Cemetery.

The matron wrote to his mother that he suffered no pain, as much of the time he was unconscious. He wanted for nothing and was well tended by the British nurses. A Memorial Service was held at Askrigg Church on Sunday evening. In paying tribute to Thomas, who was an old Sunday School scholar, Reverend Squibb said that it was only a few weeks since he met him on the road full of health and vigour. There was the same cheery smile on his face. He was a bright, lovable lad. Their hearts went out in sympathy to his parents but there was a brighter side. If these brave men and lads who had given their lives for their country could only speak they would say, "Do not grieve, but rather rejoice. We have done our part in helping towards the final victory. Go on and persevere, and right will triumph over wrong." The "Death March" in "Saul" was played at the close of the service and the National Anthem was sung after the sermon.

The previous day, an Appersett man was killed on trench duty in the Ypres Salient.

PRIVATE JOHN JACKSON
NO. 30656 1ST BATTALION
EAST YORKSHIRE REGIMENT
DIED TUESDAY 16TH APRIL 1918 AGE 23.

John Jackson was born in Hawes in 1896 but by the age of 5 he was living with his father Thomas, a farmer, and his mother Hannah and siblings Elizabeth, James and Margaret at their farm on Back Road, Appersett.

John worked on the farm, and when he enlisted at Leyburn he was eventually posted to the 1st Battalion East Yorkshire Regiment.

By April 8th 1918 the Battalion was serving in the Ypres Salient, seemingly away from the savage fighting about to open up on the Armentieres - La Bassee front further south.

However, the Messines Ridge was one of the objectives in Ludendorff's push for the Channel ports and the 1st Battalion was in that sector.

John Jackson (Hawes and Appersett).

On April 12th they took over the line at Wytschaete, on the Messines Ridge. At 5a.m. on the 16th a very heavy bombardment opened on this front line and a strong attack was launched, especially against "D" Company, which lost one of its platoons. The rest of "D" Company held fast all day although the enemy penetrated into their trenches.

At 7.30 a counter-attack was launched and penetrated through Wytschaete and consolidated on the NW slopes of the hill.

John Jackson, however, had been killed by shell fire and today his name can be found inscribed on Panel 47 to 48 and 163A of the Tyne Cot Memorial.

CORPORAL JOHN THOMAS MOORE
NO. 16144 6TH/7TH BATTALION
ROYAL SCOTS FUSILIERS
DIED FRIDAY 19TH APRIL 1918 AGE 38.

John Thomas Moore, son of John Moore, had been born in Burtersett. Marrying Clara, a Burtersett girl, they left the dale to settle in Nelson, Lancashire, some years before the start of the war. By 1918 they had a family of six young children.

John joined the Colours in December 1914, becoming a Corporal in the 6th/7th Battalion Royal Scots Fusiliers, a Pioneer Battalion.

In mid April 1918 the Battalion found itself involved in trying to prevent the German advance capturing Hazebruck and the Messines Ridge area and surging on towards the Channel ports.

On April 15th they occupied the "Army Line" behind Bailleul on the Franco-Belgian border, but on the 16th they concentrated at Locre, just over the border in Belgium and 100 men, including John, were placed at the

John Thomas Moore (Burtersett).

disposal of the Brigade for a counter-attack on the 17th and 18th April. The action at Locre was amongst the severest they had ever faced and casualties were high. One of those killed, and whose body was never recovered, was John Thomas Moore and his name is on Panel 1 of the Ploegsteert Memorial, a short distance from where he fell.

GUNNER MILES CALVERT
NO. 76751 137TH HEAVY BATTERY
ROYAL GARRISON ARTILLERY
DIED WEDNESDAY 24TH APRIL 1918 AGE 36.

Thomas Calvert, the father of Miles, was a road length man who looked after the roads in the Burtersett area on behalf of the Aysgarth Rural District Council. He and his wife Mary lived at Burtersett, with Miles and their other sons. In 1901, nineteen year old Miles was a cowman on a Burtersett farm, but by the start of the war he was in Liverpool, helping to run one of the many milk houses.

He enlisted in Liverpool on April 15th 1916 and joined the Royal Garrison Artillery, before being sent overseas in November of the same year. For a long time he acted as cook in the officers' mess but at Christmas time 1917 he expressed a wish to go to the guns, which was granted him.

In April, the 137th Heavy Battery was located in the Amiens area and carried out its role of counter-bombardment against enemy positions.

Miles Calvert (Burtersett).

Sadly, news was received by his parents that their son had died from a shell wound received in action on April 24th. The letter was from his CO and stated that he was badly wounded in the head, and became unconscious as he was carried to the dressing station at Boves, just SE of Amiens, where he died shortly after being admitted. "He was always cheerful," says the writer, "and looked on the bright side of things, so that he will be greatly missed by all his comrades."

Miles Calvert is buried in grave C.10. Boves West Communal Cemetery.

It is worth relating that it was during April 1918 that Wensleydale received news of its first and only winner of the Victoria Cross, awarded to a man born in East Witton.

Private Arthur Poulter, VC, aged 24, was the youngest son of the late Robert Poulter, a farmer, of East Witton.

Arthur left home at the age of 14 to work on farms and then at 19 he went to Leeds as a drayman for a firm of malsters and brewers. Later he became a cartman for another employer. Living at Wortley, Leeds, Arthur was married with two children.

He volunteered in March 1916, joining the 1st/4th Battalion West Riding Regiment. Arthur received the VC for most conspicuous bravery when acting as a stretcher bearer at Erquinghem-Lys. On ten occasions on April 10th 1918 he carried badly wounded men on his back to a safer locality through a particulaly heavy artillery and machine-gun barrage. Again, after a withdrawal over the river

Arthur Poulter VC
By permission of the Duke of Wellington's Regiment.

had been ordered, Arthur returned in full view of the enemy, who were advancing, and carried back another man who had been left behind wounded. He bandaged up over 40 men under fire, and his conduct throughout the whole day was a magnificent example to all ranks. On April 25th, whilst attempting another rescue, he was severely wounded to the face when a bullet went in near his ear and out near his eye. He was subsequently invalided out of the Army and went back to live in Leeds.

By the end of April Ludendorff called off the offensive. No breakthrough had been effected and the Channel ports were safe. The cost had been great, another 100,000 British casualties — but again, German casualties were almost as great. Ludendorff's carefully trained and prepared shock troops were sadly depleted, the morale of the survivors badly shaken.

PRIVATE JOSEPH DIXON RAW
(MILITARY MEDAL) NO. 30709 2ND BATTALION
YORKSHIRE REGIMENT
DIED WEDNESDAY 8TH MAY 1918 AGE 21.

Joseph Raw was the youngest son of James Raw and his wife Mary. Although both James and Mary had been born at Melbecks, Swaledale, in 1901 they were living with Joseph and their eldest son Simon in West Burton, where James was a cowman on a local farm.

Before joining up, Joseph was employed as a farm hand by Thomas Lambert of West Burton. Enlisting at Leyburn, he joined the 2nd Battalion Yorkshire Regiment and in September 1916 was at the front.

He was twice recommended for distinction and at the end of April 1918 was awarded the Military Medal for gallantry and for services rendered near St. Quentin from March 21st to the 28th. Sadly, one week later he would be dead.

On May 6th the Battalion was in the Ypres Salient, in the line near Voormezeele, just south of Ypres. The enemy guns were very active, firing many gas shells.

At 3.15a.m. on May 8th the Germans

Joseph Dixon Raw
(West Burton and Aysgarth).

laid down an exceptionally heavy bombardment on the trenches lasting four hours and causing many casualties, while the trenches were practically obliterated.

At 7.15a.m. the Germans made an attack in force upon the Battalion front line and captured it. At 7p.m. a counter-attack was ordered. "C" Company joined in the attack, gaining all the objectives, though at a very high cost, but were forced to withdraw when the Germans attacked at 9p.m.

Amongst the many casualties was Joseph Dixon Raw. He has no known grave and he is commemorated on Panel 52 to 54 and 162A on the Tyne Cot Memorial.

GUNNER JOHN MOORE
NO. 50517 "Y" 24TH TRENCH MORTAR BATTERY
ROYAL FIELD ARTILLERY
DIED WEDNESDAY 22ND MAY 1918 AGE 23.

John was the younger brother of Fred Cockett, who, as we have seen , was killed in action in October 1914. Fred's mother, Elizabeth Cockett, later married Joseph Moore, the Hawes coal merchant and haulier, and sons John and Edward Moore and daughters Mary and Agnes were born.

The death of Gunner John Moore, Trench Mortar Battery, occurred in a London hospital on May 22nd 1918. He had received shrapnel wounds in his back and to his left leg, whilst in action on May 9th. His mother went to London and was with him to the end.

At 19 years, John Moore was one of the first three Hawes lads to volunteer, in August 1914. Owing to pressure on the recruiting offices, he was sent back but he joined up two months later and had been for two years almost incessantly in action.

He was once slightly wounded and had many narrow escapes. His fatal wounds were received in a characteristically daring dash back to fire another volley when he might have escaped the surrounding enemy. His brother, Bombadier Edward Moore, who joined in 1914, had been twice wounded.

The funeral took place at St. Margaret's Church, Hawes, on Saturday May 25th. The body arrived at Hawes by the 1.17p.m. train and was met by a large crowd of towns people and friends from all parts of the district. The coffin,

John Moore (Hawes).

covered by a Union Jack and overlaid with several beautiful wreaths, was proceeded to the church by the Hawes Platoon of Volunteers under the command of Second Lieutenant H.A. Crallon of the Stone House. The "Death March" was played by Hawes Brass Band. Three volleys were fired over the grave and the "Last Post" sounded.

May 27th 1918 saw the third great German offensive on the Rivers Marne and Aisne, mainly against the French positions, but with British regiments defending as well. By May 30th they had reached the Marne but at this point the newly arrived American forces were flung against the nose of the German offensive, holding the bridges, then counter-attacking and driving the Germans back across the Marne.

Throughout June and July further German assaults were repulsed, and on July 18th the Allies went on the offensive themselves on the Aisne and Marne. The initiative had been wrested from the Germans and Ludendorff's gamble to conclude the war successfully, had failed. Allied morale soared as that of the Germans dropped.

Two Wensleydale men were killed on the first day of the new German offensive.

GODFREY METCALFE
NO. 201890 4TH BATTALION YORKSHIRE REGIMENT
DIED MONDAY 27TH MAY 1918 AGE 28.

Godfrey was born in Ellingstring, between East Witton and Masham. His father, William, was from Grewelthorpe and had married Jane, an East Witton girl. William was employed as a stockman on an Ellingstring farm and besides their son Godfrey, they had a younger child, Hilda.

Godfrey was living between Middleham and East Witton when he travelled to enlist at Bedale, joining the 4th Battalion Yorkshire Regiment.

AND
SECOND LIEUTENANT
WILLIAM ARTHUR HESELTINE SMITH
1ST BATTALION EAST YORKSHIRE REGIMENT
DIED MONDAY 27TH MAY 1918.

I have no information about William Smith, whose name is on the West Witton Memorial, except that he was not living in the village in 1901, but arrived some-time before the Great War. William had originally been in action with the 14th Battalion D.L.I. and had won the Military Cross for his conspicuous act of bravery. However, by May 1918 he was with the 1st Battalion East Yorkshire Regiment and second in command of "C" Company.

The 4th Yorkshires and the 1st East Yorkshires, part of the 50th Division which had been so badly mauled at the Battle of the Lys in April, were brought to rest in the "quiet" section on the River Aisne, in the Champagne area of France. On the tranquil Aisne they could recuperate. Large drafts of 18 year old lads arrived from England, only partially trained, and were introduced to life on the front line.

The central backbone of the Aisne's defences was performed by the historic Chemin-Des-Dames ridge, north of the river. Unfortunately, this quiet section of the front had been chosen by the German High Command for their main offensive towards Paris, planned for May 27th, and to be launched with over-whelming superiority in manpower and artillery, a force outnumbering the Allies by five to one.

At 1a.m., May 27th, a terrific storm of fire burst on the Anglo-French line between Soissons and Rheims. High Explosive and gas shells rained down for four hours, followed by smoke shells, which covered the German machine-gunners and snipers. The ordeal was made more trying by crouching, semi-suffocated in gas masks.

Then at 4a.m. the grey waves of German soldiers advanced out of the swirling mist. They reached the crest of the ridge in the centre and this uncovered the flank of the 50th Division, forcing its survivors to fall back down the slope.

By midday the Germans had reached and crossed at most points the River Aisne. The Yorkshires and East Yorkshires, their numbers considerably reduced, held firm in desperate rearguard actions. The Germans were compelled to resort to mass assault in dense waves, with tanks in close support, and creeping barrages.

The Germans began to outflank the British and a rapid retreat was necessary. The Division retired across the Aisne towards the ridge of Guyencourt, where a memorable rearguard action took place. Some

War memorial in Soissons.

of the youngest British troops made a stand alongside some of the oldest French Territorials. Boys of 18 and men of 50, they fought to the death.

On May 27th 1918, somewhere in this hellhole of carnage and desolation, Godfrey Metcalfe and William Smith met their deaths. Their bodies were never recovered and both their names are recorded on the Soissons Memorial. Both Battalions had been decimated during that day's fighting and only continued to resist as composite battalions.

PRIVATE GEORGE ERNEST DAWSON
NO. 22451 1ST BATTALION GRENADIER GUARDS
DIED WEDNESDAY 29TH MAY 1918 AGE 23.

George's father, John William Dawson, was born in Northumberland but came to work at Spennithorne House as the butler for Major General Ingilby. There he met Mary Ann Denison of Spennithorne, who was working as a maid.

They were married at Spennithorne and eventually had eight children. For the main part, Mary lived with the children in Spennithorne while John worked away in various large houses as butler, although they did live together as a family in Ireland when he was working there.

In 1906 John William died and the family returned to Spennithorne. When George Dawson left school he went to work for Groundwaters, the grocery shop in Leyburn.

George volunteered early in the war and joined the 1st Battalion Grenadier Guards. In 1916 he was wounded in the thigh but recovered and returned to France.

By May 1918 they were occupying a sector of the line between Arras and Bapaume. During the whole of that month the Grenadiers were either in the front trenches or in reserve, but when in reserve they were simply targets for the German artillery. Every day there were casualties with the result

George Dawson

that more died or were wounded when in reserve than when in the front line trenches.

On May 17th their position was subjected to a severe bombing by aircraft, with numerous losses. They were bombed with gas shells on May 20th, with even greater casualties, whilst on the 24th more men were wounded by a shell bursting.

It was during this latter period that George Dawson was wounded and taken to Bagneux, near Gezaincourt, Doullens, where he entered the Casualty Clearing Station. However, he did not recover and a few days later, on May 29th, he died from his wounds and is buried in grave 11.G.4. Bagneux British Cemetery.

*** It is of interest that George's brother Walter served in the Royal Navy throughout all the years of the two world wars. He joined the Navy as a boy signaller in March 1914 and was on board H.M.S. "Roxburgh" at Jutland, 1916, yet survived the war. He did not leave the service until May 1939 but went straight back in before war was declared, as a signaller on H.M.S. "Onslow", a destroyer.

On Christmas Eve 1941 the "Onslow" helped escort 576 Commandos in their attack on the island of Vaagso, off Norway.

The "Onslow's Captain, Robert Sherbrooke, received the VC for his actions in the Battle of the Barents Sea, December 1942, when, by laying smokesceens and threatening torpedo attacks, he kept the heavy cruiser "Admiral Hipper" and pocket battleship "Lutzow" away from Convoy JW51B, bound for Murmansk in Russia. The "Onslow", with Walter Dawson on board, was hit repeatedly in this action.

Walter Dawson

PRIVATE THOMAS SARGINSON
NO. 57467 "C" COMPANY 1ST BATTALION
LINCOLNSHIRE REGIMENT
DIED SATURDAY 1ST JUNE 1918 AGE 30.

We have already read about the Sarginson family background at Middleham and the death of Thomas's brother, Sergeant John Sarginson, on the Somme on July 4th 1916.

Thomas was living near his mother Lily in Nelson, Lancashire, when war broke out. However, it was at Richmond that he enlisted and eventually, after serving with the East Lancashire Regiment, was posted to the 1st Battalion Lincolnshire Regiment.

During May 1918 they too found themselves on the banks of the River Aisne, between Soissons and Rheims. When the German attack began on May 27th the Battalion was near Chalons-la-Verguer, which was almost surrounded by wooded country of hills and valleys.

They formed a defensive flank, keeping in touch with some French Territorials nearby, and were just in time to prevent the enemy gaining a foothold in the wood.

By 1p.m. the situation became acute: the enemy had broken through and had completely worked round the left flank. On the right he had occupied Cormicy, where "C" Company (including Thomas Sarginson) and "D" Company, after

...~~shing three successive attacks, had been compelled to withdraw to another

~~my was held until 8p.m. At that hour, however, a
"C" and "D" Companies on the right were hard-
~~rounded. Only a quick withdrawal could save them.
~~ard which kept the enemy at bay, the Battalion was
~~her ground NE of Pevy. The time was now 1a.m. on

~~rginson had been severely wounded during "C"
~~as admitted to the Casualty Clearing Station, where he
~~s buried in grave O.6. in Sissonne British Cemetery,
~~ns.

~~cene for the next fatality from the dale.

PRIVATE GEORGE WILLIAM CLARKE
NO. 235458 9TH BATTALION
YORK AND LANCASTER REGIMENT
DIED SATURDAY 15TH JUNE 1918 AGE 24.

In 1901, 7 year old George William Clarke was living at the home of his grandmother, Margaret, a widow, in Horsehouse, Coverdale. In the same household
was his 11 year old brother Peter, aunty Margaret Elizabeth and Mary Clarke, a
39 year old charwoman, who was possibly his mother. They had all been born in
Carlton Highdale and were part of the farming family from Middle Farm,
Woodale.

By 1915, George was working in Leyburn, from which place he enlisted and
joined the 9th Battalion York and Lancaster Regiment, in which he became a
member of a Lewis gun team.

At the Battle of Caporetto in October/November 1917, the Italians had
suffered a severe reversal at the hands of the Austrians, losing 275,000
prisoners, 2500 guns and 40,000 killed.

French and British reinforcements were moved in during November 1917,
with the 9th Battalion arriving on December 3rd and moving to the Asiago
Plateau sector of the front at the end of March 1918.

When, on June 15th 1918, the Austrians attacked from Mt. Grappa to Canove,
the Battalion was in the front line. A patrol of one officer and 20 men
unfortunately held on too long. Their post had been heavily bombarded and
overwhelmed by the enemy's infantry.

At 8.30a.m. the Austrian infantry advanced in artillery formation SW of

Asiago and Edelweiss Spur. They gained the shelter of woods but when they crossed the open ground the assault was stopped dead by the Battalion's fire. Over 100 of the enemy were killed in front of the wire, and many wounded. As the day wore on the Austrian attack was exhausted and the situation steadily improved.

However, during the severe fighting earlier in the day, George William Clarke had been killed. His body is buried in grave 1.D.12. Granezza British Cemetery, 9km. south of Asiago.

PRIVATE WALTER EDWARD WILKINSON
NO. 39259 5TH BATTALION
KING'S OWN YORKSHIRE LIGHT INFANTRY
DIED SATURDAY 20TH JULY 1918 AGE 19.

Walter Edward, or Eddie as he was known, was born at Wilson Yard, Grove Square, Leyburn, the home of Walter Wilkinson, the Leyburn saddler, and his wife Elizabeth. Their other children were Thomas Alfred, Cyril, Ernest, Ike, Cissie, Clare and William. The saddler's shop was on Richmond Road and their business continued into the 1930's.

Eddie enlisted at Richmond and joined the 5th Battalion K.O.Y.L.I. His brother William was an army chaplain during the war and was known as "Padre Willie".

In July 1918 the Battalion was to be found in the Marne area, the scene of Ludendorff's Offensive of May 27th, which had already resulted in the death of three Wensleydale men. This Offensive had ground to a halt by July 17th.

Between July 18th and August 5th, the French and Americans, with some support from the 62nd

Walter Wilkinson (Leyburn).

(West Riding Division), rolled the Germans back all along the line, despite their desperate resistance.

The 5th Battalion was involved in this counter-offensive and on July 20th, two days into the battle, Eddie Wilkinson was killed. On July 14th the Battalion had travelled by train, bus, and night route march to the Bois de Pourcy area of the Marne, ready for their attack on the German salient on the 20th.

The barrage opened at 8a.m. and in densely wooded country the Battalion began to work through the woods, which were thickly studded with machine-gun posts. The firing from the drive of a nearby chateau held up the centre company and "wiped out" many of the officers and men.

The left company, at a higher level of the wooded hills, also suffered severely and the whole of its contact party were shot down. It had to withdraw to the edge of the wood again. On the right, an officer and party of ten men advanced, five of whom were killed and four wounded, but they forced the enemy to leave the little wood. The position was then consolidated along the NE bank of the chateau lake.

One of the men to be killed in these series of attacks through the woods was Eddie Wilkinson. He is buried in grave 1.J.5. Courmas British Cemetery, 11km. SW of Rheims.

On August 8th 1918 Field Marshall Haig launched the first phase of the great Amiens Offensive against the Germans, who were caught off guard. Troops advanced without preliminary bombardment, preceded by tanks, and bit deep through a dense fog. More than 15,000 prisoners and 400 guns were captured. On August 11th Haig paused to regroup. General Ludendorff stated that August 8th had been the "Black Day" of the German Army.

However, on that very day, a man from Hawes was killed during the opening of the Offensive, in an action of rare manoeuvrability.

PRIVATE DAVID WILLIAM HARKER
NO. 16723 7TH DRAGOON GUARDS
DIED THURSDAY 8TH AUGUST 1918 AGE 26.

David's father, Thomas Harker, was born at Muker, Swaledale, and was employed as a lead miner. As the industry declined he concentrated instead on farming as an occupation. In 1889 he married Margaret Metcalfe from Hawes and by 1891 they were farming at Midwiddale Farm, Swineley, near Hawes, with three sons and two daughters eventually making up the family. Thomas died in 1899 and a few years before the Great War, Margaret went to live at 14

Pilgrim Street, Nelson, Lancashire.

It was from this address that David went to enlist at Ormskirk. With his farming background and his familiarity with horses he became a Trooper in the 7th Dragoon Guards, Household Cavalry.

At 10a.m. on August 8th 1918, the 7th Dragoon Guards left Cachy, 5 miles east of Amiens, by Cavalry Track to Ignacourt, crossed the tiny River Luce and formed up in the valley about 11a.m.

The Regiment moved forward with a double Advanced Guard at 11.10a.m., the objective being the SE end of Cayeux Wood, two miles away. One sub-section of the 7th Machine Gun Squadron followed in the rear.

By 11.45a.m. "A" Squadron advanced via Square Wood, which was cleared with little opposition. They then galloped the Angular Copse in the valley and two small copses, killing some Germans and taking 25 men prisoner and capturing 4 heavy machine-guns and 2 heavy long guns.

David William Harker
(Widdale, Hawes).

Meeting with heavy machine-gun fire from the SE, they then occupied the side of Angle Wood, dismounted. At the same time "D" Squadron galloped the SW end of Cayeux Wood, coming under heavy machine-gun fire from the south, but capturing 6 machine-guns, 14 prisoners and an abandoned battery in the wood.

At the sight of a good number of Germans retiring, the Regimental Scouts and part of "C" Squadron charged them. They got amongst the retreating enemy and captured one prisoner. "C" Squadron, having had nearly all their horses shot, brought a Hotchkiss Rifle into action and formed a defensive flank. At 12.30p.m. a troop advanced dismounted to the final objective and remained there until relieved by Canadian Infantry. At this position they came under very heavy fire.

At 10p.m. the Regiment was sent up dismounted in answer to a SOS call in support of the Canadian Infantry but at 11.30p.m. they were ordered to join the horses, as the situation was quiet.

During August 8th 9 officers had been wounded, 5 men killed, 29 horses killed, 22 wounded and 37 were missing. David William Harker was one of the

5 men killed. As his body was never found his name is commemorated on Panel 2 of the Vis-En-Artois Memorial, 10km. SE of Arras. All 9000 men recorded had no known graves and were killed in the "Advance to Victory" between August 8th and November 11th.

The second stage of the Amiens Offensive was launched on August 21st and 22nd and lasted till September 4th. Three more men from the dale paid with their lives on these opening days. Ludendorff ordered a general withdrawal from both the Lys Salient in Flanders and the Amiens area. The entire German situation deteriorated, necessitating retirement to the final position — the Hindenburg Line. By this time, September 4th, Haig had expended his reserves and could not further exploit his victory.

PRIVATE FREDERICK HOLMES
NO. 300131 1ST/7TH BATTALION
LANCASHIRE FUSILIERS
DIED WEDNESDAY 21ST AUGUST 1918 AGE 29.

Fred Holmes was born at Leyburn, the youngest child of Leonard Holmes, a gardener, and Annie Holmes, living at Ivy Cottage, Leyburn. Fred eventually married and he and his wife Mary lived at Hetton Villas, Leyburn. He enlisted in his home town, joining the Lancashire Fusiliers, and by the time of his death in 1918, his father Leonard had passed away.

By August 16th 1918 the 1st/7th Battalion was in front of the village of Serre, on the Somme, ready for the second stage in the Amiens Offensive. The task of the Battalion on August 21st was to capture the Beauregard Dovecot, on high ground, overlooking the village of Miraumont, north of Albert.

At 8.55a.m. "A" and "B" Companies went forward through the thick mist towards their objectives, which they succeeded in taking with the exception of the Dovecot, where the presence of many German machine-guns forbade any close approach.

The great heat on the 21st caused the mist to rise and some men found themselves on their own and advancing on a German field battery, which opened fire on them at point blank range. A gallant attempt was made to hold a position in shell holes but the enemy was in strong force and a fierce counter-attack practically wiped out the isolated party.

At 2a.m., the following day, "A" Company succeeded in taking the Dovecot, but Fred Holmes had been killed the previous day whilst taking part in the failed attempt. His grave, 11.D.8., is found in Queen's Cemetery, Bucquoup, 15km. south of Arras.

LIEUTENANT HENRY WILD (MILITARY CROSS) 14TH BATTALION NORTHUMBERLAND FUSILIERS, BUT ATTACHED TO THE 1ST LINCOLNSHIRE REGIMENT DIED WEDNESDAY 21ST AUGUST 1918.

I cannot be totally sure whether I have the correct information about his background, but I believe that Henry Wild was the son of Henry Wild senior, hotel keeper of "The White Hart", Hawes. Henry junior was born at Brough, but by 1901 the family were at the White Hart, with 6 year old Henry the youngest of six children.

By August 1918 he was a Lieutenant attached to the 1st Lincolnshire Regiment, having already been decorated for bravery. The Battalion found itself alongside Fred Holmes's Battalion, near the village of Miraumont, north of Albert, on August 21st.

Their objective was the village of Beaucourt. At 3a.m. they assembled on the road between Beaumont Hamel and Serre and reached a ravine without opposition. But now hostile machine-gun fire came from a line of German trenches ahead.

"C" Company was then sent down the ravine to attack NE through the Bois d'Hollande but were held up by machine-gun fire. Other Companies were ordered to capture a road running NW from the southern outskirts of Miraumont and in this they succeeded, before consolidating.

Thus the Battalion had helped to take Beaucourt and clear the north bank of the River Ancre. This success was not without its cost and one of the casualties was Henry Wild.His body is buried close to that of Fred Holmes of Leyburn, in grave 1.N.2. Queen's Cemetery, Bucquoup.

LANCE CORPORAL CARL DUGDALE MILNER NO. 36894 EAST SURREY REGIMENT POSTED TO 1ST/23RD BATTALION LONDON REGIMENT DIED THURSDAY 22 AUGUST 1918 AGE 32.

The Milners arrived in Wensleydale in the mid 19th Century when stonemason George Milner moved to Bainbridge from Leeds to help build the Northallerton to Garsdale stretch of the railway. He married a local girl, Martha Dugdale, and settled down. George's initials can be seen on the bridges he helped to build, over which the line crossed the River Ure, on its way down the dale.

At 14 years, his son Christopher began a six year apprenticeship with James Wheldon and Sons, drapers and mercers, in Northallerton. He married Priscilla Collett, from Northallerton, and began his own business from his house at

Bainbridge, using a handcart and back-pack to go round the district selling clothes to farming families and the navvies working on the railway.

In May 1882 he opened a shop on Bridge Street in Hawes, selling clothes and household furnishings (at the time of writing it is an antique shop). Five sons were born, with Percy taking over the Hawes shop, Cyril opening another in Leyburn, Harry one in Kirkby Stephen, whilst Tom looked after the four horses required for transportation.

Carl Dugdale Milner, the third son of Christopher and Priscilla, entered the London Joint Stock Bank at Rotherham at the age of 17. Afterwards he was employed at Richmond, Selby, Settle and Durham and finally became the manager

Carl Dugdale Milner (Hawes).

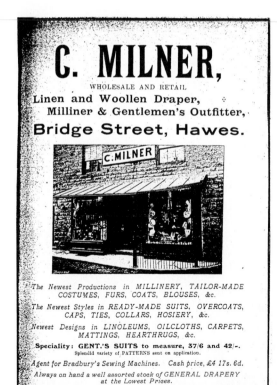

of the Barnoldswick branch at the early age of 27. It was from Barnoldswick that he enlisted in January 1917, being posted to the RFC, followed by the Tank Corps, the East Surrey Regiment and finally the London Regiment. At the time of his death two brothers were also serving overseas and another was in training.

Carl went overseas in March 1918 with the London Regiment and on August 22nd was involved in the British First Army's insertion in the Amiens Offensive.

He was killed by shell fire in a difficult operation on that first day of battle. There is no known grave, but his name is found on Panel 6 of the Vis-En-Artois Memorial.

SECOND LIEUTENANT HERBERT ALLEN
56 SQUADRON ROYAL AIR FORCE
DIED SATURDAY 10TH AUGUST 1918 AGE 19.

Herbert was the youngest son of Elijah and Alice Allen of Rose Cottage, Gayle, with two more sons, Thomas and Harry, completing the family. Alice was from Kendal.

Elijah ran a grocery shop in Gayle, whilst coal was delivered after being brought in by rail to Hawes Station. Eventually their son Thomas ran another shop in Hawes that sold animal feed to the local farmers. Elijah also kept a Livery Stables at Gayle, employing three men, with conveyances for hire and a horse drawn hearse available for funerals. The horses were looked after by Harry Allen.

Herbert attended Yorebridge Grammar School and when he left he became a motor mechanic, with a great interest in motor bikes and cars.

Herbert Allen (Gayle and Hawes).

Elijah Allen's shop at Gayle, near Hawes, prior to the Great War.
Elijah is standing with gun and dog, second from the right.

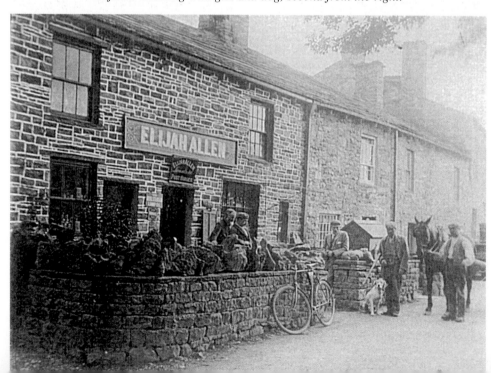

Elijah Allen on his father Thomas's conveyance at Gayle, 1895.

Inside Elijah Allen's livery stables at Gayle
(much later known as the Bus Garage, when used by United Automobile Service's buses).

His older brother, Harry, enlisted in the army and helped to look after army horses in France and Belgium. Enlisting in the army in 1917, Herbert briefly joined the Durham Light Infantry but was transferred to the Royal Flying Corps. On October 22nd 1917 he joined the Cadet Wing of 2 Squadron. By the early weeks of 1918 he was training at the Central Flying School at Upavon, Wiltshire, where, on March 7th 1918 he was commissioned as a Second Lieutenant. By April 26th he was flying solo and he graduated from Upavon on May 29th. Six weeks later he had joined 56 Squadron and, equipped with SE5a fighter planes, he made his first flight overseas on July 4th and was at Doullens airfield by the 5th.

On July 16th he was over the lines, learning the lay of the countryside and also attempting to find where Harry was stationed so that he could drop him a message, but with no luck.

July 26th saw him over the lines at Bapaume on his first offensive patrol and being fired on by anti-aircraft fire.

For the next three days he was engaged in bomb-dropping practice, for, with the Allies beginning to push the Germans back in their "Advance to Victory", the

Herbert Allen as a cadet, in training for the Royal Flying Corps 1917 (later RAF).

*Pilots and ground crew of No.1 Squadron RAF with the S.E.5a fighters,
near St. Omer, France, on 3rd July 1918.*

RAF was being deployed to bomb the German lines.

Herbert took part in his first dawn patrol on July 30th but the mist was too thick, whilst on the next day he had to leave the formation due to a "dud" engine.

On patrol between Arras and Albert, six Fokker Biplanes were spotted, whilst on August 8th, between Estrey and Albert the Squadron attacked 18 Fokkers and Herbert reported that he shot at one. Herbert's final entry into his log book is on

S.E.5a's of 56 Squadron line up at London Colney ready to fly to France 7th April 1917.

August 9th, the day before his death, when he reports that over Albert and Estrey they chased off a Fokker two-seater and came up against plenty of "flaming onions" and aircraft.

Whilst on a bombing mission over the enemy lines on August 10th, in support of ground troops advancing in the Amiens Offensive, Herbert Allen's plane went missing. Official notification of his death only came to his parents on August 26th, 1920, two years later.

His name is commemorated on the Arras Flying Services Memorial, honouring more than 1000 airmen killed on the Western Front, who have no known grave.

The following letter, posted by Herbert's mother on the day of his death, was never received by him: "My dear Herbert, Thank you very much for your letter of the 4th. I am sorry to hear you say that your nerves are

German Squadrons were highly mobile units, transferred from place to place as they were needed. They came to be called Circuses because of the temporary camps which sprang up wherever they were based.

going. You must keep them up as well as you can and get all the rest you can, which is very necessary in your case. I see from this morning's papers there are many British machines missing. Hope yours isn't one of them. Do keep sending field cards or anything to let us know you are all right. I guess you have some experiences to relate when you come back, which I hope is not long. We finished our own hay time yesterday, but we have to get Kit's yet. Your father is there mowing today. I am very busy getting all the dinners off. With much love my dear boy and many kisses."

On August 18th they received a letter from the Major commanding 56 Squadron: "I am very sorry indeed to have to tell you that your son was missing after an engagement with a large number of enemy scouts on August 10th.

Nothing whatever was seen of him at the time as all others in the fight were so busily engaged themselves.

Though he had been with us only a short time he was very popular. He had already proved himself to be a skilful and dashing fighter. I am making all enquiries possible about him and shall let you know immediately I hear anything definite. But this may take some months. It is more than probable that he is safe and well, having been forced to land behind the German lines. In the anxiety of the suspense you will experience, we offer our deepest sympathy."

The glimmer of hope was increased when a letter arrived 5 days after the Armistice reporting that he was probably a POW. In 1919 and 1920 both parents continued writing through the official channels, seeking information about his possible survival as a POW, but in August 1920 came official notification of his death.

PRIVATE GEORGE STAVELEY
NO. 29408 32ND BATTALION
MACHINE GUN CORPS (INFANTRY)
DIED MONDAY 2ND SEPTEMBER 1918 AGE 22.

We have already seen that two of George's brothers had been killed during the war, Lister in September 1916 and Edmund in June 1917 (see the relevant chapters for family background).

Living at 3 Beech Street, Padiham, near Burnley, George enlisted from that town with his younger brother Lister in December 1915, both joining the Royal Fusiliers. They were then both transferred to the Machine Gun Corps.

George was involved in the first phase of the Amiens Offensive, but was badly wounded at the start of the second phase, beginning on August 21st. From the Casualty Clearing Station he was transferred to the town of Rouen, one of the main hospital complexes for the Western Front.

Within Rouen were one British Red Cross, eight General and five Stationary hospitals as well as Number 2 Convalescent Depot. Despite these facilities, George Staveley died from his wounds on September 2nd and was buried in grave R.11.T.9. St. Sever Cemetery Extension, Rouen.

PRIVATE JAMES WILCE
NO. 28221 15TH BATTALION HAMPSHIRE REGIMENT
DIED TUESDAY 3RD SEPTEMBER 1918.

The Wilce family came to live in Harmby from Newport, Monmouthshire, when the men folk found that work in the Welsh coal fields was at a low ebb. William, their father, came to live and farm at Woodlands Farm, Harmby. His children were William, Bernard, Agnes, Ted and James.

The family was to suffer greatly during the war when James was killed and William, Bernard and Ted were badly wounded. William and Bernard had been in the regular army, with the former fighting in the Boer War with the South Wales Borderers. He went out to France in 1914, losing a leg and receiving damage to both hands. Ted was gassed and Bernard lost both his legs.

James Wilce enlisted at Leyburn and joined the 15th Battalion Hampshire Regiment. It was decided that on August 9th a small advance would be made in the Kemmel sector, south of Ypres, the 15th Battalion being selected to straighten out a nasty salient near La Clytte.

On the left, a strongly held trench, in which two machine-guns were causing damage, was rushed, the whole garrison being accounted for. An officer and 7 men captured a strong point,

William Charles Wilce,
brother of James Wilce
(Spennithorne and Harmby).

killing or taking nearly 50 enemy. Another officer promptly attacked another post with only 5 men supporting and captured its garrison of 12 soldiers and two machine-guns. Casualties had been heavy however. Over 40 men were killed or missing, whilst 110 men were wounded.

James Wilce was one of those wounded and received medical attention , well behind the lines. Despite the care and attention, James died three weeks later and was buried in grave 11.G.17. in Esquelbecq Military Cemetery, France, close to the Belgian border.

James's brother William, severely wounded in the war, learned the new trade of basket weaving at Chapel Allerton and was fitted with an artificial leg at Roehampton. Having left Spennithorne to live in Railway Street, Leyburn, with his second wife, he became well-known for his basket making.

The baskets were made in a lean to shed, using canes stored in a large tin bath. Besides the usual products, butter baskets were made for local farmers, cane chairs and seats were produced and special lily baskets were made on order for Lady Bolton, with many of the finished articles being hung on a hook for display at the front door of their house on Railway Street.

PRIVATE WILLIAM BANKS
NO. 41035 1ST BATTALION
EAST YORKSHIRE REGIMENT
DIED TUESDAY 10TH SEPTEMBER 1918 AGE 19.

William Banks senior, father of William, married Margaret Annie Bell from Nappa House and set up their home at Cringley, Askrigg. Children George, William, Alice, Fred, Peggy and John were born. William was in business as a grocer and supplier of cattle feed. The shop was next door and their warehouse, into which their horse and cart could be backed, was where the Rowan Tree Restaurant is today.

Enlisting at Richmond, William junior joined the 1st Battalion East Yorkshire Regiment and in September 1918 they found themselves taking part in the early stages of the "Advance to Victory".

On September 10th they were at Sorel, near Gouzeaucourt, between Peronne and Cambrai, ready to attack a series of enemy trenches. The bombardment was delayed and due to the darkness, the companies found themselves out of position.

The attack went in a northerly direction rather than to the NE. The enemy

George Banks, brother of William,
Northumberland Fusiliers,
standing on the right

Banks's shop in Askrigg main street can be seen at the bottom right, with the door to the warehouse immediately above (now the site of the Rowen Tree Restaurant).

anticipated the attack and was fully prepared to meet it. The right company met with very heavy machine-gun fire, and, as they had lost the barrage, had to withdraw.

The left company went too much to its left and the enemy counter-attacked and captured 20 of them. One officer and five men were killed, two officers and 36 men were missing.

William Banks was one of those killed and his body was buried in grave 1V.D.2. in Gouzeaucourt New British Cemetery.

During late September and early October the German retirement continued and the British Army made considerable progress, while the French were equally successful in hastening the retreat at St. Quentin and Soissons. In October the Germans found the retirement more and more difficult, for during September they had lost 250,000 prisoners and an immense number of guns. Their retirement had brought them to their last major defence, the Hindenburg Line, and the next two months were spent by the Allies storming these formidable positions, which were resolutely defended by the German Army.

GUNNER JOHN MOORE METCALFE
NO. 111935 "A" BATTERY 161ST BRIGADE
ROYAL FIELD ARTILLERY
DIED THURSDAY 3RD OCTOBER 1918 AGE 23.

John Metcalfe, or Jackie as he was known, was born in Settle to a single woman. His mother married later and lived in Liverpool, but Jackie was brought up from infancy with his grandfather, John Metcalfe, a stockman, and grandmother Agnes Metcalfe, at The Holme, Hawes. One of the quietest and unassuming of lads, Jackie was a favourite with his comrades. For four years prior to joining up he was a member of Hawes Church Choir and Brass Band.

He enlisted at Leyburn in October 1915 and joined up in December of that year. He went overseas with the Royal Field Artillery but was attached for two years to the Motor Transport Army Service Corps. Jackie was badly gassed whilst with a Trench Mortar Battery and was invalided home but went overseas again in July 1918 with "A" Battery RFA

John Moore Metcalfe (Jackie),
grandson of John Metcalfe.

The Hindenburg Line ran west of the village of St. Quentin. The nearby canal ran under the village in a tunnel 5km. long, and barges in the tunnel were used to shelter German reserves, whilst another tunnel at nearby Bellinglise served the same purpose

From September 29th to October 3rd 1918 the Battle of the St. Quentin Canal was fought, with the North Midland Division storming the Hindenburg Line at Bellinglise.

Jackie Metcalfe's Battery supported their attack, but on October 3rd he was killed instantly by a shell. His body lies in grave 111.1.1 in Bellincourt British Cemetery, 13km. north of St. Quentin.

PRIVATE JOHN CYRIL COLLETT HANDLEY
NO. 307623 12TH BATTALION TANK CORPS
DIED MONDAY 7TH OCTOBER 1918 AGE 24.

The Handley family was of long standing in Middleham. John's father, John Collett senior, was by 1901 a gas fitter and stoker at the gas house yard at the bottom of North Road, Middleham, supplying gas for the whole of the town. Married to Hannah, they lived across the road from the gas works, with children John, Raymond, Bob and Roland.

The gas works was owned by the Wensleydale Coal and Coke Company and John Cyril Collett Handley helped his father in providing gas. In the yard was one large gas cylinder that rose when full and sank back when empty.

Coal was brought in and gas and tar produced when it was "cooked". It was John's job to go around Middleham and light the gas mantles on the street lamps by means of a light on a long pole.

John would turn his hand to anything, for he was interested in the mechanical and engineering side of the business. He earned extra money by painting and decorating and kept rowing boats for hire on the River Ure, including a ten-seater craft.

His wife Jean had arrived in Middleham as cook for the retired Colonel Hammond at Castle Hill House. By the time John was killed in the war, the couple had one child, named John.

John C.C. Handley's brothers, Robert and Raymond, served in the Royal Navy during the Great War, but John enlisted at Richmond and because of his interest in things mechanical, he drove and maintained heavy lorries for the Royal Flying Corps.

By late 1917 the Tank Corps was short of drivers and asked for volunteers. John began training on the Mark V tanks and during September and October 1918 was at the forefront of the assault on the retreating German forces, serving with the 12th Battalion Tank Corps.

An advance was resumed in the vicinity of Havrincourt, SW of Cambrai. On October 7th they crossed the Canal in the vicinity of a wood but the Germans counter-attacked against "A" and "C" Companies. German tanks were put out of action or driven off but two of "A" Company's tanks were hit by German tank fire.

One of these tanks was driven by John Handley and he was killed in the action. He is buried nearby in grave 1V.B.9. in Anneux British Cemetery, near Cambrai.

PRIVATE WILLIAM (BILLY) MITTON
NO. 24372 1ST BATTALION GRENADIER GUARDS
DIED TUESDAY 15TH OCTOBER 1918 AGE 38.

William Mitton
(Gayle and Hawes).

"Billy" Mitton was a cousin of Ralph Alderson, who we saw was killed in March 1918. Billy's father, William Mitton, was the Hawes joiner and a farmer who lived with his wife Sarah and children William, Robert and Mary at Town Head. After leaving school, Billy helped his father in the joinery business.

He joined up with three other comrades, including cousin Ralph, in November 1915 and all were drafted into the Grenadier Guards. Standing over six feet and of fine physique, Billy Mitton was a high spirited, large hearted, jovial man. As was the case with his cousin Ralph, Billy also became a stretcher bearer.

By October 11th 1918 the 1st Battalion was near Bevillers, east of Cambrai. The country was quite open with little cover. However, they were met by heavy machine-gun fire from an orchard, which was rushed and taken. All this time the shelling was heavy and several men were hit by fragments.

October 12th and 13th proved very trying for all troops in the forward positions on account of the continual shelling, as the Germans had excellent observation and were very accurate in their shooting.

One post was rushed by a party of 80 Germans under cover of an intense trench mortar barrage and only one Grenadier escaped. The casualties during these three days of action were 3 officers wounded, 11 men killed, 3 died of wounds, 45 were wounded and 17 were missing.

Billy Mitton was severely wounded by a shell burst and died two days later, on October 15th. He is buried in grave 1.G.21. in Beugny Cemetery, 19km. SW of Cambrai.

PRIVATE HAROLD MOORE
NO. 60619 9TH BATTALION YORKSHIRE REGIMENT
DIED THURSDAY 24TH OCTOBER 1918 AGE 20.

Harold Moore was the second youngest in the family of 10 children belonging to Richard and Mary Moore. In 1901 they were living at Mirkpot Farm near Snaizholme, on the Hawes–Ingleton road, where Richard was a farmer and stonemason. By 1914, however, they were living at Catriggs Farm, between the River Ure and the main road running out of Hawes towards Bainbridge.

Harold had enlisted at Leyburn in May 1918 and only arrived in France to join the 9th Battalion Yorkshire Regiment on October 11th, just a few days before he received his fatal wounds.

Harold Moore (Hawes).

*Sapper J. H. Moore (R.E.),
brother of Harold Moore
(Catriggs Farm).*

As Harold joined his Battalion, it had just come out of the front line action, moving back to Premont, where the surrounding villages provided them with a wonderful welcome after years of German occupation.

A week later, whilst the Battalion was involved in capturing a machine-gun post in a wooded area, Harold Moore was one of a number of casualties, being severely wounded. He died from his wounds on October 24th and is buried in grave 1.B.10. Premont British Cemetery, 20km. SE of Cambrai.

By mid October 1918 a German retreat all along the line became necessary. Between October 17th and November 11th a renewed British assault advanced towards the Rivers Sambre and Scheldt. At the same time the Belgians and British began to move again in Flanders. The German Army began to crack.

PRIVATE HAROLD THOMAS WRIGHT
NO. 64933 9TH BATTALION
KING'S OWN YORKSHIRE LIGHT INFANTRY
DIED THURSDAY 24TH OCTOBER 1918.

I have no information on Harold Wright's background except to say that he was born in Nottinghamshire and enlisted in Sheffield. However I believe he could have been working on the Danby Estate and living within the parish of Thornton Steward by 1914. He joined the 9th Battalion K.O.Y.L.I. and is commemorated on the village war memorial.

On October 10th 1918 the men were comfortably billeted in Walincourt, SE of Cambrai, and in the evening the Battalion band played in the village band stand.

By October 22nd they had moved through Inchy to an attack assembly point near Neuvilly, north of Le Cateau, and advanced on the 23rd, one objective after another being taken, up to Vendegies, in this open type of warfare.

The volume of enemy artillery and machine-gun fire had been considerable, especially around the village of Ovillers, where there were many casualties. Colonel Greenwood rushed one machine-gun post single handed, killing or capturing the occupants.

A counter-attack was repulsed, whereupon the Battalion followed up the retreating enemy, whose positions were stormed and 150 prisoners, 8 machine-guns and one field gun captured.

On October 24th, the day of Harold's death, the Battalion advance was continued up to Poix-du-Nord, near Englefontaine, having attacked one position at 4a.m. and a further one at 4p.m.

After his death Harold Wright was buried in grave D.46. in nearby Englefontaine British Cemetery.

PRIVATE WILLIAM EDMUND BUSHBY
NO. 82230 20TH BATTALION DURHAM LIGHT INFANTRY
DIED SATURDAY 2ND NOVEMBER 1918 AGE 19.

Edmund Bushby, father of William, was a general labourer who lived with his wife Mary and children Margaret and William near Valley House, West Burton.

William was working in the Ulverston area, near Barrow-in-Furness, when he enlisted in the 20th Battalion D.L.I. At some stage during his service with the Battalion, William, together with his commanding officer and four other men, were awarded the Croix de Guerre by the French for bravery on the field of battle.

By November 1st, just ten days before the end of the Great War, the Battalion was advancing strongly across Belgium and had reached the River Scheldt at Kerkhove, east of Coutrai.

The last few days of October had been spent on the southern outskirts of Courtrai. Some shops were open and an abandoned German cinema was used for entertainment.

William Edmund Bushby
(West Burton and Aysgarth).

On the night of November 2nd a party of the 20th Battalion succeeded in crossing the River Scheldt by a broken bridge. It was not an easy passage and the patrol had to be withdrawn at daylight, but it is believed that these were the first British troops to cross the river.

The enemy had not been too active during these days but at dawn and dusk he put down a barrage on the main road and drenched the surrounding country with mustard gas and tear shells. 4 men were killed and 15 wounded.

William Bushby was one of those killed and is buried in grave V.C.4. Vichte Military Cemetery, 13km. east of Courtrai.

COMPANY SERGEANT MAJOR JOSEPH DAYKIN
NO. 236161 9TH BATTALION
WEST YORKSHIRE REGIMENT
DIED 4TH NOVEMBER 1918 AGE 36.

The Daykin family arrived at Manor Farm in Bellerby around 1909. Jonathan Daykin, the head of the family, was a widower who had been born at Muker, and was living at Manor Farm with his children Isabella, Mary, Hannah, Joseph, Elizabeth and Ethel, all born in Swaledale.

Early in the war, Joseph travelled to enlist at York and joined the 9th Battalion West Yorkshire Regiment, in which unit he rose to the rank of Company Sergeant Major.

In Autumn 1918, Joseph arrived on leave at Manor Farm in order to marry his fiancee, Miriam Mawer from Studda Farm and sister of James Mawer, who had been killed in September 1917. Little did she realise that she would never see her husband again, for, a few weeks later, he too was killed.

By November 3rd 1918, with only days to go before the war would finally end, the Battalion was making steady progress in its advance eastwards into France, as they pushed hard against the retreating German forces.

They were 10km. east of Valenciennes and little opposition was met from enemy infantry but opposing batteries were very active. They were ordered to dig in on rising ground forward of the railway between Curgies and Jenlain.

They continued the advance at dawn, moving forward through thickly wooded country and the River Aunelle was crossed.

Joseph Daykin (Bellerby).

Le Triez was cleared, with a number of prisoners being secured and many civilians in the village were released. The advance continued towards Roisin, but failure of the Division on the right to get into line put the right flank "in the air".

A retirement was carried out to a sunken road on the outskirts of the village, during which many casualties occurred. Heavy shelling took place till dusk, causing further casualties.

During that one day's action 18 men had been killed, 63 wounded and 41 were missing.

Joseph Daykin was one of the men killed and he was buried in grave A.35. in Sebourg British Cemetery, France, 10km. east of Valenciennes.

Joseph was the last serviceman from Wensleydale to be killed in action before the Armistice came into force on November 11th 1918. He had survived years of danger on the battlefield, only to be killed with 7 days of the war remaining.

PRIVATE GEORGE CHARLTON
ROYAL ARMY SERVICE CORPS
DIED 1918

I am disappointed that I have been unable to find out about George Charlton, both militarily and from the point of view of his home background. Four soldiers with the name George Charlton were killed during the Great War and one of these died in 1918. However, he was not serving in the Royal Army Service Corps and so is unlikely to be the one I am attempting to find out about.

All that I can say is that George Charlton had close connections to Aysgarth parish when he went off to war and was eventually killed in 1918. George's name is inscribed on Aysgarth churchyard gatepost war memorial and is honoured in this book in the same way as all of those whose stories have been discovered.

Inspired by the Communists and sparked by a mutiny of the German High Seas Fleet, disorder, revolts and mutinies flared inside Germany between October 29th and November 10th. A new Socialist government took power and proclaimed a republic on November 9th, whilst the Kaiser fled to Holland on the 10th.

A German delegation negotiated an armistice at Compiegne, France, at 5a.m. on November 11th and hostilities ceased at 11a.m. After nearly four and a half years of fighting the war had come to an end.

However, a few days after the Armistice two more men would die abroad from wounds received, whilst others had died in England during 1918 or would succumb to their wounds during 1919 and the early 1920's. Altogether, the number of men from Wensleydale who died between 1918 and the late 1920's and whose names are on the various war memorials throughout the dale totalled 65.

GUNNER TIMOTHY PERCIVAL
NO. 771813 63RD TRENCH MORTAR BATTERY
ROYAL FIELD ARTILLERY
DIED SATURDAY 16TH NOVEMBER 1918 AGE 28.

Timothy Percival was born at Carperby in 1889 and by 1901 was living there with his widowed mother, Elizabeth, a farmer, and his older brother William.

He saw action in the war with a trench mortar battery, both in the Ypres Salient in 1917 and in the "Advance to Victory" in 1918.

On one occasion, whilst on leave in Carperby, he mentioned that with his luck in the war so far, he believed that no German bullet would stop him. With only weeks to go before the conclusion to the war, however, he was wounded and taken to a hospital near Cambrai.

The problem was worsened by the onset of pneumonia, which was prevalent at this time, and he died on November 16th . Timothy Percival is buried in grave 111.A.26. in Cambrai East Military Cemetery.

DRIVER EDGAR SPENSLEY
NO. 2/1202 NEW ZEALAND FIELD ARTILLERY
DIED SATURDAY 23RD NOVEMBER 1918 AGE 29.

Edgar's father, Christopher Spensley, was born at Carperby in 1857, into a farming family. He married his wife, Sarah, a London girl, and by 1881 they were in Liverpool, where three of their eleven children were born. Christopher was a cowkeeper in the city, running a milk house at the end of the street.

They returned to live at Craken House, Harmby, a smallholding, where Christopher was a farmer and cattle dealer, gradually becoming one of the largest dealers in cattle and sheep in Yorkshire. He was a keen supporter of Leyburn Show, where, for numerous years, he was one of the judges. Before the Great War began he had bought Eastfield Lodge in Leyburn as his "town house".

Edgar Spensley was born at Harmby but before the Great War he emigrated to

Edgar Spensley of Harmby, standing on the left.

New Zealand with two other dalesmen (one a Longstaffe from Spennithorne) to start up in farming and was employed by Mr. S. Harding of Hawera, before he enlisted on December 14th 1914.

He was a Corporal, serving as a driver with the horses in the Field Artillery. They embarked for the Dardanelles in August 1915 but he was wounded in the stomach at Gallipoli. He wrote to his sister from hospital that they were dying like flies and that he expected to be "pushing up the daisies".

Edgar was admitted to St. George's Hospital on Malta with dysentery on October 15th 1915 and by January 11th he was in a Cairo hospital with enteric fever. He was invalided to New Zealand from Suez on SS "Tahiti" on February 11th 1916 and was struck off the Army Strength.

His illness did not improve and Edgar Spensley died on November 23rd 1918 His body lies in grave D.34(S) at Wellington (Karori) Cemetery, New Zealand.

During 1918 other burials of Wensleydale men serving in the armed forces had taken place in the dale.

Edgar's grave in New Zealand.

DRIVER JOHN JAMES METCALFE
NO. 501359 ROYAL ARMY SERVICE CORPS
AND LABOUR CORPS
DIED MONDAY 25TH MARCH 1918 AGE 22.

There is very little that I know about John Metcalfe except that he was the son of M.A. Metcalfe of Quaker Terrace, Masham. However, the connection with Askrigg must have been strong because he lies buried in the churchyard of St. Oswald's, Askrigg.

*The headstone of John James Metcalfe
in Askrigg graveyard.*

266

PRIVATE JOHN PERCIVAL
NO. M/279604 MOTOR TRANSPORT/R.A.S.C.
DIED MONDAY 8TH APRIL 1918 AGE 21.

John's father, William Percival, was born at Woodhall, Askrigg, in 1854. He married Mary Sayer, a Carperby girl, and with William working as a general labourer, they settled first at Drummond Cottage and then by 1914 at Hazel House, Aysgarth. Children John, Tom, William, Annie and Margaret were born.

Leaving school at 14, John had a number of jobs before becoming chauffeur to a local landowner. On enlistment in 1916 he joined a motorised section of the Royal Army Service Corps, where his days were spent delivering ammunition and rations to the dumps on the front line.

At the beginning of 1918 he suffered a severe dose of phosgene gas when a gas shell exploded nearby. He was brought back to England and discharged from the army but tuberculosis had set in and after

John Percival (Aysgarth).

some months of illness he died on April 8th 1918.

John Percival was interned in the churchyard of St. Andrew's Church on April 12th.

EDMUND ERNEST THISTLETHWAITE,
BURIED ON MAY 11TH 1918 AGE 35.

Edmund Ernest Thistlethwaite was born at Bellerby in 1882. His father, Edmund senior, was a farmer and stonemason, who, together with his wife Mary Eleanor, lived at the Marshes, along Moor Road.

In 1901, 18 year old Ernest was a railway engine linesman, working on the Wensleydale branch line, but by 1906 he had become an insurance agent, working first in the Darlington area and then travelling throughout Wensleydale for the Prudential Company.

On October 16th 1907, aged 24, he married a 22 year old Darlington girl,

Florence Atkin l' Anson, at the Congregational Church on Union Street, Darlington. They were both residing at the time at the home of her father, Edward l' Anson, a railway engine driver, at 37 Pensbury Street, Darlington. They set up home at Bellerby but sadly, in March 1912, Florence died, aged 26. Sometime before the start of the Great War Ernest married again and became an Insurance Superintendent in Ripon.

Ernest's brother, Sergeant Herbert W. Thistlethwaite, served in the regular army during the Boer War. He was killed during that conflict and, being highly regarded by his comrades, they paid for a tombstone to be erected in Bellerby churchyard, reading: "In memory of Sergeant H.W. Thistlethwaite, who was killed in action South Africa, February 11th 1902. This stone was erected by officers and

Edmund Ernest Thistlethwaite (Bellerby).

men of the 75th Company Imperial Yeomanry, as a token of respect".

Edmund Ernest Thistlethwaite served in the Great War but was invalided home in 1917, due to ill-health, made worse by the terrible conditions he experienced on the Western Front. He died at Bellerby from heart disease and consumption on May 8th 1918 and was buried on May 11th in Plot 415, Bellerby churchyard, near to the gravestone of his soldier brother, Herbert, and his first wife, Florence.

Herbert Thistlethwaite,
the brother of Edmund Ernest, who was killed
during the Boer War.

268

PRIVATE JOSEPH HUTCHINSON
COLDSTREAM GUARDS
DIED 13TH JULY 1918 AGE 28.

Alfred and Margaret Hutchinson lived at East Witton, where they raised their children, Joseph, Thomas and Florrie. Alfred worked as a sawman in the woods on Witton Fell, on the Jervaulx Estate. At the age of 14 years Joe worked as a gardener at Jervaulx. He had a fine tenor voice and was a member of the East Witton Church Choir. Joe joined the police force, serving for some time at Thirsk before transferring to the Teeside force.

During the Great War, Joe's younger brother Thomas falsified his age and joined the army. As a policeman, Joe was not allowed to volunteer, but in the Spring /Summer of 1918, as the Allied push began, policemen were finally allowed to enlist and Joe signed up. He was placed in

Joseph Hutchinson (East Witton).

the Coldstream Guards and was based at their headquarters at Caterham.

He never saw service abroad, however, for he became a victim of the flu pandemic that was starting to wreak havoc around the world. He developed pneumonia and his heart failed. Joseph was brought back for burial in East Witton Churchyard. A large attendance of parishioners took part in a choral service and at the close there was a muffled peal of bells.

CORPORAL JOHN GEORGE TOWLER
ROYAL ARMY SERVICE CORPS
DIED 11TH AUGUST 1918 AGE 36.

The Towlers had kept the Cover Bridge Inn, near Ulshaw Bridge, from the 18th Century until the 1920's. John was the son of Christopher Towler, a journalist, who came back into the area to run the establishment.

John joined the Colours at the outbreak of war and was in active service abroad for three and a half years, on the Western Front and finally in Egypt. He was invalided home in the Spring of 1918 with sunstroke and died after a

The Cover Bridge Inn at the time of the Great War.
It was run by Private John Towler's father, Christopher Towler.

painful, lingering illness at York on August 11th 1918.

On August 16th there was a military funeral in the churchyard for John Towler, with a large attendance.

CAPTAIN SIR DAVID DURRELL BARCLAY
LATE 19TH HUSSARS
DIED 2ND OCTOBER 1918 AGE 60.

David Edward Durrell Barclay was the 12th Baronet of Pierston Ayrshire. He had been a Captain in the 19th Hussars and had seen service in the Egyptian Campaign of 1882 and Sudan Campaign 1884. He had retired from army life and was living in Middleham with his wife Letitia, daughter of the Honourable Amias Orde-Powlett of Thorney Hall, Spennithorne.

During the Great War we have seen in Chapters One and Two how he was greatly involved in the recruitment campaign throughout the dale as Recruitment Officer.

His main task, though, throughout the war, was as Railway Transport Officer for a large region of the North.

SECOND LIEUTENANT WILLIAM LOGAN RAYNER, KING'S LIVERPOOL REGIMENT DIED 28TH OCTOBER 1918 AGE 24.

William was the son of E. Vyvian Rayner and Eva Mary Rayner of Clarendon House, Middleham. Having survived the dangers on the field of battle whilst serving his country, William was another who fell victim to the flu pandemic and died of pneumonia. The names of both Sir David Barclay and William Rayner were added to the plaque on Middleham War Memorial.

LANCE CORPORAL ALFRED WARD SALMON 5TH BATTALION YORKSHIRE REGIMENT DIED 16TH FEBRUARY 1919 AGE 36.

Alfred had been born in 1882 at Thornaby, South Stockton, in the Middlesborough district, the son of Thomas Salmon, a foreman brewer, and Ann Salmon (nee Appleton). Alfred eventually became an assistant grocer, and I believe came to work at Leyburn before the start of the Great War, at either Reeds Store or Groundwaters.

It was at Leyburn that he courted Lizzie Chilton, sister of James Chilton, who we have seen was killed in action during June 1917. Alfred joined the 5th Battalion Yorkshire Regiment. By early 1917 he was seriously wounded and was admitted to hospitals and convalescent homes in England during 1917 and part of 1918.

Discharged from the army before the end of the war, Alfred received a pension, and was to be found living at Waverley Terrace, Darlington. It was at this address that he died from Lobar pneumonia, exacerbated by his war wounds, on 16th February 1919.

Alfred Ward Salmon of Leyburn (Wensley and Darlington).

Alfred Ward Salmon, middle of back row. Convalescing after being wounded.

PRIVATE JOHN (JACK) HENRY RUECROFT
4TH BATTALION YORKSHIRE REGIMENT
DIED 26TH FEBRUARY 1919 AGE 27.

Jack's father, William Ruecroft, married Isabel Fowler from Castle Bolton and they raised their children Annie, Isabel, James William and John Henry in the village of Redmire.

William was employed by the Urban Council to keep the roads in good repair and was skilled at his job. He had been a pupil teacher at Redmire School and intended to be a school teacher, but in an accident whilst felling a tree, he lost his leg and was later fitted with a wooden one.

Though he gave up the idea of teaching, William would still help the village children in their reading. His wife died at an early age, in 1895, and Annie helped to bring up the family.

Jack Ruecroft, who was working on a farm after leaving school, thought he could do better for himself by going to work in a Liverpool factory but he soon came back and began work on a Teesdale farm.

His brother, James William, joined the army early in the war and urged his brother Jack to enlist. He joined the 4th Battalion Yorkshire Regiment and worked with the horses in bringing the ammunition up to the front line.

In 1916 his father William died and it was at this time that Jack was severely wounded. He lost his right arm and was shot in the chest, resulting in the loss of a lung. He spent a great deal of time in a Nottingham hospital and when he came home he was discharged from the army.

By the end of 1918 Jack had recovered as much as he ever would and went to Osmotherley on a Government run scheme for promoting poultry keeping. Sadly he caught a flu germ and pneumonia set in. His condition was made worse by only having one lung. He did not recover and died on February 26th 1919. John Henry Ruecroft was brought back to Redmire and buried in the churchyard.

A memorial commemorating the names of members of the village reading room who died as a direct result of the Great War was made. Jack's was the only grave that was accessible and so the memorial was erected by the side of his grave. It remained there for the next 65 years until Nancy McGregor, a niece of Jack Ruecroft, persuaded the Church Council to place it inside the church for its safety and preservation.

War memorial in Redmire Church.

PRIVATE WILLIAM FAWCETT
83RD TRAINING RESERVE BATTALION
DIED 12TH APRIL 1919 AGE 22.

William was born at Sedbusk, the son of Edward Fawcett, a farmer from Simonstone, and Margaret Fawcett from Woodhall. By 1901 Edward and his family, consisting of children William, Kate, Thomas, Mary and Edward were living at Stalling Busk. Eventually they moved to Low Fors Farm, between Bainbridge and Semer Water.

William Fawcett joined the army in the later stages of the war but suffered from tuberculosis and died in April 1919 aged 22. On the 12th April he was buried in the peaceful setting of Stalling Busk churchyard, close to the shore of Semer Water.

The old Stalling Busk church, erected in 1602 and rebuilt in 1722, overlooking Semer Water. The graves of Thomas Hodgson and William Fawcett are in the churchyard. Semer Water is the largest natural lake in Yorkshire.

The stone laying ceremony of the new church at Stalling Busk, in May 1909. Two Stalling Busk servicemen would be laid to rest in the graveyard of the old church, close to Semer Water.

JAMES (JIM) MOORE
DIED OCTOBER 28TH 1919 AGE 30.

We have seen that in Chapter 4, William Moore, the brother of Jim Moore, was killed during April 1917. Jim was also in the army but was badly wounded and suffered dreadfully from shell shock. He returned to England and spent a considerable time in hospitals. By October 1919, 30 year old Jim Moore was in the North Riding Asylum, at Clifton, York, where he died on October 28th. During the 19th century the establishment was known as the North Riding Lunatic Asylum but during the Great War it played a second role when large numbers of disabled and shell shocked soldiers were cared for on the premises and many stayed there throughout the 1920's. James's body was brought back to the dale and was buried in Hardraw churchyard.

PRIVATE THOMAS SPENCE
NO. 2425 4TH BATTALION YORKSHIRE REGIMENT
DIED FRIDAY 18TH APRIL 1919 AGE 23.

Thomas's father, John Spence, was a farmer at Hargill Haw Farm, three quarters of the way down Walden Dale. His wife Margaret had been born at Newbiggin and their children were Thomas (the youngest), Margaret, Grace, Sarah and John.

Thomas returned safely from the war but in early 1919 he contracted influenza, which developed into pneumonia. He died on April 18th and was interned in the churchyard at Aysgarth.

Thomas Spence
(Walden Dale, West Burton and Aysgarth).

The Bowes family at Ulshaw Cottage c1915.
Back row: Thomas Joseph Bowes, John Emmerson Bowes, May Bowes,
Leonard Matthew Bowes, Veronica Bowes.
Front row: Annie Bowes, Winnifred Bowes, Leonard Fisher Bowes, Evelyn Bowes,
Mary Ann Bowes.

GUARDSMAN JOHN EMERSON BOWES, COLDSTREAM GUARDS DIED 18TH OCTOBER 1920 AGE 22.

John was born at Eagle Lodge, on the Danby Estate of the Scrope family. His father was Leonard Fisher Bowes and his mother was Mary Ann. From 1908 the family settled in Ulshaw Cottage, near Ulshaw Bridge, where Leonard worked as a general estate labourer. After the Great War he was one of the first in the dale to possess a Ford lorry, using it for carting during his spare time.

John was in the Coldstream Guards, whilst his brother Leonard was in the Royal Engineers. At some point in 1917 John Bowes was gassed in France and returned to the dale as an invalid. He greatly suffered over the next three years, for he never recovered, and he died in Becketts Park Hospital, Leeds, on October 18th 1920, aged 22.

The family was Roman Catholic and John was buried in the Catholic Cemetery at St. Simon and St. Jude Roman Catholic Church on October 22nd 1920.

The Kirkbride family of Town Head Farm, Askrigg c1905.
Back row: Jack, Fred, James, Tom, Lizzie.
Middle row: Esther, Annie, Margaret, Thomas, William.
Front row: Ernest, Margaret, Laura, Harry, Jenny.

PRIVATE JAMES KIRKBRIDE
NO. 44445 3RD BATTALION ESSEX REGIMENT
DIED SUNDAY 24TH OCTOBER 1920 AGE 25.

Thomas Kirkbride, from Worton, near Askrigg, married Margaret Terry from Askrigg in 1890. They then came to farm at Town Head Farm, Askrigg, where Thomas was a cattle dealer. He had land on which he could fatten cows that he had bought at the Auction Market and which he had driven home along the roads in the dale. He would then walk them to another market and sell them on at a profit.

James Kirkbride was one of 13 children: Fred, Tom, Mary Elizabeth, Annie, James, Ernest, Esther, John (Jack), William, Margaret, Henry, Agnes and Laura. Tom, Fred and Ernest served in the Army and Jim joined them when he was posted to the Essex Regiment. Sadly, he was severely affected by a gas attack on the Western Front and returned to England.

James suffered terribly and for a considerable period he was in a convalescent home in the Durham house provided by the mother of the future prime-minister, Sir Anthony Eden. On October 24th 1920 James Kirkbride died and was later buried in Askrigg graveyard. (we shall see later that his nephew, Sydney Chapman Kirkbride, would be killed in action in 1940, whilst serving in the RAF).

JAMES WILLIAM HUTCHINSON
DURHAM LIGHT INFANTRY
DIED SOMETIME IN THE MID 1920'S.

William Hutchinson, James's father, was a carter on a farm belonging to the Orde-Powlett family of Spennithorne. He and his wife Elizabeth raised six children.

By 1901, 16 year old James was working as a cattleman and lodging at Thorney Farm, again belonging to the Orde-Powletts.

Whilst serving with the Durham Light Infantry James William was wounded in the hip and invalided out of the army. From that time onwards he had to walk with the aid of a crutch and found work difficult.

He spent a great deal of time fishing on the River Ure, and the Vicar of Middleham presented him with a boat, which he used for fishing.

James would often visit his sister in Newhaven, Sussex, and whilst there in the mid 1920's the wound to his hip turned septic and he died in Newhaven, where he was buried.

During the 1930's, the Spennithorne blacksmith, John William Metcalfe, worked to ensure that James William Hutchinson's name was added to the Spennithorne and Harmby memorial.

LANCE CORPORAL THOMAS METCALFE COATES
(MILITARY MEDAL)
4TH BATTALION YORKSHIRE REGIMENT
DIED 21ST JANUARY 1925 AGE 32.

George Coates, father of Thomas, was a farm worker who was born in Thwaite, Swaledale, whilst Thomas's mother Margaret came from Reeth. By 1901 they were living at Marsett, in Raydaleside, where sons George, Thomas and Albert were born.

The children went to Stalling Busk School and when Thomas left he worked in the Council Offices at Hawes, before he enlisted and joined the 4th Battalion Yorkshire Regiment, the same Battalion as John William Horn from nearby Burtersett.

Thomas became a Lance Corporal, and on September 26th 1916, during the attack against Flers he won the Military Medal for bravery in the field and was severely wounded. We have seen already that in the very same battle, on the following day, his Wensleydale colleague John Horn was killed.

Thomas was wounded in an attack on a German trench. A German soldier threw a bomb which caught him just below his left eye. It was too close to burst in his face but exploded under his foot, with the result that he received severe injuries to his leg and to his face. Despite this he was still able to save a colleague close by when he despatched the German who had thrown the stick bomb, with his bayonet.

He was in hospital at Rouen for 11 weeks, where he underwent four operations and had two more operations in English hospitals. He was then discharged from the army.

Eventually he went back to his old job until he married Elizabeth Watson in 1921. They went to live at The Heugh, a large, isolated house on the hillside above Nappa Scar, which they ran

Thomas Metcalfe Coates, seated, bottom left (Stalling Busk).

Thomas Metcalfe Coates and wife Elizabeth on their honeymoon.

279

as a guest house. It was here that their two daughters, Margaret and Mary were born.

On January 21st 1925, after only three day's illness, Thomas Metcalfe Coates died from meningitis, partly attributed to the war wound to his head. He was buried in Stalling Busk graveyard and his name was added to the Stalling Busk war memorial.

Elizabeth Coates kept the guest house running throughout the 1925 season with the help of her mother, but then sold it and moved into a cottage in Askrigg.

And so we come to an end of the account of the men of Wensleydale who were killed or died during the Great War, or who died later from injuries or illness associated with that period.

There has probably never been a more prolonged and appalling experience for ordinary soldiers in all the history of the British Army than the four years of Trench warfare, 1914 – 1918. And now, after living through such nightmare conditions, the survivors could look forward to returning to the beautiful surroundings of Wensleydale.

Though victory had been achieved, the cost was enormous in both man-power and material, with 900,000 Empire troops killed and a further two million wounded. Those who survived came back to a "land fit for heroes" and were promised that the Great War had been "the war to end all wars". The sentiments seemed appropriate at the time but history would make a mockery of them.

As a silence fell over the battlefields, Wensleydale counted its loss of so many dalesmen, but those who arrived safely back gave thanks that they had survived the horror of war. A saddened dale was also grateful for the war's end and wished to see the survivors take up their civilian lives again. However, within the space of 19 years the dales folk would once again find themselves confronting the prospects of conflict against Germany and the possibility of world wide confla-gration.

The news of the Armistice on November 11th 1918 had been received very calmly by the people of Upper Wensleydale. Flags floated from churches, busi-ness premises and houses, whilst church bells rang out. The brass band turned out in Hawes and played patriotic selections.

A thanksgiving service was held at St. Margaret's Church, Hawes, on Wednesday night, conducted by Reverend S.D. Crawford. Special prayers and thanksgiving collects were said and the hymn "Now thank we all our God" was sung, as was the National Anthem at the close.

At Askrigg a thanksgiving service was conducted by Reverend Squibb in St. Oswald's on Monday evening, when the bells, silent for so long, summoned the people. For the first time since early in the war trained bell ringers rang merry peals. At night a bonfire was set alight and fireworks let off.

On Wednesday, after a thanksgiving service led by H.G. Topham, a meeting was held in Middleham Town Hall to consider the form of a memorial by the parish to those who had lost their lives. After some discussion it was decided to place a memorial in the parish church and a committee of five was appointed to arrange further proceedings.

To celebrate the suspension of hostilities a bonfire was lit in Hawes Market Place on Saturday night, November 16th. A number of blazing tar tubs, carried on the heads of enthusiastic youths, were taken, along with effigies of the ex-Kaiser and Crown Prince, through the town and then cast on to the fire. The Hawes Brass Band turned out and played patriotic tunes and dance music. A number of couples danced, whilst a band of young girls sang all kinds of popular melodies. Fireworks and bonfires were lit in many surrounding villages.

Unfortunately, the people of the dale were facing another enemy that was taking its toll of their lives. Spanish Flu! The flu pandemic that was sweeping the world during 1918/1919 had taken a strong hold in Wensleydale, with higher than average the number of deaths reported in the district, especially amongst the young and old.

These included, on Sunday November 10th 1918, the 36 year old vicar of St. Bartholomew's Church, West Witton, Reverend Richard Thomas Ainscow. He had contracted influenza a week before, which turned to pneumonia. His brother, an Oxford graduate and former POW was staying with him. The vicar had only been inducted on January 2nd 1918 and was a very fit young man, having been a rower at university and had won the mile races at school.

For this First World War generation there was no protection. For them this epidemic was a cruel epilogue to the suffering they had endured in four years of fighting. It was, as one historian has written, the gleaner of the war's harvest.

On a somewhat brighter note, a national holiday was held on July 19th 1919 when Peace Celebrations were held in towns and villages throughout the land. In East Witton a tea was provided for everybody and there were sports and contests for young and old. Prizes a plenty were distributed by the local squire, Mr. Christie, and there was a display of fireworks in the evening. A dance provided by Mrs. Shields of the "Blue Lion" Inn for all East Witton servicemen who had so far returned from the war was much appreciated.

At Hawes, however, Peace Celebrations were held on Wednesday August 27th 1919, a fine, cold, blustery day. There was singing of the National Anthem on Kiln Hill, followed by a procession that formed at Town Foot and, headed by Hawes Brass Band, marched through the town and the village of Gayle. Horsemen rode in double file, vehicles were decorated and children and adults were adorned in costumes. One entry was Dr. Anderton's famous donkey cart, carrying Dr. Macfarlene's daughter dressed as Britannia and pulled by Frank Parker, Dick Jones (later to be killed in the 2nd World War), Eric Avery, John Anderton and Harold Watson.

After judging, the procession wended its way to Haylands Pasture, lent by Mr. C.M. Fawcett as a venue for the sports. A free tea was served in the Market Hall for adults of 60 years and older, all servicemen and their wives, as well as children up to 14 years. Tea was served to others for the cost of one shilling. In the evening a cycle parade rode through the town, headed by the Brass Band riding in Elijah Allen's charabanc and at the rear of the cyclists was the "Russian Quartet" on a wagon.

After a Punch and Judy entertainment, souvenir medals were presented to the children. Sadly, the non-arrival of the fireworks prevented the fireworks display taking place. A crowded dance in the Market Hall ended the day's celebrations.

A few months later East Witton witnessed the "Welcome Home" for the returning soldiers. On Friday February 6th 1920 a delightful evening was spent in the National Schoolroom, when the servicemen and their friends, 70 in all, were entertained by the parishioners at a "Welcome Home" dinner and social

19th July 1919 at Redmire Peace Day celebrations.

Nicholas Albany Lum-Robinson receives the Military Medal from Mr. W.R. Burrill-Robinson on 19th July 1919 at Redmire.

The service which was held on Peace Day at Redmire. Willis Hartley plays the Wesleyan Sunday School harmonium. Mr. Lee, station master and church warden, stands hatless in the centre of the front row. David Stringer Calvert, joiner, sits in the wheelchair (his son started Redmire Quarry c1919).

By permission of Clive Torrens.

evening. Lieutenants Maughan and Towler and Driver Garbutt were unable to attend since they were still on service.

A silver-mounted walking stick was handed to each serviceman, to be engraved later on with the words "East Witton 1914 – 1918". After dinner there was a short whist drive. Then came musical entertainment, interspersed with games, followed by a dance which lasted till the small hours of the morning.

It was during the years just after the war that Wensleydale's parishes raised money to provide some sort of memorial to honour the names of those who had died.

The date set for the unveiling and dedication of the East Witton War Memorial was Sunday June 24th 1923 at 4p.m. The Memorial

East Witton War Memorial.

had cost £250 and all of the material, except for the tablet of Roman marble, had come out of the parish.

Placed in a recess outside the west end of the Georgian church, the handsome cenotaph was from a design by Vernon Crompton, and was covered with Union flags. From far and near the people flocked, with a space reserved for the volunteers and ex-servicemen.

The ceremony began with the singing of the National Anthem and then the choir and clergy filed into the church. Later, with a deep crowd standing round the cenotaph, Brigadier General W.H.L. Allgood unveiled the War Memorial. He hoped the relatives of those who were commemorated on the monument would look on it with feelings of pride and not with feelings of sorrow. Two buglers from the Yorkshire Regiment sounded the "Last Post" and "Reveille". The relations of the fallen then deposited their wreaths and flowers on its base.

In October 1919 a meeting had been held in Aysgarth to discuss how the village should honour its dead from the Great War. As electricity was being cabled to the village shortly, it was thought that providing lamps for the village would be a suitable "Peace Memorial".

Aysgarth War Memorial.   *Memorial gatepost at Aysgarth Church.*

George Dougill, a local builder, designed an unusual but practical memorial and on February 13th 1920 submitted plans and estimate for a memorial lamp to be fixed on a stone pedestal, with a seat around. The ratepayers would pay through a collection. It would be 10 feet in height , circular in shape and built of locally quarried limestone. The plinth would be a millstone from the local corn mill, incorporated to form a seat. On top would be an ornamental metal standard, the apex incorporating a candelabra of electric lights. The inscription would read "They heard. They felt. They gave. They died.".

Each member of the community would help to carry the stone from the quarry to the site on the village green. The day for the collection of stone proved to be wild and bitterly cold, keeping the older people indoors. The vicar, Reverend W.K. Wyley, gathered the local Aysgarth school children to him and together with members of the Red Cross walked down to Seata Quarry, between the main Hawes road and the minor road to Thornton Rust, to collect the locally prepared limestone.

The building work commenced and the coping blocks of Pateley stone delivered. Delays in the delivery of the ironwork caused the committee to decide on the unveiling of the unfinished structure.

On January 10th 1922 the ceremony took place, a cold and windy day, with hail showers. A large gathering attended. After the hymn "The Supreme Sacrifice" and short prayer, Colonel Morrough Wilson, M.P. for the Richmond district, addressed the gathering and unveiled the Memorial. The "Last Post" was sounded by Mr. Bushby of Bainbridge.

Twenty names were to be commemorated in the parish church, three of them being Aysgarth men, and these same three names appeared also on the new Aysgarth Memorial, etched onto a brass plaque and reading: "Remember all who shared in the Great War, these of Aysgarth gave their lives – James P. Bell, William Hemsley, John Percival".

Hawes eventually found

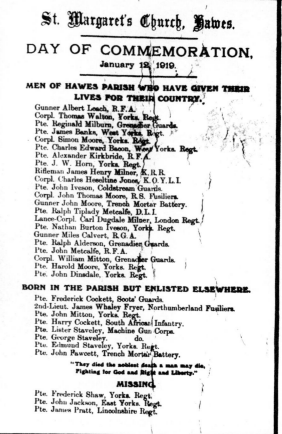

itself with two memorials to the fallen of the parish. On January 12th 1919 there was a "Day of Commemoration" at St. Margaret's Church. A fine wooden screen was placed in the church with the names of those who lost their lives carved into the wood. Sometime later, an organ was placed in the beautiful Methodist Church in Hawes, with these words engraved on a brass plaque:

"This organ is erected in grateful memory of the men of this town and neighbourhood who laid down their lives in the Great War 1914 — 1918. Precious shall their blood be in His sight".

Neither did Gayle forget their men folk, for 7 names are also to be found inside Gayle Chapel.

Although the men from Bellerby who were killed in the war were honoured when a plaque was placed on a wall inside the church, their memory was further honoured when, in the late 1920's, a splendid Memorial Hall was constructed in the village. Built by Richmonds, a building firm from nearby Hunton, the stone was hewed in a quarry on Manor Farm land belonging to the Scott family and was transported on a horse and cart belonging to John Mawer and his sons, of Studda Farm, Bellerby.

Throughout all the other parishes in the dale, similar memorials were erected. Tragically, events around the world were conspiring to increase international tension between certain nations, especially in Europe, and the prospects for war were building up once again.

Leyburn War Memorial at its unveiling and dedication service.

Photograph showing the unveiling and dedication service for Leyburn War Memorial. According to a contemporary diary entry the service took place in September 1920. It was not until around 1924 that a low wall with railings was added. The memorial is on the site of an old market cross that was knocked down in 1834 when a tree fell on to it during a storm.

Unveiling and dedication of Leyburn War Memorial 1920.

Bolton Castle and Castle Bolton in the 1930's. Wensleydale's largest sited building was erected by the first Lord Scrope, Chancellor of England in 1379. From July 1568 until January 1569 Mary, Queen of Scots was imprisoned at Bolton.

DALES LIFE DURING THE INTER-WAR YEARS: A PHOTOGRAPHIC RECORD

Castle Bolton in the 1920's. The Temperance Hotel can be seen on the right, in the foreground.

1935 Jubilee celebrations for George V and Queen Mary at Castle Bolton.
Fancy dress parade.
Back row: Gladys McGregor, Jimmy Iveson, Rita Appleton, Ernest Spensley, Mec Spensley,
Cissie Wilson, X, Georgina Rutter, Selina Appleton, Percy Dinsdale.
Front row: Norman Appleton, Kenneth Spensley, Joe Bostock, Josephine Henderson,
Clifford Rutter, Rebecca Dinsdale, Hilton Rutter, Jessie Rutter, Nancy Bostock,
Hazel Spensley, Mary Bostock.

Leyburn Market Place, 1934.

Leyburn Market Place c1938.
(The bus in the foreground is travelling to Skipton via Grassington.)

Market day on Richmond Street, Leyburn, 1928, looking towards the King's Head Hotel.

Market day in Leyburn, 1928.

Market day in Leyburn, 1928. Facing the Golden Lion Inn.

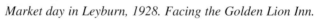

Askrigg, 1920's, showing the Old Hall to the left, which was burnt down in 1935. The main street is bordered by elegant three-storey 18th and 19th century houses, arising from Askrigg's prosperity through leadmining, textiles and clock making.

The Old Hall in Askrigg in 1933, when it was a hotel. Sadly it burnt down in 1935. Built in 1678 by William Thornton, the balcony between the gables was reputedly a viewing area for the old sport of bull baiting.

Bow Bridge, Low Abbotside and Askrigg residents on a charabanc trip, 1920's.
The driver is Jack Airey from Middleham.

Askrigg sports in the 1930's.

Tommy Hunter at work in Redmire Quarry in the 1920's. He is drilling without a hard hat and balanced precariously on a drum. His wages were 35 shillings a week (£1.75).

Middleham Castle in the 1920's. Built in 1170, it passed into the hands of the Neville family. Richard, Duke of Gloucester, later Richard III, married Anne Neville in 1472. The Swine Cross in Middleham's upper market place commemorates Richard's 1479 ratification of the Market Charter given to the town a century earlier by Ralph Neville.

Town Head, Hawes, c1940's.

Hawes market place, early 1920's.

Hawes market place 1920's.
By permission of the Dales Countryside Museum.

The first Wensleydale bus service, in 1926.
By permission of the Dales Countryside Museum.

*Ernest Heseltine taking the milk from Hogra Farm, Redmire, to Redmire Station
(up the Grinton road) in 1928.*

Ernest Heseltine at Hogra Farm, Redmire, in 1928.

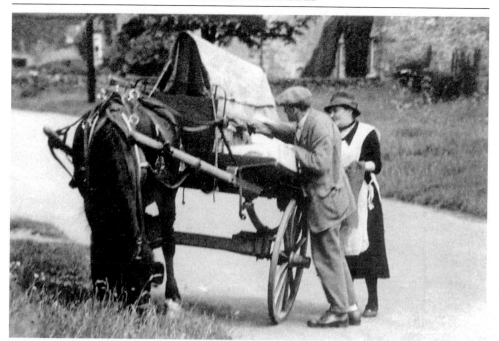

Greengrocer's cart in Redmire village 1930. W. Percival from Preston under Scar is the greengrocer.

Delivery by butcher's van in Redmire village 1930 (by the side of the Drill Hall/Village Hall). Morton's from Preston under Scar often made a delivery.

*Mr. William Scott, farmer from Redmire, milking one of his cows, in 1930.
The Scotts lived at East Farm.*

A steam train on the Wensleydale line, nearing Redmire, in 1930.

Christopher Smithson, son of the well-known photographer and producer of postcards,
J.B. Smithson, ran West Witton Post Office and stores in the late 1930's and 40's.
Christopher also produced postcards in a darkroom at the post office.
Frank Ward is shown driving the post-van.

By permission of Clive Torrens.

Fancy dress parade at West Witton Feast 1933.
Back row left to right: Rene Hammond, X, Greta Walker, Alice Watson, Stanley Walker,
John Spence, Albert Yeoman, Kenneth Styan.
Middle row: Barbara Robinson, Mary Walker Marion Walker, Evelyn Bushby,
Margaret Bushby, Cyril Harker, X, Brian Sowerby, Teddy Dawson.
Front row: X, Florie Spence, Joyce Robinson.

By permission of Clive Torrens.

CHAPTER SIX

THE SECOND WORLD WAR 1939 — 1945

The early years of the 1930's had been the "Depression Years". The bottom had fallen out of the Wall Street Stock Market of late 1929, resulting in a faltering in investment, less money for people to spend, factories closing due to a lack of markets, with demand reduced still further as men were thrown out of work. Whilst people "tightened their belts", farmers found that no one could afford the food they had grown. As Great Britain abandoned her policy of free trade, international trade virtually collapsed and further men were thrown out of work as more factories, shipbuilding yards and industries were closed down.

Wensleydale people could not avoid being affected by these national and international ramifications in the business and industrial world, but the availability of jobs in farming, on the railways and in the quarries helped a little to ward off the worst ravages of the "Depression" that descended upon the large urban conurbation.

What could not be avoided in Wensleydale or elsewhere, were the repercussions from the growing tensions on the international diplomatic scene. The political climate in Europe was changing and "war clouds" loomed on the horizon. The strains imposed by economic collapse and the bitterness caused by the outcome of the Versailles Peace Treaty, settled in 1920, had found certain country's democratic institutions wanting. Fascist and Nazi regimes had won favour, determined to push their aggressive foreign policies in the belief that the remaining democracies were ill-prepared to defend their rights.

The likely victory of Fascism on the Iberian Peninsula, during the Spanish Civil War of 1936 — 1939, only emboldened the aggressive plans of Adolf Hitler's Nazi Germany. In 1938 a German ultimatum led to the appointment of several Nazi representatives in the Austrian Cabinet. On March 11th German troops entered Austria and the Anschluss, or forbidden union of Austria with Germany, was established.

Tension increased in Czechoslovakia, where Hitler demanded the handing over of areas of Bohemia to Germany, particularly those occupied by Sudetan Germans. Czechoslovakia agreed to this demand, under pressure from France and Britain, but Hitler demanded further considerable concessions by October 1st 1938, in default of which Germany would "march". The Czech army mobilised on September 23rd, France on the next day, whilst on the 28th the British Fleet was mobilised.

Prime Minister Neville Chamberlain visited Hitler at Bad Godesberg and Berchtesgaden, without result, and on September 28th Hitler invited the British and French premiers to meet with Mussolini at Munich the next day. At this meeting, to which no Czech representative was admitted, it was agreed that German occupation of the areas demanded should proceed in stages between October 1st and the 10th. Chamberlain was able to return to London, claiming "Peace in our time" and most of Britain breathed a collective sigh of relief.

Relief turned to concern, when, in March 1939, Hitler ignored certain conditions of the Munich Agreement and occupied both Bohemia and Moravia without British or French government intervention. Sensing a weakness of resolve throughout the European democracies, Hitler turned his attention to Poland during the summer months. War clouds were looming once again over Europe, for at last, Chamberlain spelt out clearly in Parliament British condemnation of Hitler's latest aggression and made it clear that an attack on Poland would not be tolerated. On April 26th Britain reintroduced conscription.

There was an unprecedented fear in 1939 of devastating air attack with immediate dangers and horrors in store. Air Raid sirens were tested throughout the dale during these months of tension, with Air Raid Precaution exercises taking place to test the blackout.

The weakness displayed by Britain and France in Munich was Hitler's most powerful incentive to plan the attack on Poland, first for August, then for September 1939. He believed that Poland could be defeated in isolation, as Czechoslovakia and Austria had been before, especially when, on August 23rd, Germany and Soviet Russia signed a Non-Aggression Pact. Hitler's way to Poland seemed open, but on August 25th the signing of the Anglo-Polish Alliance was announced in London and Hitler realised that his attempts to isolate Poland had failed.

As the might of Germany's armed forces swept across the Polish frontier on Friday September 1st and Britain still remained at peace, the reality of the situation was brought home to the people of Wensleydale with the arrival at Leyburn Station of special trains bringing evacuee school children from the industrial North East to be billeted in the dale. The evacuees had arrived, and with them the realisation that this time there was no "turning back".

More than 600 children from St. Joseph's Roman Catholic School, Gateshead, the first of Leyburn District Council's 1200 evacuees, arrived at the station, with the remainder who were under school age, to be received the next day.

Detraining at Leyburn occurred without mishap. Mr. W. Sutton, Sanitary Inspector to Leyburn Rural Council was in charge, assisted by voluntary helpers. A first aid post in the waiting room was staffed by district nurses and a first aid officer. Evacuees were handed emergency rations, and, with the exception of evacuees to be billeted in Leyburn, were provided with refreshments. Others for towns and villages in the district were conveyed to their destinations by buses, or continued by rail to Aysgarth, Askrigg and Hawes. The Women's Voluntary Services Organisation, led by Lady Jane Scrope of Danby Hall, would arrange for the welfare of the children after they had been billeted and organise communal recreation for them.

At Askrigg the reception and distribution of the first batch of 500 children from Gateshead took place and as the train arrived, crowds of young folk waved a welcome. At Yorebridge Grammar School they were given a meal and a rest. The Askrigg contingent went to the Temperance Hall, where refreshments were served by members of the Women's Institute, whilst the rest went by bus to their distribution centres.

Emergency rations sufficient for 48 hours were handed to each child and adult. Mrs. F.S. Graham, Aysgarth leader of the Women's Voluntary Services Organisation was responsible for much of the preliminary work of receiving the evacuees. Mr. R.C. Shorter and staff of Yorebridge Grammar School were in charge of the detraining arrangements. Another trainload of 500 children under school age were expected the following day.

Some Gateshead pupils settled down well, but as the months passed, not everything went smoothly. By October 1939 Leyburn and District Council were receiving many complaints about "the disgusting behaviour of some of the pupils and the outbreaks of diseases such as impetigo". By January 1940 Askrigg billeting officers, working on a voluntary basis, were threatening to resign if they did not receive further help. The tact required to be shown to all concerned was making their lives very stressful,

East Witton had received 22 children from Gateshead on September 1st, but on the following weekend, West Park Central School, Sunderland, and the boys of the Junior Technical School, Sunderland, set out by rail, via Durham, to Northallerton, thence on to Leyburn Station. The Primary School children travelled to the Selby area, whilst Bede Grammar School pupils, Sunderland, were billeted in and around Richmond.

West Park Central were allowed to bring their younger brothers and sisters with them and so we find that 14 year old Olive Wright was taking care of her younger sister Elizabeth and brother Norman. Detraining at Leyburn, they watched from the platform as the boys of the Technical School continued on towards Hawes, trading friendly insults with the girls from West Park.

At Leyburn they were provided with an orange drink and biscuits, whereas the Gateshead pupils had received tea and buns just one week earlier. Olive, together with her maths teacher, a second adult, and 19 other children, arrived by bus at the Parish Room, Lowerthorpe, East Witton, on a damp September afternoon. She had been separated from a friend, Margaret Chalk, who had departed with 9 other pupils for Thornton Steward.

By this stage, some of the Gateshead pupils had returned home, for they had found it difficult to settle. Olive and her group sat in the window seats around the Parish Hall waiting for the East Witton ladies to arrive and choose which ones they wanted. It had been a sad day and the only two smiles that Olive could remember seeing all day came from the East Witton head teacher Rosamund Thwaite and the Jerxaulx Estate Secretary Miss Florence Cutter.

At 11.15a.m. on Sunday September 3rd 1939, Neville Chamberlain announced to a hushed nation that Britain was at war with Germany. It was the beginning of the greatest conflict the world has yet seen and it was not long before the people of Wensleydale learned that they would not be spared. If anyone still

Evacuees from Sunderland with their teacher in front of Redmire School, early 1940's.
Dorothy Murrell, who later married into the Heseltine family is third from the left
on the front row.

Winter (January 1941) schoolboy evacuees from Sunderland at Redmire (on the Carperby road).

doubted the serious implication for families within Wensleydale, resulting from the new world wide conflict, any such false hopes were dashed when news came just one day into the war that the first dalesman had lost his life whilst serving King and Country.

CORPORAL GEORGE WILLIAM PARK
NO. 524855 "A" FLIGHT 9 SQUADRON RAF
DIED MONDAY 4TH SEPTEMBER 1939 AGE 23.

William Park was the son of Thomas and Alice Maude Park from Redmire. Tom came from a long standing Redmire family and married his wife Maude, a Sunderland girl. He ran a small holding as a tenant of Lord Bolton, but also opened a shop in a room of their house in the early 1930's, selling a wide variety of goods. Tom's father had also run a shop from the same premises during the 1870's. One son, Ernest, helped to run the farm, daughter Eleanor (Nellie) studied to be a teacher during the war years, whilst their son Tom worked in a Leyburn electrical shop.

The Redmire shop was a "going concern". Tom Park senior became the Bus Agent and parcels would be dropped off, to be delivered in the village. With motorised transport helping to make the dales villages more accessible, bread was delivered and sold from the premises.

William (Bill) Park left Yorebridge Grammar School in 1934, having intended to go into banking, but, during the intervening period of waiting to enter that profession, he decided instead to join the airforce, and in late 1935 entered RAF Cranwell as a cadet.

By 1939 he was a Corporal in 9 Squadron RAF, the first squadron to be equipped with the Vickers Wellington bomber. At the beginning of August the Squadron had taken part in Defence Exercises, involving long hours in the sky.

On August 10th Bill took two weeks leave, spending some time at home in Redmire, but on August 25th he returned to his Squadron at RAF Honington, in Suffolk. On September 3rd 1939 Bill posted his last letter to his parents. He wrote that he believed the international

William Park (Redmire).

Tom and Maud Park's shop in Redmire, between the wars c1930.

The Park family.
Back row: Maude Park, Tom Park.
Front row: Bill (William) Park,
Tom Park, Ellen Park,
Ernest Park, Eleanor Park.

Ernest Park and Nellie Park,
brother and sister of
George William Park, Redmire.

Tom Park milking in the fields.

*Farmer Tom Park,
father of George William,
carrying pail and back can
for transporting milk.
The village shop was
run by the family.*

309

tension seemed to have eased slightly, but says, "Take it from me, though, we are ready for any emergency." The following day he was killed in action.

The sea-borne war had begun almost as soon as Chamberlain had risen from his microphone in Downing Street. Blenheim aircraft had photographed the German Fleet refitting at Wilhelmshaven on September 3rd and the movement of naval capital ships near Brunsbuttel in the mouth of the Kiel Canal on the morning of September 4th. At 4.05p.m. Wellington L4268, piloted by Flight Sergeant Borley, with Bill Park and three other crew on board, took off from Honington, their target Brunsbuttel.

On the afternoon of September 4th the pocket battleship "Admiral Scheer" lay peacefully in the German naval anchorage of Wilhelmshaven. Suddenly three British Blenheims were spotted and air raid warning bells sounded.

The first Blenheim dropped two 500 lb. bombs clanging on to the deck but they failed to explode. The bombs of the second Blenheim hit the water along-side the ship, but again did not explode. The three remaining aircraft failed to make their attack. As they jettisoned their bombs one received a direct hit and crashed in flames.

Five other Blenheims approached the naval vessels in the second wave. With the flak by now fully alerted, they were met by a storm of fire. One aircraft after another crashed in flames. Only the Squadron Leader succeeded in carrying through his attack, the target being the light cruiser "Emden".

Though his aircraft was already blazing, the pilot still held his course and his bombs splashed down between the jetty and the ship. Seconds later the Blenheim itself crashed against the "Emden's" bows and tore out the side of the ship, the pilot taking over a dozen German sailors with him to his death.

Almost simultaneously the battleships "Scharnhorst" and "Gneisenau", anchored off Brunsbuttel in the River Elbe, and at the entrance to the Kiel Canal, were subjected to attack by high level Wellington bombers — fourteen of them. This time the British planes were harassed by German ME109 fighters, so that their bombs fell at random and no hits were scored on the targets. Two Wellingtons, including Bill's plane, spun down in flames, but the others arrived safely back in England.

All five crew members of L4268 were killed in the crash and their names are commemorated on the RAF Memorial, Panel 2, Runnymede, Surrey. Out of a total force of 29 bombers, 24 had attacked, 7 were lost and most of the remainder returned severely damaged. Despite the daring and resolute action of the two squadrons, the result was disappointing for Bomber Command.

Sadly, Maude Park never really believed her son had been killed and thought that he would return. Throughout the war years she constantly wrote to former Squadron colleagues and the authorities, asking questions and trying to find out what happened. Even in the years after the war she still did not accept that he would not be coming back.

With news of Bill Park's death, Wensleydale families once again faced the prospects of losing loved ones for the second time within living memory. 53 Wensleydale men were to die during the Second World War, compared to the 168 combatants who perished in the Great War. The 1939 – 1945 conflict was spread even more world wide, but did not suffer from the stalemate conditions of trench warfare experienced on the Western Front. Nevertheless, 53 more families would receive the sad news of bereavement and the war would be brought closer home to the civilian population by the ever present threat of aerial bombardment during the "Blitz".

**** In reality, there were few incidents in the dale with regards to bombing from the air. There was of course the constant reminder of that danger, as night

Photograph showing the Leyburn retained fire brigade c1943. The members were retained fire personnel who had to dash from their places of work to man the green fire engine and water tender. If they missed the action they lost their call-out pay of 12s 6d. They were on the scene soon after the German bomb was dropped behind Thornborough Crescent, Leyburn. Amongst their many extra harrowing war-time duties was to attend the scene of aeroplane crashes, of which there were many during the five years of war.
Standing, X, Eddie Taylor, X, Oswald Tallentyre, X, X, Frank Rumford, Bill Hunter, Jimmy Rumford, Norman Hoisten, Joe Blenkinsop, Vince Ward, Ted Metcalfe.
Seated: Barbara Burton, Mary Ward, Bill Ward (chief fire officer),
Annie Vollands (nee Gow), Jean Wood.

Photograph showing the old fire station on Shawl Terrace, Leyburn, before it moved to its present site. John Ward (chief fire officer) stands by the side of the horse-drawn appliance (he lived next door at number 4). Standing on the top is Leyburn blacksmith Bill Blenkinsop. The horses which were used to pull the appliance grazed in a field belonging to the Bolton Arms Hotel (where Leyburn Dental Practice is nowadays). In the later inter-war years the fire station moved to the old Leyburn electricity power station building, which had been operated by Eric and Leslie Dobson (who also owned 'The Elite' cinema).

after night the drone of aircraft could be heard as the Luftwaffe searched for targets in the North East, or crossed the country to bomb the North West, Belfast or even the Ribbleshead Viaduct.

Some bombs did land though. Masham suffered the most, when, on the night of April 16th 1941, a bomb partially destroyed the White Boar Inn, killing Mr. and Mrs. H. Scaife and Mr. and Mrs. D. Watkinson.

In Leyburn, a bomb landed in a field behind Thornborough Crescent, where nowadays Woodburn Drive is situated. Shrapnel and rock was showered over a wide area. Many Leyburn properties had their windows smashed, whilst the ceilings were brought down in a number of homes in the Crescent. Fortunately no one was killed or seriously injured. A large crater was produced, however, and local children searched for shrapnel souvenirs (a 14 pound specimen was found in the garden of No. 12 Thornborough Crescent).

On another occasion a bomb which landed close to Nellholme, near Aysgarth, failed to explode. An Army Bomb Disposal team sent to deal with it left their work when torrential rain fell and 15 minutes later the bomb exploded.

The houses in West Burton and Aysgarth were shaken by the blast from another bomb that exploded in "Tom Metcalfe's Pasture", near Aysgarth Station. Fortunately, other than these events, the dale was spared the horrors emanating from air warfare.

During the Autumn of 1939 the British Expeditionary Force embarked for France, but no hostile action was pursued, as the opposing sides faced each other across the Siegfried and Maginot Lines during the winter of 1939/1940, in the period known as the "Phoney War".

However, during that bitterly cold winter, one of the worst on record, a member of the RAF ground staff from Leyburn, died whilst working at a Yorkshire air base.

1940 – THE END OF THE PHONEY WAR

AIRCRAFTMAN 2ND CLASS JOHN ERNEST TAYLOR
NO. 747494 RAFVR
DIED THURSDAY 8TH FEBRUARY 1940 AGE 47.

Ernest Taylor was to serve his country in both World Wars. The son of John and Annie Elizabeth Taylor, he was born at Sinderby, a small village to the west of Thirsk. During the Great War he volunteered and served in France and Belgium, in the Royal Horse Artillery.

Eventually he married Mary Ann Cooper Wilkinson, daughter of the Leyburn saddler and sister of Walter Wilkinson, who had been killed during the Great War. For some years they were licensees of the Cross Keys Inn at Bellerby. Later, living at Riseber Lane, Leyburn, they brought up their family of Eddie, Harry, Arthur and Edna, with Ernest employed as a civilian maintenance worker in the Royal Ordnance, at Catterick Camp.

When war was declared in September

John Ernest Taylor, as a member of the Royal Horse Artillery, during the Great War.

313

1939 Ernest was already 47 years of age, but feeling the call of duty he once again volunteered to defend his country.

As an Aircraftman, he became a serving member of the Motor Transport Section of the RAF, and by January/February 1940 was working very long hours at RAF Dishforth, a bomber squadron aerodrome.

During the last week of January he was working in the rain, sleet and cold and often slept in his wet clothes. Ernest caught pneumonia and though admitted to the Military Hospital at Catterick, he died on Thursday 8th February, leaving a widow and four young children.

Ernest was accorded military honours at the funeral in Leyburn. A firing party of the RAF attended, and the coffin, draped in the Union Jack, was carried by RAF personnel. A service was held at Leyburn Church, at which he had been sexton. He was buried in grave 34, Section C of Leyburn Cemetery.

Ernest Taylor and Mary Ann Wilkinson on their wedding day at Leyburn.

Throughout Wensleydale, rationing was introduced in January 1940, although ration books had been stored ready ever since 1938. Butter, sugar, bacon and ham were first on the list, but things did not get really bad until 1942.

The dire military situation of the Allies and the British Army was brought home to Wensleydale folk in early June 1940, when soldiers who had been evacuated from the beaches of Dunkirk arrived by train at stations throughout the dale. The first troops arrived at Hawes, exhausted and dirty. During their week long stay, they were fed in Hawes Market Hall and the Sunday Schools. The officers were billeted in people's homes whilst the men were accommodated in the chapels, National School, Methodist Sunday School Rooms, Band Room and empty houses and huts.

Soldiers also occupied Askrigg Village Hall (called the Casualty Clearing Station) and large houses in the parish. For a few weeks after Dunkirk, five large Midland Red buses were parked in the market square, ready to take soldiers any-where they were required, such was the fear of imminent invasion.

During these dark days of 1940 Wensleydale folk rallied to the cause, when, on May 14th, Anthony Eden broadcast to the nation that volunteers were required for a new force called the Local Defence Volunteers (nicknamed "Look, Duck and Vanish"). People were asked to give in their names to the local police stations. Eventually the organisation would be renamed the Home Guard, with the whole of Wensleydale forming the 11th Battalion North Riding Home Guard.

The Leyburn contingent was mainly made up of older men, some of whom had seen service in the Great War, and younger men not yet called up into the armed services. In charge were commissioned officers Malcolm Scott, the local solicitor, and Herrick Peel, manager of the Shawl Quarry at Leyburn, whilst

Carperby Platoon Home Guard c1941. Sitting on Carperby Market Cross after the 'Wings for Victory' Methodist Church Parade.
Top: Lance Corporal Alice Foster (ATS)
Back row: Kenneth Percival, George Scott, Edgar Percival, John Layborn.
Middle row: Robert Foster, William Percival, William Preston, William Suttil, Richard Heseltine, Frank Dinsdale, George Percival.
Front row: Ernest Coulthard, Edward Percival, John Wood, John Moore, Harold Jackson.

Full Carperby Platoon of the Home Guard.
Harold Jackson, William Preston. W. Moore, Harry Weatherald, William Percival,
Percy Oliver, Alan Raw, George Percival, William Percival, Kenneth Percival,
Edward Percival, Richard Heseltine, Robert Foster, John Wood, John Layborn,
Frank Dinsdale, Ernest Coulthard, Edgar Percival, George Scott, Jack Moore,
James Firby, William Suttil, Oliver Amsden, Eric Amsden, Corporal Atkinson.

Arthur Chaploe from the Leyburn building firm of C. Chaploe and Son was one of the sergeants.

The headquarters was in a small building off Riseber Lane, although the Town Hall was used frequently for practices, as was the Conservative Club (nowadays the Dalesman Club). The latter premises housed the Communication Centre (or Signallers Section), consisting of two telephones manned mainly by local women, including Marjorie Metcalfe and Betty Archer. They were kept very busy on the occasions when the platoons went on training manoeuvres.

Target practice with ·22 rifles was held in Leyburn Town Hall, with the required 25 yard distance obtained by opening up an intervening door to provide a view of the target. Rifle practice with the Lee-Enfield took place in a section of the Shawl Quarry and at the nearby Bellerby camp and range. Three rifles were available in the early days, kept by the police and handed out to those they thought could use them best. Training with Mills Bombs was undertaken on the moors near Catterick Camp, Leyburn, and indeed the whole dale was fortunate in being in close proximity to Catterick and Bellerby Camps and regular army personnel were always on hand to help in training and to offer advice.

Carperby Platoon's headquarters was in the Village Hall, where two parade nights a week were held. In overall charge of the Aysgarth district was Major R.H. Whitehead, of Thornton Hall, Thornton Rust, but former Great War soldiers John Wood, Edward Percival, Ernest Coulthard and John Moore taught members to drill and shoot.

A depot Regimental Sergeant Major from the Green Howards came fort-nightly to train them, with each weekend spent either on the Bellerby ranges or taking part on manoeuvres, their transportation a lorry from Catterick, reeking of petrol fumes. Between Carperby and Aysgarth Station, half a mile from the village, a camouflaged caravan was sited in a field. It was here that night time guard duty took place with two men on duty and two resting.

In charge of West Witton's detachment was John Christopher Smorthwaite, the local saddler, who had seen service during the Great War. The headquarters was in the village Reading Room, now an annexe of the "Wensleydale Heifer", just across the road from the inn.

The Scout Hall in the grounds of Middleham vicarage, near to the church, was the headquarters for Middleham Platoon. They sometimes paraded inside the Castle grounds and in the early days were not always "up to scratch". Private Clapham was admonished for being out of step on parade but replied, "It's not me sir, it's the rest of these buggers!"

Doug Weatherill remembers his first night time experience of guard duty on the top of William Hill. He and the Captain were due to be on duty at 4a.m. but as the clock struck 4.30a.m., then 5a.m., still there was no sign of the Captain, and he was the only one with a gun. Suddenly a shadowy figure appeared. It was the Captain. He certainly had the rifle, but only to help him up the hill, for there was no ammunition for it. On this particular occasion the "Dads' Army" theme was continued when the Captain opened up his great coat to reveal he was wearing civilian clothes so that he could quickly arrive at his place of work when he went off duty.

The men from West Burton met in the village Reading Room (now made into flats) and received their equipment and uniforms quite quickly. Sten gun practice was always held in the fields at Broad Bottom, with regular army officers arriving to test the members' skills as they fired into the hillside.

On manoeuvres at Edgley Farm a mock battle was held between army regulars and the Home Guard, who were asked to defend the farm. A referee oversaw the action and gained the displeasure of Home Guard members. As the regulars came over the beck, firing live ammunition and using thunder flashes, the West Burton men believed that they would have "picked them off" as they crossed the beck. The Home Guard retreated into the lofts of farm buildings but felt extremely annoyed when told by the referee they had been captured.

West Burton Home Guard. Photograph taken in the field known as Broad Bottom.
Back row: William James Lawson, Jack Miller, George Nicholson, Laurie Nicholson,
Donald Gedge.
Middle row: John Ewbank, Leslie Slater, Herbert Capstick, Kenneth Capstick.
Front row: John Dinsdale, Arthur Hazle, Rob Close, Jimmy Dickson, Bob Ewbank.

Sergeants Rob Close and George Shepherd, both old soldiers, were in charge
in the village, with regular army officer Captain Simpson, whose wife kept the
Fox and Hounds, helping to organise them. They travelled to Catterick by car for
hand grenade practice, using an old army tank as the target. Church parades were
held on the green, as was regular practice in hand grenade throwing by the
Special Constables, with the detonators removed of course.

West Burton Platoon had their guard hut in a hollow in the ground at the top
of Morpath Scar, above West Burton. Three men went on duty at 7p.m. and
returned at 7a.m. One soldier went on duty, with two men resting inside the hut.
During one night's guard duty they saw a large flash from the direction of the
Ribbleshead Railway Viaduct, the attempted target of a bomb (members of
Hawes Home Guard were often transported to Ribbleshead to help keep guard
on the viaduct).

In charge of East Witton Detachment was the Jervaulx Estate Agent, Ralph
Maughan, from Abbey Hill. The main guard post was in a hut high on Witton

Hawes Home Guard c1941. Phil Marlein is second from the right on back row (tin hat) and Jos Hutchinson is second from the left on the back row.

East Witton Headquarters Section 1942.
Back row: Cecil Fawcett, John Hanslip, Bill Croft, Bob Pickard, Sid Batty, Jack Yeoman, Tommy Ianson.
Middle row: John Thwaites (dispatch rider), Alan Wilson (Company Sergeant Major), Ken Foster.
Front row: Harold Fawcett, Frank Craggs, Wilson Foster, Ralph Maughan (C.O.), Ernest Dinsdale, Fred Clarkson, Jack Perrigo.

Thoralby, Newbiggin and Bishopdale Home Guard Platoon.
Back row: Harold Webster, Frank Heseltine, Roland Fawcett.
Middle row: Vic Close, Bob Spraggon, Tom Dinsdale, Albert Heseltine, Joe Scarr,
Albert Spence, Matthew Heseltine, Joe Chapman.
Front row: John Sayer, William Atkinson, Bill Spence, Tom Percival, Robert Heseltine,
John Dinsdale, Chris Thompson, Arthur Heseltine.

Fell, and it was from there one evening that 80 German planes were counted as they headed westwards to bomb Belfast.

In the early days of the Home Guard, before uniforms and weapons were issued, the men from East Witton set up road blocks to check passing motor vehicles at Harker Bridge, near Jervaulx. In civilian clothes and carrying 12 bore shotguns, they improvised a road barrier by dragging sheep racks filled with rocks across the public highway. Searchlight Batteries were stationed nearby, lighting up the night sky, at High Jervaulx Farm (today Brymor Farm) and at Parson's Barn, Collywath Lane, near Spennithorne.

The Askrigg Home Guard Post was high up on the moor land road to Muker, in the stone built Greets gamekeeper's hut. Reporting for duty at 7.30p.m., the members left their post at 6.30a.m. One man kept a watch whilst the others played cards inside the hut or cooked food on a fire.

Their log book indicates that on most nights there was nothing to report, although on Sunday 12 October 1941 an air raid was reported, with three salvos of bombs due south and very heavy bombing seen due east at 11.45p.m. On Sunday May 10th 1942 Captain Edmonds (the biology teacher at Yorebridge Grammar School) inspected the post at midnight and wrote, "Hut dirty — grease and egg shells lying around. Not good enough, Lance Corporal Atkinson!!"

By mid June 1942, however, we find that the members only went on duty from 4a.m. to 6a.m., for Germany had just invaded Russia and the likelihood of invasion of the British Isles had diminished.

In overall charge was Major Rendell from Newbiggin, with Captain J.V. Edmonds as his deputy, together with Lieutenants Wilkinson and C.J. Dinsdale, Sergeants Hopper, Charles Bell, Hammond, Scarr and Halton and Corporals Hodgson and Lance Corporals Humble and Atkinson. James Dinsdale (known as Flute) was the quartermaster.

Wensleydale proved to be a splendid area for keeping army stores, including ammunition and petroleum. The dale from Bedale to Hawes was wooded and provided camouflaged cover for this undertaking. The Royal Engineers brought in ammunition trains to Leyburn Station, and places such as Hornby Park,

Aysgarth and Thornton Rust Home Guard 1940's.

Members of the Downholme Platoon, Home Guard, (Swaledale) in November 1940.
Top left: In front of the Bolton Arms Inn, forming up for the Armistice Day Church Parade, 1940.
Back row: Joe Dixon, Jack Whitehead, Ernest Whitehead, Douglas Webster, X,
Harold Weller, Richard Allison, X, Ian Raine.
Front row: Michael Webster, Ronald Calvert, Thomas Brown, Eric Lochart, Jack Dixon, X,
Kenneth Calvert, Matthew Lambert (officer in charge).

Photograph on right: Jack Weller and Ian Raine.
Photographs and information from Mary Sanderson (nee Brown).

between Catterick and Bedale, were used to store petroleum in barrels, under cover of the trees and camouflage netting. Large houses, empty buildings and barns were requisitioned throughout the dale, and with the help of local building firms such as C. Chaploe and Son and Sandersons of Leyburn, fresh buildings, often in the form of Nissan huts, were provided for the army.

Simonstone House, near Hardraw, became the Staff Headquarters for the Army in the Upper Dale and Nissan huts were erected. Bricklayers and joiners were drafted to C. Chaploe, some men even being brought out of the services for this task, as these were works of national importance.

Thornborough Hall, Leyburn, was requisitioned and the Royal Engineers and Canadian forces arrived, many housed in Nissan huts, with their food canteen sited on Riseber Lane. The Canadians, including the Rocky Mountain Rangers, were favourites amongst the children, for they would often give their sweet ration coupons to the children of Leyburn and Spennithorne Schools. Some Leyburn children also took jars to school and received cocoa from the Canadian soldiers as well as large red apples from British Colombia.

The Tank Corps arrived in the Upper Dale, with soldiers billeted in wooden huts at Tupgill House, Coverdale (nowadays The Forbidden Corner), and Middleham Town Hall was used as the Naafi. They were also stationed in Bainbridge, behind the Village Hall (the site of the present Council Depot), with the officers' mess at Sedbusk. At Castle Bolton, Scots Guards troops camped in tents in the Ellerands Pasture, and tanks often rumbled past the side of the village green. One of these servicemen at Castle Bolton was to become the future Archbishop of Canterbury, Robert Runcie.

It was found that Hawes and its environs was a good centre for armoured vehicle training and tanks were a common sight on Hawes main street. Gayle Green was resurfaced with concrete as a standing ground for armoured vehicles (the bus garage being used to make repairs), with other vehicles parked behind the Auction Mart. Nissan huts appeared throughout the town, including on

Scottish Regiment marching through Hawes. The car belongs to Annie Ryland of the Green Dragon Inn, Hardraw. Note the blackout covers on one of the headlamps.

Armoured vehicles manouevering on the village green at East Witton.

Marridales Lane between Gayle and Bainbridge Ings and on what is now Hawes children's playground, whilst soldiers from the Border Regiment and Scots Guards were billeted on the upper floor of Gayle Mill. Soldiers from the Scots Guards, Argyll and Sutherland Highlanders, Border Regiment, Royal Engineers and the London Fusiliers were all stationed in Hawes at one time or another. Some were billeted in Gayle Sunday School, whilst their Naafi (canteen) was housed in newly constructed corrugated Nissan huts at Little Ings. Clints House at Gayle, used as accommodation for Belgian refugees during the Great War, was now requisitioned for use as an officers' mess.

Whilst using their Churchill tanks, the Scots Guards certainly tested the strength of Gayle Bridge, which in peacetime had a weight restriction of four tons. The Regiment also used Gayle Mill pond (known locally as the Washdub) for submerged tank training, in preparation for the landing of tanks on the D-Day Normandy beaches in June 1944. The tanks were sealed beforehand and when they emerged from the pond water, their engines were revved to a certain level, which blew the seals away, without the necessity of the crew exposing them-

324

selves to enemy fire.

One consequence of tank training in the dale and across the moors was the demolition of many roadside walls. The farmers needed to be recompensed by the War Office and Sergeant Hopper from Askrigg Home Guard, whose daytime job was as an auctioneer, liaised with army officers to observe and note the damage. One of the officers detailed for this task was Willie Whitelaw, who later became Deputy Prime Minister in Margaret Thatcher's Government.

The dale helped play its part in the war effort in other ways. The quarries throughout Wensleydale, with three in Leyburn alone, became extremely busy, providing limestone for the Middlesborough steel works, especially those of Dorman Long. Former quarry workers, by now serving in the forces, were released from duty to go back to work in these quarries. Shawl Quarry at Leyburn had its own large rail sidings where limestone could be loaded onto rail wagons and sent directly to Middlesborough by rail.

It is true to say that civilian workers were often at risk and in great danger of their lives whilst transporting ammunition and other war supplies throughout the dale and it's environs. It was to be the case that in 1944 a man from Downholme, but with strong Leyburn and Richmond connections, was to be involved in a horrific accident whilst transporting munitions and was eventually awarded the George Cross for his heroic endeavours.

Jack Weller (George Cross medal), standing by the bonnet of his lorry c1932.
At the time he was working for his uncle Matthew Brown of Brentwood, Leyburn.

Jack (John) Weller was born in 1912 at Kirkbymoorside, the eldest son of William and Cecilia Weller. William was killed in action in 1916 and Cecilia married John William Brown from Leyland, the family moving to the village of Downholme, near Bellerby.

John William Brown was a tree feller and dealer who travelled the country felling trees on large estates. Sadly, in 1928, he was badly injured and with his compensation he later bought a lorry and set up in business as "haulage contractors, furniture and cattle removers". Jack had meanwhile left school to work on a Coverdale farm, but by 1935 was driving the lorry in the family's haulage business.

In 1939 John William Brown died and his step-son, Jack Weller, was later given dispensation by the Darlington Military Tribunal to continue operating the business during the war instead of joining the services. As a civilian driver he was employed by the War Ministry to transport munitions throughout the district and by North Riding District Council to carry limestone from the many quarries in the dale.

On February 4th 1944, 12 people were killed and 102 injured in an ammunition explosion at Catterick Bridge Railway Station. The munitions consisted of anti-tank grenades and incendiaries. Six railway wagons of incendiaries had been loaded a few days before, ready to be despatched to Norwich for use by the RAF. Other lorries were arriving loaded with grenades, to be sent to army units practising for the forthcoming Normandy landings in June.

Just before 4p.m. that afternoon Jack Weller arrived with a load of grenades from nearby Hornby Park, the last load of the day. Four soldiers began unloading his lorry, whilst Jack went to report at the traffic hut, thirty yards away.

Suddenly, a violent explosion occurred. The hut collapsed and Jack Weller was blown a considerable distance. The explosion was followed immediately by extensive fires and explosions in the surrounding area. Jack returned to the hut, which was on fire, and extricated three injured men from the ruins and then assisted in the rescue of killed and injured from other wrecked buildings. Jack knew that the area contained other loads of high explosives which might well have exploded. His behaviour showed courage, initiative and determination of a high order.

The four soldiers who were off-loading Jack's lorry were killed outright and are buried in a grave in Hornby churchyard. In June 1944, Jack Weller was awarded the Edward Medal by King George VI in recognition of his gallantry and some years later he was presented with the George Cross for his action.

Although by May/June 1940 some Wensleydale men were experiencing action in Belgium and France as the German invasion pushed ahead in those countries, others being involved in taking the war to Germany as members of Bomber or Fighter Commands, and still others in naval actions on the High Seas, it was not until July 1940 that word arrived confirming the death of a second person from the dale.

SERGEANT PILOT SYDNEY CHAPMAN KIRKBRIDE NO. 566117 37 SQUADRON RAF DIED MONDAY 15TH JULY 1940 AGE 24.

Sydney was born on August 16th 1915 at Cringley Farm, Askrigg, the eldest son of Tom and Isobel (nee Chapman) Kirkbride. His father was a dairy farmer and cattle dealer. Children Margaret, Thomas and Shelagh completed the family.

Cringley Farm was on Silver Street, the lane that begins near the cross and led past the blacksmith's forge and then on to the fields across to Worton. Tom was a cattle dealer and often travelled throughout Swaledale buying cows and sheep. Often, as teenagers, Sid and his brother Thomas would walk across the moor to meet the Swaledalers halfway at Jinking Gate with the stock their father had bought, and sometimes as far as Summer Lodge Hill. As brother Thomas recalls, they were jaded by bringing the stock home, for it could be a "right pantomime".

Sydney Chapman Kirkbride of Askrigg.

Sid was mainly brought up by his grandmother, Mrs. Chapman, who thought the world of him, for he was a kind and sensible, caring lad. For a period, trainspotting became a passion and Sid and Thomas would pursue their hobby at Garsdale and even at Danby Wiske on the East Coast line.

Sydney attended the nearby Yorebridge Grammar School and went straight from there to RAF Cranwell as a 17 year old cadet on September 6th 1932. By August 1935 he was a wireless operator mechanic, whilst by December 1938 he was training to be a pilot, which he accomplished by August 1939, as war was about to be declared.

During his career he had been posted as a wireless operator to Iraq in October 1936, based at Air Depot Habbanyia, west of Baghdad, on the Euphrates, and also saw service in Palestine, before returning to Britain by September 6th 1938. It was now that he began his training as a pilot.

As a Sergeant Pilot he was eventually posted to 37 Squadron, at Feltwell in Norfolk, on December 20th 1939, flying Wellington bombers. Three months before this, on September 30th, Sydney had married Kathleen Mary Middlebrook from Bradford.

On December 18th 1939, just two days before he joined his squadron, six Wellingtons from 37 Squadron had joined in a disastrous raid to locate German warships along the German coast near Heligoland. They were pounced on by enemy fighters and five of the six planes were shot down. The Wellington was barred from taking part in such future ventures.

Instead, the Squadron concentrated on attacking targets in Northern Europe, the majority of them night bombing operations, as well as targeting sites in Norway during the period of German invasion of that country. Sydney's worst experience at this point was when they ran into a heavy snowstorm returning from Norway. They had to fly dangerously low to avoid the worst of it.

In a letter written to his wife Kathleen, dated May 14th 1940, he talks about standing by and participating in night raids, including one on Rotterdam. On May 22nd he writes, "Very busy lately and four flights out of six have been on bombing raids destroying railways and bridges. We were out on Wednesday, Friday, Sunday and last night. So we're doing our share all right. We lost one plane last night but none on the other trips. Last night we were in Aachen in Germany and bombing railway sidings. Did you hear it on the 1 o'clock news today?" (** these raids were attempting to stem the German invasion of the Low Countries and France, beginning on May 10th).

In his next to last letter he writes, "I feel much better than I did yesterday. I was awfully tired when I wrote to you. I can't for the life of me sleep through the day but I shall see the doctor soon and he'll probably be able to help me. Apparently I'm not the only one who suffers in this way."

Within a few days Sydney was dead.

At 10p.m. on July 14th 1940, Wellington L7792, piloted by Sergeant McCaulay and with Sergeants Kirkbride, Read, Johnson and Grimson on board, took off from Feltwell, Norfolk, in a raid over Hamburg, together with 79 other bombers. The objective was to bomb widespread targets in the port and drop mines in the harbour and estuary mouth. Out of the 80 aircraft that set off on the mission, just one failed to return, Wellington bomber L7792.

Three men were killed, including Sydney Kirkbride, whilst two escaped death and were taken prisoner by the Germans. Sydney and his colleagues Sergeants McCauley and Read were buried with full military honours by the German Army in Bremen, but after the war were removed to Becklingen War Cemetery near Soltau, between Hamburg and Hannover.

The sad news was received by his wife, Kathleen, who, twelve days later gave birth to their daughter Terry. Desperate for news of what had happened, Sydney's mother wrote to the father of one of the crew members taken prisoner after the raid. Eventually, on March 16th 1941, Sergeant Johnson, POW, wrote this letter to Isobel Kirkbride;

"Thank you very much for your kind letter. My father has told me that you were writing to me and I was very glad to hear that he had written to you and was able to put your mind at rest by letting you know what happened to Syd.

"I can hardly believe Syd has gone, for I have flown on his crew all the time. I always experienced the utmost confidence in his ability as a pilot. I shall always remember Syd by his cheerful smile and optimistic attitude during moments of great danger, it made me feel proud to be flying with him.

"We were victims of a direct hit, which struck the cockpit, the pilots received the full force of the blow, killing them instantly. The only survivors were the rear gunner and myself who escaped by parachute. Syd was buried with full military honours in Bremen. I was unfortunate to be in hospital at the time. I gained details of the funeral from a guard who described it "as a procession worthy of a gallant flyer."

"No words can express the deep sympathy I feel for you. But as you say, we have many happy memories of Syd, these are immortal."

Syd's brother, Thomas, recalls, "Syd was proud of being English and had

Burial, with full military honours, of Sergeants Sydney Kirkbride, J.F. McCaulay and C.E. Read by the German Army at Bremen.

Burial of Sydney Kirkbride.

great respect for King and Country. He loved the dales. I can still picture him riding his bike on a fine morning, his face beaming with pleasure".

With the German armed forces seemingly poised to invade Britain during August and September 1940, the main thrust of the country's retaliation was an attempt to defeat the German Luftwaffe in the skies above Southern England and to continue the night time bombing raids across Germany and occupied Europe.

It was in late September 1940, two months after Sydney Kirkbride's death, that confirmation came of the loss of another Wensleydale pilot's life, this time a man with connections in the tiny village of Hardraw.

PILOT OFFICER FRANCIS JOSEPH WATSON DFC NO. 42945 AIR GUNNER 83 SQUADRON RAF DIED TUESDAY 24TH SEPTEMBER 1940 AGE 27.

Joseph Watson was the eldest son of Francis Fowler Watson and Sarah Ann Beckett Watson. In 1936 Joe arrived in Hardraw with his parents and siblings Robert and Mary, when his mother took up the post as headmistress of the small village school. All three children would serve their country during the war, with Joseph joining the RAF, Robert the army and Mary becoming a nurse.

Training as an air gunner and pilot, Joe Watson joined 83 Squadron, based at Scampton, Lincolnshire, and flying Handley Page Hampden bombers. It was not until April 1940 that the Squadron was able to operate regularly and in that month it flew 45 sorties, more than half of them "Gardening" or mine-laying operations. During August the Squadron's aircraft took part in an attack on an aqueduct forming part of the Dortmund-Ems Canal, flying at a height of 150 feet. During the same month 83 Squadron made its first raids on Berlin and also attacked the battleships Scharnhorst, Tirpitz and Von Scheer.

On September 8th 1940 Invasion Alert No. 1 was in force and a major effort was made by the Squadron directed against German invasion preparations. Many attacks were made on invasion barges in Antwerp and other harbours. By this time Joe Watson had been awarded the Distinguished Flying Cross for his exploits.

On the evening of 23rd/24th September the Squadron took part in a raid by 129 aircraft despatched to 18 separate targets in Berlin.

Hampden bomber L4049, piloted by Squadron Leader Bridgman and crewed by Sergeants Blatch and Gorwood and Pilot Officer Joe Watson, set off on the same mission. Three aircraft were lost that night, one of them being L4049. It was hit by flak (anti-aircraft fire) and crashed near Bethen in Germany. Although Squadron Leader Bridgman survived and became a POW, Joe Watson and the other two aircrew were killed and were buried in collective grave 13.E.9. in Becklingen War Cemetery, and so sadly joined Sydney Kirkbride.

The grief that shrouded the Watson family was unfortunately added to later in the war when Joseph's brother Robert was killed whilst fighting against the Japanese in February 1942.

Meanwhile, during the late summer and autumn of 1940, the German Navy was attempting to destroy or capture enemy ships, dislocate shipping movements and force the dispersion of British warships for escorts and patrol to counter the menace. By September 1940 five disguised German merchantmen, powerfully armed, had been set loose upon British trade routes, sinking or capturing 36 ships, amounting to 235,000 tons. Worse was to follow as one of Germany's capital ships was let loose upon the sea lanes, resulting in the death of a merchant seaman with strong Wensleydale connections.

RICHARD HESELTINE JONES FIRST RADIO OFFICER SS "MAIDAN" (LIVERPOOL) MERCHANT NAVY DIED 5TH NOVEMBER 1940 AGE 34.

We have seen in Chapter Four how Charles Heseltine Jones, eldest son of Christopher (Kit) Jones, landlord of the Crown Hotel, Hawes, was killed in action in June 1917. His youngest brother, Richard, eventually joined the Merchant Navy during the inter-war years, rising to the rank of First Wireless Operator. He had received his education at Yorebridge Grammar School and, although making his home at Barnard Castle, when not at sea, Richard maintained strong contacts with

Hawes, the town in which his father still lived.

In October 1940, Richard was on board the 7908 ton vessel SS "Maidan" in Halifax harbour, Nova Scotia. Being taken on board as cargo was explosives, bound for Liverpool, and preparations were made to join 36 other ships bound for that port, in Convoy H.X.84.

On October 27th the 12,000 ton pocket battleship "Admiral Scheer" left Germany and broke out into the Atlantic through the Denmark Strait, with orders to attack the North Atlantic convoys, from which the battleship escorts had been withdrawn to reinforce the Mediterranean. Captain Krancke believed that Convoy H.X.84 had left Nova Scotia on October 27th and he planned to intercept it.

Richard Heseltine Jones
(Hawes and Barnard Castle).

On November 5th his aircraft sighted a single ship, the "Mopan", which was sunk, after taking on board the crew of 68. At 4.50p.m. the 37 ships of H.X.84 appeared over the horizon.

On board the convoy's escort, the armed merchant cruiser "Jervis Bay", her commanding officer, Captain Fegen, realised that he was faced by hopeless odds. As darkness approached he engaged the enemy in order to give the convoy a chance of dispersing and escaping.

While the convoy scattered, the "Jervis Bay" closed at speed with the "Admiral Scheer", with the shots of the old 6 inch guns of "Jervis Bay" falling well short. By 6p.m. the "Jervis Bay", heavily on fire and out of control, was abandoned and sank by 8p.m., taking down with her Captain Fegen and 190 crewmen. The Captain was later posthumously awarded the VC.

Night had closed in by now, the ships had scattered and the "Admiral Scheer" was able to overtake and sink only five ships before darkness closed in.

The final ship to be sunk by the "Scheer's" 11 inch guns was SS "Maidan", with Richard Jones on board. The vessel went down with its full complement of 90 crew, due mainly to the effect of the tremendous blast generated as the cargo of explosives erupted.

Richard Heseltine Jones is commemorated on Panel 66, Tower Hill Memorial. Christopher and Ann Jones had therefore lost their eldest son in the Great War and now their youngest son had perished in the Second World War.

Thankfully the year 1940 ended without the loss of any other dalesman serving in the armed forces and it would be April of the following year before such news arrived.

1941 – THE BRITISH EMPIRE ALONE AND AT BAY

During January and early February 1941 the British and Empire troops of the Western Desert Force had advanced 500 miles in North Africa, destroying nine Italian divisions in the process. By the end of February, however, the German Luftwaffe had arrived in Sicily, barring the use of the port of Benghazi as a base for the Western Desert Force. General Erwin Rommel arrived in North Africa with his Afrika Korps in March 1941 and drove back the British forces between March 24th and May 30th. The isolated fortress of Tobruk held out against the Germans and Italians, in order to deprive Rommel of a base port to support further advance into Egypt.

Throughout the rest of 1941, the world witnessed the evacuation of British forces from Greece and the German conquest of the Mediterranean island of Crete. However, 1941 saw important developments in widening the war into a truly world wide conflict. The main new German sphere of interest now became Russia, when on June 22nd Operation "Barbarossa" was launched against the Soviet Union, and toward the close of the year America was drawn into the war when the Japanese launched their surprise attack on Pearl Harbour, on December 7th.

This third year of the war would see the loss of seven men from the dale whilst serving in a military capacity. Five of these servicemen died on home territory due to accidents or from natural causes, but each man was in uniform, serving his country during these dangerous, trying times. For some, their deaths would not have occurred if it had not been for the war disrupting their civilian lives and their loss was felt deeply by their families back in the dale.

PRIVATE ROBERT HAMMELL HESELTINE NO. 7634237 (RAOC) ATTACHED TO 9TH BATTALION LANCASHIRE FUSILIERS DIED SATURDAY 19TH APRIL 1941 AGE 19.

Robert Heseltine was born at Hogra Farm, just off the main street in Redmire, the eldest child of Ernest Heseltine and his wife Elizabeth (nee Hammell). The five other members of the family were Jack, Matthew, Betty, Margaret and Eileen.

When Robert left school he went to work for his uncle, Vic Hammell, at

Aysgarth Garage, where he became a qualified motor mechanic. He also helped his father at Hogra Farm. A feature on all the farms in Redmire and Castle Bolton during the 1920's and 1930's was the use made by the farmers of donkeys to transport the milk from the fields to the farm or up Dairy Hill to Redmire Dairy, close to the railway station. Whey was brought back to the farm from the dairy to feed to the pigs, after the milk had been made into cheese.

Although he could have remained working on the farm in a reserved occupation, Robert was encouraged to volunteer for the services and, with his skills as a mechanic, he joined the Royal Army Ordnance Corps.

By 1941 he was attached to the 9th Battalion Lancashire Fusiliers as a motor

Private Robert H. Heseltine, Royal Army Ordnance Corps (Redmire).

Matthew Heseltine, brother of Robert, aged 11 years, with the family donkey, bringing the milk back to Hogra Farm after milking in the fields, 1930's. They are on Dairy Hill.

cycle despatch rider and was working in the Colchester area. Sadly, he was killed in a traffic accident whilst riding his motor bike on service, on April 19th 1941. Robert was brought back home to Redmire and is buried in the village church-yard.

ORDINARY SEAMAN JAMES METCALFE
NO. D/JX241291 HMS DRAKE RN
DIED MONDAY 5TH MAY 1941 AGE 26.

James Metcalfe was the only child of Thomas Metcalfe and his wife, Sophia Isabel. Thomas was from a farming family at Hellgill, on the Moorcock Inn to Kirkby Stephen road. It was here that James was born in 1915, but in December 1918 his father died, aged 35, in the flu pandemic that resulted in greater loss of life than from the casualties of the Great War.

Sophia was left a young widow, with a three year old child to raise. For some years she kept house for her brother, but eventually she went to live with James in Hawes, near to the Cattle Market.

James, a serious minded youth, left Hawes School and eventually began work for the Customs and Excise branch in the office of a whisky distillery at Campbell-town, in Scotland.

Called up during the early part of the war, James joined the Royal Navy and was posted to the RN Shore

James Metcalfe (Hawes).

Establishment, HMS Drake, an Accounting Base at Devonport, where his clerical skills could be put to good use. As the work load became ever greater he was sent to the overflow establishment at Bristol, known as HMS Cabot.

It was here that James was taken seriously ill and rushed into hospital with a form of Purpura, a blood disease associated with a diseased bone marrow. His mother and aunty travelled by rail to Bristol but he died shortly after their arrival. James Metcalfe is buried in grave 19 in St. Margaret's Churchyard, Hawes.

Two days later. Another serviceman from Hawes died, killed in action in the skies above the French coast.

SERGEANT NORMAN HENRY MEANWELL
NO. 755671 18 SQUADRON RAFVR
DIED WEDNESDAY 7TH MAY 1941 AGE 29.

On the outbreak of the war Norman Meanwell, son of Percy and Florence Ethel Meanwell, lived with his wife Margaret and baby daughter June in Caister-on-Sea, on the outskirts of Great Yarmouth.

Norman Meanwell.

He enlisted for training as an observer in the RAF and was posted to 18 Squadron, which in early 1941 was operating twin-engined Bristol Blenheim fighter bombers from Portreath Airfield on the north coast of Cornwall, between St Ives and Newquay.

Prior to this the squadron was stationed at RAF Oulton, near Aylsham, which was not too far from his home, where he took a friend and colleague Jim Moore, from Hawes, to visit his family.

The Squadron had an extremely busy April. Anti-shipping operations dominated, though night time raiding featured on two occasions early in the month when the port of Brest on the Brittany coast was the focal point of attention. Losses were particularly heavy between April 15th and 23rd whilst attacking enemy coastal shipping. The Commanding Officer of 18 Squadron was last seen flying towards the French coast following an attack on an armed trawler.

More and more attacks were made against mainland Europe. In the period between the end of April and 9th May, operations had been mounted on six consecutive nights. Daytime operations over the same period had witnessed the despatch of 131 Blenheims, continuing their hazardous anti-shipping strikes. These raids were at a cost of seven Blenheims and one of these was the machine crewed by Norman Meanwell, lost on May 7th.

At 10.25a.m., Blenheim R3741 took off from Portreath, crewed by Squadron Leader Barker, Sergeant Norman Meanwell and Sergeant Hughes, their mission

The R.A.F. Memorial at Runnymede.

to patrol Beat 15 and strike at enemy shipping.

Approaching the Brittany coast, off the small port of Paimpol, the aircraft attacked a cargo ship, sailing with an armed escort, and at 11.16a.m. crashed into the sea, streaming flames. On impact a plume of smoke was seen rising to over 100 feet. All three crewmen were killed and, as no bodies were recovered, their names are commemorated on Panel 48 of the RAF Memorial at Runnymede.

Great Yarmouth was receiving a lot of unwelcome attention from the Luftwaffe at that time. The parents of Norman's friend, Jim Moore, invited Norman's wife Margaret and daughter June to stay with them at West Bank, Hawes. She accepted and never returned to Caister.

Although the threat of invasion had receded a little in people's minds, the Home Guard and its activities still performed a vital role in the defence of the British homeland. These activities sometimes came at a cost, for during the wartime years fatalities within Home Guard ranks were numbered in their hundreds. Indeed, the next casualty in Wensleydale came from within the ranks of Leyburn Home Guard Platoon.

PRIVATE GEORGE MILES LUMLEY, LEYBURN HOME GUARD DIED FRIDAY 15TH AUGUST 1941 AGE 31.

George Miles Lumley (Leyburn).

George, one of twin brothers, was born in 1909, the son of John and Ada Lumley of Birkby, near Appleton-on-Wiske. He married a local girl, Millicent Herring, at Hamposthwaite church, near Harrogate, and they came to live at the recently built Thornborough Crescent, Leyburn, at No. 9.

George Lumley was a lorry driver employed by the Central Road Motor Services of the LNER Railway. He was based at Leyburn Station Yard, where 3 ton Fordson flat bodied lorries and a tipper lorry for delivering coal were garaged. Five lorries were kept at Leyburn, three at Bedale, two at Hawes and one each at Aysgarth, Jervaulx and Leeming Bar.

Another large wooden garage was across the yard from the workshop, containing four Albion and one Guildford horse boxes. All the race horse trainers from Middleham and Coverdale used railway transport in those days. On race days, four drivers, including George Lumley, would appear in their fine uniforms, double breasted with gold buttons, topped off with peaked chauffeur's hats.

One of these boxes had a plaque on its side after 1945, noting that it was the box that transported "Dante", trained by Middleham trainer Matthew Peacock, when it won the 1945 "Derby".

However, George would not live to see that day. During 1940 he joined Leyburn Home Guard. On July 15th 1941 George was taking part in a shooting match between Leyburn and Hunton Home Guards, in a field at Hunton, when a shot from a rifle in the hands of Sergeant George Parsley of the Leyburn detachment, entered his right foot. He died a month later as a result of injuries received.

George Parsley, a Leyburn station worker and former corporal in the Great War, was a great friend of George Lumley. Whilst lying down to fire his ·22 rifle at the target, the cocking pin had slipped and caused the cartridge to fire, at the same time as his left hand slipped, turning the rifle in the direction of his friend.

Whilst visiting her husband in Darlington Hospital, George Lumley had told his wife Milly that George Pashley was not to blame and at the inquest the sergeant was exonerated. However, one month after the accident George Lumley had died from a heart condition resulting from the injury to his foot.

The Coroner recorded "This man has died in the service of his country in the same way as if he had been engaged on active service."

George Lumley was buried on Tuesday 19th August at Leyburn Cemetery. Leyburn Home Guard, with Platoon commanders J.C. Beswick and R. Lambert, formed a guard of honour and representatives from other detachments were in attendance.

Two months later another accident claimed the life of the son of a well-known dales family from Thornton Rust.

PRIVATE FRANCIS JOHN CHAPMAN NO. 4466393 16TH BATTALION DURHAM LIGHT INFANTRY DIED WEDNESDAY 8TH OCTOBER 1941 AGE 31.

Francis Chapman was the eldest son of John and Ella Mary Chapman of Thornton Hall, Thornton Rust. John Chapman from Cliff Lodge, Leyburn, had married Ella Matthews, also of Leyburn, and set up home at Thornton Hall, where Francis was born in 1910, sister Ruby in 1911 and brother Robert in 1915. Their father died in 1915, at the early age of 37.

Francis attended Sedbergh School and by this time his mother had married Major R.H. Whitehead, an officer who had served in the Great War.

The head of the Chapman family had for many years been Master of the Wensleydale Harriers, and in 1931 Francis John Chapman became Master. The family owned land, moors and farms in the dale and the gentry would arrive to take part in the grouse shooting.

However, it was the hunting of hares and occasionally foxes, on foot, using the pack of hounds from the Wensleydale Harriers, that provided the main field sport in the dale. The hunts went on for a number of days and the trails extended across the dale towards Thoralby.

In the "Kennel Field" at Thornton Rust was a barn where cows and sheep which had died, were skinned

Francis John Chapman (Thornton Rust), Master of the Wensleydale Harriers.

Francis John Chapman with some of the Wensleydale Harriers' hounds pre-1939.

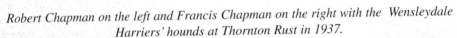

Robert Chapman on the left and Francis Chapman on the right with the Wensleydale Harriers' hounds at Thornton Rust in 1937.

Gathering to shoot foxes on the Stake Road across Stake Allotments between Bainbridge and Wharfedale, 1938, just beyond Carpley Green.

and their meat placed in a "set pan", together with meal and water, which was then boiled. This tasty dish was then fed to the pack of hounds.

Major Whitehead was in charge of Aysgarth and Thornton Rust Home Guard and his step son, Francis, became a member, before joining the army as a private in the 16th Battalion Durham Light Infantry. By October 1941 Francis was serving in the south of England.

It was there that Francis was killed in a road accident involving a military vehicle on October 8th, whilst off duty, and his body was returned to be buried in the north part of Aysgarth Churchyard.

An escort of men from the D.L.I., represented by Sergeant Knight, attended and after the internment, the Last Post and Reveille were sounded by a bugler. The guard of honour consisted of members of the Aysgarth Home Guard, commanded by Major Whitehead and Askrigg Home Guard was represented by Lieutenant Wilkinson and Sergeant R. Hopper.

In the Britain of today, with its proliferation of light pollution in all our cities and towns, it is difficult to imagine the intensity of the ink-black darkness that was the norm during the blackout, experienced by the population of these islands in the 1940's. It is not surprising that in such conditions the number of road accidents increased dramatically. The next fatality to a serving dalesman came in just such a way eight days later.

AIRCRAFTMAN SECOND CLASS FREDERICK WILLIAM LAWSON NO. 948576 RAFVR DIED THURSDAY 16TH OCTOBER 1941 AGE 25.

The Lawson family had long standing West Burton connections. Frederick's grandfather, William Lawson, was married twice, first to Ann Fawcett who died young, and then to Margaret Jacques of Finghall. A son, James, came from the first union, whilst William Anthony Lawson was born to William and Margaret.

When he became older, James kept the West Burton shop selling mainly groceries, whilst his half brother, William Anthony became the sub-postmaster for the village and kept a general store, known as Wensleydale Stores (now a house called Hazeley). He kept items that reflected the life of the dale — cattle drenches, pig powders and cartridges. He used to issue Game Licences on the Post Office side, as August 12th, the start of the grouse shooting, was an important occasion in the area. Between 3a.m. and 5a.m. on August 12th the locals

Frederick William Lawson
(West Burton).

West Burton c1910. The two shops belonging to the Lawson families can be seen.
On the left is the Post Office (now called 'Hazeley'). In the 1930's
Freddie Lawson's parents ran the shop.

would hear many cars travelling through Walden Dale, on their way to the shooting on Walden Moor.

By this time, William Anthony Lawson had married a West Burton girl, Margaret (Maggie) Tomay, a teacher at West Burton School, and two children, Frederick and Kathlene, were born. On leaving Yorebridge Grammar School, where he had been a high achiever academically, Fred went on to Leeds University to take a degree in English. He was also a good sportsman, especially keen on cricket, playing the game throughout the dale and at University. Poetry was a passion and a number of his poems were published.

Fred volunteered for the RAF at the beginning of the war, leaving his work as a teacher at the Methodist School in Richmond. Serving first in Wiltshire and Lincolnshire, before being sent to the Yorkshire bomber squadron base at Dishforth, his job in the RAF was teaching Polish airmen English. However, unbeknown to his family he was also training to be an air-gunner.

Freddie Lawson on Graduation Day
at Leeds University.

Fourth row: Tommy Brown (extreme right),
Lawrence Lidell (3rd from the left).
Third row: Renee Shorter (3rd from left),
Mrs. Shorter (5th from left).
Second row: R.C. Shorter,
headmaster Yorebridge Grammar School
(3rd from right).
First row: Roger Johnson (extreme left),
Fred Lawson (2nd from left),
Len Kirby (3rd from left).

1941 at RAF Dishforth, Yorkshire.
Freddie Lawson is sitting first on the right, middle row.

He died in a night time traffic accident on October 16th near his base, during the blackout. A military truck mounted the pavement whilst he was walking, and struck him down.

Frederick Lawson was brought home to West Burton and was buried in the SW part of Aysgarth Churchyard.

An article in the Darlington and Stockton Times reads, "It was his fine, dauntless spirit, his gay and courageous personality that won the hearts of all those with whom he came in contact. None could resist that flashing smile and cheery voice. Affectionately known throughout the dale as "Freddie", he was loved by old and young, rich and poor, high and low. Wensleydale is proud to have nurtured one so brilliant, so charming and so loveable."

A poem Freddie wrote during the war reads :

> "There was a time when men could walk
> Beneath the jewelled dome of night,
> Deriving from the very stillness of the air,
> The simple beauty of the star-lit sky,
> A calm of mind — a peace of soul.
> But now, strange darting beams of light
> In wanton violation of the heavens,

Attempt to pierce the virgin veil which hides
The cherished secrets of the stars.
For night no longer offers peace and calm,
The frantic throb of engines cut the air,
The retching sirens wail in warning blast,
Portending grim destruction, chaos, death.
The fall of bombs, the angry roll of guns
Combine discords of war, whilst bursting shells
Encase the wondering stars with rings of fire.
For though this race is so advanced in mind
In science, reason and enlightened thought,
War is permitted to destroy
The Peace and sanctity of our dreams,
The lovely silence of our night."

The final casualty from Wensleydale during 1941 was a Royal Navy officer who went down with his ship in desperate fighting in the waters of the Mediterranean Sea, off the coast of North Africa.

LIEUTENANT FRANK V. PERCIVAL (ENGINEER) HMS "BARHAM" RN DIED TUESDAY 25TH NOVEMBER 1941 AGE 26.

During 1935/1936 Frank Percival's father, Arthur, a retired police superintendent, and his mother Caroline, arrived with Frank's elder sister Ann to live at Winville, on the Main Street in Askrigg. Later they moved to The Lodge. Ann set up in business as a hairdresser in the village.

Frank was an engineer with a Bachelor of Science Honours Degree from London University, who worked for one of the electricity companies in Sheffield. He would drive over to the family home in Askrigg each weekend. It was at dances held in the locality that he met Ann Scarr from Gill Gate Farm, near Helm, and started dating her. Sometimes they would drive on Saturdays to Morecambe to attend the dancing at the resort. He also enjoyed working on the Scarr's farm, especially during hay making.

Frank joined up early in the war as a sub-lieutenant and rose to the rank of Lieutenant, in charge of the engine room of HMS "Barham", a First World War battleship. By 1941 it was part of Admiral Cunningham's cruiser-carrier force in the Eastern Mediterranean.

With the arrival of the Luftwaffe Corps in Sicily and Rommel's Afrika Korps in Libya, Allied surface and air activities were disrupted and Malta bombed incessantly. Shipping from England to North Africa had to be re-routed via the Cape of Good Hope and the Red Sea.

In anticipation of German intervention in the Balkans and Greece, the British sent their best troops from North Africa to Greece in March 1941. Due to the German's rapid progress, these forces withdrew to the coast and Royal Navy ships evacuated 43,000 troops, 14,000 of these being landed on Crete to prepare its defences. A total of 24 Royal Navy vessels were lost to German air attacks.

Whilst German air-borne troops assaulted the island of Crete on May 20th, the Royal Navy routed a German amphibious operation bringing reinforcements, with the loss of 5000 German lives. Naval forces managed to evacuate 15,000 hard pressed defenders from Crete but many vessels were lost, with naval casualties totalling 2000 men.

The arrival of 12 more U-boats into the Mediterranean complicated the British naval situation. The submarines soon had a devastating effect on Royal Navy strength, for on November 12th HMS "Ark Royal", with her complement of aircraft, was sunk by torpedo and this was the beginning of a series of grievous losses to the fleet.

At 4.25p.m. on November 25th HMS "Barham" was hit by three torpedoes

The death of the Barham on 25th November 1941, in the Mediterranean Sea.

from submarine U-331, 200 miles WNW of Alexandria. The salvo, fired at close range, struck Barham on the port side, between the funnel and the after turrets. She immediately took a heavy list to port and when she was on her beam end, about 4 minutes after being hit, her magazine blew up. She sank with the loss of 861 officers and men, including Lieutenant Frank Percival.

More was to follow. On the night of December 18th an Italian submarine launched three "human torpedoes" against Alexandria. Penetrating the harbour boom, time bombs were fixed to the battleships "Queen Elizabeth" and "Valiant", which were put out of action for months. In the course of a few weeks the whole of the Eastern Fleet was eliminated and Rommel's position in the Western Desert was rapidly strengthened.

No bodies were recovered from HMS "Barham" and Frank Percival is commemorated on Panel 45, Column 2 of the Portsmouth Naval Memorial.

1942 – THE WAR WIDENS DRAMATICALLY

As 1942 dawned, just over two years of war had resulted in 12 deaths among Wensleydale's servicemen. However, the coming year, with its ever widening spheres of conflict, witnessed five more deaths of men from the dale. The Japanese advance through Malaya and their capture of Singapore claimed one victim, an RAF Bomber Command airman lost his life over Germany, as embattled Britain carried the war to the enemy by air bombardment, whilst the three remaining victims lost their lives in the battle for supremacy in North Africa.

CAPTAIN ROBERT WATSON
NO. 56898 9TH BATTALION
NORTHUMBERLAND FUSILIERS
DIED SUNDAY 15TH FEBRUARY 1942 AGE 27.

We have already seen that Robert's elder brother, Pilot Officer Joe Watson, was killed whilst attacking targets over Berlin in September 1940.

Robert Watson joined the army and by late 1941 he was a Captain in the 9th Battalion Northumberland Fusiliers (the Divisional Machine Gun Battalion), in charge of "Y" Company.

On October 30th 1941 they sailed from Liverpool on board "Warwick Castle", in convoy, bound for Egypt via Halifax, Nova Scotia, and the Cape of Good Hope in South Africa.

At Cape Town on December 9th they heard news of the Japanese attack on Pearl Harbour on December 7th. The USA were now allies at war with Germany,

Italy and Japan.

Whilst off Mombasa, the decision was made to divert the 18th Division to the Far East, to help ward off the Japanese threat. On arrival at Bombay, on January 6th 1942, the Battalion went into camp, where they heard of an unbroken series of Japanese successes.

On January 21st they embarked on "Felix Roussel" on the final stage of their long journey. Although well trained, well equipped and with excellent morale, the Battalion had spent 14 weeks in the confined space of a crowded troop ship. The men had therefore become somewhat "soft". As they approached Singapore on February 5th the convoy was attacked by 27 enemy aircraft, with 5 men killed and 14 wounded on board the ship.

The Battalion moved to the NE side of the island, making do with impressed civilian lorries of doubtful reliability. The Japanese were now preparing to assault the island across the Johore Straits, crossing on the night of February 8th/9th and establishing a bridgehead. By February 12th the situation had become very grave and the decision was made to form a perimeter on the south of the island, covering the city. At 2p.m. the Battalion withdrew within the perimeter.

On the 13th, enemy gun, mortar and small arms fire and bombing continued throughout the day and the Battalion had lost many of its vehicles owing to enemy action. During February 14th the Battalion took up fresh defensive positions, with "Y" Company in the centre and on the 15th enemy pressure from both ground and air was intensified. Many isolated engagements took place in which heavy casualties occurred on both sides.

By this time the Japanese held all the water reservoirs and at 6p.m. on February 15th the garrison surrendered to the Japanese forces.

For Captain Robert Watson it was too late, however, for on the very day of the surrender he had been struck down during one of the isolated engagements with the enemy.

A senior officer of the Fusiliers later wrote to Robert's parents, "I knew Robert well as my second in command at Whitley Bay and then in "Y" Company before we embarked. I always found him a most loyal and hardworking comrade, and felt very upset at his death. His leadership of the Company in action was typical of his earlier work in the training stages, to do his best at any cost; and he upheld the highest traditions of our Regiment to the end."

Robert Watson was buried in grave 34.A.10. at Kranji War Cemetery, Singapore, on the north side of Singapore Island, overlooking the Straits of Johore. His parents left Hardraw shortly after the war ended and retired to the Swaledale village of Thwaite.

SERGEANT ERNEST KEITH STEVENS
WIRELESS OPERATOR/AIR GUNNER
214 SQUADRON RAFVR
DIED THURSDAY 2ND APRIL 1942 AGE 22.

Keith Stevens arrived in the dale as a youth during the mid-1930's when his mother, Lily Stevens, took up her position as a teacher at Bainbridge School. Together with an older brother Reg, they lived at Bow Bridge, Low Abbotside, where their father Josiah Dickens Stevens was a self employed joiner.

Ernest Keith Stevens of Bow Bridge, near Askrigg.

Josiah was musical, helping with the choir at Askrigg Church and during the 1935 Silver Jubilee Celebrations at Bainbridge, he was the leader of a band that led the procession, playing on home made instruments such as combs.

Keith Stevens worked at Swain's Shop in Hawes and in his leisure time was great friends with local lads, Jack Hindle and David Middleton. During the summer months they often went swimming in the River Ure, near Yorebridge, being charged a few pence by Mr. Bell to use a diving board fixed on the river bank in his pasture. The lads also made a flat bottomed wooden boat that they launched on the same stretch of the river.

As soon as war was declared, Keith Stevens joined the Royal Air Force Volunteer Reserve and was soon training as a wireless operator/air gunner. By mid 1941 he was a member of 214 Squadron, based at RAF Stradishall in Suffolk and flying Wellington bombers. During that year they flew many missions against naval and industrial targets in Fortress Europe and played an active part in "Gardening" or mine-laying operations.

On the night of April 1st/2nd, fourteen Wellingtons from 214 Squadron joined with 21 other Wellington bombers and 14 Hampdens to carry out a dangerous low-level attack on railway targets at Hanau, Germany, 10 miles east of Frankfurt. They met with fierce resistance, both from night fighters and flak, and 214 Squadron received catastrophic losses, with 7 Wellingtons failing to return out of the 14 that departed. One of those that crashed was Wellington

Z8805. The crew of E. Dixon, T. Best, A.G. Richards, J. MckHenderson, Keith Stevens and E.T. Albrighton were killed and all are buried in the Rheinberg War Cemetery in Germany. Keith Steven's grave is 1.D.3. By the close of the war Keith's parents had left the dale and were living at Anerley, in Kent.

Meanwhile, Rommel's Afrika Korps and their Italian allies forced the British Army eastwards through the Libyan desert towards the Egyptian border during May and June 1942. A serviceman from Middleham was killed during these defensive operations, whilst a Spennithorne man was captured and died as a POW. A third Wensleydale casualty occurred when a RAF ground crew man from Wensley drowned whilst returning to England from North Africa when his transport ship was torpedoed by a German U-boat.

PRIVATE THOMAS HENRY HAMMERTON
NO. 4540397 2ND BATTALION
WEST YORKSHIRE REGIMENT
DIED FRIDAY 5TH JUNE 1942 AGE 23.

Thomas Hammerton, 3rd from the left. (Middleham and South Otterington).

Thomas (Sonny) Hammerton was born at Masham, the eldest son of Robert and Maude. Robert had served as a gunner in the horse artillery during the Great War and became a groom in a hunting stable in the Ripon area after being de-mobbed. He married a girl from Mickly and they moved to the Masham area, where Robert was again employed as a groom. Other children born were

Kathleen, Betty, Les, Ted, Billy and Maude.

The family moved to Clematis House at South Otterington, near Northallerton, but in the mid-1930's Sonny went to work as a stable hand at Matthew Peacock's Manor House Racing Stables, Middleham.

Sonny Hammerton entered the war early and joined the 2nd Battalion West Yorkshire Regiment. By late 1941 the Battalion found itself in North Africa and involved in stemming Rommel's assault. The defence against Rommel's drive across Cyenaica towards Suez consisted of a number of strong points or "boxes" linked by deep minefields. Those nearest the Axis forces were held by the infantry, while those further back served as a base from which the armour could operate. The key position was the "box" known as "Knightsbridge".

The German armour and their air support were superior to the British at this point and the German Stuka dive bombers could take up again their role of flying artillery.

Rommel attacked on May 26th, forcing a gap through the minefield, and threw the mass of his armour against the strong point of Got el Oualeb. It capitulated on June 2nd with the loss of 3000 prisoners.

As the British counter-attacked in the battle known as "The Cauldron", the German position was skilfully held behind minefields protected by batteries of 88mm. guns and these thwarted the most gallant attacks of the British forces.

Rommel then re-doubled his armoured attack, which drove hard into the British rear. As night fell on the "Knightsbridge" battlefield, the Germans counted 4000 Allied prisoners and 50 tanks destroyed. Many other soldiers had been killed and one of those missing was Sonny Hammerton. It would be many months before his death was confirmed and he was later buried in grave 8.H.22. in Knightsbridge War Cemetery, Libya.

During the same battle, a Spennithorne man was taken prisoner and sadly died some months later.

PRIVATE FRANK WILKINSON
NO. 4393757 5TH BATTALION
GREEN HOWARDS REGIMENT
DIED FRIDAY 13TH NOVEMBER 1942 AGE 26.

Frank's father, George Wilkinson, was born at Tunstall and started work in Hornby Castle gardens for the Duke of Leeds, before working in the quarries at Piercebridge. When work became scarce in 1911 he travelled to Wensleydale, settling at Spennithorne and working in the quarries at Harmby and Leyburn. Marrying a local girl, Mary Dodsworth, they lived at Abbey Cottage, where they

Frank Wilkinson (Harmby).

Mr. and Mrs. Wilkinson, Harmby,
parents of Frank.

raised Joseph, Annie, Frank and Harry. In 1929 George left quarrying and took up road work for the County Council as the "lengthman" for Harmby and Spennithorne, until he retired in 1939.

Frank left school and worked for the Co-operative Shop on Richmond Road, Leyburn, before entering the army early in the war and joining the 5th Battalion Green Howards Regiment. Sister Annie joined the WAAF, Harry was a member of RAF ground crew and Joseph also joined the army.

The 5th Battalion travelled via the Cape of Good Hope to Egypt. In February 1942 they entered the line south of Gazala, making ready for the next Axis push.

During the next month they adapted to desert fighting as they dug, wired, laid mines and patrolled aggressively from their strong point, the "Knightsbridge Box". When Rommel struck on May 26th, the "Box" was by-passed, but eventually attacks intensified. For five days they doggedly defended the area of desert called "The Cauldron" against 6 separate attacks from Rommel's panzers and dive bombers.

Then on June 1st, tanks, self-propelled guns and infantry were unleashed from every direction. The Brigadier was killed and most positions were overrun. Though desperate in their defence, fighting to the last of their ammunition, it was

Henry (Harry) Wilkinson.

Wilkinson brothers, Joseph, Frank, Harry.

all over by midday. The Brigade had ceased to exist and thousands of soldiers were taken prisoner. One of these men was Frank Wilkinson.

He was taken to a POW camp in the captured port of Tripoli, well behind the lines, where the conditions were very poor. Unfortunately, due to the dreadful sanitary conditions, Frank succumbed to dysentery and died on November 13th. He was buried in grave 11.C.10. in the Tripoli War Cemetery.

It was between the deaths of Thomas (Sonny) Hammerton and Frank Wilkinson that a Wensley man was reported as lost at sea.

CORPORAL FREDERICK STANLEY HUMBLE
NO. 523212 RAF
DIED SATURDAY 12TH SEPTEMBER 1942.

Stanley's father, John Humble, was born in Manchester but by 1901 he was the 21 year old poultry manager on the Bolton Hall estate at Wensley. However, by the start of the Great War he was chauffeur for Lord Bolton. He married into the Pearson family and set up home in a cottage near Wensley church.

John Humble only entered the Great War in June 1918, aged 39, when his skills as a mechanic were utilised by the RAF as an Air Mechanic. Less than a month later he sailed for Egypt but when the war ended he was de-mobbed in April 1919, returning to become eventually the head chauffeur at Bolton Hall.

Two children, Frederick Stanley and Clarice, were born. Clarice became the post mistress at Wensley, whilst Stanley worked in the joiners' shop at Wensley Sawmill. Soon after war was declared Stanley joined the same service as his father when he became a Corporal in the RAF, and was stationed in Egypt and the North African desert.

Involved in the rout of the Italian forces in 1941, Stanley later found himself on board Her Majesty's Transport Ship SS "Laconia" in early September 1942, bound for England.

The 19,695 ton SS "Laconia" was sailing independently from the Middle

John Humble in the RAF in 1918. He was the father of Frederick Stanley Humble of Wensley.

East to the United Kingdom via the Cape. She had on board over 3,500 passengers and crew, including British service personnel and 1,800 Italian POW's.

The ship was torpedoed and sunk by the German U-boat U-156 at 8p.m. on September 12th, about 300 miles NE of Ascension Island in the Atlantic Ocean. No distress signal was received by any British authority until September 15th, when naval authorities in West Africa ordered "Corinthian" and SS "Empire Haven" to search for survivors, without success.

In the meantime, Korvettenkapitan Hartenstein of U-156 had himself made an SOS signal. In Germany, Admiral Donitz ordered other U-boats to go to the rescue and requested the French Vichy Government to send help from Dakar. The French sloop Annamite had also picked up a SOS and passed it on to Dakar.

The French cruiser "Gloire" and escort vessels Annamite and Dumont D'Urville picked up 1041 survivors, of which about 600 were British. In addition, 16 survivors landed from a lifeboat near Freetown on October 10th, and a further 4 were picked up from another lifeboat by HMS "Wistam" on

October 21st. 2,500 people were therefore lost when the "Laconia" sank, including Stanley Humble.

While U-boats were collecting survivors they were bombed by American aircraft. The news was transmitted to the German Admiralty and led Donitz to issue the order, subsequently known as the "Laconia Order", directing that survivors of ships sunk were not to be rescued in future.

Frederick Stanley Humble's name is commemorated on Column 263 of the Alamein Memorial, Egypt.

1943 – THE TIDE BEGINS TO TURN

As the year 1943 unfolded it would witness an increase in the number of casualties from the dale. For British soldiers in 1943, the main theatre of operations was North Africa and the Mediterranean, where 3 men from Wensleydale would lose their lives. In Northern Europe, the sole means of striking at the enemy came from the air and sadly 6 airmen would also be lost during the year. The "Forgotten Army" was still fighting the Japanese in the Far East and it was as a POW that a Bellerby soldier would die, due to the atrocious living conditions he was made to suffer and the treatment meted out to him by his Japanese captors.

FLIGHT SERGEANT HARRY TERRY
NO. 1091871 WIRELESS OPERATOR/AIR GUNNER RAFVR
DIED FRIDAY 5TH MARCH 1943 AGE 21.

Harry Terry was the son of Harry and Margaret Alice Terry (nee Dolphin). Harry senior worked as a cowman for Middleham farmer and landowner Mr. Topham, at Middleham House, looking after his herd of Jersey cows (each cow with a bell round its neck).

The Terry family lived first in a cottage behind Castle Hill, Middleham, and then moved to Magpie Cottage, Kirkgate, where Evylene, Fred, Harry and Roland were raised.

Harry Terry attended Yorebridge Grammar School and was then employed by Messrs. Wilkinson and Co., Solicitors, of Leyburn. In his spare time he was a member of Middleham Church Choir, a sidesman at the church, Honorary Secretary of Middleham Tennis Club and in 1940 was a member of the Home Guard.

However, he had offered his services in the Royal Air Force Volunteer Reserve when war began and eventually joined the RAF, becoming a wireless operator/air gunner in Bomber Command, serving on an airfield in the south of

Harry Terry (Middleham). *Parents of Harry Terry.*

Harry Terry with his aircrew. He is 3rd from the left.

Fred, Roland and Norah Terry.

England. On Friday March 5th he met with an accident whilst in training and died, aged 21 years.

Wellington bomber DV923 took off from Westcott airfield, Buckinghamshire, for a night navigation exercise. It returned to base about 1.55a.m. but overshot its approach and crashed at Long Crendon, 9 miles WSW of Aylesbury. Sergeants Terry and Black were killed, whilst the other four crew men were injured.

Harry's body was returned to Middleham and on Tuesday March 9th he was buried with full military honours in Middleham Churchyard. The coffin, draped with the Union Jack, was borne shoulder high by a military escort.

Brother Fred had joined up in September 1939, joining the 1st Border Regiment and being attached to the Airborne Division when it was formed. Stationed in North Africa, he trained on gliders and in parachuting, taking part in the airborne invasion of Sicily and Italy, where he was wounded.

Returning to England, Fred trained in preparation for the Arnhem landings in Holland, September 17th 1944, and went in with the gliders of the 1st Airborne Division. He was hit by a sniper and was taken to a local convent by the Dutch villagers and attended to by local doctors until he recovered.

For the rest of the war he remained a POW in Stalag 11B, in Germany. It was not until December 1st 1944, however, that his family received news that he was alive, bringing great comfort to them, for they believed that they may have lost a second son.

One week after the death of airman Harry Terry, Middleham received further news of the death of another RAF flyer from the town.

FLIGHT SERGEANT GEORGE EDWARD BENSON NO. 1143366 AIR GUNNER 78 SQUADRON RAFVR DIED FRIDAY 12TH MARCH 1943.

George Edward Benson was born at Middleham and lived with his parents and five older sisters, including Kathleen, Florence, Grace and Muriel, in a cottage immediately below the present day "Nose Bag Cafe" and Richard III Inn. With a bright, cheery disposition, his nickname was "Sunny" and like Harry Terry, he

George Edward Benson (Sunny), standing on extreme left together with three friends, outside the Middleham Picture House, a few days before all four went off to join the Armed Services.

359

too was a member of the church choir.

His father was a cowman working for Mr. Rayner at The Grove, Middleham, whilst his mother worked for the Rayners in the laundry. After "Sunny" Benson left school he went to work for Mr. Paulter in Middleham, as an apprentice cobbler, and was still employed there when he enlisted in the RAF near the start of the war. Joining 78 Squadron, he began training as an air-gunner.

By September 1942, 78 Squadron was based at Linton-on-Ouse, just north of York. They first used four-engine Halifax bombers on April 30th 1942 in a bombing attack against Ostend.

By mid 1942 onwards the US Airforce arrived in Britain with their Flying Fortresses and the task of bombing was divided around the clock equally between the British and Americans, the former by night and the latter by day. By day the Americans performed "precision" bombing whilst by night Bomber Command performed area bombing, applying an anti-city strategy. Air Chief Marshal Sir Arthur Harris of Bomber Command wished to destroy the morale of the German people as well as destroy the 3rd Reich's war potential.

The Squadron had participated in the historic 1000 bomber raid on Cologne on May 31st 1942, but Bomber Command's Battle of the Ruhr began on March 5th/6th with an attack on Essen. 442 aircraft were despatched, using a blind-bombing device called "Oboe" fitted in each aircraft, resulting in the first effective attack on Essen. Between March 1st and July 1st 1943, the night attacks on the industrial complex of the Ruhr, when 18,506 sorties were made, cost 872 bombers and 5,600 aircrew. One of these casualties was George Edward Benson.

On the night of March 12th/13th 1943, 457 aircraft set out on an air operation against Essen, the primary target being the Krupps Steelworks.

At 7.08p.m. Handley Page Halifax DT774, piloted by Canadian Sergeant Marean, with Sonny Benson as air-gunner, took off from Linton-on-Ouse. 23 aircraft were lost on the raid, 5% of the total force, with DT774 being one of the planes that failed to return. It was shot down by a night fighter and crashed at 9.48p.m., close to a farm building near the hamlet of Grafwegen, on the western edge of the Reichswald and practically straddling the Dutch-German border, some 3km. south of Groesbeck, Holland. All 7 crewmen were killed and are buried in Uden War Cemetery, Holland. George Edward Benson's grave is 4.C.7.

During April 1943 a guardsman from Carperby lost his life in the final push against the Axis forces in North Africa.

SERGEANT THOMAS FOSTER
NO. 2618396 5TH BATTALION GRENADIER GUARDS
DIED THURSDAY 29TH APRIL 1943 AGE 25.

Tom Foster of Thoresby, Carperby.

The Fosters had come from Bishopdale to farm at Thoresby Green Farm, near Carperby. Father Robert and mother Emily brought up a large family consisting of Frank, Tom, James, Robert, Fred, Marmaduke, Alice, Mary, Barbara and Hilda. All six of the lads eventually worked on the farm.

Although in a reserved occupation, Tom Foster enlisted and joined the 5th Battalion Grenadier Guards, whilst his brother James joined the Guards Armoured Division.

Whilst on his embarkation leave, ready to join the fighting in North Africa, Tom Foster married local girl Irene Holmes from Carperby. Nearing the end of his leave he was walking up through Thoresby with the postman, Robert Raw, a veteran of the Great War, when he commented, "I don't think I will come back from this!" The postman replied that of course he would, telling him how he went through the Great War, had become a POW and yet still survived. But after just six weeks of marriage, Tom Foster would be killed.

Prior to embarkation, Tom had instructed soldiers on the use of the bren-gun carrier. He had very little trust in them for they were open-sided and he knew that bullets could ricochet around inside the vehicle.

The campaign the 5th Battalion was joining in had begun on November 8th 1942 when Empire, American and French troops made a series of landings in Algeria and Morocco (Operation "Torch"). The Germans had responded immediately by sending a force from Sicily to northern Tunisia which checked the Allied advance eastwards in December. In the Western Desert the Axis forces that had been defeated at El Alamein withdrew into Tunisia, pursued by the British 8th Army. By mid-April 1943 the combined Axis force was hemmed into a small corner of NE Tunisia and the Allies were grouped for their final offensive.

Carperby Undenominational School 1933.
Standing in front of the school and the Jubilee Tree (planted for Queen Victoria's Diamond Jubilee). This is the same year that Adolf Hitler came to power, with far-reaching consequences for all those on the photograph.
Fourth row: Agnes Scott (teacher), Tom Foster, Alice Foster, Betty Raw, Annie Wood, James Foster, Ruth Preston, Miss Florence Siddell (teacher).
Third row: Annie Lishman, Frank Dinsdale, Eric Dinsdale, Walter Haig, James Percival.
Second row: ? Pickthall, Olive Pickthall, Gwen Dinsdale, Isobelle Atkinson, Emily Raw, Renee Holmes, Bessie Percival, Mary Foster, Hilda Haig, Phyllis Boyce, Nellie Dinsdale, Nellie Percival, Frank Dinsdale.
First row: Freda Pickthall, Mary Percival, Mary Dinsdale, Kenneth Percival, Robert Foster, Roy Wood, George Percival, Edward Pickthall, Gordan Bousfield, Raymond Pickthall, Frank Percival, Fred Percival.

Through the last week of April and the first week of May, the attack against Tunis, spearheaded by the British 1st Army (including the 5th Grenadier Guards Battalion) and the US 2nd Corps went ahead, advancing slowly, losing some encounters but winning most. The first five days of hard fighting failed to break the enemy's resistance and losses were heavy on both sides. Tom Foster was one of these casualties.

On April 7th the 5th Battalion faced north at Medjez, occupying the area for several days. They were attacked on April 20th whilst in position on "Banana Ridge".

The following day they observed a tank battle from this position, whilst the Battalion's mortars and machine guns tore great gaps in the German troops out in the open below. 5 men were killed and 12 wounded during this period.

A night attack took place on April 23rd, with the Battalion assaulting point 134, one of the isolated hills nearby, and taking it as it grew light. The next few hours were spent digging in, with a company detached to dig out various pockets of enemy resistance in the surrounding hills.

Tom Foster (Thoresby) and Irene Holmes (Carperby) on their wedding day.

At 1a.m. on April 26th they set out for "Hill Ridiculous", which they found abandoned by the enemy. Another attack was planned for the evening of April 27th, this time resulting in heavy casualties. Eventually, over the next two days Hills 154 and 171 were taken and the positions occupied for a further 8 days. It was during these actions that Tom Foster was killed on April 29th.

Thomas Foster is buried in grave 9.E.2. Medjez-el-Bab War Cemetery, Tunisia. Sometime after the war, Irene Foster married Thomas's brother James.

SERGEANT STANLEY (PETER) MOORE
NO. 1125511 218 (GOLD COAST) SQUADRON RAFVR
DIED THURSDAY 27TH MAY 1943 AGE 21.

Peter Moore was born at Hawes in 1921, the youngest son of Harold and Helena Moore who had a shop in the Market Place. Brother James and sister Kathleen completed the family. Peter was educated for a short spell at Ripon Grammar School but mainly spent his schooldays at Hawes. He loved fishing, rabbiting,

Peter Moore (Hawes).

Peter Moore cycling home from work as an electrician at Askrigg and stopping to chat with his friend Norman Routh, c1938.

Peter Moore, playing for the Hawes Schoolboy's Football Team, winners of the 1934 Wensleydale Cup by a score of 9 – 0 in the final.
Back row, left to right: John Walker, James Heseltine (Jammy James), Harold Moore (Whitey), Arthur Kirkbride, Harold Jameson, Jackie Irving.
Front row, from left to right: Jim Blades Moore, Jimmy Metcalfe, Peter Moore, Sidney Carter, X.

The mill at Askrigg producing electric light for the Burton's 'Askrigg Electric Lighting Company'. Note the cast iron conduit providing the flow of water from Mill Gill Force.

The cast iron water conduit supplying water from Mill Gill Force to power the generators and turbines in Burton's Mill.

soccer and walking, and in 1934, despite his lack of height, was the goalkeeper in the Hawes Schoolboys' XI which successfully won the Wensleydale Cup.

Peter Moore was employed by Askrigg electrician Ernest (Cloggy) Burton. The Burton family were strong Methodists, with Cloggy being a local lay preacher. They owned West Mill on Mill Lane, Askrigg, producing electricity for the village from before the Great War until after the 2nd World War. The turbine and generator were operated using water from the Mill Gill Waterfalls above Askrigg. It was due to the Burtons that Askrigg possessed electric street lighting before the Great War.

Ernest's father, William

Handley Burton, a millwright, joiner, builder and maker of hand rakes, had seen the possibilities of producing hydro-electric power by harnessing the force of the water tumbling over the 70 feet falls at Mill Gill. West Mill, formerly a corn mill producing Askrigg oatmeal, was set up for operation and in 1908, the Burton home, Mill Gill House, was the first in the dale to be lit by electric light.

A reservoir lake was constructed half a mile above Mill Gill Force. From here it descended 129 feet through a cast iron pipe to the power house in the gorge below. A water supply pipe was laid in a trench cut into the side of the gorge. When the weather was dry, they held the water back in daytime and saved it for the night. The Burtons also introduced lighting to Reeth in 1910, Bainbridge in 1912 and West Burton in 1913.

At the end of 1940 Peter enlisted in the Royal Air Force for training as an electrician and was posted first to his brother James's squadron No.18 in Norfolk. His brother was a wireless operator – air-gunner and the squadron suffered losses during daylight operations.

Within twelve months Peter was promoted to the rank of corporal. He volunteeed for training as an air-gunner and began the process in the autumn of 1942. Having been with his brother's squadron when they were suffering heavy losses he had no illusion about the danger. In May 1943, as the mid-upper gunner in the crew of a four engined Stirling bomber he was posted to 218 Squadron at Downham Market in Norfolk.

At 10.52p.m. on Thursday May 27th Stirling bomber BF405 took off from Downham Market piloted by Flight Sergeant Mills and Pilot Officer True, with Peter Moore as air-gunner. It was a "Gardening" sortie (mine-laying), the target being the sea area off the Friesian Islands along the Dutch and German coasts. It was the 21 year old's first mission of the war and it would be his last. The plane was lost without trace and six months later he was officially presumed dead. No wreckage or bodies were recovered and so the family was never sure what happened on that night. Peter's name is commemorated on Panel 159 of the RAF Memorial, Runnymede.

48 years later his brother James, who had also served in the RAF, received a letter from a history student at Groningen University in the Netherlands, asking for his wartime experiences. James asked the student if there was any way of finding out what happened to his brother. By coincidence, the student's friend

The Blenheim crew from 18 Squadron that parachuted Douglas Bader's artificial leg during a raid over St. Omer, France. One month later they were all killed over the Dutch coast. Left to right: Pilot John Nickelson age 19 (Canada), Walter Meadows, 26, the Observer of Garswood and Wireless Operator/Gunner John Pearson, 24, of Birmingham.

had interviewed a German pilot, Oberfoldwebel Karl George Pfeiffer, who claimed to have shot down a Stirling in the same area at that same time. Only one Stirling had been operating that night. At long last James had confirmation of what had happened to his brother.

*** It is interesting to note that whilst serving as an electrician on 18 Squadron, Peter's colleague, Walter Meadows (Observer) was shot down off Zandvoort, over the coast of Holland in his Blenheim during September 1941. Walter had strong connections with Askrigg, for his brother Alan was the physics teacher at Yorebridge Grammar School, who later retired in the village. The Meadows family had originated from Garswood, near Wigan, where Walter was a buyer for a carpet firm before the war. His mother also came to live at Askrigg in 1940 and Walter was a regular visitor to the village. Walter was 26 years old when he was killed on a 'sweep' of enemy shipping. His aircraft flying into the bomb bursts of another Blenheim during an attack on a convoy and crashed into the sea. He is buried at Bergen op Zoom.

Only the previous month, Walter's crew had had the honour of dropping Wing Commander Douglas Bader's artificial leg by parachute over St. Omer in France, after Douglas Bader had been taken prisoner.

CRAFTSMAN LEONARD SCOTT
NO. 5121868 ROYAL ELECTRICAL
AND MECHANICAL ENGINEERS
DIED WEDNESDAY 9TH JUNE 1943 AGE 23.

Born in 1921, Leonard was the son of Leonard and Nellie Scott of Manor Farm, Bellerby. Educated at Bellerby Church of England School and Richmond Grammar School, he found himself sent to Singapore in late 1942.

During the battle for Singapore Island, in which we have seen that Robert Watson was killed, Leonard Scott was taken prisoner by the Japanese on February 15th 1942. Together with thousands of other POW's he was sent to work on the notorious Burma-Siam Railway, built by Commonwealth, Dutch and American POW's, together with the local civilian population. It was a Japanese project driven by the need for improved communications to support the large Japanese army in Burma. During its construction 13,000 POW's died and were buried along the railway. Between 80,000 and 100,000 civilians also died.

Two labour forces, one based in Siam, the other in Burma, worked from opposite ends of the line towards the centre. The work began in October 1942 and the line, 425 kilometres long, was completed in December 1943.

Working on the railway, the POW's suffered terrible deprivations and abuse from their guards. Leonard Scott died of cholera on June 9th during an epidemic at the Ricke POW camp, in which 300 men died.

His body was cremated in the camp burial ground and later his name was commemorated on Special Memorial 9.M.4. in Kanchanaburi War Cemetery, 129km. WNW of Bangkok, Thailand.

Whilst Leonard was away in the war, two young German Jews who had escaped to England prior to the war on the Kindergarten Scheme, were evacuated to Bellerby from Sunderland and taken in by Leonard's parents at Manor Farm. They became lifetime friends of the family.

As a memorial to Leonard, Nellie Scott presented to Bellerby Church two brass vases to sit on shelves either side of the war memorial plaque inside the

Leonard Scott (Bellerby).

church, as well as a silver communion cup and paten, engraved to her lost son and reading, "To the glory of God and in memory of Leonard Scott who died on active service 9th June 1943."

GUNNER WILLIAM HOUSEMAN
ROYAL ARTILLERY
DIED FRIDAY 18TH JUNE 1943.

William's father and mother, John and Ruth Houseman, came to Middleham from Darley, near Pateley Bridge, in 1919. They lived in a house at the West End and John earned his living as a farm worker for race horse trainer and farmer Matthew Dobson Peacock at Manor Stables. Their children were Raymond, Albert, William, Leslie, Ronald, Phoebe, Stanley, Wilfred and Peter.

In 1939 the family moved to No. 1 Dairy Cottages at Coverham Dairy (run by Rowntrees). John was employed as the pig-keeper at the Dairy, with young pigs brought from Masham to Thoralby to be fed, then transferred to Coverham Dairy to be fattened up on the whey produced from the cheese making at the dairy. Finally the pigs were sent by rail to Leeming Bar for slaughter. Pig breeding at Coverham Dairy stopped in 1941 when tanker lorries began arriving to transport the whey elsewhere.

William Houseman was employed as a cobbler (shoe repairer), working for Middleham cobbler Mr. Poulter and then for Jimmy Barnett, three doors down from Manor House (in the late 1930's there were as many as 18 shops in Middleham, including drapers and saddlers).

In 1941 William enlisted in the Royal Artillery, although his health was not strong. His mother wanted him to get permission from the doctor to be excused from service but William would not hear of it.

However, he was eventually discharged from the army with rheumatic fever, brought on by the soakings he received whilst on manoeuvres.

For a few months he went back to

William Edward Houseman of Middleham and Coverham with youngest brother Peter, just after William was discharged from the army.

work but the illness worsened and he was admitted to Northallerton Hospital, where he died. William was buried in the graveyard of Coverham Church.

By this stage of the war, brothers Raymond, Albert and Leslie were all serving in the army. Albert had joined the Artillery in July 1939 and went to France. He came out at Dunkirk after spending a week on the beaches. Later, he was involved in Operation "Torch" in North Africa and the landings in Sicily and Italy. Leslie, in the Royal Corps of Signals, also saw service in the same three theatres of operations.

However, three months after William's death, the family would be devastated by news of the death of their son Raymond whilst serving in the Mediterranean.

PILOT OFFICER GEORGE DAYKIN COCKBONE NO. 139493 175 SQUADRON RAF DIED SATURDAY 19TH JUNE 1943 AGE 26.

George's father, John Cockbone, came from four generations of a Bainbridge family, whilst his mother, Alice Daykin, came from Nappa Scar. John's father had owned a great deal of property in the area, including Bainbridge Corn Mill.

During the 1920's the mill became a cheese dairy, with the family living nearby. John also kept a few animals on land near Semer Water and ran a

George Daykin Cockbone (Bainbridge).

George Daykin Cockbone, speedway rider.

Bainbridge Sports 1946. The motorbike climb.

Bainbridge Sports 1946. Preparing for the horse race.

Bainbridge Sports 1946. Spectators on the valley side.

butcher's shop in Bainbridge (now Hammond's butchers), with a slaughterhouse at the back.

George was second youngest in the family, his siblings being Richard, John, Guy, Doris, Sidney, Harry, Kenneth and Joan.

From Bainbridge School George went on to Yorebridge Grammar School, before becoming a mechanic at Kettlewell's Central Garage in Hawes. He developed a passion for motor bikes and, allied with his dare devil spirit, he became a semi-professional speedway rider during the 1930's, taking part in events at Belle Vue and Liverpool.

Bainbridge Sports was one of the main social events in the calendar, taking place on a Saturday and Monday in June. The venue was the pasture land along-side the River Ure, near Yorebridge. Athletics, fell races, trotting and harness racing (sulkie racing) all took place on the Saturday and bookies would be on hand to take any bets.

One of the main events was a motor bike hill climb up the steep valley side to see who could reach the top. During the late 1930's the only rider to succeed in this endeavour was George Cockbone, who would complete the climb standing on the seat of his bike (eventually, the "Cockbone Cup" was presented to Bainbridge Sports as a prize for motor bike racing). On the following Monday the children's sports and fancy dress competition were held on the village green.

George Daykin Cockbone (Bainbridge).

George enlisted soon after war broke out and it was no surprise when he joined the RAF as a fighter squadron pilot. In 1940 he married Beatrice (Beatty) Jean Fawcett, a girl from neighbouring Dent, at Cowgill Church. They lived at Spice Gill, Dent, where their son Desmond was born.

By mid 1942 George had joined 175 Squadron, a fighter squadron in the south of England, flying Hurricanes. Just two months before he was killed, the squadron was equipped with the Hawker Typhoon fighter plane, capable of firing from machine-guns or using rockets for low level strafing of ground targets.

On June 2nd, they moved to a new base at Apuldram, near Chichester, on the Selsey peninsula in West Sussex. On the morning of June 19th Pilot Officer George Cockbone took off from the airfield in Typhoon EK184 on a "Rhubarb" mission (RAF slang term for a small scale freelance fighter sortie against ground targets of opportunity).

Crossing the English Channel he passed over the French coast at low level, west of Dieppe, and headed inland looking for targets on the railway line or military vehicles on the highway.

As he followed the main railway line between Rouen and Le Havre he was shot down in the Motteville area, 20 miles south of Dieppe, with no chance of using his parachute.

George Cockbone is buried in grave H.57. in the Dieppe Canadian War Cemetery.

FLIGHT SERGEANT MATTHEW THOMAS METCALFE NO. 1068354 (PILOT) 458 (RAAF) SQUADRON RAFVR DIED TUESDAY 13TH JULY 1943 AGE 22.

"Mattie" Metcalfe was born at Spennithorne in 1921, the elder son of John William and Florence Metcalfe. A younger brother, Alan, completed the family. Their father carried on the family tradition as the village blacksmith for Spennithorne and Harmby, shoeing heavy horses and repairing harrows etc., whilst Florence ran the village post-office after taking over that position from the Blade family.

Mattie Metcalfe had a distinguished career at Yorebridge Grammar School, where, in 1938, he gained his higher school certificate and with it a County major Scholarship to Leeds University. He won the Graham Cup — the most coveted trophy in the school. An all round sportsman, he captained the school cricket and football teams, and was a member of the local cricket, football and tennis clubs.

A talented musician, he had won many awards for pianoforte playing at the Wensleydale Tournament of Song, and as

Leonard Jackson (left) and Matthew Metcalfe whilst on holiday at Morecambe during the 1930's.

Matthew Thomas Metcalfe (Matty) of Spennithorne.
Left: Playing for Yorebridge Grammar School 1930's.
Right: Serving in the RAF.

The Post Office and shop at Spennithorne.

The blacksmith's smithy at Spennithorne. William Metcalfe on the left,
Matthew Thomas Metcalfe on the right.

a boy he frequently played the organ for the children's services at Spennithorne Church, where he was a member of the choir.

He studied for teaching and came through each term with first class results. In 1940, while sitting for his BA degree he volunteered for the RAF.

Mattie joined 458 Squadron but in January 1942 it was transferred to the Middle East and its air crews subsequently ferried 36 Wellington bombers safely to Egypt. Before the sea party arrived at Suez in May the Wellingtons were issued to existing hard-pressed squadrons. 458 Squadron reformed in September 1942 at Shallufa, Egypt, as a Wellington torpedo-bomber unit and rendered valuable service in the Mediterranean Sea. It performed low-level operations over the sea, searching for enemy naval surface vessels or U-boats, often using powerful searchlights at night.

Matthew was serving with the Middle East Training School when he was killed. His Wellington bomber HX734 crashed into the ground 6 miles SE of Cgport Rock while flying low during a training flight. Four other crew members were also killed. He is buried in grave 3.C.7. in the Suez War Memorial Cemetery, Egypt. A memorial service for Matthew Metcalfe was held at Spennithorne Church on Sunday September 12th. The Harmby Methodists made a fine gesture by closing their chapel and attending the service in a body.

PRIVATE JOHN DIXON CHAPMAN
NO. 4470492 9TH BATTALION
DURHAM LIGHT INFANTRY
DIED TUESDAY 17TH AUGUST 1943 AGE 20.

The Chapman family lived near Leyburn Railway Station on Harmby Road. James Chapman, a local postman, had married his wife Margaret Alice and John Dixon was their only child.

John joined the 9th Battalion Durham Light Infantry. Taking part in the invasion of Sicily, the Battalion was moving towards the Primosole Bridge, 15 miles south of Catania, by July 10th 1943. This important river crossing was being held by a small party of British parachutists.

Awaiting the 9th Battalion was the German 1st Airborne Division, recently airlifted in from France. It was vital that the 9th Battalion relieve the hard-pressed parachutists, but they arrived just too late, for they had been driven off the bridge.

During the next 3 days the Battalion took part in an epic battle against a strong position, well defended by first class enemy troops. Heavy losses were inflicted on the 9th Battalion during bitter and prolonged fighting. Many were shot and drowned attempting to swim the river. It was not until July 18th that the Germans finally surrendered their position and the bridge was captured.

I have been unable to discover with certainty whether John Chapman was one of those who was wounded during the battle and died later from his wounds.

What is known is that on August 17th he was buried in grave 2.7.3. in Imtarfa Military Cemetery on the nearby island of Malta. It is most likely that he was evacuated from the battlefield to the care of the hospital on Malta, but there is the possibility that he could have been taken ill and transferred to Malta, where he died from natural causes.

PRIVATE RAYMOND HOUSEMAN
NO. 4461208 1ST BATTALION
DURHAM LIGHT INFANTRY
DIED MONDAY 4TH OCTOBER 1943 AGE 27.

We have already seen how Raymond's brother William died in June 1943 and was buried in Coverham Graveyard.

Living at No. 1 Dairy Cottages, Coverham, Raymond worked as a lorry driver collecting milk churns from local farms and delivering them to Coverham Dairy.

Enlisting on April 18th 1940 he joined the 8th Battalion Durham Light

Infantry and fought with them in North Africa. He escaped from Tobruk but went sick with desert sores and recuperated in Alexandria. Later he was transferred to the 1st Battalion DLI.

With the defeat of Rommel's Afrika Korps, the attention turned to the invasion of Sicily but the 1st Battalion remained in training in Palestine and Syria. In September, with Italy having capitulated, the Battalion were ordered on board aircraft, their destination the Italian held island of Kos in the Dodecanese group of Aegean Sea islands, off the coast of Turkey.

The island was occupied by some 3000 Italians and contained the only airstrip in the Dodecanese, except for those at Rhodes, the chief island. The occupation of the Aegean islands of Kos, Leros and Samos was carried out between

Private Raymond Houseman (Middleham).

September 15th and 18th. Possession of the Dodecanese not only denied to the enemy airfields and bases from which he had done untold damage in the Eastern Mediterranean, but made possible the bringing in of Turkey into the war as an ally and the use of air bases from which Greece, Romania and Bulgaria could be bombed.

However, the air support, the shipping and the troops were lacking for its execution at the right time, which was the moment Italy collapsed. At this point Rhodes was taken over by a German garrison on September 11th. A more limited operation was therefore improvised.

The 1st Battalion was assigned to Kos, not the largest, but, by reason of the airfield at Antimachia, the most important of the islands, next to Rhodes. "C" Company was carried there in transport aircraft early on the 16th, with most of the remainder following during the course of the next few days in commandeered launches, coastal craft and fishing boats. By the end of September the garrison amounted, with detachments, to about 1400, with Italian support.

The Germans reacted with a vigour that came as a complete surprise. Their aircraft started bombing from the first moment and it increased steadily until the airstrip was neutralised, and casualties mounted. As a result, "A" and "B"

Companies, including Raymond Houseman, were withdrawn to a position in olive groves 5 miles west of Kos Harbour, while "C" Company was posted in the outskirts of the town.

It was known that enemy landing craft were assembling at Piraeus, the port of Athens, and in harbours in Crete and on the evening of October 2nd a convoy was sighted by aircraft off the island of Naxos, but it was assumed to be making for Rhodes. By a stroke of ill-fortune the RN destroyers able to intercept the armada were forced to return to port to refuel and two British submarines ordered to intercept the convoy off Kos failed to arrive in time. When the enemy sea-borne assault began at 5a.m. October 3rd, the garrison was unprepared.

Landing on the north side of the island under a heavy air bombardment from JU-88's (Stuka dive bombers) and JU-87's, the 2000 German troops rapidly advanced inland and severed the Kos/Antimachia road, while a strong force of German parachutists flown in from Greece were dropped on the airstrip. "D" Company, defending the airstrip, were isolated, but fought gallantly until almost all were either killed, wounded or taken prisoner.

"A" and "B" Companies were placed in position astride the main road, where an obstinate pitched battle with the enemy raged throughout the day. With virtually no British air support and the Germans greatly superior in strength, "B" Company, north of the road, was overrun after a stubborn resistance. "C" Company lost a whole Platoon early in the fighting, whilst to the south of the road "A" Company became cut off and received orders to retire to the outskirts of Kos.

The Battalion had inflicted heavy casualties on the Germans by this time but was reduced to less than 200 effective fighting personnel and withdrew to form a perimeter round the approaches to the town of Kos. Fighting continued into the night of October 3rd/4th.

An attempt was made to organise a counter-attack, but a salvo of mortar bombs fell on the assembly point, wounding the commanding officer and killing other officers.

During that night the officer remaining in charge received orders from Force Headquarters to split the Battalion into parties of a dozen, which were to attempt to make their way through the hills to a rendezvous at Kargliou. Throughout the next 10 days about 60 men managed to accomplish this task and on October 13th the remnants of the 1st Battalion escaped in a local fishing craft to Casteloriso, and thence to Cyprus. The Battalion had suffered near extinction.

During the savage fighting of October 3rd/4th, Raymond Houseman was one of those killed. Near the end of the war, a survivor colleague reported to the family that he had been with Raymond, who was last seen swimming in the sea, as the Germans overran their position. Raymond's body was never recovered and his name is honoured on Face 7 of the Athens Memorial, Greece (within the Phaleron War Cemetery).

The loss of a second son bore down heavily upon the family, especially their mother Ruth, who for many years had been an invalid, wheelchair bound, and in 1948 she died. Their father lost his hair with the shock and the worry.

The final casualty for 1943 was a Pathfinder pilot from Hawes.

PILOT OFFICER THOMAS WATSON
NO. 161042 97 SQUADRON RAFVR
DIED FRIDAY 26TH NOVEMBER 1943 AGE 23.

Tommy Watson's father, Charles, had arrived in Appersett from Garsdale, as a boy. During the Great War he served as a battery quartermaster sergeant in the Royal Field Artillery, seeing action in Salonika.

Charles married a local girl, Alice Moore from Rose House, Hawes, and two children, Thomas and Mary were born. Charles worked as a Solicitor's clerk for Willan and Johnson at Hawes. Simon Willan kept trotters at his stables at Nether Bar, Appersett, and Charles Watson was the jockey when they performed at Dent and Hawes Sports Days.

His wife Alice did all the catering at the Market Hall, Hawes, whilst Charles was the Secretary. However, in 1935 Alice died.

Tommy Watson was educated at Hawes Council School and Yorebridge Grammar and was captain of the football team. He was an all round sportsman and a good athlete, having won the two sprint races at the Yorebridge School Sports in record time for two years in succession and also won the half mile race the second year.

Tommy Watson (Hawes).

Popular in the Hawes, Northallerton and Wensleydale districts, he was a playing member of Hawes United and Northallerton Alliance Football Clubs. He was articled clerk with Willan, Jefferson and Metcalfe, Solicitors, Northallerton, and had completed his statutory law course at Leeds University and passed the intermediate law examination prior to volunteering for the RAF in November 1940.

Tommy joined for training in May 1941, spending time in the USA, before returning to England in October 1942, having passed out as a navigator and receiving his commission.

Shortly afterwards he joined 97 Squadron flying Lancaster bombers and in April 1943 they moved to Bourn, on the Cambridge road. It was at Bourn that they joined No. 8 Group as a Pathfinder or marker squadron.

Crews of high navigational ability were used to lead the main force and drop brilliant target indicators. In June 1943 the Squadron illumunated the Zeppelin works at Friedrichshafen and the Italian naval base at Spezia on the occasion of the first "shuttle bombing" raid. The aircraft landed in Algiers and attacked Spezia on the return journey three days later.

At 00.30 hours on the night of November 26th, 262 aircraft took off for a raid on Frankfurt, including Lancaster JB221 piloted by Flight Lieutenant Brown and navigated by Tommy Watson as part of the Pathfinder force. 12 aircraft were lost, including the lone Lancaster JB221, which crashed at Brandau, 12km. SSW of Reinheim. All 7 crew members were killed and Thomas Watson's name is commemorated on Panel 133 of the Runnymede Memorial.

1944 – INVASION OF FORTRESS EUROPE

The year 1944 opened with the Axis Powers on the defensive in the West. Hitler's Russian gamble was lost, the eastern front crumbling. Italy was eliminated, North Africa cleared and the Mediterranean Sea lanes opened. In the United Kingdom, American strength was accumulating in astounding abundance.

However, the U-boats still menaced the Atlantic, Arctic and Mediterranean Sea lanes and the embattled German economy was producing war materials at ever increasing rates, despite the ravages of Allied bombing. The war was still far from a decision, especially as the Japanese were fighting tenaciously in the Far East Theatre of War.

From their bridgehead in the British Isles, the Allies held the priceless advantage of strategic interior lines and could, in principle, attack Germany at any point. But where, when and how? We now know of course that the invasion, code-named Operation "Overlord", would come in Normandy on D-Day, June 6th 1944. Meanwhile, the difficult assault on the mainland of Italy continued against highly motivated soldiers.

During 1944, as more and more servicemen became engaged in the ever-widening campaigns, the number of casualties from Wensleydale increased dramatically to a total of 18 killed.

FLIGHT LIEUTENANT JOHN ALAN BROADLEY
DSO, DFC, DFM
NO. 47690 NAVIGATOR 487 SQUADRON RAF
DIED FRIDAY 18TH FEBRUARY 1944 AGE 23.

John Alan Broadley, known to everyone as Alan, was born at Leyburn in 1921, the son of Thomas Pearson Broadley and wife Irene. Three years earlier, a daughter Ann had been born. Thomas and his brother John ran the family butcher's shop in Leyburn town centre, with Tom also attending their meat stall at Richmond on market days.

*John Alan Broadley
(Leyburn and Richmond).*

Very shortly after giving birth to Alan, Irene sadly died and was buried in Bellerby graveyard, in the village where the Broadleys owned property. Tom found great difficulty in raising a family whilst running a business and so the two children came to live with their maternal grandmother, Mrs. Adamson, in Leyburn.

At the age of 3, Alan, together with his sister, went to live with their aunt, Peggy Broadley, and when she married Jack Siddall, proprietor of the radio and electrical shop on the market square, the two youngsters were brought up by Peggy and Jack as if they were their own children.

Meanwhile, Tom frequented the Fleece Hotel whilst in Richmond and there he met the landlady, Ada Kitchen, whom he married.

In the summer of 1931 Alan went to Yorebridge Grammar School, but at the age of 13, in 1934, he left Leyburn and Yorebridge to live with his father and step mother at The Fleece, Richmond. However, Alan spent the weekends and holidays in Leyburn, where his heart really belonged.

Shortly after his 18th birthday, in 1939, Alan left Richmond Grammar School with the ambition to be a pilot, and, with the call for men to join the RAF as war loomed, he volunteered for that service in April 1939 and was accepted.

He left his family in Richmond and Leyburn and the girl he loved, farmer's daughter Kitty Ovesby. To Alan's disappointment he failed the selection for pilot but was selected to train as an air observer and was posted to Navigation School,

Richmond Grammar School Rugby Team 1937-1938.
John Alan Broadley is on the extreme left, back row.

John Alan Broadley, sitting second from the left.

where eventually he was awarded his flying badge and was promoted to Sergeant.

By September 10th 1939 he was flying with 215 Squadron, the crews converting to the Wellington bomber. By March 8th 1940 Alan was with 99 Squadron at Newmarket and on the 31st flew on his first sortie over the German mainland in a "Nickel" raid, dropping leaflets over Hamburg.

On April 27th 1940 Alan acted as navigator on a 30 minute engine test flight in a Wellington captained by Flying Officer Charles Pickard. This almost casual meeting was to be the start of one of the most famous flying partnerships of the entire war.

Charles Pickard was a pre-war RAF officer with a flare for flying. He and Alan struck up a rapport and developed a

Percy Charles Pickard (Pick).

strong friendship that was to bring them together again and again on many operational sorties.

When the German invasion of the Low Countries began on May 10th 1940 Alan and Pickard flew 10 bombing sorties in aid of the British Expeditionary Force during the next 20 days, attacking German forward airfield bases. It was after this series of sorties that Pickard recognised that he had in the newly promoted Flight Sergeant Broadly a navigator of extraordinary ability.

On June 19th 1940 their Wellington bomber was struck by "flak" over the Ruhr city of Essen and their plane came down in the North Sea, the crew taking to the dinghy. Some 14 hours later the sodden and tired airmen were hauled aboard a rescue launch.

Charles Pickard and Alan were split up and it was not until June 1st 1941, when Alan was posted to 9 Bomber Squadron based at Honington in Suffolk that he returned to operational flying with Charles Pickard. On his arrival Alan was told that he had been awarded the Distinguished Flying Medal in recognition of his skilful navigating on more than 30 operational sorties and for bravery under fire.

In August Alan, now a Pilot Officer, was posted back to Newmarket with 1419 Flight, without Pickard. 1419 Flight was a Clandestine Special Duties

Flight operating modified Whitley bombers engaged in dropping supplies and agents of the Special Operations Executive into enemy occupied territory. Navigation on these flights had to be precise and only the best navigators were called to fulfil this role.

Alan's first trip was on August 6th 1941when they dropped 6 SOE agents by parachute over Chateaureauroux, France, but by December 10th Alan was posted to 51 Bomber Squadron based at RAF Dishforth and commanded by Charles Pickard. It was at the air base that 51 Squadron began training Whitley crews for Operation "Biting", with the aim of obtaining components from a German radar station based at Bruneval, on the French coast. It was decided to drop commandos by parachute and take them off by sea. On February 13th 1942 the pair made a photographic reconnaissance of the dropping zone near Le Havre. The operation went with precision and was a stunning success.

By October 1st 1942 Pickard and Alan Broadley had been posted to 161 Squadron based at Tempsford in Cambridgeshire. This base was used by Special Operational Flights using Whitley bombers flying at low altitudes and many nerve wracking operations were carried out by Alan. Having to navigate into a field in a foreign country, with only torch light to tell him that they were over the field that had been selected for the drop, was quite an ordeal.

On November 8th, whilst returning from a trip to Gibraltar, engine trouble caused them to divert to neutral Portugal and crash land the plane. Though interned in Portugal, the crew escaped over the border into Spain, from where they were spirited back to England.

Alan arrived back at Tempsford in January 1943 and by April he was navigating a new type of aircraft, the Lockheed Hudson, on Special Duties. This aircraft could land in a very short distance and was used to actually touch down in occupied territory to drop agents and return other agents to England.

Alan received notice that he had been awarded the Distinguished Flying Cross and by now he had become the Squadron's Navigation Leader, responsible for organising and routing all operational sorties for the other navigators of the Squadron.

By May 1943 the Pickard/Broadley partnership was again broken up when Pickard was posted in command of a Yorkshire bomber station. Alan continued on the SOE clandestine work and by this time he had been promoted to the rank of Flight Lieutenant.

September 1943 saw the team together again when Alan joined Pickard at RAF Sculthorpe, near Fakenham, Norfolk, the Squadron being part of the newly formed Tactical Airforce. It was at Sculthorpe that Alan and Charles became familiar with their new aircraft, the Mosquito. Made chiefly of wood and glue, this fighter/bomber was arguably the best twin-engine aircraft of the war.

Their first operation was on October 3rd 1943, a low level daylight raid against the power station at Pont Chateau, France. After this successful operation, Alan Broadley was awarded the Distinguished Service Order, a high reward rarely given, other than to pilots. Alan was one of only three navigators to be awarded the DSO at this stage of the war.

On November 23rd Alan, Kitty Ovesby, Uncle Jack and Aunt Peggy were at Buckingham Palace, where the DSO was pinned to Alan's chest by King George V1.

On December 2nd 1943 the next target was a group of barges at Cleve and Ijmuiden on the Rhine. On both these missions their Mosquito was badly damaged by flak, but managed to get back to England.

On Kitty's 21st birthday on December 4th, Alan asked her if she would marry him and she replied, "Yes." However, the low level training continued, ready for the start of a special mission on December 22nd to attack V1 (Doodlebug) rocket sites at St. Nicholas, near Dieppe, which posed a threat to the Home Counties and to the forthcoming invasion plans against Fortress Europe.

After returning to the dales for Christmas leave, Alan and Kitty announced their engagement but a few days later Alan was back with 21 Squadron at RAF Hunsdon, preparing for a very special operation.

As a result of infiltration, German counter-intelligence had penetrated the French Resistance Movement in Northern France and 700 Resistance workers were in Amiens Prison in late 1943. With the forthcoming invasion of Normandy planned for 1944, it was vital that the French Resistance Movement could still operate its sabotage missions in conjunction with the invasion. Many of the prisoners were under sentence of death, with a deadline of February 19th 1944. Plans were therefore prepared for their release by means of a low level bombing raid attacking the prison walls. The man put in charge of the bombing plans in Operation "Jericho" was Charles Pickard.

Six aircraft from Nos. 487,464 and 21 Squadrons would carry out the bombing, with a film unit Mosquito to record what happened, and a fighter escort of Typhoons. Ten days before the operation Alan reached his 23rd birthday.

Although Pickard and Alan were in 21 Squadron, they were to fly in the last aircraft of 464 Squadron, allowing Pickard to make an assessment of the results. 487 Squadron was to bomb the outer walls and German guardroom just as the Germans were having their midday meal. 464 Squadron was to breach the actual prison walls, thus allowing the prisoners to break free. 21 Squadron was held in reserve, ready to bomb the whole area if the breach had not been made. They all realised that in reality their job was to kill the inmates before the Germans could take their revenge. The inmates had informed the British that they preferred to die by RAF bombs than at the hands of the Gestapo.

By 10a.m. on February 18th the weather had improved very slightly and the operation was on. 18 Mosquitoes took off to rendezvous with the Typhoon escort, but in the blackness and murk, 4 Mosquitoes became lost, leaving 14 for the raid. The weather was better over the French coast and the run in to Amiens was along the Albert — Amiens road, from the east. The flak was accurate and intensely dense. A leading Mosquito was badly damaged, pulling clear and dropping its bombs in open countryside.

The five remaining bombers of the first wave headed for the prison, three bombing the walls, the other two coming in after the bombs had exploded, and dropped their bombs from 10 feet above the ground.

After the explosions the four Mosquitoes of 464 Squadron came in low and fast. In the last of these planes were Charles Pickard and Alan Broadley. Alan released the bombs and the plane climbed sharply, but they saw the walls of the prison collapse.

As the other Mosquitoes headed back, Pickard circled the area in order to make his assessment of the damage. Hundreds of people were running out of the broken down walls and he decided the mission had been successfully achieved. As he began his turn for home, Pickard saw a Mosquito in trouble, after being hit by flak. He went to investigate and saw the crippled plane crash land in a snow covered field.

Suddenly, two Focke Wulf 190 fighters of Adolf Galland's Squadron dived upon Alan's circling Mosquito from the advantage of height. The tail of the Mosquito was shot away, resulting in the aircraft cart wheeling and crashing into the ground near St. Gratien, a few kilometres from Amiens. Both air crew died in the wreckage of their plane.

French peasants nearby hurried to the scene and wrapped the two bodies in their parachutes and carried them to the mayor's house. However, German soldiers arrived on the scene and took the bodies away.

Although scores of French people had died in the attack on Amiens prison, the mission had been a success, for more than 250 Resistance workers survived, continuing their work against the Germans.

News that Alan was reported missing arrived for his family and Kitty. At Easter, a sergeant from 487 Squadron arrived to see Kitty, bringing with him the engagement ring bought by Alan for Kitty. From that day Kitty wore Alan's ring as her talisman.

Alan Broadley is remembered both on the war memorial and parish church in Leyburn, at Richmond Grammar School and on the town memorial and in the Central Church of the RAF St. Clement Danes, London, and at St. Pierre Cemetery, Amiens, where he is buried in grave 3.A.11.

On December 5th 1944 a Memorial Service to the memory of Alan Broadley and Charles Pickard was held at St. Martin in the Fields, London.

ORDINARY TELEGRAPHIST FRED HARRISON NO. D/JX577478 ROYAL NAVY HMS "GOULD" DIED WEDNESDAY 1ST MARCH 1944 AGE 19.

Fred Harrison (Middleham and Skelton).

Fred Harrison came from Skelton (in Cleveland), near to Saltburn-by-the-Sea, and arrived in Middleham during the early war years to work as an apprentice jockey in the stables of Matthew J. Peacock (on one occasion riding in an Apprentices Race at Stockton). He remained there for around eighteen months until he was called up and entered the "Senior Service". His father, Fred Harrison, a bus driver, had married Mary Elizabeth Colledge, a Co. Durham girl from Fence Houses, near Houghton le Spring, and Fred junior was the second eldest of five brothers and two sisters.

Fred's father, Fred Harrison senior, had been born at Stanley, Co. Durham, whilst his maternal grandfather, Mr. Colledge, had been employed as an ostler, tending the horses at the King's Head, a Darlington coaching inn.

Fred Harrison senior was one of the earliest bus drivers in the Durham/North Yorkshire areas, for United Services. His son Fred was born at West Pelton, near Chester le Street, but the family moved first to the village of Lingdale, North Yorkshire, and then the short distance to Skelton, from where Fred attended Guiseborough Grammar School.

By late 1943 Fred had trained as a telegraphist in the Royal Navy and was a crew member of the Frigate HMS "Gould", an ex-American Destroyer Escort. Launched in Boston, USA, in June 1943, she had a displacement of 1085 tons and a crew of 200, captained by Lieutenant Unged.

HMS "Gould" was one of a number of escorts chasing a submarine contact NNE of the Azores, in the North Atlantic. Contact had been made initially by HMS "Garlies" with U-boat U-358 captained by Rolph Manke, at 5.07a.m. on

February 29th but the U-boat proved determined and cunning, constantly manoeuvring and changing depth throughout the 29th and most of March 1st, though with one or other of the Frigates in contact most of the time.

At 7.20p.m. on March 1st HMS "Gould" had just completed an attacking run and had lost contact with the U-boat, which was off her port quarter. The next ship astern, HMS "Affleck", had just acquired the contact when a sudden improvement in the echo was observed. U-358 had come shallow and promptly torpedoed HMS "Gould", with the loss of 123 crewmen and just 14 survivors. Fred Harrison was not one of these survivors.

U-358 was eventually sunk by HMS "Affleck" with the loss of all crew members. Fred Harrison is honoured on Panel 88, Column 3 of the Plymouth Naval Memorial.

ORDINARY SEAMAN JAMES IVESON
NO. D/JX420974 HMS "ASPHODEL" RN
DIED THURSDAY 9TH MARCH 1944 AGE 19.

James was the only son of Thomas and Agnes Iveson of Gayle and worked for Elijah Allen in his grocery shop in Gayle. His father, Thomas, worked on the Wensleydale branch of the railway and had been a POW during the Great War. James joined the Royal Navy and by March 1944 was on board a Flower Class Corvette HMS "Asphodel". A small vessel of 925 tons, with a complement of 97 men, it was commanded by Lieutenant Halliday, Royal New Zealand Navy.

On March 9th it was in the Atlantic WNW of Cape Finisterre when it came under attack from U-boat U-575, commanded by Oberleutnant Zur See Rudolf Boehme. It was sunk by torpedo with the loss of 92 lives, there being only 5 survivors.

James Iveson (Gayle).

Four days later the U-boat was sunk by USS "Bogue" with the loss of 16 hands. 14 survivors were taken prisoner. James Iveson is commemorated on Panel 88, Column 1 of the Plymouth Naval Memorial.

Both HMS "Gould" and HMS "Asphodel" were lost protecting the vast quantities of American men and material pouring across the ocean, both to the United Kingdom and the Mediterranean Basin. This became supremely important between January and June 1944, as the time for the cross channel invasion of Europe neared.

Groups of warships hunted the packs of submarines in both the North and South Atlantic. Improved methods of detection prevailed, even though the "schnorkel" — a tube providing air for Diesel engines while submerged assisted the latest submarines to remain underwater for longer periods. By the beginning of March 1944 more than one million American troops had been safely conveyed to the United Kingdom. Both Fred Harrison and James Iveson sacrificed their lives in helping make this possible.

On May 14th two men, one from the Upper Dale and the other from West Burton were killed by Japanese forces on the Indian frontier with Burma, whilst serving in the same Battalion.

PRIVATE CHARLES HENRY WARD
NO. 3608420 9TH BATTALION BORDER REGIMENT
DIED SUNDAY 14TH MAY 1944 AGE 29.

Charles Ward was born in Dent, the son of William and Annie Ward, and married a Garsdale Head girl, Mary Elizabeth Brunskill. They settled down to married life at No. 3 Moorcock Cottages, next to the Moorcock Railway Viaduct, in Lunds and Hardraw Parish. When Charles enlisted he eventually joined the 9th Battalion Border Regiment, based at Carlisle.

PRIVATE ALAN LEWIS SMITH
NO. 4393245 9TH BATTALION BORDER REGIMENT
DIED SUNDAY 14TH MAY 1944 AGE 27.

Alan was the youngest son of John and Emily Smith of West Burton, where the family of Wilf, George, Albert, Frank, Hugh, John, Arthur, Maurice, Alan, Elsie, Emily and Florrie lived in Gardeners Cottage.

Before the war Alan and his father had been gardeners for Mr. and Mrs. Ritchie at The Grange and Alan was a trainee local preacher on the Wensleydale Methodist Circuit.

Alan entered the forces at the beginning of the war and spent time at Catterick Camp before joining the 9th Battalion, Border Regiment. In 1940 he married Alice Brown from Burtersett, who was working for local shopkeeper James Lawson, and they settled into married life at "Sunnyside", West Burton. Late in

Alan Lewis Smith (West Burton).

1940, a son, Maurice, was born.

In April 1944 the 9th Battalion, part of Field Marshal Slim's 14th Army, were in the Imphal area of North East India, on the border with Burma. Imphal was a focal point in the defence of India against the Japanese. New airfields were constructed and army and airforce reinforcements arrived. Strategically well placed for attacks on Allied lines of communication into Burma, Imphal, with its airfields, was a main objective when the Japanese made their thrust towards India in the Spring of 1944. They were within 50 miles of a crucial railhead and the gateway to the plains. Beyond lay Delhi, the jewel in the crown of the British Empire.

There was severe fighting in the surrounding hills and the Japanese succeeded in cutting a long section of the Imphal-Kohima road and holding it for over three months. The 14th Army held on grimly, inflicting heavy punishment on the Japanese.

On May 14th 1944 9th Battalion were ordered to clear Potsangbam village of Japanese troops. At 10.30a.m. "C" Company came under heavy fire from the woodland. The troops were shelled as they crossed the open paddy field, with several casualties resulting. Heavy fire from rifles and machine-guns was met in the first 20 yards on both flanks and a Platoon of "B" Company was pinned down in the paddy field.

It became obvious at 5p.m. that the whole area could not be taken in day light with the troops available, so the gains were boxed and wired in. During the day

17 men had been killed and 45 wounded. Amongst those killed were Alan Smith and Charles Ward.

Taken from the beautiful valley of the Ure to fight in a landscape and climate alien to both of them, they were buried close together in the Imphal War Cemetery, India, Charles Ward in grave 2.C.8. and Alan Smith in grave 1.A.19.

The three months of bitter fighting proved to be a turning point in the fight against Japan. After 4000 men had died on each side, the Japanese were forced into retreat and the 14th Army's push into Burma began.

CORPORAL JACK HINDLE
NO. 7360813 ROYAL ARMY MEDICAL CORPS
ATTACHED TO THE 6TH/10TH BATTALION
(ROYAL WELCH FUSILIERS), PARACHUTE REGIMENT
DIED SUNDAY 4TH JUNE 1944 AGE 25.

Jack's father, Lewis Hindle, was born in Halifax and married Harriet Louise Holdsworth. Lewis was a master baker and they went to Blackpool when he began work at the "Cash Bakery". A daughter Ellen had been born in 1905, but Jack was born in Blackpool in 1918. The family arrived in Bainbridge in 1927, where Lewis started a bakery business at Riversdale, at the top of the green. Jack went to the village school before transferring to nearby Yorebridge Grammar School.

Jack Hindle (Bainbridge).

In 1934 his father died of tuberculosis but Harriet and daughter Ellen kept the bakery going and opened a shop in Askrigg, with Jack eventually delivering bread as far as Bishopdale in a Ford van.

Called up just before the war began, Jack joined the Royal Army Medical Corps and went to France with the BEF, tending the wounded in an Army Field Ambulance Section, before being rescued at Dunkirk.

At Askrigg Church on October 11th 1942 Jack married Irene (Rene) Fawcett, a farmer's daughter from Nappa Hall. Whilst stationed on Salisbury Plain, he was joined by his wife, who began work at an aircraft factory.

The RAMC captain in charge of Jack's unit desired greater military action and volunteered his unit for training to go into action with the newly formed Parachute Regiment. Some men were not too keen but did not wish to appear afraid.

By the middle of 1943 the 6th/10th Battalion Parachute Regiment were in the Mediterranean and when Jack's daughter Ann was born in November 1943, it proved to be the case that she would never see her father.

Jack died on June 4th 1944. A letter from his Commanding Officer, Captain Stock, to Renee Hindle explained what happened.

The Hindle Family (Bainbridge).
Lewis, Harriet with Jack, Ellen.

"I was with Jack for a short while in the old 127th Field Ambulance before we became parachutists. We did no fighting in North Africa, it was a period of hard training and we did three parachute jumps.

"We were prepared to take part in the invasion of Sicily but our part was

The Hindle home at the top of the Green, Bainbridge. The bakery
was in the small building on the extreme right.

393

Yorebridge Grammar School Football Team 1933-1934.
Three players, Jack Hindle, Freddie Lawson and William Park would die during the war.
Back row: David Peacock, Jack Hindle, F. Lawson, Geof Harrington, George Metcalfe.
Middle row: W. Walker, W. Park, L. Liddell, T. Metcalfe, R. Metcalfe.
Front row: Jack Kilburn, Dick Fawcett.

cancelled while we were on the airfield waiting to take off. Then came the landings in Italy, sailing to Taranto, and it was in the harbour that Jack was ship-wrecked.

"We were the first Allied ships into the harbour. Most of our men were on deck, though some were below getting their equipment together, when there was a sudden and violent explosion and the ship split in half. A mine had struck the vessel. Jack and about 20 other men were down below when they were thrown to the floor and water poured in.

"In the dark no one could find the way out and panic was starting. Jack got

Keith Stevens and Jack Hindle in their home-made boat.

them moving out in an orderly way without panic. He found and opened a second escape hatch and got the rest out that way, staying below himself and shining the torch until everyone else was out. Without Jack they would certainly have perished."

Jack was recommended most highly for a decoration but nothing ever came through, being not exactly "in action

Nappa Hall, Askrigg. A 15th century fortified house.

against the enemy". On December 1st 1943 we were sent into the line near Canoli and saw service in the line for the next six months, rather like the fighting in the last war. Jack did very well, frequently collecting the wounded under shell fire and displaying complete coolness and judgement. There was no one in the Company valued more highly than Jack and to the men he was "our doctor".

"Though involved in the Battle for Cassino, we were brought back to Salerno to prepare for a parachute operation. The plan was to drop behind the German lines, north of Cassino, and to get in position beside the main German supply road in that area, there to shoot up German transport.

Jack Hindle and Irene Fawcett on their wedding day 14th October 1942.

"Two medical corporals were to be sent in and two medical orderlies. We were much against Jack going but there was no one else as good as him so he went.

"The drop was perfectly successful. They climbed over a mountain range into the next valley, where the road they had to attack lay. This they did that night, and the next morning they split into four parties. Jack was with the headquarters, remaining high up in the mountain and responsible for supplying the fighting patrols. They were relying on moving around in the area to avoid detection, working by night and hiding by day.

"There was less cover available than was expected so the party was further sub-divided into small groups, all fairly close together. The Germans reacted very strongly and we believe a whole brigade of them were sent to deal with the British parachutists.

"Anyway, on June 4th a party of Germans greatly outnumbering our party found Jack and his companions and overpowered them after a brief fight. Jack was shot clean through the head and must have died immediately.

"Some of our men got clean away, including the officer, and he revisited the area the next day, found Jack's body and arranged for him to be buried. He was buried high up in the hills at the side of the main road 40 miles north of Cassino, near Arezzo. From Jack's operation 30 of our men are missing or prisoners. The rest went into hiding and got back in ones and twos.

"As for the success of the operation, the German guns were withdrawn from that area and 4 days later the advancing New Zealand Division encountered no opposition in the area in which the parachutists operated.

"I was glad to hear from you Mrs. Hindle. It seems to me that you have the same brave philosophy as Jack had, and I am so glad that you have got the baby."

Jack's body was never recovered from its mountain grave and his name is commemorated on Panel 12 of the Cassino Memorial, Italy.

PRIVATE ROBERT WILLIAM MARKS
NO. 3776520 ARMY CATERING CORPS ATTACHED TO
5TH BATTALION THE KING'S REGIMENT (LIVERPOOL)
DIED TUESDAY 6TH JUNE 1944 AGE 28.

Robert Marks (Bob) was the eldest son of R.M. and Charlotte Marks of 213, Guildford Road, Birkdale, Southport, Lancashire. Bob had been in the Army for the past four years, and had served in the Catering Corps. An old boy of St. John's School, Birkdale, he was a keen sportsman and attended Liverpool Road Methodist Church. Prior to joining the forces he was employed by Houghs, cycle mechanics, on Sussex Road. A brother, Walter, was serving with the Motor Transport Corps. I do not know Bob Mark's connection with Leyburn but it was strong enough for his name to be later commemorated on the Leyburn War Memorial.

By the Spring of 1944 Robert Marks was attached to the 5th Battalion, The King's Regiment, which was taking part in a period of intense training, part of which took place in Scotland. Exercises were carried out, some on land, some from ship to shore, for they were training for their part in the Allied invasion of Europe, the Normandy landings.

The 5th Battalion moved to the south of England in May, assembling in their respective "Marshalling Areas", ready to form part of the 3rd British Division's attack on Fortress Europe.

Between June 1st and 3rd the beach group of the Battalion departed for its port of embarkation, not to meet again until they re-united on the beaches of Normandy.

The area in which the assault landings were to be made lay between Lion-Sur-Mer on the right and Ouistreham on the left. The German defences included under-water obstacles with mines attached, continuous deep belts of wire along the shore, exits from the beaches heavily mined, whilst the strong points of Lion-Sur-Mer and Ouistreham covered the beaches with the cross-fire of small arms and mortars.

*Robert (Bob) William Marks
(Southport and Leyburn).*

Seven miles off the coast the assault troops transferred to Landing Craft Assault vessels. The shore batteries opened against the advancing craft. These first troops ashore pushed inland to seize their objectives while others set about their special tasks, marking out the beach, neutralising mine-fields and improving the exits from the beaches. The shore was swept with small arms fire and heavily mortared from enemy batteries. The Battalion suffered a serious loss early in the battle when Commanding Officer, Lieutenant Colonel Board, was killed. One enemy position was attacked by "A" Company and eventually cleared, with the capture of 14 German soldiers, though several of the Battalion were killed in the action.

Meanwhile, troops and vehicles were arriving in succeeding waves of landing craft, including the next detachments of the 5th Battalion. Considerable gun and mortar fire was still opposing the landings, and craft were being hit and holed as they approached.

By the end of the first day, by which time the whole of the 5th Battalion were ashore, the beaches were already becoming congested with both transport and stores. But in spite of continuing shell fire and occasional air-raids the Battalion worked throughout the night and by morning, the congestion was greatly relieved.

Considering the magnitude of the undertaking, the casualties on the first day had been relatively insignificant, but one of those killed was Robert Marks. Bob did not even make it to the beach, for his landing craft was one of those that was holed and his body was lost in the waters of the English Channel. His name is commemorated on Panel 19, Column 1 of the Bayeux Memorial.

FLIGHT SERGEANT BARNARD BENSON HAYTON NO. 1435704 WIRELESS OPERATOR/AIR GUNNER 4 (OBSERVERS) ADVANCED FLYING UNIT RAFVR DIED MONDAY 12TH JUNE 1944 AGE 21.

Barnard's grandfather, Thomas Henry Hayton, had been landlord of the Bolton Arms at Redmire, with the inn remaining under Hayton management into the 1930's. A son, Ernest, married Mary Ellen Viggars and they settled in Bellerby, where their son Barnard, born at Redmire in 1922, attended Bellerby day school

William Robinson, the Redmire blacksmith, shoeing a horse, 1930's. The Hayton family ran the Bolton Arms, seen in the background. Barnard Hayton's family lived in an attached cottage.

and Sunday school and was in the choir. Ernest and Mary Ellen were landlords of the Cross Keys Inn for several years. Ernest eventually took his family to live at Spalding in Lincolnshire, where Ernest worked as a representative for the Singer Sewing Machine Company.

Later, the Hayton's returned to Redmire, living in a small cottage attached to the Bolton Arms, which was still run by a close relative (the cottage on longer exists).

Barnard joined the RAF as a wireless operator/air gunner, eventually serving with 4 (Observers) Advanced Flying Unit based at RAF West Freugh, Dumfries and Galloway.

The Flight Sergeant was on board an Avro Anson aircraft No. N9589 that crashed on Cairnsmore of Fleet, Kirkudbright, on June 12th at 2.45a.m. while on a navigational exercise. All five crew men were killed.

The aircraft was flying too low and flew into the side of the hill in low cloud and crashed into the ground. Low cloud was possibly a contributory factor.

Barnard Benson Hayton was buried in Redmire graveyard, next to his father, Ernest, who had died in 1941 at the relatively early age of 45.

TROOPER RENNY CHRISTIAN MURE FITZHUGH NO. 7940389 4TH COUNTY OF LONDON YEOMANRY (SHARPSHOOTERS) ROYAL ARMOURED CORPS DIED TUESDAY 13TH JUNE 1944 AGE 32.

Reverend Canon Victor Christian Albert Fitzhugh, the father of Renny Fitzhugh, took up his position as the vicar of Wensley in 1926, and resided at Wensley Rectory with his wife Alice Vara Fitzhugh. As one of the best livings in the country, he was to remain as vicar until 1956.

His son Renny was away from the village at school and university and eventually worked in London, where he married his wife, Evelyn Mary. He worked in the City of London as an assistant at the Chamberlain's Office at the Corporation of London's Guildhall, the main governing body of the City of London. He was also a Freeman and Livery Man of the Merchant Taylor's Company, which exercised its traditional functions of charity and education.

His father, the Canon, had relatives in New Zealand and during the war years received food parcels containing lots of cheese but little butter. He would visit the homes in the parish and provide cheese, in return for butter.

Lord Bolton's box pew was opposite the pulpit. Before the service each Sunday, Lord Bolton told the Rector how long the sermon should be. If it went on for five minutes longer, a row of half crowns laid out in full view was reduced and taken off the cushion one at a time. Whatever was left went onto the collection plate.

Renny Fitzhugh joined the Royal Armoured Corps as a trooper in the 4th County of London Yeomanry. Throughout April 1944 training in tank warfare took place in the Thetford area of Norfolk, ready for the imminent invasion of Normandy.

June 1st witnessed the loading of armoured vehicles at Felixstowe docks and on June 5th they sailed into the English Channel. On D-Day plus 1, 7th June, they unloaded their vehicles on the beaches, moving to the concentration area.

A move was made on June 10th but progress was slow. The bocage (a checkerboard of small fields boxed by deep hedgerows) reduced the Allied advance to a crawl. German resistance centred about Caen and Field Marshal

Reverend Canon Victor Christian Albert Fitzhugh, of Wensley Rectory, father of Trooper Renny Christian Mure Fitzhugh.

Montgomery's efforts to take the town on June 13th were rebuffed.

On June 13th Renny's Battalion moved forward at first light towards Villers Bocage. "A" Squadron, with Trooper Fitzhugh, led into the village but the column was split by two German Tiger tanks and "A" Squadron took up battle positions. "B" Squadron held the village but was unable to get through to "A" Squadron.

By 10a.m. "A" Squadron was surrounded and attacked by Tiger tanks and infantry, calling for immediate assistance, but none could get through. Withdrawal of "A" Squadron was impossible. "B" Squadron was ordered to hold the village at all costs and, after a six hour street battle, destroyed 4 Tiger tanks and 3 Mark 1V tanks.

By 4p.m. "B" Squadron still just held the village but British infantry failed to clear the opposing infantry. "B" Squadron withdrew, covered by "C" Squadron.

At the end of the day 12 officers and 76 other ranks were missing, 3 officers and 5 men wounded, 4 men killed and 20 Cromwell tanks, together with 11 other armoured vehicles, destroyed or badly damaged.

One of those missing, whose body was never recovered, was Trooper Renny Fitzhugh. His name is commemorated on Panel 10, Column 1 of the Bayeux Memorial.

LIEUTENANT JAMES ROWLAND MAY
NO. 269350 5TH BATTALION
EAST YORKSHIRE REGIMENT
DIED FRIDAY 16TH JUNE 1944 AGE 25.

James May was born in Leyburn, the son of Rowland and Mary Helen May. His sister Marjorie completed the family. Their father Rowland ran a plumbing business in Leyburn and introduced the piping of water into people's homes in the town, instead of using wells. Mary May was in business on the High Street, in Leyburn, running a small confectionery shop.

James married a London girl from Streatham Hill, Elizabeth Dorothy May, and a daughter was born to them. When war was declared James joined the army, becoming a Lieutenant in the 5th Battalion East Yorkshire Regiment, whilst his sister Marjorie joined the Wrens.

On D-Day Plus 1, the 5th Battalion received their carriers and ammunition and began to move forward into the village of St. Leger, Normandy, where snipers harassed their positions. They remained there until June 11th.

They were now entering the difficult countryside of the bocage, of small stone walled fields, high hedges, deep ditches and sunken lanes, ideal for concealing German snipers but unsuitable for tank operations. On June 11th the 5th Battalion advanced to Oristot, but received heavy casualties in a German counter-attack with tanks.

For the next two days they were not involved in the fighting, sending out patrols while holding on to their base. On June 13th they moved to a rest area and visited Bayeux, the first French town to be captured.

At Les Orailles, on the morning of June 16th , the Battalion, supported by a Squadron of tanks, moved forward with the cross roads at La Taille as the objective. As they advanced they were met with fire from mortars and Spandau machine-guns and by 4p.m. were held up about a mile from the objective. Although further attempts were made to capture La Taille, it was not until June 27th that La Taille was reached.

However, in the first attack on June 16th, Lieutenant James Rowland May had been cut down by the concentrated fire power of the German defenders. He was later buried in grave 111.C.5. of the Hottot-Les-Bagues War Cemetery.

CAPTAIN THOMAS DAWSON WHALEY
NO. 101178 83RD FIELD REGIMENT ROYAL ARTILLERY
DIED MONDAY 17TH JULY 1944 AGE 34.

Thomas Dawson Whaley, known to everyone as Dawson, was born in 1909 at Widdaleside, a farm in Widdale, two miles out of Hawes on the Ingleton road. His parents, James and Mary (nee Moore) farmed in Widdale. Another son, James, was born in 1911.

Dawson went to Gayle School and then Yorebridge Grammar School, where he met his future wife Renee Shorter, daughter of the headmaster. Whilst working as a solicitor in Romford, he married Renee in 1934 and they went to live in Newport, Wales, where a daughter, Greta Mary was born in 1938.

A great deal of Dawson's spare time was spent training with the Territorial Army and when war was declared he joined the Army and received his commission in 1940, in the Royal Artillery.

Thomas Dawson Whaley (Gayle and Hawes).

In 1941 Dawson was stationed at Down Patrick, Northern Ireland, with Renee and daughter living nearby. In the same year a son, Thomas, was born. Whilst in training with their 25 pounder guns the Regiment practised firing by "lobbing" shells into the waters of Strangford Lough.

The Regiment was then stationed in Sutton Valence, south of Maidstone, Kent, with Dawson's family following. When he went into training for the Normandy landings, Renee, who was pregnant, moved back to Gayle, into the family home of Rookhurst.

The 83rd Field Regiment went into Normandy in the second wave after D-Day, between June 7th and 12th. It was not until July 9th that the British 2nd Army was able to capture Caen, its D-Day objective. Throughout the ferocious fighting of June and July we hear of Sherman tanks burning like torches, Cromwell tank riddled like sieves and Churchill tanks never surviving a direct hit.

An honourable mention must be made of the artillery, for which Rommel's grenadiers had a special dislike, for it fired quickly and accurately. In particular, the 25 pounder gun-howitzer fired so rapidly that the Germans believed it must have been fitted with a system of automatic loading.

And this fact goes a long way to explain the form which the fighting took in the Caen sector, for if the British tanks failed in all their attempts at breakthrough whenever they came up against the German Panthers, Tigers and the 88mm. anti-tank guns of Panzergruppe West, the German counter-attack collapsed under the murderous fire of the British artillery concentrations whenever they went beyond purely local engagements.

With Caen now captured, Montgomery planned for Operation "Goodwood" to be launched on July 18th in order to engage and tie down the Panzers on his front and, if possible, to advance the armoured units into the region around Falaise. On July 18th, at 5.30a.m., the thunder of 720 guns signalled the beginning of Operation "Goodwood".

But Dawson Whaley was not taking part in this huge bombardment. A few hours earlier, on July 17th, he had been acting as a forward observer, in preparation for the coming attack, when the position was shelled by the Panzer artillery and then strafed by a Luftwaffe plane, resulting in his death.

Thomas Dawson Whaley was buried in grave 1X.J.1. at Tilly-sur-Seulles War Cemetery, 12km. SE of Bayeux. One week after Dawson's death, a son, David, was born.

FLIGHT SERGEANT FRANCIS STANLEY SEYMOUR NO. 1475129 FLIGHT ENGINEER 49 SQUADRON RAFVR DIED WEDNESDAY 19TH JULY 1944 AGE 22.

In 1922 Stanley Seymour was born at Leyburn, the son of Frank and Florence Seymour. A daughter, Peggy, completed the family. Frank Seymour had travelled from Lancashire to work in the racing stables at Middleham, "mucking out". Eventually he took a job as a line lengths man on the railway, until finally he went to work for the Ministry of Defence establishment at Catterick.

He married a Leyburn girl, Florence Metcalfe, and they began married life on High Street, near Grove Square.

After war was declared Stanley joined up, entering the RAF. Although an engineer, he also trained as a pilot so that he could take over the controls if required.

In early April 1944 Stanley Seymour was posted to 49 Squadron, flying Avro Lancaster bombers out of Fiskerton aerodrome, 5 miles east of Lincoln. In charge of his Lancaster JB178 was New Zealand pilot, Flying Officer Bill Green.

On the night of May 3rd/4th an attack was made on a military camp housing 21st Panzer Division near the Northern France village of Mailly, by 346

Lancasters and 16 Pathfinder Mosquitoes, led by Wing Commander Leonard Cheshire. German night fighters roamed at will, resulting in dreadful losses in men and machines (41 Lancasters).

JB178 was on its bombing run when a Lancaster dead ahead of them blew apart. Debris crashed through the perspex nose of the aircraft and logs and charts disappeared. Harassed by fighters after leaving the target, Bill Green and the crew gratefully managed to make their base.

On May 27th/28th five coastal battery positions along the French coast were the target, with 49 Squadron's objective being the medium battery at Morsalines.

D-Day, 6th/7th June, saw attacks being made by the Squadron on Caen in Normandy and communications targets in the vicinity.

Francis Stanley Seymour (Leyburn).

The Wesseling synthetic oil plant, 15 miles south of Cologne, was the target on June 21st/22nd. Night fighters over Holland and Germany played havoc with the bombers. When JB178 landed back at Fiskerton the crew reported, "We saw many aircraft shot down — we were attacked twice and the rear guns became unusable. After another attack the port inner engine had to be feathered and the bomb load jettisoned as we were losing height rapidly. My crew behaved exemplary." For his actions Bill Green received the DFC.

Sadly, within a month, Bill and his crew would all be killed. Six aircraft from 49 Squadron had been lost that night, with 42 men, including its CO and Squadron Leader, killed.

Between June 24th and July 18th Stanley Seymour took part in raids against V1 rocket storage sites, launching pads and railway centre targets. On July 4th/5th and 7th/8th raids were made on underground flying bomb stores at St.-Leu-D'Esserent in France, accurately bombing the tunnels in which V1 rockets were stored.

A daylight raid took place on July 18th on fortified villages around Caen in Normandy, in support of the British 2nd Army's armoured attack, Operation "Goodwood". The crews returned exhausted from their pre-dawn exploits, but were roused from their beds to be told that they were to be back in action that night, July 18th/19th.

The raid was to take place on Revigny, a railway centre and V1 storage depot, east of Chalons-sur-Marne, in eastern France, take off time 10-50p.m. The target was hit, severing the railway line to the battle front. The planes, however, ran into the full fury of the German night fighters, especially near the River Aube turning point. Four planes from 49 Squadron were lost, including JB178, which crashed at Herbisse, just NNW of Arcis-sur-Aube. All seven crew men were killed and Stanley Seymour lies in the joint grave in Herbisse churchyard.

Stanley was reported missing and his mother Florence would spend hours listening to the "wireless" broadcasts by the traitor William Joyce (Lord Haw Haw) on German radio, as he gave out the names of POW's. She listened and hoped. Many months later his death was officially announced.

His sister Peggy had joined the WAAF as a winch operator in a barrage balloon battalion, protecting the port of Hull. Shortly after Stanley's death she married a paratrooper, Jack Carr, but sadly he too was killed a short while later at the Battle of Arnhem.

MAJOR THOMAS BOULBY MAUGHAN
NO. 154951 IRISH GUARDS
DIED SATURDAY 29TH JULY 1944 AGE 45.

Thomas (Tommy) Maughan was the elder son of John and Frances Maughan of Abbey Hills, Jervaulx. His father, John, had been the agent for the Jervaulx Estate. John had married twice and his son from his first marriage, Captain John Maughan, had been killed during the Great War.

Two sons, Tommy and Ralph, and daughter Nancy, were children of his second marriage. It was Ralph who was CO of the East Witton Home Guard Platoon.

In the previous war Tommy had served as Agricultural Organising Officer for the whole of Northern Ireland, and later for the Northern Command. During the inter-war years his work took him overseas, with his journeys taking him as far afield as Hong Kong.

He joined the Irish Guards during the 2nd World War and on July 29th was returning home on leave for the weekend from his Regiment, based in Northumberland, when his car left the road near Haltwhistle and he was killed when it plunged over a 20 feet embankment and through a stone wall.

The funeral service took place on Tuesday August 1st at East Witton Church. The whole Jervaulx Estate was represented, in addition to many of his brother officers. The coffin, draped in the Union Jack, was borne by friends from Jervaulx Estate.

GUNNER ALBERT ROBERT JAMES
NO. 1568410 122ND BATTERY
13TH LIGHT ANTI-AIRCRAFT REGIMENT
ROYAL ARTILLERY
DIED SUNDAY 20TH AUGUST 1944 AGE 32.

Albert, or "Bal" as he was affectionately known, was born at Castle View, Harmby. His father, Albert, a Harmby man, worked at the Shawl Quarry, Leyburn, whilst his mother, Mary Catherine (nee Mallaby) was a farmer's daughter. Children Frank, Albert, Betty, Marion, Wilfred (Bill) and Ada completed the family. Sadly, their mother died during the 1930's and Betty died from tuberculosis just before the war began.

Working at Harmby Quarry, Bal drove a lorry that took the limestone away to be used for road surfacing. Quarrying could be a dangerous occupation and tragedy struck the family when during the

Albert Robert James ('Bal') of Harmby. He is sitting on the extreme right in the North African desert.

war years brother Frank broke his back in a quarry accident and was killed.

Bal was a warm hearted man who looked after his young sister Ada, when they lost their mother. He would take her in the wagon when he was working and treat her to sweets from the shop at the top of Harmby Bank.

He joined the Royal Artillery during the war, training in the use of anti-aircraft guns, and by late 1942 he was in Tunisia, North Africa, as Montgomery's 8th Army advanced from the east and the Allied forces pushed from Algeria in the west, squeezing the life out of Rommel's Afrika Korps in Tunisia.

However, Bal James was captured during the fighting and interned in an Italian POW camp. When Italy capitulated on September 8th 1943, the Germans transported the prisoners by rail through Austria into Germany. Bal became POW number 220115 in POW camp Stalag 1VB.

He would write home on occasions, sometimes to "Dear little sister" and comment that he was somewhat happier than he had been in Italy because he was allowed to work on neighbouring German farms.

Tragically, on Sunday August 20th 1944 the camp appears to have been mistakenly bombed by American planes and amongst those killed was Albert Robert James. He has no grave and since he was captured in North Africa his name is commemorated on Column 35 on the Alamein Memorial.

FLIGHT LIEUTENANT (PILOT) RAISBECK DENNIS BELL NO. 63454 51 SQUADRON RAFVR DIED FRIDAY 6TH OCTOBER 1944 AGE 24.

Dennis Bell arrived in Bellerby from Blackhall, near Durham, during the mid 1920's. His father was Raisbeck Bell, headmaster at Bellerby School. Dennis's mother had died shortly after his birth and his father had married again, taking on the responsibility for his second wife's daughter.

Dennis Bell attended Richmond Grammar School at the same time as Alan Broadley. He was a fine cricketer, with both he and his father playing for Bellerby and Hawes.

It was at the Grammar School that Dennis met his future wife, Margaret Hilda Metcalfe of Richmond. They settled in that town and two children were born.

Having joined the RAF, Dennis spent part of his training in Canada. He eventually joined 51 Squadron at Snaith

Dennis R. Bell (Bellerby).

in Yorkshire, where they were equipped with Halifax bombers from November 1942.

On February 27th/28th 1942 the Squadron, then equipped with Whitleys, had participated in Operation "Biting", when a raiding party was parachuted in to capture a complete German Wurzburg radar installation at Bruneval, near Le Havre (we have seen that Alan Broadley also participated).

On April 19th 1944 a plan was approved to begin systematic attacks on the German synthetic fuel industry. It was on one of these missions that Dennis Bell lost his life.

At 2.39p.m. on October 6th 1944 the Halifax carrying Dennis Bell departed

Snaith airfield, destination Sterkrade-Holten, an oil production target in the Ruhr. The plane was shot down by flak and all seven crew men on board were killed. Dennis is buried in grave 8.A.8. in the Reichswald Forest War Cemetery near Kleve, in Germany.

FLYING OFFICER EDWARD PARKER (DFM) NO. 54422 AIR GUNNER 576 SQUADRON RAF DIED THURSDAY 2ND NOVEMBER 1944 AGE 27.

Eddie Parker's parents, James and Ada Parker, were Lancashire folk from Nelson. Born in 1882, James served in the Boer War as a regular soldier in the East Lancashire Regiment and was afterwards posted to India for six years, where he took part in several skirmishes. He then spent some time in Canada before the Great War, where he farmed and spent a short while in the Mounted Police. During the Great War he served as a signaller attached to the Royal Artillery and was gassed.

A son, Roland, had been born, and in 1917 Eddie completed the family. In 1919 the family arrived at Castle Bolton, where James helped in the opening up

Edward Parker of Castle Bolton, standing on the extreme right (back row).

of Redmire Quarry. Ada ran a small shop from their house next door to the church, baking bread, cakes and confectioneries and providing cream teas for any visitors.

Leaving Redmire School, Eddie Parker worked for awhile on a local farm but then decided to make a career in the RAF. In 1938 he went to India and also served in Singapore and Malaya until 1941. He trained as a sergeant gunner in Rhodesia until 1942. Returning to Britain he joined first of all 101 Squadron, before being posted to 576 Squadron and took part in many missions over Europe. He gained the DFM in late 1943 for devotion to duty.

During this period he met May, a Lancashire girl serving as a Corporal in a WAAF Barrage Balloon section in London and they were married. In Wensleydale, his father James became a member of Castle Bolton Home Guard, whilst Roland, living at Preston under Scar and working at the quarry, also became a member there.

By October 1944, 576 Squadron, equipped with Lancaster heavy bombers, was based at Fiskerton in Lincolnshire. At 4p.m. on November 2nd, Lancaster NE115 departed Fiskerton, with Eddie Parker on board. It was part of a 992 aircraft raid on the industrial city of Dusseldorf and was the last major Bomber Command raid of the war on that city.

19 aircraft failed to return, one of these being Eddie Parker's Lancaster. The only survivor was Flying Officer Muirooney, who was taken prisoner. The other crew men were eventually buried in Rheinberg War Cemetery. Eddie Parker had planned to take his wife to Rhodesia after the war but sadly he was laid to rest in grave 11.D.12. in Germany.

FLIGHT SERGEANT VICTOR SINCLAIR WILLIS NO. 1546247 AIR BOMBER 9 SQUADRON RAFVR DIED FRIDAY 22ND DECEMBER 1944 AGE 23.

Victor Sinclair Willis was born in Bellerby, the elder son of Thomas Sinclair Willis and Elsie Barker Willis. Thomas, born in 1894 into a farming family from Preston under Scar, came to Bellerby to run Eastfield Farm (situated where Sayers Bus Company presently park their buses). During the Great War Thomas had served in the Royal Flying Corps. In 1919 he married a Sheffield girl and brought her back to the Bellerby farm. As he took his bride into the farmhouse he followed the ancient custom of throwing coins to the waiting Bellerby children.

Victor and his brother Teddy (Edwin) were born at the farm, with Victor attending Richmond Grammar School. He volunteered to join the RAF and by 1944 was serving with 9 Squadron.

By this time Tom and Elsie Willis had left Bellerby. In 1943 Tom had become landlord of the Strines Inn, in the Strines Valley, near the village of Bradfield, close to Sheffield. They remained there until 1955. It is a beautiful but isolated site, on the moors above the local reservoirs.

In August 1943, 9 Squadron, based at Bardney in Lincolnshire and flying Lancasters, took part in the epic raid on the Peenemunde V Weapons experimental station on the Baltic coast. In October and November 1944 detachments based at Lossiemouth took part in operations to sink the battleship "Tirpitz" as it sheltered in Tromso Fjord, Norway. Using 12,000 lb. Tallboy bombs 9 Squadron, in conjunction with 617 Squadron, put an end to the famous German battleship on November 12th 1944.

At 4.33p.m. on December 21st, Lancaster PD213, piloted by Flying

Victor S. Willis (Bellerby).

Officer Read and with Victor Willis as one of the air crew, departed Bardney. It was participating in an attack by 207 Lancasters and one Mosquito Pathfinder on the synthetic oil refinery at Politz, near Stettin, on the Baltic coast. Three Lancasters were shot down and five more crashed in England. Victor's plane was one of these five aircraft.

The crew were exhausted after the gruelling ten hour journey and on the return to base the visibility was extremely poor. Whilst trying to land, the Lancaster collided with a tree and crashed at 2.35a.m. near the airfield. Sergeant White and Flight Sergeant Willis were both killed and the other five crewmen injured.

Victor Sinclair Willis is buried in St. Nicholas Churchyard, Bradfield, in grave 269, close to the war memorial bearing his name. The inscription reads, "In grief and sorrow too deep to tell, We long for the son that we loved so well."

The final Wensleydale casualty for 1944 lost his life on Boxing Day, when a Bainbridge serviceman died in Holland.

TROOPER WALTER ARNOLD BROWN
NO. 14508382 11TH HUSSARS ROYAL ARMOURED CORPS
DIED 26TH DECEMBER 1944 AGE 27.

Walter Brown (Bainbridge).

The Brown family farmed at Gill Edge, on the road towards Semer Water, just above Bainbridge. It was here that Edward (Ned) and Annie Brown (nee Brockhill) raised Jenny, Percy, John, Harry and Walter.

Walter worked on his father's farm but when war broke out he eventually went down the mines near Durham as a "Bevan Boy". Disliking the experience, he joined up as a Trooper in the Royal Armoured Corps, as the driver of an armoured car.

The 11th Hussars went into France after D-Day and took part in the Allied advance into Belgium and Holland. On October 1st 1944 he wrote home explaining that they had gone through Belgium four weeks before and had received a good reception from the population. The troops had been showered with gifts of fruit and beer, whilst local children swarmed over their vehicles. He had been driving with one hand and taking gifts from the Belgians with the other. The vehicle looked like a grocer's van.

In the letter he reported that he was "somewhere in Holland" and had milked some cows, whilst he remarked that the windmills were a grand sight. By December 17th, nine days before he was killed, he wrote home that the shell fire was becoming nerve racking.

Walter was in 3 Troop "B" Squadron and was the driver for Sergeant McGuire, its commander. The Sergeant had won the Military Medal earlier in the campaign and on November 28th he had been presented with his ribbon by Field Marshal Sir Bernard Montgomery.

By November, the 11th Hussars were near Bree in Holland, in reserve, but at the start of December they were in the Maaseik and Ophoven area, just south of Roermond on the River Maas, and crossing the river to go into the line at Roosteren and Illikhoven.

"B" Squadron was responsible for about 3000 yards of front with no defences except the Juliana Canal, whose bridges were blown. The only plan was for each patrol to form a strong point at night and endeavour to observe by day without being seen. They also had the support of 40 Dutch Resistance men, equipped with all manner of German weapons. Defences were continually being thickened up by mines and wire.

At intervals "B" Squadron had four days of rest, mainly spent in hot baths procured in a local colliery. Some cinema shows were enjoyed together with a general clean up and sort out.

"B" Squadron's War Diary reports that, "on the 16th December there was a draw for leave in January. 23 out of 86 names were the lucky ones drawn by the head lady of Roosteren Red Cross, who had not one word of English. She wore glasses and was very plain, in spite of strict instructions from the Squadron leader to the sergeant major to pick the "best looker" in the place. Perhaps he had lost his torch!"

On December 17th "B" Squadron had the idea of broadcasting propaganda from the Canal bank in German but that night the wind was in the wrong direction and by the second night, the German counter-offensive through the Ardennes was going so well that it seemed inopportune to try and persuade them to desert.

On Christmas Eve, a discordant carol service by drunken German soldiers in Old Roosteren was heavily engaged by the artillery and peace reigned again.

At 5a.m. on Boxing Day, gunfire and machine-gun fire began to the right, for the Germans had attacked "D" Squadron in Gebroek village. They overran the village but the troops got out with minor casualties. As the enemy were now in Gebroek, 3 Troop and Walter Brown, were sent to just outside Illikhoven to watch the Canal in case the enemy attempted to cross and reach the River Maas.

Just as a counter-attack was about to go in, a few shells burst around 3 Troop, one landing on the house which they were behind, killing Trooper Walter Brown. This was extremely bad luck as they were unobserved by the enemy and the shells must have been "overs" from the Gebroek battle.

Walter was later buried in grave 23.H.5. of the Jonkerbos War Cemetery, Nijmegan. For many years after Walter's death, the family did not celebrate on Boxing Day.

1945 – DEFEAT FOR THE AXIS AND JAPANESE POWERS

During the Winter and Spring of 1945 British forces continued their advance towards the River Rhine and across the mighty river defences into the heart of

Germany. The German Reich would surrender at midnight on May 8th/9th 1945 and the following day the parishes throughout Wensleydale were able to bring out the bunting, ring the church bells and light bonfires to celebrate VE Day (Victory in Europe).

The celebrations in Middleham continued in even greater style in early June when "Dante", a three year old horse from Manor House Racing Stables won the Derby, the greatest of the five English Classics, at Newmarket (the race was probably run at Newmarket in 1945 instead of Epsom, in Surrey, because Epsom Downs were still covered with wartime necessities such as POW camps and vehicle parks).

Dante's Derby success led to scenes of wild excitement at Middleham. The winner bell at the Manor House Training Establishment, only rung when a race of £1000 or over was won, was pulled so heartily that the iron chain broke. Seven stable lads had dead heated to reach the chain.

Middleham people turned out to wave flags and handkerchiefs amid cheering, although the result was no surprise to them. Middleham Forces Welcome Home Fund Committee had arranged a week ago a "Dante Victory Ball", which took place on Saturday night in Middleham Picture Hall (the building now houses Middleham Motors). The cinema was packed for the Saturday night show, and requests were made to cut the programme short so that

Middleham Picture House in the 1930's. This was the scene for the celebrations in 1945 when 'Dante' won the Derby that year. It is now the building used by Middleham Motors for their garage.

By permission of Clive Torrens.

413

the ball could begin. Stable lads quickly adjusted the seats, the floor was swept, powder put down and upwards of 500 people filled the hall, as the local schoolmaster, Mr. H.C. Pybus, led off on the piano a lively dance tune.

During the dance cheers were given for Dante, Sir Eric Ohlson (owner), Matthew J. Peacock (trainer), Willie Nevett (jockey) and the stable lads. The highlight was reached when Willie Nevett, who arrived from Newmarket, was carried shoulder high into the hall and placed on top of the piano, amid deafening cheers. "By winning three wartime Derby's," he said, "I have beaten Steve Donaghue's wartime record of two winners. Dante is a jolly good horse, the best I have ridden, and it has been trained by a good man."

Just before midnight the National Anthem was sung and the crowd dispersed, but many friendly arguments continued around the Market Cross until the early morning hours about Dante's misfortune in the Guineas and his chances in the St. Leger.

Out in the Far East, however, despite the celebrations in Britain for the end of the conflict in Europe, British forces (the so called "Forgotten Army") would continue the desperate fight against the Japanese in Burma, Malaya and elsewhere, until the surrender of Japan on September 2nd.

Wensleydale would lose a further four servicemen during these months, three from natural causes and the fourth whilst fighting in the jungles of Burma.

LEADING AIRCRAFTMAN FRANK BURTON
NO. 983749 946 BALLOON SQUADRON RAFVR
DIED SATURDAY 6TH JANUARY 1945 AGE 25.

Frank, James, Barbara, Ernest, Mary and Dennis were the children of John (Jack) and Mary Burton, living in Grove Square, Leyburn. Their father was a painter and decorator employed by Ernest Metcalfe of Railway Street (Mary was a member of the Raw family from Thoresby, Carperby). For several years Mary and a daughter also opened a small fish and chip shop in Leyburn, along the alleyway between the present day Towler's Newsagents and the toilet block. A newspaper business was also run from Mary's home.

Frank Burton (Leyburn).

414

After leaving Leyburn Council School, Frank began work in Leyburn Quarry. One of his jobs was to blow a trumpet to warn his colleagues that blasting was about to commence. Each week he would supplement his wages by taking a box of cigarette packets into the quarry to sell to his fellow workers.

Frank joined the RAFVR in late 1939 and by 1940 he had been posted as a leading aircraftman to 946 (City of Glasgow) Balloon Squadron. Operating in Glasgow its purpose was to protect important buildings by using a balloon barrage as an aerial minefield and so causing enemy aircraft to fly much higher than they would wish. The Squadron, in 1940, consisted of five flights of eight balloons each, a total of 40 balloons.

Frank was not in the best of health and later in the war he was discharged, suffering from tuberculosis. He died from consumption on January 6th, aged 25, and was buried in Leyburn Cemetery. Sadly, his mother Mary, who had nursed him devotedly during his illness, contracted the disease and died of TB just one year later, February 7th 1946, aged 50 years and was laid to rest alongside her son.

LIEUTENANT NORMAN RICHARD MOORE NO. 258318 DURHAM LIGHT INFANTRY ATTACHED TO 5TH BATTALION NIGERIA REGIMENT, ROYAL WEST AFRICAN FIELD FORCE, DIED SATURDAY 20TH JANUARY 1945 AGE 21.

Norman was born at Burtersett, the son of Richard and Annie Margaret Moore. Richard had lived as a child at Catriggs Farm, just outside Hawes, and was the brother of Harold Moore, who had been killed during the Great War. Richard married Annie Pratt from Burtersett and they settled in that hamlet, with Richard running the family farm at Catriggs in partnership with brother Frank. Three

Norman Richard Moore
(Hawes).

Norman Richard Moore in the Far East,
April 1944.

Norman Richard Moore with sisters, Rosemary and Vera.

children were born at Burtersett, Norman, Rosemary and Vera.

In 1929 their father Richard died, aged just 34 years. Some years later Annie Moore married again, her husband being John Mason who farmed "Thorns", just outside Hawes, on the road to Appersett.

Norman was educated at Yorebridge Grammar School, of which he was head boy for a time, and gained both his school certificate and higher certificate. In May 1940 he became one of the first members of Hawes Home Guard.

Soon afterwards he joined the Durham Light Infantry and for awhile became a physical training instructor at Aycliffe, near Darlington. He was granted his commission in December 1942 and promoted full Lieutenant six months later.

Going to West Africa in September 1943, he was seconded to the West African Frontier Force, where he was a Lieutenant in the Nigeria Regiment. They trained in jungle warfare and in June 1944 went to the Burma front.

On December 12th the Regiment took part in the offensive on the Arakan coastal strip, aiming to clear the way towards Rangoon. Good progress was made with amphibious landings helping to capture Ramree Island, and Akyab airfield was abandoned by the Japanese. Meanwhile, the West Africans pushed southwards, inland.

The Japanese sent a covering force to delay the advancing 81st and 82nd West African Divisions for as long as possible and established full scale defensive positions in the region of Kangaw. The British attack on Kangaw began on January 21st 1945 and was fought over two days, with fierce resistance from the Japanese, before the position fell.

However, the day before the Battle of Kangaw began, Norman Moore had been killed elsewhere, fighting against the Japanese covering force that had been sent out to hold up their advance.

Buried in the Akyab battlefield Cemetery, Norman's body was later brought to be buried in grave 3.H.7. at Taukkyan War Cemetery, just outside Rangoon, Burma.

AIR COMMODORE JOSEPH RYLANDS (CBE), RAF DIED SUNDAY 4TH FEBRUARY 1945 AGE 59.

With a long standing career in the RAF behind him, Joseph Rylands worked at a desk job in London during the 2nd World War as a Senior Service Accountant with the Air Ministry Unit, associated with Technical Training Command.

In the early stages of the war he had brought his wife Annie to Wensleydale, to escape the London Blitz, and she settled in Hardraw, where she became the landlady of the Green Dragon Inn.

On February 4th Joseph Rylands died from natural causes and was buried in

Green Dragon Inn at Hardraw c1945.
The landlady was Mrs. Annie Rylands, wife of Air Commodore Joseph Rylands.

Watford North Cemetery in Hertfordshire. His wife remained as landlady of the Green Dragon for awhile, before returning south.

SERGEANT ALAN EDWARD WARRINER
NO. 2372600 ARMY EDUCATIONAL CORPS
DIED WEDNESDAY 13TH JUNE 1945 AGE 38.

Sergeant Warriner, a fine musician, being a member of the Academy of Music, brought his wife Edith and daughter Shirley to live at Leyburn and later on Moor Road, Bellerby, during the war years. Edith was a teacher who started work at Leyburn Council School and lived at "Windyridge", Harmby Road, Leyburn (she became the headmistress at Downholme C. of E. School and later a teacher at Bellerby School).

At the age of 20 Alan Warriner had spent two years in the Territorial Army (1926-1928). Born in Sunderland, he had married Edith (nee Scriven), a Sunderland girl, in 1934.

Alan enlisted at Ossett, between Dewsbury and Wakefield, in August 1941 and was posted to the Royal Signals as a signalman. On January 6th 1943 he embarked for Algeria in North Africa for the final part of Operation "Torch" (the Allied landings in Algeria) and remained in North Africa until March 1944, when he was posted to the Middle East Command.

It was here that he was transferred to the Army Education Corps and was

Unveiling and dedication of the Second World War memorial at Middleham.

Castle Bolton celebrations just after the Second World War.
Back row: X, Ronnie Richardson, Tom Peacock, Harry Weatherill, Fred Peacock,
Kit Spenseley, Mary Ann Richardson, Maria Storey, X, X, X, Lilian Richardson,
Cissie Peacock, X, X.
Front row: Carole Parker, X, Joan Parker, John Peacock, Colin Peacock, X,
Dennis Lambert, Alan Peacock, X, ? Hunter, Billy Horn, Margery Batty,
Nancy Bostock, Jane Dinsdale, Elizabeth Hunter, Mary Dinsdale, Eve Spenseley,
Mabel Hunter.

Castle Bolton celebration shortly after the Second World War.
Fourth row: Kit Spenseley, Muriel Peacock, X, X, Lilian Richardson, Maggie Metcalfe,
X, Gwen Wilson, ? Wilson, Audrey Spoors, X, X, Fred Lawson, Bessie Peacock.
Third row: Ronnie Richardson, Frank Lambert, Jack Richardson, Jim Peacock,
Irene Peacock, Mary Dinsdale, Margaret Iveson, X, Mary Ann Richardson, Florrie Iveson,
Flo Spenseley, Essie Lambert, Maria Storey, Cissie Peacock, Nancy Bostock,
Jane Dinsdale, Fanny Horn.
Second row: X, John Peacock, X, Godfrey Lambert, X. ? Wilson, Colin Peacock,
Billy Horn, David Horn, Stella Spenseley, Eva Spenseley, X, ? Wilson, Margery Batty,
Joan Parker, Jim Storey, Mabel Hunter and Elizabeth, Robert Hunter.
First row: X, Dennis Lambert, Thomas Hunter, X, Carole Parker, X, X, X.

posted to Benghazi in Libya.

During the war years three large educational programmes were run by the AEC:

"British Way and Purpose" helped to explain to the servicemen why Britain was in the war and what its aims were.

The Army Bureau of Current Affairs. Every two weeks this department produced maps and text for the servicemen on the theatres of war and explained what was currently happening, in order to update them on events.

"The Release Scheme". This was a resettlement scheme in the latter part of the war providing courses set up to help servicemen when they left the Army, especially as there was a great deal of illiteracy amongst the soldiers.

Alan Warriner was stationed at the small Benghazi office, engaged in this release scheme as the Regimental Educational Instructor, when he died on 13th June 1945. He was taking part in a game of cricket on the field and died of a heart attack. He was buried in grave 4.A.12. in the Benghazi War Cemetery, Libya.

A few months later, on September 8th 1945, Japan surrendered after the dropping of atomic bombs on Hiroshima and Nagasaki, and the war was finally over. It brought to a conclusion Wensleydale's participation in the second global conflict to shatter the peace of the 20th Century. The families from the dale could look forward to a return to peacetime conditions. Throughout late 1945 and into 1946 servicemen and women began their return to civilian life, and husbands, sons and daughters readjusted to the novel experience of being back permanently within the bosom of their families.

There was sadness, though, within the dale and especially within the hearts of members of those families who had lost their loved ones. 50 dalesmen had not survived the war and although the number of those killed did not reach the horrendous scale of the Great War, 50 families mourned the loss of their men folk.

Yet even with an end to the conflict, it was not to be the end of the story of the men whose names are inscribed on the village war memorials. During the late 1940's and early 1950's three more men who had served during the war years, and suffered as a result of the conflict, would die and have their names commemorated within the dale.

MAJOR DAVID SHORTER GURKHA RIFLES
DIED 1947 AGE 25.

David Shorter was the only son of R.C. Shorter, headmaster of Yorebridge Grammar School. His father had served in the Great War and had been gassed on the Western Front. R.C. Shorter ended the war in Ireland, working with a gas development unit. Prior to the war he had read Classics and then the Sciences at Cambridge University. Teaching first at Taunton, then Northallerton, he arrived at Yorebridge Grammar School in 1922 and set up home with his wife and daughter Renee at Bainbridge. In 1922 the family was completed when David was born.

From Yorebridge, David went to Durham School in 1935, where he played in the rugby and cricket teams. Joining up in 1940, at the age

David Shorter (Bainbridge).

of 18, he was commissioned in 1941 and went to India early the following year and saw action on the Indo-Burmese border and in Burma as a major in the Gurkha Rifles.

It was whilst he was in India that he contracted a mild form of polio but recovered sufficiently to enable him to continue his career.

On April 28th 1945, in Lahore, David married Audrey, a girl he had met whilst on the sub-continent. When war with the Japanese ended in September 1945 he remained in the army. In 1947, having returned home on leave, he was embarking on a ship at Liverpool, bound for India, when he was taken ill and rushed to one of the city hospitals, where he died. David Shorter's name is commemorated on the Askrigg Memorial.

R.C. Shorter, headmaster of Yorebridge Grammar School, in 1930, standing on the site of the new school at Askrigg.

The old Yorebridge Grammar School and schoolhouse at Yorebridge, near Bainbridge. Anthony Besson founded the school in a riverside location at Bainbridge (by the River Ure) in 1601 and it remained in that building until 1931 when the school transferred to new buildings at Askrigg. The new school closed in 1971 when it became Askrigg Primary School and part of Craven College. Former members of the Grammar school are known as Old Bessonians.

The newly constructed Yorebridge Grammar School, Askrigg, opened 1931.

David Shorter with his Ghurka platoon 1944
(standing second from the right on next to back row).

CHARLES NORMAN HARRISON
1ST BATTALION TYNESIDE SCOTTISH (BLACK WATCH) DIED 1955.

Norman was the youngest of four boys and two girls (Fred, Rodwell, Harold, Norman, Carrie and Clara), the children of William and Mary Harrison. The Harrisons were a farming family living at Manor Farm on Harmby Bank.

Fred, Rodwell and Norman all worked on the farm, but Norman was called up near the start of the war. He joined the newly reformed 1st Battalion of the Black Watch, which in May 1940 had been badly mauled by confronting the attack of a German Armoured Division in France.

The unit was selected as part of the force to occupy Iceland — an outpost liable to attack and invaluable to the defence of Britain.

Relieved of this task, the Battalion was at the forefront of the Normandy landings, where its fighting qualities brought it especial mention and a reputation maintained in the swift advance through France and Holland towards Germany.

It was in Holland, in December 1944, that Norman was badly injured by the shrapnel from a mortar shell and was left for dead. However, he managed to creep back to the British lines, where he was found and brought back to England.

After coming out of hospital, he was still in a poor state of health. He could not move his arm at all, but with the support of his mother, he started to recover and began work on the family farm. In 1953 he married a Barden farmer's daughter,

Norman Harrison (Harmby).

Norman Harrison on bren-gun carrier in Iceland. The polar bear logo on the back of the carrier became the symbol of the Iceland garrison.

424

Muriel Terry, at Hauxwell Church and they came to live at "Woodlands", Harmby, where a daughter, was born. However, in 1955 a piece of shrapnel that had not been removed caused meningitis and Norman died. His name is commemorated on the Spennithorne and Harmby war memorial.

PATRICK (JACK) O'CONNOR
NAVIGATOR RAF
DIED 1952.

Patrick was a citizen of the Irish Republic, a neutral country during the war years, but against the main view of the Irish people he volunteered to join the RAF and fight against Fascism. He became an officer and navigator, flying on many bombing missions over Europe.

It was whilst he was in the Newcastle, Sunderland area that he met a young widow, Roma, whose husband, Lieutenant Lambert Russel RN, had been killed whilst commanding his Motor Torpedo Boat on a hazardous operation off the coast of Tunisia.

Patrick and Roma married and she followed him to live in the Stratford upon Avon area, where he was based. However, Patrick was starting to have problems with his lungs, the onset of tuberculosis, which was worsened by his flying missions.

John Patrick O'Connor (Hawes).

In 1946 they arrived in Hawes, where Roma O'Connor bought for £500 the Chemist Shop and the goodwill of its customers achieved by its former owner, Mr. Bowness.

Patrick trained to be an optician but he was diagnosed with tuberculosis. The RAF regarded his illness as being partly a result of his wartime service and paid for him to attend a sanatorium in Switzerland for the next few years, with short spells of leave back in Hawes.

In June 1951 a son, Terry, was born but in 1952 Patrick O'Connor died whilst receiving treatment in hospital. His name was added to the memorial screen in Hawes parish church.

With the death of Patrick O'Connor, the 221st serviceman to have his name inscribed on a Wensleydale war memorial, it would appear that we have come to the conclusion of our story of the sacrifice made by families throughout the dale.

In reality, the suffering went much deeper, for many men who survived the war were wounded or scarred by their wartime experiences. Even worse was the suffering and sadness experienced by numerous dale's women folk who had married men from outside the dale and whose husbands were killed during the six years of conflict. The names of such men are only to be found on war memorials in other parts of the country, but the suffering was still felt deeply within Wensleydale.

I will relate the story of Kenneth and Joyce Fawcett to show how one must look beyond the war memorials scattered throughout Wensleydale to reveal the true depth of suffering within this northern dale.

FLIGHT SERGEANT KENNETH FAWCETT
NO. 1196180 547 SQUADRON RAFVR
DIED WEDNESDAY 26TH APRIL 1944 AGE 29.

Kenneth was the eldest son of John Thomas Fawcett and Dora Annie Fawcett of Great Smeaton, a village between Darlington and Northallerton, where John Thomas continued the family tradition as the village blacksmith.

Having attended Northallerton Grammar School, Kenneth began work in the offices of County Hall, Northallerton, where he rose to the position of chief clerk. He was an all-round sportsman and as a cricketer was well-known in the Langbaurgh West, Northallerton and Thirsk district leagues.

In September 1939, Joyce Hamilton, daughter of the Thornton Steward post mistress, Emily Hamilton, began work at County Hall and she and Kenneth were

Kenneth and Joyce Fawcett and baby John at Thornton Steward in 1943.

seconded as members of "War Ag" (War Agricultural Executive Committee), issuing coupons to the dale farmers, amongst their many duties.

Eventually they began courting, but in early 1941 Kenneth volunteered for the RAF and began training as a wireless operator/air gunner. On June 28th 1941 they were married at Northallerton Church. By Spring 1942 Joyce was expecting and returned to live with her parents at the post-office in Thornton Steward. Whenever Kenneth was on leave, he too regarded Thornton Steward as his home village and attended church there. On December 27th 1942 their son John was born.

By 1943/1944 Kenneth was serving in 547 Squadron of Coastal Command, flying Liberator aircraft based at RAF St. Eval, near Wadebridge in Cornwall. Their main duty was to participate in the fight against German U-boats in the Bay of Biscay and in the North Atlantic approaches.

Coastal Command was known as Cinderella Command, its contribution to victory in the Second World War largely eclipsed in history by the glamour and sacrifice of the fighter and bomber squadrons of the RAF. 10,875 members, however, lost their lives between 1939 and 1945. Service with Coastal Command required a distinct personality, involving as it did long and mainly fruitless patrols, often at night and usually hundreds of miles from land. There was no glamour flying, searching for U-boats day after day. Then there was the loneliness and the endurance. A 20-hour sortie was common and took the crew far out into the Atlantic Ocean. When boredom was replaced by sudden, swift action the result could be a slow death on the empty, savage sea.

It was to grow into a formidable force, helped by an influx of more modern, often American, aircraft like the Catalina and Liberator. The latter helped to plug the Atlantic Gap, an area previously free from air patrol which provided U-boat commanders with some of their happiest hunting grounds.

By the end of the war, Coastal Command had accounted for 189 U-boats, and another 24 sunk in joint actions with surface ships. The cost in aircraft was enormous, however, the Command losing 2000 in six years of fighting.

Kenneth was on leave for virtually the whole of March 1944 and spent it with Joyce and John at his mother-in-law's house, the post office, Thornton Steward. He loved his time there and spent most of it digging the garden plot and sewing seed. He returned to RAF duties on March 31st and 26 days later he was killed whilst on operational duties.

The ten men crew of the Liberator aircraft, including Kenneth Fawcett, took off from St. Eval on a night training exercise flight on the evening of Wednesday April 26th 1944. The training was in conjunction with a Royal Navy submarine, 9 miles off the port of Fishguard, on the Pembrokeshire coast. The submarine captain reported that the aircraft flew low overhead and then flew straight on into the sea. It broke up at once and an intensive search was launched.

One of the occupants of the aircraft was rescued and two others were found dead, but no trace of Kenneth or the six other crew members were found.

Kenneth Fawcett's name was commemorated on Panel 217 of the RAF Memorial at Runnymede and his name is honoured on the Great Smeaton war memorial and at Northallerton. He left a young widow and 16 month old son at Thornton Steward.

Sadly, his brother Vernon, also serving in the RAF, was at Singapore when the naval fortress was captured by the Japanese, and was killed. Stanley, another brother, was taken prisoner by the Axis Poweres and became a POW of the Germans. Although escaping on one occasion, he was recaptured and was not repatriated until the end of the war.

And so ends an epic story of sacrifice, heartache and tragedy for many families within this northern dale during the two world wars of the 20th Century. It is a story that deserves to be told, and, though it is a sad tale, it is one that can be told with pride. Here is not the place to argue the rights and wrongs of war, brought about by the machinations of governments or regimes. This is simply the story of ordinary men, who, in extraordinary times, attempted to do their duty and in doing so, paid with their lives.

Neither I, nor others born at the end of the 2nd World War, have had to experience the horrors of world wide conflict. For that I am extremely grateful and I believe that it is partly due to people such as those whose stories are related in this book, that my generation has not had to bear arms as they had to do. It is in recognition of their sacrifice that I have attempted to throw light upon their lives so that their stories will be remembered and honoured within the wider community.

The headstone of Barnard Benson Hayton, in Redmire churchyard.
He was killed in an air crash whilst training in Scotland (see page 398).
The words at the base of the headstone provide a fitting epithet for all the
Wensleydale servicemen who lost their lives during the Second World War.

'FOR HONOUR, LIBERTY AND TRUTH, HE GAVE HIS YOUTH. HE DIED THAT WE MIGHT LIVE.

WENSLEYDALE'S WAR MEMORIALS

HARDRAW CHURCH

1st World War.
Harold Bell d.10-4-18
Samuel Kirk (Lambert) d. 12-11-17
William Moore d. 23-4-17
Edmund Staveley d. 9-6-17
Robert Sharples d. 23-4-17

2nd World War
Joseph Ryland 4-2-45
Charles Ward d. 14-5-44
Robert Watson d. 15-2-42
Joseph Watson d. 24-9-40

HAWES CHURCH AND GAYLE CHAPEL

1st World War
Michael Akrigg d. 13-3-18
Herbert Allen d. 10-8-18
Ralph Alderson d. 28-3-18
Charles Edward Bacon d. 26-1-17
James Banks d. 26-7-16
Miles Calvert d. 24-4-18
Frederick Cockett d. 29-10-14
Harry Cockett d. 20-9-17
John Dinsdale d. 28-9-17
John Fawcett d. 12-12-16
James Whaley Fryer d. 1-7-16
David Harker d. 8-8-18
John William Horn d. 27-9-16
John Iveson d. 14-3-17

Nathan Burton Iveson d.4-10-17
John Jackson d. 164-18
Charles Heseltine Jones d. 1-6-17
Alexander Kirkbride d. 17-2-17
Albert Leach d.12-7-16
John Chaytor Metcalfe d. 7-7-16
John Moore Metcalfe d. 3-10-18
Ralph Tiplady Metcalfe d. 21-11-17
Reginald Milburn d. 16-9-16
Carl Dugdale Milner d. 22-8-18
James Henry Milner d. 17-9-16
John Mitton d. 9-4-17
William Mitton d. 15-10-18
Harold Moore d. 24-10-18
John Moore 22-5-18
John Thomas Moore d. 19-4-18
Simon Moore d. 5-11-16
James Pratt d. 5-4-18
Fred Shaw d. 7-6-17
Edmund Staveley d. 9-6-17
George Staveley d. 2-9-18
Lister Staveley d. 15-9-16
Thomas Thwaite d. 11-4-18
Robert Walton d. 6-3-17
Thomas Walton d. 14-9-16
Henry Wild d. 21-8-18

2nd World War
James Iveson d. 9-3-44
Norman Henry Meanwell d. 7-5-41
James Metcalfe d. 5-5-41
Norman Richard Moore d. 20-1-45
Stanley (Peter) Moore d. 27-5-43
Thomas Watson d. 26-11-43
Thomas Dawson Whaley d. 17-7-44
John Patrick O' Connor d. 1952

STALLING BUSK AND MARSETTE

1st World War
James Bell d. 11-4-18
William Fawcett d. 12-4-19
Thomas James Allen Hodgson d.8-4-16

Herbert Lawson Metcalfe d. 20-11-17
Thomas Pickard Outhwaite d. 19-6-17
Thomas Metcalfe Coates d. 21-1-25

ASKRIGG CHURCH

1st World War
William Appleton d. 25-1-17
William Banks d. 10-9-18
James Chapman d. 1-7-16
Frank Dinsdale d. 1-7-16
John W. Horn d. 27-9-16
James Kirkbride d. 24-10-20
Bemard Grime Lodge d. 24-8-17
John J. Metcalfe d. 25-3-18
Robert Pickering Metcalfe d. 24-8-17
John Mitton d. 9-4-17
Robert Mudd d. 13-4-17
Thomas Miller d. 17-4-18
James G. Preston d. 2-11-17
William H. T. Webster d. 5-8-17

2nd World War
Sidney C. Kirkbride d. 15-7~0
Walter A. Brown d. 26-12-44
George D. Cockbone d. 19-6-43
Ernest K. Stevens d. 2-4-42
Jack Hindle d. 4-6-44
Frank V. Percival d. 25-11-41
David C. B. Shorter d. 1947

CARPERBY MEMORIAL

1st World War
Jack Harker d. 6-8-15
Herbert Kilburn d. 3-9-16
Timothy Percival d. 16-11-18
Albert Senior d. 22-4-16
John Shannon d. 1-7-16
Henry Storey d. 2-8-16

2nd World War
Thomas Foster d. 29-4-43

AYSGARTH CHURCH GATEWAY MEMORIAL

1st World War
James Bell d. 4-10-16
Harold Binks d. 22-3-18
William Edward Bushby d. 2-11 -18
George Charlton d. 1918
James Bell Fawcett d. 7-6-17
John Mills Gould d. 9-4-15
George Sidney Gould d. 9-4-17
George Iveson Hammond d. 3-9-16
William Hemsley d. 4-10-17
Matthew Heseltine d. 14-9-16
Matthew Heseltine d. 14-9-16
William Herbert Kilburn d. 3-9-16
John William Lodge d. 23-8-17
Arthur Mawer d. 11-2-16
Robert Pickering Metcalfe d. 24-8-17
John Percival d. 8-4-18
Timothy Percival d. 16-11-18
Joseph Dixon Raw d. 8-5-18
John Shannon d. 1-7-16
Thomas Spence d. 18-4-19

AYSGARTH VILLAGE MEMORIAL

1st World War
James P. Bell d. 4-10-16
William Hemsley d. 4-10-17
John Percival d. 8-4-18

AYSGARTH CHURCH

2nd World War
Francis John Chapman d. 8-10-41
Thomas Foster d. 29-4-43
Frederick William Lawson d. 16-10-41
Alan Lewis Smith d. 14-5-44

REDMIRE CHURCH

1st World War
John H. Ruecroft d. 26-2-19

Fred Lealman d. 10-4-18
John E. Rider d. 26-4-16
Francis H. Rider d. 13-4-18

2nd World War
George William Park d. 4-9-39
Robert Hammell Heseltine d. 19-4-41
Barnard Benson Hayton d. 12-6-44

CASTLE BOLTON CHURCH

1st World War
Robert Henry Lambert d. 17-9-16
John Fawcett d. 16-6-17
Fred Kilding Shields d. 29-9-17
Thomas Storey d. 21-3-18
Fred Lealman d. 10-4-18
George Beckwith d. 30-3-18

2nd World War
Edward Parker d. 2-11-44

WENSLEY CHURCH

1st World War
Joseph Alderson d. 9-11-15
Henry Beswick d. 21-3-18
James Chilton d. 14-6-17
William Deighton d. 21-9-17
Frederick Holmes d. 21-8-18
Alfred Kilding d. 17-9-16
Harry Kilding d. 27-8-17
Leslie Loftus d. 3-5-17
Percy Orde-Powlett d. 17-5-15
Alfred Salmon d. 16-2-19
Charles Scott d. 4-10-17
Harold Scrivener d. 31-5-16
Edward Spence d. 12-4-18
Willie Smith d. 26-9-17
John Teasdale d. 8-7-16
Thomas Wardman d. 25-3-18
Edward Wilkinson d. 20-7-18
Harry Wilson d. 31-5-16

2nd World War
Frederick Stanley Humble d. 12-9-42
Renny Christian Mure Fitzhugh d. 13-6- 44

LEYBURN WAR MEMORIAL

1st World War
Joseph Alderson d. 9-11 -15
Henry Beswick d. 21-3-18
George William Clarke d. 15-6-18
James Chilton d. 14-6-17
J. Raymond Clapham d. 21b-17
William Truefit Deighton d. 21-9-17
Frederick Holmes d. 21-8-18
Alfred Ward Salmon d. 16-2-19
William Smith d. 26-9-17
John William Teasdale d. 8-7-16
Thomas Lawson Wardman d. 25-3-1
Walter Edward Wilkinson d. 20-7-18

2nd World War
John Alan Broadley d. 18-2-44
Frank Burton d. 6-1-45
John Dixon Chapman d. 17-8-43
George Miles Lumley d. 15-8~1
Robert William Marks d. 6-6-44
James Rowland May d. 16-6-44
Francis Stanley Seymour d. 19-7-44
John Ernest Taylor d. 8-2-40
Alan Edward Warriner d. 13-6-45

MIDDLEHAM WAR MEMORIAL

1st World War
Thomas E.M. Rumford d. 10-6-16
William H. Turner d. 10-7-17
Harold L. Collinson d. 26-10-17
Charles R. Nicholson d. 14-7-17
John William Weatherill d. 23-4-17
Thomas Sarginson d. 1-6-18
John Sarginson d. 4-7-16
John W. Teasdale d. 8-7-16
Digby G. Beswick d. 14-2-16

Henry Peacock d. 28-4-17
Charles B. Miller d. 22-8-15
Frank Collinson d. 1-7-16
Frederick Clarkson d. 10-4-18
Bertie Potter d. 10-8-17
William T. Deighton d. 21-9-17
John C.C. Handley d. 7-10-18

Died in England
David Durrell Barclay d. 2-10-18
William Logan Rayner d. 28-10-18

2nd World War
George Edward Benson d. 12-3-43
Thomas Henry Hammerton d. 5-6-42
Fred Harrison d. 1-3-44
Raymond Houseman d. 4-10-43
William Edward Houseman d. 18-6-43
Harry Terry d. 5-3-43

EAST WITTON WAR MEMORIAL

1st World War
Joseph Allen d. 8-2-17
Frank Atkinson d. 23-3-18
Robert S. Atkinson d. 17-9-16
John Bowes d. 18-10-20
John Carruthers d. 15-4-18
Bertie William Greenhalgh d. 24-5-15
Joseph Hutchinson d. 13-7-18
John Leake d. 3-11-14
John Maughan d. 17-2-16
Godfrey Metcalfe d. 27-5-18
John G. Towler d. 11-8-18
Mansell Waite d. 16-1-16
Edwin Wright d. 25-9-16

2nd World War
Thomas B. Maughan d. 29-7-44

SPENNITHORNE AND HARMBY WAR MEMORIAL

1st World War
Hugh Clervaux Chaytor d. 31-10-14
Percival Van Straubenzee d. 1 -11-14
George W. Stayman d. 2-6-16
Sidney C. Allinson d. 8-9-17
George E. Dawson d. 29-5-18
Charles Oswald Sewell d. 17-3-15
Edgar Spensley d. 23-11-18
James Wilce d. 3-9-18
ThomasWynne d.27-9-15
James William Hutchinson d. mid-1920's

2nd World War
Albert Robert James d. 20-8-44
Matthew Thomas Metcalfe d. 13-7-43
Francis Wilkinson d. 13-11-42
Charles Norman Harrison d. 1955

THORNTON STEWARD CHURCH

1st World War
J. Horn d. 21-3-18
Frank Atkinson d. 23-3-18
Harold Thomas Wright d. 24-10-18
Robert S. Atkinson d. 17-9-16
Douglas Bernard Priestley d. 31-7-17

BELLERBY CHURCH

1st World War
George C. Beck d. 21-5-17
James Robinson Mawer d. 20-9-17
Robert Thomas Davison d. 11-4-18
Joseph Daykin d. 4-11-18
George Martin Raw d. 11-10-15
Edmund Ernest Thistlethwaite d. May 1918
Christopher Gregg d. 15-9-16
Anthony Ward d. 3-5-17

2nd World War
Dennis R. Bell d. 6-10-44

Leonard Scott d. 9-6-43
Victor Sinclair Willis d. 22-12-44

WEST WITTON CHURCH

1st World War
William A.H. Smith d. 27-5-18
John A. Harland d. 23-10-16
William Thompson d. 26-12-16

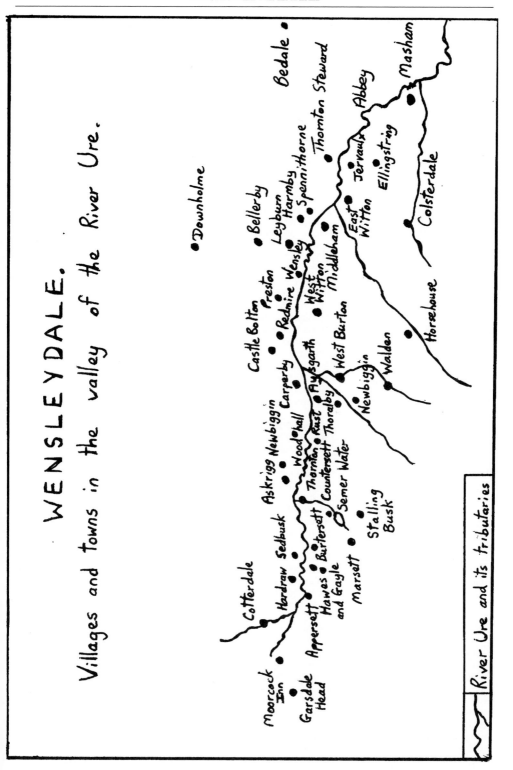

WENSLEYDALE.

Villages and towns in the valley of the River Ure.

River Ure and its tributaries

INDEX

443